VICE

VICE
An Anthology

Compiled by Richard Davenport-Hines

VIKING

VIKING
Published by the Penguin Group
Penguin Books USA Inc., 375 Hudson Street,
New York, New York 10014, USA
Penguin Books Ltd, 27 Wrights Lane,
Penguin Books Australia Ltd, Ringwood, Victoria, Australia
Penguin Books Canada Ltd, 10 Alcorn Avenue, Toronto, Ontario, Canada M4V 3B2
Penguin Books (NZ) Ltd, 182–190 Wairau Road, Auckland 10, New Zealand

Penguin Books Ltd, Registered Offices: Harmondsworth, Middlesex, England

First American edition published in 1994 by Viking Penguin,
a division of Penguin Books USA Inc.

The acknowledgements on pages 547–52 constitute an extension of this copyright page

1 3 5 7 9 10 8 6 4 2

Copyright © Richard Davenport-Hines, 1993
All rights reserved

ISBN 0-670-85548-0

Printed in England
Set in Monotype Garamond

For Hugo and Cosmo

Contents

A King of Shreds and Patches
His Preface

In old mystery plays a character representing Vice was dressed as a mimic king in tattered, parti-coloured clothes and was known as the King of Shreds and Patches. The phrase was later applied to hacks who compiled books at the demand of publishers without original thoughts of their own. Anthologists after all have always ranked low in literary precedence. 'Of all authors', wrote Montesquieu, 'there are none whom I despise more than compilers.' I must be at a double hazard of being despised as a King of Shreds and Patches, for I have compiled an anthology of vice. But some ideas and feelings have gone into my selection: I should indicate what they are.

A celebratory tone has been my aim. A vice like drug-taking may wreck people's lives; another like motoring may kill people; others like snobbery are a bore; and vicious cruelty is detestable. But overall I think cheerful vice is preferable to stubborn virtue (virtues like patience or fidelity being no more than a version of obstinacy). This selection reflects my feeling that virtuous people are often dupes or hypocrites: that few vices prevent someone from finding love, or slaking desire, as an excess of virtues may do. Vices may be as amiable as virtues can be obnoxious, but there are no universal rules in any of this. The pleasures of the rich often seem the boring dissipations of convention; the vices of the vainglorious are usually the dreariest.

Nevertheless one person's pleasure can excite pleasure in others. Food

and Voyeurism are examples which I have chosen as categories in this
collection. The themes of this book are given by a belief in pleasure, a
dislike of mean behaviour and a delight in the varieties and contradic-
tions of epicureanism. Versatility seems best to me. I have wanted to celebrate voluptuousness, which is why I have included such categories as
Alfresco Sex. Flirting has been included because it can be pleasurable,
although it can also cover several of the meaner and paltrier vices. I did
not want my anthology to be dull. Avarice was called 'a good old-gentle-
manly vice' by Byron, but according to Sir Thomas Browne is 'not so
much a vice as a deplorable piece of madness'. Certainly avarice is not
life-enhancing: so it has been a relief to omit it. Apart from the section
Short Views on Mean Vices I have similarly ignored drab vices like envy
and pedantry – both I hope unknown to all reviewers of this anthology.
More regrettably, a few of my favourite authors, such as Caroline
Blackwood, Elizabeth Bowen and Edith Wharton, have been omitted
because their evocations of vice defy that process of abstraction and
abridgement which makes anthologies. Other writers are excluded
because permission to quote them was withheld: lines 139–72 of *The
Waste Land* by T. S. Eliot (demonstrating the viciousness of pub gossip),
are omitted for this reason.

Most fools can be dissolute, but pleasures take time and thought. 'The
greatest Drunkards are the worst Judges of Wine. The most Insatiable
Leachers the most Ignorant Criticks in Women, and the Greediest
Appetites, of the best Cookery of Meats – for those that use *Excess* in
any Thing never understand the Truth of it, which always lies in the
Mean': so wrote Samuel Butler in the seventeenth century. One of the
characteristics of Vice is the tendency to swerve away from the Mean to
extremes. Cumulatively there is something habitual, or obsessive, or
compulsive about viciousness. It can turn into thraldom or hard
drudgery. 'People do not persist in their vices because they are not weary
of them, but because they cannot leave them off,' wrote Hazlitt. 'It is the
nature of vice to leave us no resource but in itself.' These negative
aspects of vice have to be represented in my selection too.

Anthologies are personal, even narcissistic; any collection which
tried to be comprehensive of all ages, cultures and temperaments would
be characterless. Two of the anthologists whom I most admire are

W. H. Auden and Lord David Cecil. Auden described *A Certain World* as 'a map' of his 'personal planet'; Cecil saw his anthology 'as a sort of self-portrait; myself, as mirrored in the looking-glass of my reading'. I would have died long ago if I had practised all the vices mirrored in this book, but I have tried to emulate Auden and Cecil in one respect. My choices represent nothing but my own taste. They have their origins in a commonplace book which I began compiling in 1969. There is nothing here which I find ill-written, or boring, or monstrously untruthful. Chaucer on drink and lust, Lamb's 'Farewell to Tobacco' or supposedly erotic intervals in D. H. Lawrence's novels have been omitted, for example, because I found the appropriate passages either uninteresting, too familiar, or plain silly. No specimens have been included merely to represent some phase of literary history or to acknowledge an author who has been popular with other anthologists. I have consulted my own pleasures, which is what I hope my readers will do.

The compilation of this anthology has been a delight, not least because it has required so many visits to the London Library. Several individuals whom I have met there have given generous advice: Jonathan Sinclair Carey, for example, Tiffany Stern, Francis Wheen and Marina Majdalany; but supremely Christopher Phipps. For other corrective hints I am grateful to Adrian Maddox, of PROD (Public Relations Over Dose). My wife has been a sure and cheerful guide around the sleazier corners of classical literature. I thank them all.

Dates of publication are only given for the most obscure works, but the dates of birth and death of the authors are given in the index. Many of the shorter translations from French and German are my own; other translators are indicated in the acknowledgements. Every effort has been made to trace copyright holders of the material which has been used. There are sure to be omissions, for which I apologise; my publishers will be grateful for notification in appropriate cases.

Adultery

Whosoever looketh on a woman to lust after her hath committed adultery with her already in his heart.

MATTHEW, V: 28

Adultery is in your heart not only when you look with excessive sexual zeal at a woman who is not your wife, but also if you look in the same manner at your wife.

POPE JOHN PAUL II

Marriage is but a ceremonial toy.

CHRISTOPHER MARLOWE

It is better to love two too many than one too few.

SIR JOHN HARINGTON

Adultery

Wear dark glasses in the rain.
Regard what was unhurt
as though through a bruise.
Guilt. A sick, green tint.

New gloves, money tucked in the palms,
the handshake crackles. Hands
can do many things. Phone.
Open the wine. Wash themselves. Now

you are naked under your clothes all day,
slim with deceit. Only the once
brings you alone to your knees,
miming, more, more; older and sadder,

creative. Suck a lie with a hole in it
on the way home from a lethal, thrilling night
up against a wall, faster. Language
unpeels to a lost cry. You're a bastard.

Do it do it do it. Sweet darkness
in the afternoon; a voice in your ear
telling you how you are wanted,
which way, now. A telltale clock

wiping the hours from its face, your face
on a white sheet, gasping, radiant, yes.
Pay for it in cash, fiction, cab-fares back
to the life which crumbles like a wedding-cake.

Paranoia for lunch; too much
to drink, as a hand on your thigh
tilts the restaurant. You know all about love,
don't you. Turn on your beautiful eyes

for a stranger who's dynamite in bed, again
and again; a slow replay in the kitchen
where the slicing of innocent onions
scalds you to tears. Then, selfish autobiographical sleep

in a marital bed, the tarnished spoon of your body
stirring betrayal, your heart over-ripe at the core.
You're an expert, darling; your flowers
dumb and explicit on nobody's birthday.

So write the script – illness and debt,
a ring thrown away in a garden
no moon can heal, your own words
commuting to bile in your mouth, terror –

and all for the same thing twice. And all
for the same thing twice. You did it.
What. Didn't you. Fuck. Fuck. No. That was
the wrong verb. This is only an abstract noun.

CAROL ANN DUFFY

Against Constancy

Tell me no more of constancy,
    The frivolous pretense
Of cold age, narrow jealousy,
    Disease, and want of sense.

Let duller fools, on whom kind chance
    Some easy heart has thrown,
Despairing higher to advance,
    Be kind to one alone.

Old men and weak, whose idle flame
    Their own defects discovers,
Since changing can but spread their shame,
    Ought to be constant lovers.

But we, whose hearts do justly swell
    With no vainglorious pride,
Who know how we in love excel,
    Long to be often tried.

Then bring my bath, and strew my bed,
    As each kind night returns;
I'll change a mistress till I'm dead –
    And fate change me to worms.

EARL OF ROCHESTER

Cuckold Contented

My wife told me
I go to the market
I too went to the market
Where I did not
Where I did not find my wife.
My friend told me
I go to my shop
I too went to the shop
Where I did not
Where I did not find my friend.
Walking on the beach
At the end of the day
I see the friend
Stretched out
On top of my wife.
With a thrust of my knife

I could have certainly
Certainly killed him
If he would not just in time
Just in time have awoken.
Just to give me
To give me five pounds
Five pounds which I took
And taking back with me
Taking back with me my wife.
Because water takes off the scent
The scent of love
And money doesn't smell
And money smells of nothing.

Traditional Yoruba poem (Africa)

Domestic Doings, Love's Antithesis

In her first passion woman loves her lover,
    In all the others all she loves is love,
Which grows a habit she can ne'er get over,
    And fits her loosely – like an easy glove,
As you may find, whene'er you like to prove her:
    One man alone at first her heart can move;
She then prefers him in the plural number,
Not finding that the additions much encumber.

I know not if the fault be men's or theirs;
    But one thing's pretty sure; a woman planted
(Unless at once she plunge for life in prayers)
    After a decent time must be gallanted;
Although, no doubt, her first of love affairs
    Is that to which her heart is wholly granted;
Yet there are some, they say, who have had *none*,
But those who have ne'er end with only *one*.

'Tis melancholy, and a fearful sign
  Of human frailty, folly, also crime,
That love and marriage rarely can combine,
  Although they both are born in the same clime;
Marriage from love, like vinegar from wine –
  A sad, sour, sober beverage – by time
Is sharpen'd from its high celestial flavour
Down to a very homely household savour.

There's something of antipathy, as 't were,
  Between their present and their future state;
A kind of flattery that's hardly fair
  Is used until the truth arrives too late –
Yet what can people do, except despair?
  The same things change their names at such a rate;
For instance – passion in a lover's glorious,
But in a husband is pronounced uxorious.

Men grow ashamed of being so very fond;
  They sometimes also get a little tired
(But that, of course, is rare), and then despond:
  The same things cannot always be admired,
Yet 'tis 'so nominated in the bond,'
  That both are tied till one shall have expired.
Sad thought! to lose the spouse that was adorning
Our days, and put one's servants into mourning.

There's doubtless something in domestic doings
  Which forms, in fact, true love's antithesis;
Romances paint at full length people's wooings,
  But only give a bust of marriages;
For no one cares for matrimonial cooings,
  There's nothing wrong in a connubial kiss:
Think you, if Laura had been Petrarch's wife,
He would have written sonnets all his life?

All tragedies are finish'd by a death,
    All comedies are ended by a marriage;
The future states of both are left to faith,
    For authors fear description might disparage
The worlds to come of both, or fall beneath,
    And then both worlds would punish their miscarriage;
So leaving each their priest and prayer-book ready,
They say no more of Death or of the Lady.

LORD BYRON

Etiquette for an Adulteress

Your husband will be with us at the treat;
May that be the last supper he shall eat.
And am poor I, a guest invited there,
Only to see, while he may touch the Fair?
To see you kiss and hug your nauseous Lord,
While his lewd hand descends below the board?
Now wonder not that Hippodamia's charms,
At such a sight, the Centaurs urged to arms;
That in a rage they threw their cups aside,
Assailed the bridegroom, and would force the bride.
I am not half a horse (I would I were):
Yet hardly can from you my hands forbear.
Take then my counsel; which, observed, may be
Of some importance both to you and me.
Be sure to come before your man be there;
There's nothing can be done; but come howe'er.
Sit next him (that belongs to decency);
But tread upon my foot in passing by.
Read in my looks what silently they speak,
And slily, with your eyes, your answer make.

My lifted eyebrow shall declare my pain;
My right-hand to his fellow shall complain;
And on the back a letter shall design;
Besides a note that shall be writ in wine.
Whene'er you think upon our last embrace,
With your forefinger gently touch your face.
If any word of mine offend my dear,
Pull, with your hand, the velvet of your ear.
If you are pleased with what I do or say,
Handle your rings, or with your fingers play.
As suppliants use at altars, hold the board,
Whene'er you wish the Devil may take your Lord.
When he fills for you, never touch the cup;
But bid th' officious cuckold drink it up.
The waiter on those services employ.
Drink you, and I will snatch it from the boy:
Watching the part where your sweet mouth hath been,
And thence, with eager lips, will suck it in.
If he, with clownish manners, thinks it fit
To taste, and offer you the nasty bit,
Reject his greasy kindness, and restore
Th' unsavory morsel he had chewed before.
Nor let his arms embrace your neck, nor rest
Your tender cheek upon his hairy breast.
Let not his hand within your bosom stray,
And rudely with your pretty bubbies play.
But above all, let him no kiss receive;
That's an offence I never can forgive.
Do not, O do not that sweet mouth resign,
Lest I rise up in arms, and cry, 'Tis mine.
I shall thrust in betwixt, and void of fear
The manifest adulterer will appear.
These things are plain to sight; but more I doubt
What you conceal beneath your petticoat.
Take not his leg between your tender thighs,
Nor, with your hand, provoke my foe to rise.

How many love-inventions I deplore,
Which I, myself, have practised all before!
How oft have I been forced the robe to lift
In company to make a homely shift
For a bare bout, ill huddled o'er in haste,
While o'er my side the Fair her mantle cast.
You to your husband shall not be so kind;
But, lest you should, your mantle leave behind.
Encourage him to tope; but kiss him not,
Nor mix one drop of water in his pot.
If he be fuddled well, and snores apace
Then we may take advice from Time and Place.
When all depart, when compliments are loud,
Be sure to mix among the thickest crowd.
There I will be, and there we cannot miss,
Perhaps to grubble, or at least to kiss.
Alas, what length of labour I employ,
Just to secure a short and transient joy!
For night must part us; and when night is come,
Tucked underneath his arms he leads you home.
He locks you in; I follow to the door,
His fortune envy, and my own deplore.
He kisses you, he more than kisses too;
Th' outrageous cuckold thinks it all his due.
But, add not to his joy, by your consent,
And let it not be given, but only lent.
Return no kiss, nor move in any sort;
Make it a dull and a malignant sport.
Had I my wish, he should no pleasure take,
But slubber o'er your business for my sake.
And what e'er Fortune shall this night befall,
Coax me tomorrow, by forswearing all.

OVID *(translated by John Dryden)*

The husband who decides to surprise his wife is often greatly surprised himself.

FRANÇOIS MARIE AROUET DE VOLTAIRE

Two or three visits, and two or three bows,
Two or three civil things, two or three vows,
Two or three kisses, with two or three sighs,
Two or three Jesus's – and let me dies –
Two or three squeezes, and two or three towses,
With two or three thousand pound lost at their houses,
Can never fail cuckolding two or three spouses.

ALEXANDER POPE

When a lover is seen in public with his mistress's husband, it is only decent that he should make himself look the more attractive of the two.

SEBASTIEN CHAMFORT

So heavy is the chain of wedlock that it needs two to carry it, and sometimes three.

ALEXANDRE DUMAS

A Foolish Marriage Vow

Why should a foolish marriage vow,
    Which long ago was made,
Oblige us to each other now,
    When passion is decayed?

We loved and we loved, as long as we could,
   Till our love was loved out of us both;
But our marriage is dead, now the pleasures are fled;
   'Twas pleasure first made it an oath.

If I have pleasures for a friend
    And further love in store,
What wrong has he, whose joys did end,
    And who could give no more?
'Tis a madness that he should be jealous of me,
   Or that I should bar him of another.
For all we can gain is to give ourselves pain,
   When neither can hinder the other.

JOHN DRYDEN

For My Lover, Returning to His Wife

She is all there.
She was melted carefully down for you
and cast up from your childhood,
cast up from your one hundred favorite aggies.

She has always been there, my darling.
She is, in fact, exquisite.
Fireworks in the dull middle of February
and as real as a cast-iron pot.

Let's face it, I have been momentary.
A luxury. A bright red sloop in the harbor.
My hair rising like smoke from the car window.
Littleneck clams out of season.

She is more than that. She is your have to have,
has grown you your practical your tropical growth.
This is not an experiment. She is all harmony.
She sees to oars and oarlocks for the dinghy,

has placed wild flowers at the window at breakfast,
sat by the potter's wheel at midday,
set forth three children under the moon,
three cherubs drawn by Michelangelo,

done this with her legs spread out
in the terrible months in the chapel.
If you glance up, the children are there
like delicate balloons resting on the ceiling.

She has also carried each one down the hall
after supper, their heads privately bent,
two legs protesting, person to person,
her face flushed with a song and their little sleep.

I give you back your heart.
I give you permission —

for the fuse inside her, throbbing
angrily in the dirt, for the bitch in her
and the burying of her wound —
for the burying of her small red wound alive —

for the pale flickering flare under her ribs,
for the drunken sailor who waits in her left pulse,
for the mother's knee, for the stockings,
for the garter belt, for the call —

the curious call
when you will burrow in arms and breasts
and tug at the orange ribbon in her hair
and answer the call, the curious call.

She is so naked and singular.
She is the sum of yourself and your dream.
Climb her like a monument, step after step.
She is solid.

As for me, I am a watercolor.
I wash off.

ANNE SEXTON

The Forsaken Wife

Methinks, 'tis strange you can't afford
One pitying look, one parting word;
Humanity claims this as due,
But what's humanity to you?

　　Cruel man! I am not blind,
Your infidelity I find;
Your want of love my ruin shows,
My broken heart, your broken vows.
Yet maugre all your rigid hate,
I will be true in spite of fate;
And one preeminence I'll claim,
To be for ever still the same.

　　Show me a man that dare be true,
That dares to suffer what I do;
That can for ever sigh unheard,
And ever love without regard:
I then will own your prior claim
To love, to honour, and to fame;
But till that time, my dear, adieu,
I yet superior am to you.

ELIZABETH THOMAS

The Four Nights Drunk

The first night when I come home, drunk as I could be,
I found this horse in the stable, where my horse ought to be.
  'Come here, little wifey! Explain yourself to me:
  Why is there a horse in the stable, where my horse ought to be?'
    'Why, you durn fool, you blame fool, can't you plainly see?
    It's only a milk cow my momma give to me?'
Now, I been living in this here world forty years and more,
And I never seen a milk cow with a saddle on before.

The second night when I come home, drunk as I could be,
I found a coat in the closet, where my coat ought to be.
  'Come here, little wifey! Explain yourself to me:
  Why is there a coat in the closet, where my coat ought to be?'
    'Why, you durn fool, you blame fool, can't you plainly see?
    It's only a coverlet my momma give to me.'
Now, I been living in this here world forty years and more,
And I never seen a coverlet with buttons on before.

The third night when I come home, drunk as I could be,
I found a hat hanging on the rack, where my hat ought to be.
  'Come here, little wifey! Explain yourself to me:
  Why is there a hat hanging on the rack, where my hat ought to be?'
    'Why, you durn fool, you blame fool, can't you plainly see?
    It's only a chamberpot my momma give to me.'
Now, I been living in this here world forty years and more,
And I never seen a J. B. Stetson chamberpot before.

The fourth night when I come home, drunk as I could be,
I found a head lying on the bed, where my head ought to be.
  'Come here, little wifey! Explain yourself to me:
  Why is there a head lying on the bed, where my head ought to be?'

'Why, you durn fool, you blame fool, can't you plainly see?
It's only a cabbage head my momma give to me.'
Now, I been living in this here world forty years and more,
And I never seen a cabbage head with a mustache on before.

ANONYMOUS

Give Me a Little Romance

18 November 1819: She met me affectionately enough & seemed rather nervous. Dinner was ready. In taking off my hat & front, the firelight did not let M— see my hair was in paper. She thought it cut close to my head & started back, saying I was not fit to be seen. She could not make it look decent. I said Anne could & sent for her. I was before, when I saw M— nervous, beginning to be a little pathetic, but this little incident cured me. I laughed it off, said M—'s horror had done me a great deal of good, put on a neat waist & went down grinning & looking the neatest of the party …

Not much conversation before getting into bed. C— made no objection to her coming to Manchester when he heard she was to meet me, tho' before he did not wish her to go farther than Wilmslow, he hurried them off before seven in the morning that she might have more time to be with me, & on this account, would give her till eight o'clock to be at home tomorrow … Asked her how often they were connected &, guessing, found it might be at the rate of about twenty times a year. Got into bed. She seemed to want a kiss. It was more than I did. The tears rushed to my eyes. I felt I know not what & she perceived that I was much agitated. She bade me not or she should begin too & I knew not how she should suffer. She guessed not what passed within me. They were not tears of adoration. I felt that she was another man's wife. I shuddered at the thought & at the conviction that no soffistry [*sic*] could gloss over the criminality of our connection. It seemed not that the like had occurred to her. (I said, just before we got up, 'Well, come, whatever

C— has done to me, I am even with him. However, he little thinks what we have been about. What would he do if he knew?' 'Do? He would divorce me.' 'Yes,' said I, 'it would be a sad business for us both, but we are even with him, at any rate.' 'Indeed,' said M—, laughing, 'indeed we are.' Shewed no sign of scruples … What is M—'s match but legal prostitution? And, alas, what is her connection with me? Has she more passion than refinement? More plausibility than virtue? Give me a little romance. It is the greatest purifier of our affections & often an excellent guard against liberties.) From the kiss she gave me it seemed as if she loved me as fondly as ever. By & by, we seemed to drop asleep but, by & by, I perceived she would like another kiss & she whispered, 'Come again a bit, Freddy.' For a little while I pretended sleep. In fact, it was inconvenient. But soon, I got up a second time, again took off, went to her a second time &, in spite of all, she really gave me pleasure, & I told her no one had ever given me kisses like hers.

ANNE LISTER, *I Know My Own Heart*

The Horns of Derision

In the county of Alletz there lived a man named Bornet, who being married to an upright and virtuous wife, had great regard for her honour and reputation, as I believe is the case with all the husbands here present in respect to their own wives. But although he desired that she should be true to him, he was not willing that the same law should apply to both, for he fell in love with his maid-servant, from whom he had nothing to gain save the pleasure afforded by a diversity of viands.

Now he had a neighbour of the same condition as his own, named Sandras, a tabourer and tailor by trade, and there was such friendship between them that, excepting Bornet's wife, they had all things in common. It thus happened that Bornet told his friend of the enterprise he had in hand against the maid-servant; and Sandras not only approved of it, but gave all the assistance he could to further its accomplishment, hoping that he himself might share in the spoil.

The maid-servant, however, was loth to consent, and finding herself hard pressed, she went to her mistress, told her of the matter, and begged leave to go home to her kinsfolk, since she could no longer endure to live in such torment. Her mistress, who had great love for her husband and had often suspected him, was well pleased to have him thus at a disadvantage, and to be able to show that she had doubted him justly. Accordingly, she said to the servant –

'Remain, my girl, but lead my husband on by degrees, and at last make an appointment to lie with him in my closet. Do not fail to tell me on what night he is to come, and see that no one knows anything about it.'

The maid-servant did all that her mistress had commanded her, and her master in great content went to tell the good news to his friend. The latter then begged that, since he had been concerned in the business, he might have part in the result. This was promised him, and, when the appointed hour was come, the master went to lie, as he thought, with the maid-servant; but his wife, yielding up the authority of commanding for the pleasure of obeying, had put herself in the servant's place, and she received him, not in the manner of a wife, but after the fashion of a frightened maid. This she did so well that her husband suspected nothing.

I cannot tell you which of the two was the better pleased, he at the thought that he was deceiving his wife, or she at really deceiving her husband. When he had remained with her, not as long as he wished, but according to his powers, which were those of a man who had long been married, he went out of doors, found his friend, who was much younger and lustier than himself, and told him gleefully that he had never met with better fortune. 'You know what you promised me,' said his friend to him.

'Go quickly then,' replied the husband, 'for she may get up, or my wife have need of her.'

The friend went off and found the supposed maid-servant, who, thinking her husband had returned, denied him nothing that he asked of her, or rather took, for he durst not speak. He remained with her much longer than her husband had done, whereat she was greatly astonished, for she had not been wont to pass such nights. Nevertheless, she endured it all with patience, comforting herself with the thought of what she would say to him on the morrow, and of the ridicule that she would cast upon him.

Towards daybreak the man rose from beside her, and toying with her as he was going away, snatched from her finger the ring with which her husband had espoused her, and which the women of that part of the country guard with great superstition. She who keeps it till her death is held in high honour, while she who chances to lose it, is thought lightly of as a person who has given her faith to some other than her husband. The wife, however, was very glad to have it taken, thinking it would be a sure proof of how she had deceived her husband.

When the friend returned, the husband asked him how he had fared. He replied that he was of the same opinion as himself, and that he would have remained longer had he not feared to be surprised by daybreak. Then they both went to the friend's house to take as long a rest as they could. In the morning, while they were dressing, the husband perceived the ring that his friend had on his finger, and saw that it was exactly like the one he had given to his wife at their marriage. He thereupon asked his friend from whom he had received the ring, and when he heard he had snatched it from the servant's finger, he was confounded and began to strike his head against the wall, saying – 'Ah! good Lord! have I made myself a cuckold without my wife knowing anything about it?'

'Perhaps,' said his friend in order to comfort him, 'your wife gives her ring into the maid's keeping at night-time.'

The husband made no reply, but took himself home, where he found his wife fairer, more gaily dressed, and merrier than usual, like one who rejoiced at having saved her maid's conscience, and tested her husband to the full, at no greater cost than a night's sleep. Seeing her so cheerful, the husband said to himself –

'If she knew of my adventure she would not show me such a pleasant countenance.'

Then, whilst speaking to her of various matters, he took her by the hand, and on noticing that she no longer wore the ring, which she had never been accustomed to remove from her finger, he was quite overcome.

'What have you done with your ring?' he asked her in a trembling voice.

She, well pleased that he gave her an opportunity to say what she desired, replied –

'O wickedest of men! From whom do you imagine you took it? You thought it was from my maid-servant, for love of whom you expended more than twice as much of your substance as you ever did for me. The first time you came to bed I thought you as much in love as it was possible to be; but after you had gone out and were come back again, you seemed to be a very devil. Wretch! think how blind you must have been to bestow such praises on my person and lustiness, which you have long enjoyed without holding them in any great esteem. 'Twas, therefore, not the maid-servant's beauty that made the pleasure so delightful to you, but the grievous sin of lust which so consumes your heart and so clouds your reason that in the frenzy of your love for the servant you would, I believe, have taken a she-goat in a nightcap for a comely girl! Now, husband, it is time to amend your life, and, knowing me to be your wife, and an honest woman, to be as content with me as you were when you took me for a pitiful strumpet. What I did was to turn you from your evil ways, so that in your old age we might live together in true love and repose of conscience. If you purpose to continue your past life, I had rather be severed from you than daily see before my eyes the ruin of your soul, body, and estate. But if you will acknowledge the evil of your ways, and resolve to live in fear of God and obedience to His commandments, I will forget all your past sins, as I trust God will forget my ingratitude in not loving Him as I ought to do.'

If ever man was reduced to despair it was this unhappy husband. Not only had he abandoned this sensible, fair, and chaste wife for a woman who did not love him, but, worse than this, he had without her knowledge made her a strumpet by causing another man to participate in the pleasure which should have been for himself alone; and thus he had made himself horns of everlasting derision.

However, seeing his wife in such wrath by reason of the love he had borne his maid-servant, he took care not to tell her of the evil trick that he had played her; and entreating her forgiveness, with promises of full amendment of his former evil life, he gave her back the ring which he had recovered from his friend. He entreated the latter not to reveal his shame; but, as what is whispered in the ear is always proclaimed from the housetop, the truth, after a time, became known, and men called him cuckold without imputing any shame to his wife.

QUEEN MARGARET OF NAVARRE, *The Heptameron*

I Like My Mistresses' Husbands

The chief pleasure that a bachelor gets from taking a married woman as his mistress is that she gives him a comfortable, pleasant home in which everyone cares for him and spoils him, from the husband to the servants. Every pleasure is there: love, friendship, the bed, the table, even paternity, in fact every happiness in life, together with the inestimable advantage of being free to change your household intermittently, installing yourself by turns where you will, in the country, during summer, in the home of a workman who lets you a room in his house; in the winter, with the middle classes, or even with aristocrats, if you are ambitious.

I have another weakness: I like my mistresses' husbands. Admittedly there are husbands, vulgar or coarse, who inspire in me disgust for their wives, however charming these may be; but when the husband has wit or charm, it is inevitable that I become infatuated. I am careful, if I break with a woman, not to break with her husband. In this way I have made my best friends.

GUY DE MAUPASSANT, 'Misti'

May I Feel Said He?

> may i feel said he
> (i'll squeal said she
> just once said he)
> it's fun said she
>
> (may i touch said he
> how much said she
> a lot said he)
> why not said she

(let's go said he
not too far said she
what's too far said he
where you are said she)

may i stay said he
(which way said she
like this said he
if you kiss said she

may i move said he
is it love said she)
if you're willing said he
(but you're killing said she

but it's life said he
but your wife said she
now said he)
ow said she

(tiptop said he
don't stop said she
oh no said he)
go slow said she

(cccome? said he
ummm said she)
you're divine! said he
(you are Mine said she)

                      e e cummings

A Meanness and a Stealing

Presently I had a martini to pull myself together, and then went out to a kiosk and telephoned to Vere, and on account of the martini and talking to Vere, I stopped feeling neurotic and felt instead happy and at peace and as if nothing mattered but that we should be together in an hour. And then I thought how odd it was, all that love and joy and peace that flooded over me when I thought about Vere, and how it all came from what was a deep meanness in our lives, for that is what adultery is, a meanness and a stealing, a taking away from someone what should be theirs, a great selfishness, and surrounded and guarded by lies lest it should be found out. And out of this meanness and this selfishness and this lying flow love and joy and peace, beyond anything that can be imagined. And this makes a discord in the mind, the happiness and the guilt and the remorse pulling in opposite ways so that the mind and soul are torn in two, and if it goes on for years and years the discord becomes permanent, so that it will never stop, and even if one goes on living after death, as some people think, there will still be this deep discord that nothing can heal, because of the great meanness and selfishness that caused such a deep joy. And there is no way out of this dilemma that I know.

DAME ROSE MACAULAY, *The Towers of Trebizond*

No Complaints

Not long ago there lived at Perugia a rich man called Pietro di Vinciolo, who took a wife, not from desires of his own, but to blind others and mitigate the ill repute in which he was held by all Perugians: and such being his motive, Fortune gave him just the wife he deserved. For the wife of his choice was a sturdy, red-haired wench, so hot-blooded that two husbands would have satisfied her better than one, though she was saddled with one whose interests were altogether different. In time she realised this, and knowing herself to be fair and lusty, feeling game and fresh, she felt aggrieved, and had high words with her husband, with whom she was always now at odds. Then, seeing that she was fretting away without stopping her husband's depravity, she resolved to herself: 'This wretch deserts me to walk in overshoes in dry weather, so I will take others on board ship in wet weather. I brought a fine great dowry when I married him, knowing that he was a man, and expecting him to have manly desires; had I not thought him a man, I would never have married him. He knew that I was a woman; if women were not to his taste, why did he marry me? It is insufferable. If I had wanted to renounce the world, I should have become a nun; now, having chosen a worldly life, if I have to wait on that man for my pleasures, I will have a long wait indeed; and then, too late, when I am old I shall bemoan that I wasted my youth. As to obtaining satisfaction, I can find no better guide than him, who finds his delights where I should find mine; seeing that I will offend the law alone, whereas he defies both law and Nature, what is disgraceful in him will be more excusable in me.'

So the lady reasoned more than once; and then, reflecting how she might discreetly compass her end, she confided in an old crone, resembling Saint Verdiana, foster-mother of vipers, who was always going to confession with beads in her hands, talked of nothing but the lives of the Holy Fathers, or the wounds of St Francis, and was reputed to be saintly. 'My girl,' replied the crone, 'God who knows all things, knows that you would do rightly indeed: neither you nor any other woman should waste their youth, for there is no grief so arid as knowing that it has been wasted. And what the devil are we women good for when old except to guard the cinders of the hearth? No one knows this better than I, who am now old, and suffer sore gnawing remorse at the chances I missed; for though I was not a complete fool and my youth was not entirely wasted, still I did not make the most of it ... We women are always ready for it, which is not the case with men; besides which, one woman can tire out many men at the game, although many men cannot satiate one woman. Seeing that this is what we are born for, I tell you again that you would be right to give your husband your loaf for his cake, so that in your old age you will have nothing to rue. You only get as much of life as you take: this is especially true for women, who far more than men should take their chances while they can, for when we age, neither husband nor any other man will spare us a glance; but instead, will banish us to the kitchen, there to gossip with the cat and count the pots and pans; or worse, they make rhymes about us ...'

So the lady arranged with the old crone, that as soon as she saw a boy who came often along that street and whose every feature she described, she would know what to do; then giving her a chunk of salted meat, she bade her God-speed. Before long the crone smuggled this boy into the lady's chamber; and a little while after, another; and then another; as took the fancy of the lady who, despite her dread of her husband, would not stint herself any longer. It chanced one evening that, the husband going to sup with a friend named Ercolano, the lady charged the crone to procure her a youth, who was one of the most luscious and amenable in all Perugia. But hardly had the lady and her boy sat at the table to eat, but lo, Pietro's voice called at the door for it to be opened to him. She, hearing this, despaired of herself as lost; but wanting to hide the boy if she could, and not thinking of anywhere better to conceal him, pushed him under a hen-coop that stood outside the chamber where they were supping, and threw over it the sacking of a mattress that she had only that day emptied of its straw.

This done, she hastened to open the door to her husband, saying to him, 'You have guzzled your supper quickly tonight.' 'We have not so much as tasted it,' he replied. 'Why's that?' enquired the lady. 'I will tell you,' said Pietro. 'No sooner were we at table, Ercolano, his wife, and I, than we heard a sneeze close by, which we ignored, though it was repeated; but the sneezer sneezed a third, and a fourth, and a fifth, and many more times, till we began to wonder, and Ercolano, who was displeased with his wife because she had kept us standing a long time at the door before she opened it, demanded irritably, "What means this? Who is it sneezing?" Rising from the table, he made for a nearby staircase, beneath which was a wooden cupboard. As it seemed the sneezing came from there, he opened the cupboard's door, and no sooner had he done so, than the foulest stench of brimstone billowed forth. Something of this smell had already reached us, and when we complained of it, the lady had put us off, saying; "I was just bleaching my veils with brimstone, sprinkling it on a dish so that they might catch its fumes, and it's still smoking a little."

'When the smoke was less thick, Ercolano peered in the cupboard, and saw the fellow who had sneezed, and who still kept sneezing at the pungency of the brimstone. By this time he was so choked by the fumes that he was soon like neither to sneeze nor do aught again. Ercolano, seeing him, yelled, "Now, wife, I see why it was that when we came here, we were kept waiting so long before you opened. By thunder, I will pay you for this!" Whereupon, the lady, seeing that all was discovered, made no excuse, but fled the table, I know not where. Ercolano, ignoring her flight, again and again ordered the sneezer out; but the latter, who was at his last gasp, would not stir, for all that was said; whereupon Ercolano, seizing a foot, dragged him from his hiding-place, and ran for a knife to kill him; but I, fearing the magistrates on my own account, rose and would not suffer him to kill the fellow, or do him any hurt, and for his protection, gave the alarm, whereupon some neighbours took the boy, more dead than alive, and bore him off, I know not whither. Our supper being disrupted by all this, I not only have not finished it, I have not even tasted it.'

Pietro's story showed his wife that there were other women like her, whom misfortune might sometimes catch out; gladly would she have defended Ercolano's wife, but thinking that by condemning another's vices she would secure more scope for her own, she began to exclaim. 'Fine doings indeed, a holy and virtuous woman she must be! The worst of it is, she is no longer young, and should be setting a better example! Curses on the hour that she came into the world! Curses on the vile, per-fidious, faithless woman! How shameful for the rest of her sex, that she casts aside all regard to her honour, her marriage vows, her reputation, and lost to shame, disgraces so worthy and honourable a citizen as her husband, who has treated her so well! God save me, there should be no mercy for such women! They should be put to death! They should be burnt to ashes!' Then, remembering her lover so near by in the hen coop, she began to coax Pietro off to bed, for the hour grew late; but he was more inclined for food than sleep, and asked for supper. 'Supper,' answered the lady, 'as if there'd be supper for anyone when you've gone out for the night. Do you take me for Ercolano's wife? Why don't you go to sleep now? It would be better for you.'

Now it chanced that some of Pietro's husbandmen had come to the house that night with various things from the farm, and had put their asses away without watering them. One of the asses, being thirsty, slipped his halter and broke loose from the stable, and went nosing for water: whereby he came upon the hen-coop in which the youth crouched. The latter, who was down on all fours, had put out the fingers of one hand on the ground outside the coop, and as ill-luck would have it, the ass trod on them; whereupon the boy, in agony, set up a great howling, to the surprise of Pietro. Perceiving that the noise came from his own house, he went out, and hearing the boy moaning and groaning, for the ass still kept its hoof hard down on the fingers, cried, 'Who's there?' Then running to the hen-coop, he raised it, and saw the fellow, who beside the pain of having his fingers crushed, trembled in every limb for fear lest Pietro should do him a mischief.

The boy was one that Pietro had long been after for his lewd ends, so Pietro, recognising him, asked him what he did there. The boy made no answer, save to beseech him for the love of God to do him no hurt. Then Pietro said, 'Get up, and have no fear that I will hurt you, but tell me how you came here, and for what purpose.' The boy then told all, whereupon Pietro, as stimulated by the discovery as his wife was woeful, took him by the hand, and led him into the room, where the lady waited in an extremity of terror. Seating himself directly in front of her, he said: 'A moment ago you cursed Ercolano's wife, and averred that she should be burned, and was a disgrace to all women: why did you not speak of yourself? Or even if you didn't choose to speak of yourself, how had you the effrontery to abuse her, knowing that you were no better than she? Truly it was for no other reason than that you are all like that, and cover your vices with the delinquencies of others: would that fire might fall from heaven and burn you all, brood of iniquity that you are!'

The lady, marking that in his first flush of wrath he had given her nothing worse than hard words, and discerning that he was secretly elated to hold so beautiful a boy by the hand, took heart and said: 'I don't doubt that you would be pleased if fire should fall from heaven and consume all women, seeing that you are as fond of us as a dog is of the stick; but by Christ, you will not get your wish. Of what do you dare to complain? It would be fine enough for me if you put me on a level with Ercolano's wife, who is a sanctimonious old hypocrite, but has of her husband what she will, and is cherished by him as a wife should be. That is not my case. Granted that I am well clad and shod by you, but you know too well how I fare for the rest, and how long it is since you did lie with me; yet I would rather go barefoot, in rags, and be well used by you in bed. Understand me, Pietro, be reasonable; I am a woman like other women, with the same cravings; if you deny me their gratification, it's not my fault if I look elsewhere; and at least I do you this much honour, that I do not do it with stable-boys and knaves.'

Pietro perceiving that words were not likely to fail her all night, and indifferent as he was to her, said: 'Wife, enough of this; I will content thee; but let us have supper first, for I think this boy, like me, has not yet eaten.' 'True enough,' said the lady, 'he has not supped, for we were sitting down to table when you made your ill-timed entrance.' 'Go then,' rejoined Pietro, 'get us supper, and afterwards I will arrange things so that you have no cause to complain.' The lady, seeing her husband's tranquillity, rose, had the table laid and spread with the supper which she had ready; so they made a merry meal of it, husband, lady and boy. What after supper Pietro devised for their mutual satisfaction I cannot recall; but this much I know, that on the following morning, the boy left, not sure which he had been more that night, wife or husband. This only I would say to you, my dear ladies, whoever does it to you, do it to him; and if you cannot do it at once, keep it in mind until you can, so that he may get as good as he gives.

GIOVANNI BOCCACCIO, *Decameron*

Nothing to Fear

All fixed: early arrival at the flat
Lent by a friend, whose note says *Lucky sod*;
Drinks on the tray; the cover-story pat
And quite uncheckable; her husband off
Somewhere with all the kids till six o'clock
(Which ought to be quite long enough);
And all worth while: face really beautiful,
Good legs and hips, and as for breasts – my God.
What about guilt, compunction and such stuff?
I've had my fill of all that cock;
It'll wear off, as usual.

Yes, all fixed. Then why this slight trembling,
Dry mouth, quick pulse-rate, sweaty hands,
As though she were the first? No, not impatience,
Nor fear of failure, thank you, Jack.
Beauty, they tell me, is a dangerous thing,
Whose touch will burn, but I'm asbestos, see?
All worth while – it's a dead coincidence
That sitting here, a bag of glands
Tuned up to concert pitch, I seem to sense
A different style of caller at my back,
As cold as ice, but just as set on me.

SIR KINGSLEY AMIS

Our Shopboy, Jack

In these words to his tearful wife the dying butcher spake:
     'Since slaughtering needs a strong man's help, dear, if I go,
Our shopboy Jack's an honest lad and smart. Then why not take
     Him as a husband, for you might do worse, you know?
In sheets no less than shambles a stout partner he would make.'
     'I've tried him oft,' she sobbed, 'and ever found him so.'

BARRATON

It is sometimes pleasant for a husband to have a jealous wife, for then he constantly hears about the woman he loves.

DUC DE LA ROCHEFOUCAULD

Platonic love is a bawd to adultery.

DUCHESS OF NEWCASTLE

No man worth having is true to his wife, or can be true to his wife, or ever was, or ever will be.

SIR JOHN VANBRUGH

Matrimony hath many Children; Repentance, Discord, Poverty, Jealousy, Sickness, Spleen, Loathing.

JONATHAN SWIFT

Questions of Paternity

A grave wise man that had a great rich lady,
Such as perhaps in these days found there may be,
Did think she played him false and more than think,
Save that in wisdom he thereat did wink.
Howbeit one time disposed to sport and play
Thus to his wife he pleasantly did say,
'Since strangers lodge their arrows in thy quiver,
Dear dame, I pray you yet the cause deliver,
If you can tell the cause and not dissemble,
How all our children me so much resemble?'
The lady blushed but yet this answer made:
"Though I have used some traffic in the trade,
And must confess, as you have touched before,
My bark was sometimes steered with foreign oar,
    Yet stowed I no man's stuff but first persuaded
    The bottom with your ballast full was laded.'

SIR JOHN HARINGTON

A Song on the Beautiful Wife of Dr John Overall

The Dean of Paul's did search for his wife
    And where d'ee think he found her?
Even upon Sir John Selby's bed,
    As flat as any flounder.

ANONYMOUS, 17th century

But for his funeral train which the bridegroom sees in the distance,
Would he so joyfully, think you, fall in with the marriage-procession?

ARTHUR HUGH CLOUGH

When charged with infidelity, a husband says: 'I admit it, but I did not love her', and a wife says: 'I loved him, but I stayed faithful.'

COMTESSE DIANE

Fidelity. A virtue peculiar to those who are about to be betrayed.

AMBROSE BIERCE

A marriage proves itself a good marriage by enduring an occasional 'exception'.

FRIEDRICH NIETZSCHE

Those who are faithful know only the trivial side of love: it is the faithless who know life's tragedies.

OSCAR WILDE

Taken in Adultery

Shadowed by shades and spied upon by glass
Their search for privacy conducts them here,
With an irony that neither notices,
To a public house; the wrong time of the year
For outdoor games; where, over gin and tonic,
Best bitter and potato crisps, they talk
Without much zest, almost laconic,
Flipping an occasional remark.
Would you guess that they were lovers, this dull pair?
The answer, I suppose, is yes, you would.
Despite her spectacles and faded hair
And his worn look of being someone's Dad
You know that they are having an affair
And neither finds it doing them much good.
Presumably, in one another's eyes,
They must look different from what we see,
Desirable in some way, otherwise
They'd hardly choose to come here, furtively,
And mutter their bleak needs above the mess
Of fag ends, crumpled cellophane and crumbs,
Their love-feast's litter. Though they might profess
To find great joy together, all that comes
Across to us is tiredness, melancholy.
When they are silent each seems listening;
There must be many voices in the air:
Reproaches, accusations, suffering
That no amount of passion keeps elsewhere.
Imperatives that brought them to this room,
Stiff from the car's back seat, lose urgency;
They start to wonder who's betraying whom,

How it will end, and how did it begin –
The woman taken in adultery
And the man who feels he, too, was taken in.

VERNON SCANNELL

Proud and vaine-glorious persons are certainly mad, and so are lascivious, I can feele their pulses beate hither, horne mad some of them, to let others lye with their wives, and winke at it.

ROBERT BURTON

The cruellest revenge of a woman is to remain faithful to a man.

JACQUES BOSSUET

Deare wife hath ne're a handsome letter,
Sweet mistris sounds a great deale better.

RICHARD CRASHAW

The more one loves a mistress the nearer one is to hating her.

DUC DE LA ROCHEFOUCAULD

To Divide is Not to Take Away

I never was attached to that great sect,
Whose doctrine is, that each one should select
Out of the crowd a mistress or a friend,
And all the rest, though fair and wise, commend

To cold oblivion, though it is the code
Of modern morals, and the beaten road
Which those poor slaves with weary footsteps tread
Who travel to their home among the dead
By the broad highway of the world, and so
With one chained friend, perhaps a jealous foe,
The dreariest and the longest journey go.

True love in this differs from gold and clay,
That to divide is not to take away.
Love is like understanding, that grows bright
Gazing on many truths; 'tis like the light,
Imagination! which from earth and sky,
And from the depths of human phantasy,
As from a thousand prisms and mirrors, fills
The universe with glorious beams, and kills
Error, the worm, with many a sun-like arrow
Of its reverberated lightning. Narrow
The heart that loves, the brain that contemplates,
The life that wears, the spirit that creates
One object, and one form, and builds thereby
A sepulchre for its eternity.

PERCY BYSSHE SHELLEY

Treasure

She had given orders that she wished to remain undisturbed and more-over had locked the doors of her room.

The house was very still. The rain was falling steadily from a leaden sky in which there was no gleam, no rift, no promise. A generous wood fire had been lighted in the ample fireplace and it brightened and illu-mined the luxurious apartment to its furthermost corner.

From some remote nook of her writing desk the woman took a thick bundle of letters, bound tightly together with strong, coarse twine, and placed it upon the table in the centre of the room.

For weeks she had been schooling herself for what she was about to do. There was a strong deliberation in the lines of her long, thin, sensitive face; her hands, too, were long and delicate and blue-veined.

With a pair of scissors she snapped the cord binding the letters together. Thus released the ones which were top-most slid down to the table and she, with a quick movement thrust her fingers among them, scattering and turning them over till they quite covered the broad surface of the table.

Before her were envelopes of various sizes and shapes, all of them addressed in the handwriting of one man and one woman. He had sent her letters all back to her one day when, sick with dread of possibilities, she had asked to have them returned. She had meant, then, to destroy them all, his and her own. That was four years ago, and she had been feeding upon them ever since; they had sustained her, she believed, and kept her spirit from perishing utterly.

But now the days had come when the premonition of danger could no longer remain unheeded. She knew that before many months were past she would have to part from her treasure, leaving it unguarded. She shrank from inflicting the pain, the anguish which the discovery of those letters would bring to others; to one, above all, who was near to her, and whose tenderness and years of devotion had made him, in a manner, dear to her.

She calmly selected a letter at random from the pile and cast it into the roaring fire. A second one followed almost as calmly, with the third her hand began to tremble; when, in a sudden paroxysm she cast a fourth, a fifth, and a sixth into the flames in breathless succession.

Then she stopped and began to pant – for she was far from strong, and she stayed staring into the fire with pained and savage eyes. Oh, what had she done! What had she not done! With feverish apprehension she began to search among the letters before her. Which of them had she so ruthlessly, so cruelly put out of her existence? Heaven grant, not the first, that very first one, written before they had learned, or dared to say to each other 'I love you'. No, no; there it was, safe enough. She laughed with pleasure, and held it to her lips. But what if that other most precious and most imprudent one were missing! in which every word of untempered passion had long ago eaten its way into her brain; and which stirred her still to-day, as it had done a hundred times before when she thought of it. She crushed it between her palms when she found it. She kissed it again and again. With her sharp white teeth she tore the far corner from the letter, where the name was written; she bit the torn scrap and tasted it between her lips and upon her tongue like some god-given morsel.

What unbounded thankfulness she felt at not having destroyed them all! How desolate and empty would have been her remaining days without them; with only her thoughts, illusive thoughts that she could not hold in her hands and press, as she did these, to her cheeks and her heart.

This man had changed the water in her veins to wine, whose taste had brought delirium to both of them. It was all one and past now, save for these letters that she held encircled in her arms. She stayed breathing softly and contentedly, with the hectic cheek resting upon them.

She was thinking, thinking of a way to keep them without possible ultimate injury to that other one whom they would stab more cruelly than keen knife blades.

At last she found the way. It was a way that frightened and bewildered her to think of at first, but she had reached it by deduction too sure to admit of doubt. She meant, of course, to destroy them herself before the end came. But how does the end come and when? Who may tell? She would guard against the possibility of accident by leaving them in charge of the very one who, above all, should be spared a knowledge of their contents.

She roused herself from the stupor of thought and gathered the scattered letters once more together, binding them again with the rough twine. She wrapped the compact bundle in a thick sheet of white polished paper. Then she wrote in ink upon the back of it, in large, firm characters:

'I leave this package to the care of my husband. With perfect faith in his loyalty and his love, I ask him to destroy it unopened.'

It was not sealed; only a bit of string held the wrapper, which she could remove and replace at will whenever the humor came to her to pass an hour in some intoxicating dream of the days when she felt she had lived.

KATE CHOPIN, *Her Letters*

What is more disheartening to think of than the unremitting monogamy of grim couples?

LOGAN PEARSALL SMITH

I can only admit two schools: either sensuality practised as an art, with specialised slaves and all that one reads of in Suetonius: or marriage, the perfect realisation of the promise given me by Nature when I awoke in shame at puberty. But adultery, that half measure, that commonplace literary thing: the whole world may go into it, but it shall not have me.

VALÉRY LARBAUD

He had the three badges of nonentity: a receding chin, the Legion of Honour, and a wedding ring.

NATALIE BARNEY

There are few who would not rather be taken in adultery than in provincialism.

ALDOUS HUXLEY

A man never forgives a woman who forces him to tell lies.

GEORGES SIMENON

When a man marries his mistress, it creates a vacancy.

SIR JAMES GOLDSMITH

Finally – the Perfect Relationship

I was sustained at this time – and indeed for just over a year longer – by perhaps the most intimate and delicious friendship of the many with which I have been blessed. I never saw her. I never knew who she was. I was to call her Egeria because like that nymph she was so elusive, and she so quickly melted into tears and laughter. It was not of course her real christian name. Inevitably she called me Numa, the mortal who accepted Egeria's instructions in the art of living.

Late one night in London, during an in-between hospital period, I was endeavouring to telephone to a friend. Instead of getting through to him my line was crossed with that of a woman, also wanting to telephone. 'My number is Grosvenor 8527,' I heard her tell the operator, 'and I want a Hampstead number. Instead of which you have hitched me up to Flaxman something. This poor man doesn't want to talk to me at all.' 'Oh yes, I do,' I joined in, for I liked her voice immensely. It was harmonious and clever. Instead of being cross this woman was very good-humoured about the muddle. After mutual apologies we both rang off. A minute or two later I dialled again, and again got on to her, although there was no resemblance between her number and the one I was trying to get. Since it seemed that our lines were predestined to link up, we talked to each other for twenty minutes. 'Why were you wanting to speak to a friend after midnight, anyway?' she asked. I told her the reason which I have now forgotten. 'And why were you?' I asked her. She explained that her old mother slept badly, and she often talked to her late at night. Then we discussed the books we were reading, and of course the war. Finally I said, 'I don't remember enjoying a talk so much for years.' 'It was fun, wasn't it? Well, I suppose we ought to stop now,' she said. 'I suppose we must. Good-bye.' 'Good night,' she said. 'Pleasant dreams.'

All next day I thought of our conversation. I thought of her intelligent remarks about Balzac. I thought of her spontaneity, her enthusiasm, and her sense of fun. I thought too of her distinctive accent which was soft and seductive, without being the least insinuating. Its musical modulation haunted me. I am not good at remembering telephone numbers, but for some reason Grosvenor 8527 stuck. I kept repeating it to myself in buses and on pavements, and I wrote it down for fear of forgetting.

That evening in bed I paid little attention to what I was reading. By midnight Grosvenor 8527 was recurring so often in my head that I could bear it no longer. I got up, went to the telephone and with trepidation dialled the number. I heard the swift, disengaged purr of the bell at the other end, the note that was soon to become as familiar and welcoming as the high-pitched, frenzied engaged signal was rebarbative. In course of time I got to know by the pitch of the very first ring whether she was at home, or not. If she was at home the ring was warm and joyous. If she was away, it took on a hollow sound like a desolate voice crying for mercy in a tomb. The longer one let it continue the more deathlike and tragic it sounded. On this occasion however the receiver at the other end was picked up instantly, as it always was to be when she was there. 'Hello! it's me. So sorry to be a bore, but may we continue our conversation where we left off last night?' I asked. Without saying no or yes, she straightway launched upon a dissertation on *La Cousine Bette* which was highly original and funny. Within minutes we were joking and laughing as though we had known each other for years.

This time we talked for three quarters of an hour. She was enchanting. The late hour and our anonymity broke down all those absurdly conventional reserves which usually hedge two people during preliminary meetings after an introduction. At the end of this talk I suggested that we ought to introduce ourselves. But she would not have it. It might spoil everything, she said. 'I don't recognise your voice, nor you mine. If we found that we had friends or even relations in common, there would be a restraint upon our totally unguarded talks. Let's not even mention our friends by name in case one of us has a clue who the other may be.' Her only concession was to make a note of my telephone number.

We had several more midnight talks before I went to the Birmingham hospital from which I occasionally rang her up in London. But from a public call-box trunk calls, which must necessarily be short, were not as satisfactory as local ones which could last as long as we wanted them to. Before I left for Birmingham I extracted a promise from her that we would reveal our identities when the war ended. Even so she gave it with some reluctance. All I ever learned about her circumstances was that she had been married at seventeen to a disagreeable man from whom she was separated. She was thirty-six. Her only child had recently been killed flying at the age of eighteen. He meant everything to her and she spoke of him as though he were still alive. After a month or two I got to know him almost as well as her, and found myself saying things like, 'Do you remember how Billy flew over Hamburg and couldn't bring himself to release his bombs over the suburbs?'; or, 'It seems to me that remark of yours was just how Billy would have expressed it.' His was an infinitely endearing personality; and he became like a son to me. Since she once described him as being beautiful as the dawn, and another time as resembling her in every feature, I had a picture of her which once formed never changed. When I told her how beautiful she was to contemplate, she merely laughed and asked, 'How do you know I am?'

We grew to depend upon each other. There were no subjects we did not discuss. Our views on most were identical, including the war. She gave me counsel and strength. The only fault I could find in her was an over-scrupulosity in her relations with others, in particular her husband towards whom her loyalty and help seemed excessive. We took to reading the same books for the fun of discussing them, and because we both belonged to the London Library each undertook not to find out from the librarians the name of the other. When I was discharged from hospital for good I rented a minute house in Chelsea for the rest of the war. Never a night passed when we were both in London that we did not telephone, no matter how late she or I might be back from dinner, and sometimes I was horribly late. I would look forward to our next talk the whole preceding day. If I went away for the weekend and was unable to telephone she complained that she could hardly get to sleep for loneliness. At times I found it unbearable not to see her. I would threaten to jump into a taxi and drive to her at once. 'Let's stop this pantomime. We know each other much better than any couple in the world. And we love each other as much.' But she would not give in. She said that if we met and found we did not love, as then we did, it would kill her. 'Perhaps,' she said, 'I made a mistake in the first place. Now it's too late.' 'All right, my darling,' I said, 'I won't come. Anyway I can't, so long as you refuse to tell me who or where you are. But the war shows little sign of ending. And we may have ages to wait.'

Whenever there was a bad raid at night I would ring up, after it was over, to find out how she was. This always amused her. But I noticed that whenever she imagined there was one over Chelsea she did the same. When my telephone was out of order I would send a telegram addressed simply to Grosvenor 8527 and signed Numa, just to say that I was alive. And whenever my work took me out of London for a few days I felt anxious.

For twelve months I lived in an extraordinary state of inner content. Extraordinary because the times through which we were living were grim, and our love was in a sense unfulfilled. But it had compensations. It was the first I ever experienced that lacked agony. There was nothing to provoke a twinge of jealousy, that terrible and almost invariable accompaniment of love which undermines the spirit. I knew that our passage was entirely free from the usual shoals and reefs that beset the turbulence of passion. There seemed no reason why it should not flow on this even course for ever. After all, the language of words is more powerful and more lasting than that of the eyes, or the hands.

But the sable of fate's brooding wings is intensified by the contrasting brightness of the heavens in which the innocent prey are disporting themselves. Fate struck swiftly. One night I got back to London late from the country. I picked up the receiver and dialled her number. Instead of the clear, healthy ringing tone, instead of the high-pitched and hysterical engaged signal, there was a prolonged, piercing scream. I can never listen to that signal now without feeling faint. It means the line is out of order, or the line no longer exists at all. Next day the same banshee scream was repeated. And the next. No telegram signed Egeria came. In great distress I asked Enquiries to find out what had happened. I begged them to give me the address of Grosvenor 8527 even at the risk of breaking my solemn promise to her. The number was, I knew, ex-directory in order to prevent the husband's unwelcome attentions. At first Enquiries would say nothing. They thought it odd that I could not even tell them the subscriber's name. Finally an obliging operator agreed for once to disregard Post Office regulations. After all, she said, why should she not oblige me? 'We may all be blown sky high any moment.

And you seem worried. The fact is that the house to which this number belonged received a direct hit three days ago. There can be no harm now in giving you the subscriber's name.'

'Thank you,' I said, 'for your help. I would much rather you didn't. So please, please don't.' And I rang off.

JAMES LEES-MILNE, *Another Self*

Alfresco Sex

For those that know, the alfresco fuck is the original fuck.

DEREK JARMAN

Hooray, Hooray, the first of May,
Outdoor fucking begins today.

Old Thurleston saying

Assignations

In the Feeldes and Suburbes of the Cities thei haue Gardens, either palled, or walled round about very high, with their Harbers and Bowers fit for the purpose. And least thei might be espied in these open places, they have their Banquetting houses with Galleries, Turrettes, and what not els therein sumptuously erected: wherein thei maie (and doubtlesse doe) many of them plaie the filthie persons. And for that their Gardens are locked, some of them have three or fower keyes a peece, whereof one they keepe for themselves, the other their Paramours have to goe in before them, least happely they should be perceived, for then were all

42

their sports dasht. Then to these Gardens thei repaire when thei list, with a basket and a boy, where thei, meeting their sweet hartes, receive their wished desires. These Gardens are exelent places, and for the purpose; for if thei can speak with their dearlynges no where els, yet there thei maie be sure to meete them, and to receive the guerdon of their paines: thei know best what I meane.

PHILIP STUBBES, *Anatomie of Abuses* (1583)

The Dutch Lover

Amyntas led me to a Grove,
    Where all the Trees did shade us;
The Sun it self, tho it had strove,
    Yet could not have betray'd us.
The place secure from human Eyes,
    No other fear allows,
But when the Winds that gently rise
    Do kiss the yielding Boughs

Down there we sat upon the Moss,
    And did begin to play
A thousand wanton Tricks, to pass
    The Heat of all the Day.
A many Kisses he did give,
    And I return'd the same:
Which made me willing to receive
    That which I dare not name.

His charming Eyes no aid requir'd,
    To tell their amorous Tale;
On her that was already fir'd,
    'Twas easy to prevail.

He did but kiss, and clasp me round,
   Whilst they his thoughts exprest,
And laid me gently on the Ground;
   Oh! who can guess the rest?

APHRA BEHN

The Faithless Wife

And believing she was a maid,
I took her by the river,
but already she was married.

It happened as if by pledge
upon Saint James's night.
Only the crickets glowed
now that the lamps were out.
In the furthest confines of the town
I touched her sleeping breasts,
and like branches of the hyacinth
they opened at once to my caress.
The starch of her petticoat
was sounding in my ears
like a piece of silk
that is rent by ten knives.
The trees by the roadside
spread their unlit tops
and far from the river
barked an horizon of dogs.

The bramble-bushes were passed,
the thorns and the furze.
With the back of her head
she made a hollow in the earth.
I took off my tie,

and she took off her dress.
I threw off my revolver belt,
and she her four bodices.
Neither spikenard nor snail
ever had skin so smooth,
nor did any crystal shine
so brilliant in the moon.
Her thighs escaped from me
like two startled trout,
one half of them cold,
and the other full of light.
By the finest of roads
that night I galloped
on a mother-of-pearl filly
without bridle nor stirrups.

The things she said to me,
as a man, I won't repeat.
The light of understanding
has made me discreet.
Soiled with sand and with kisses,
I carried her from the river.
In the night-wind, the swords
of the irises shivered.

A genuine gypsy,
I behaved as is proper,
and gave her a large work-box
of straw-coloured satin.
But I wished not to love her,
for though she was married,
she told me she was single
when I took her by the river.

FEDERICO GARCIA LORCA

The Geranium

In the close covert of a grove,
By nature formed for scenes of love,
Said Susan in a lucky hour,
Observe yon sweet geranium flower;
How straight upon its stalk it stands,
And tempts our violating hands:
Whilst the soft bud as yet unspread,
Hangs down its pale declining head:
Yet, soon as it is ripe to blow,
The stems shall rise, the head shall glow.
Nature, said I, my lovely Sue,
To all her followers lends a clue;
Her simple laws themselves explain,
As links of one continued chain;
For her the mysteries of creation,
Are but the works of generation:
Yon blushing, strong, triumphant flower,
Is in the crisis of its power:
But short, alas! its vigorous reign,
He sheds his seed, and drops again;
The bud that hangs in pale decay,
Feels not, as yet, the plastic ray;
Tomorrow's sun shall bid him rise,
Then, too, he sheds his seed and dies:
But words, my love, are vain and weak,
For proof, let bright example speak;
Then straight before the wondering maid,
The tree of life I gently laid;
Observe, sweet Sue, his drooping head,
How pale, how languid, and how dead;
Yet, let the sun of thy bright eyes,
Shine but a moment, it shall rise;
Let but the dew of thy soft hand

Refresh the stem, it straight shall stand:
Already, see, it swells, it grows,
Its head is redder than the rose,
Its shrivelled fruit, of dusky hue,
Now glows, a present fit for Sue:
The balm of life each artery fills,
And in o'erflowing drops distils.
Oh me! cried Susan, what is this?
What strange tumultuous throbs of bliss!
Sure, never mortal, till this hour,
Felt such emotion at a flower:
Oh, serpent! cunning to deceive,
Sure, 'tis this tree that tempted Eve;
The crimson apples hang so fair,
Alas! what woman could forbear?
Well hast thou guessed, my love, I cried,
It is the tree by which she died;
The tree which could content her,
All nature, Susan, seeks the centre;
Yet, let us still, poor Eve forgive,
It's the tree by which we live;
For lovely woman still it grows,
And in the centre only blows.
But chief for thee, it spreads its charms,
For paradise is in thy arms. –
I ceased, for nature kindly here
Began to whisper in her ear:
And lovely Sue lay softly panting,
While the geranium tree was planting.
'Til in the heat of amorous strife,
She burst the mellow tree of life.
'Oh, heaven!' cried Susan, with a sigh,
'The hour we taste – we surely die;
Strange raptures seize my fainting frame,
And all my body glows with flame;

Yet let me snatch one parting kiss
To tell my love I die with bliss:
That pleased, thy Susan yields her breath;
Oh! who would live if this be death!'

RICHARD BRINSLEY SHERIDAN

Italian Shepherds

As for boys under twenty (maybe it was a trick of the milk or the cheese) we relieved our horniness in every way possible. The valleys, the forests, the woods, and the hills, all whistled with our furious and ravenous jacking-off. The bushes were shaken by the storm of our hands. When we were tending the sheep or were at work, we were often seized by these attacks: shortness of breath, lump in the throat, and prick stiff as a rod, harder than the handle of the hoe we were holding.

If a boy was alone he holed up in the first bush he found, opened his fly, and strangled his monster fiercely, lying down with his eyes closed in order to 'see' the charms of some girl, of some patch of thigh he might have glimpsed occasionally. Then nothing else existed, neither flock nor hoe (which, often as not, had been left sticking out of the ground), neither rain nor ice. It was just as in the case of *thius* Antoniccu and Diddia.

Under the sun and in the silence of the woods we stretched out to enjoy this concession; the release of beating off. Often the bush – our woman – wavered spasmodically with the jerks of the unstoppable right hand, and of the galvanised writhing body. If the shepherd boys did happen to meet by chance, they had contests in jerking off, a way like any other to demonstrate our strength and show others what we could do.

'Ciao, pal! Today I'm going to beat you. I've been in training. The other day I got up to eight!'

'And why shouldn't I be able to do eight? Day before yesterday I did it four times in a quarter of an hour. I've been in training, too. When my father goes away I stretch out under a tree and stay there. I just roll over to follow the shade when it shifts with the sun.'

When I was twelve or thirteen and was with three friends, a thing happened to me that I am almost ashamed to confess. It happened a few days before the grape harvest took place. Papa had brought some girls of eighteen or twenty to pick the grapes. All day long we boys had been casting sidelong glances at their asses. It wasn't every day that we got to do this, and naturally, en masse, we attempted two or three jackings-off, one boy with one girl, another with a different one – in our jealous fantasies. Several days later we came upon the place where those girls had gone to piss and shit. At the sight of the now dried turds we imagined this one had made, or that one, we jerked off as violently as possible. Each boy stretched out wherever he imagined his favourite had pissed.

Otherwise we had a different but still rather common resort: the animals. Coming back from Siligo one day, just past Tuvu, G. and I saw a spectacle of this kind. From the backs of our donkeys we were able to see over the enclosure walls, which meandered along the main road, and we caught sight of a shepherd boy trying to get a hold of his she-ass.

'We'll end up doing the same thing,' said G.

The boy, who was around fourteen, kept trying but couldn't make it from the ground, so he made his 'lady' stand near a heap of stones. He climbed up onto it and finally his legs allowed him to join soft with hard. He dropped his pants and mounted his animal in an enterprising way, as though he had every right: she was his. He shook his little ass and quickly calmed down, embracing his lover and relaxing against her after having done his job.

'Would you screw your donkey?' I asked G.

'I've done it already in Capiana. A prick's frenzy respects nothing.'

They weren't the only ones; most of the boys did it and everybody thought about doing it, preferably with the ewes and nanny-goats.

Thanne tried it often when his father sent him alone to water the flock, along the path, behind the usual big cloud of dust. Generally he did it at the gate which blocked his flock's exit from the enclosure. The sheep surged toward the opening, and the boy passed through them to reach the gate but did not always succeed in opening it: the usual urges overcame him. Then he lay down in the middle of the bunched-up flock, choosing the ewe he found most attractive. He stretched her out, on her back to feel the swelling of her dugs on his belly, and went at it in a hurry, pants halfway down his thighs, while the flock waited in the sun for the shepherd to open the gate. At that moment not even a cannon could have distracted the lover, inventing the woman. One time in Siligo, during one of the rare free hours which Papa granted me, some friends convinced me to storm a poultry yard. We were still young, around ten years old; there were three of us. Inside, while the hens made a racket, each boy chose one and went to work, amidst great laughter.

'Listen, pal, this one with no feathers on her neck has a really hot ass. She's great.' Everyone wanted to try her, and it was really true.

For the servant shepherds, and the longtime bachelors, the sexual deprivation was total. They frequented the bushes until they married and some until they died, if their sexual vigour permitted them this solitary bliss. For the hired hands, another rule prevailed. At around eighteen, the master began taking them to brothels, at least once a year, and this gave them titillating material for their fantasies which carried them for at least a few months in the underbrush.

I heard a curious but true anecdote from the Siligo shepherds. A master had promised to take his good hired hand to Sassari to get him laid, but kept putting it off, partly because he couldn't find the time and partly because he didn't want to spend the money. The worker kept insisting, month after month.

'*Thiu* Anto! But when are you taking me there? Eh? … You promised me!'

'All right. We'll go on Sunday.'

And that time they did go. For the hand, Giommari, it was the first time. When he returned to the sheepfold, all the younger hired hands, for whom the great day was still to come (always supposing they had decent masters) wanted to be the first to hear.

'Well, Giommari. What's it like to make love?'

'Oh! Another thing altogether. No tails!'

GAVINO LEDDA, *Padre Padrone*

Move On

They made love under bridges, lacking beds,
And engines whistled them a bridal song,
A sudden bull's-eye showed them touching heads,
Policemen told them they were doing wrong;
And when they slept on seats in public gardens
Told them, 'Commit no nuisance in the park';
The beggars, begging the policemen's pardons,
Said that they thought as it was after dark –

At this the law grew angry and declared
Outlaws who outrage by-laws are the devil;
At this the lovers only stood and stared,
As well they might, for they had meant no evil;
'Move on,' the law said. To avoid a scene
They moved. And thus we keep our cities clean.

WILLIAM PLOMER

The Orchard

Leave go my hands, let me catch breath and see;
Let the dew-fall drench either side of me;
   Clear apple-leaves are soft upon that moon
Seen sidelong like a blossom in the tree;
   And God, ah God, that day should be so soon.

The grass is thick and cool, it lets us lie.
Kissed upon either cheek and either eye,
   I turn to thee as some green afternoon
Turns toward sunset, and is loth to die;
   Ah God, ah God, that day should be so soon.

Lie closer, lean your face upon my side,
Feel where the dew fell that has hardly dried,
   Hear how the blood beats that went nigh to swoon;
The pleasure lives there when the sense has died,
   Ah God, ah God, that day should be so soon.

O my fair lord, I charge you leave me this:
Is it not sweeter than a foolish kiss?
   Nay take it then, my flower, my first in June,
My rose, so like a tender mouth it is:
   Ah God, ah God, that day should be so soon.

Love, till dawn sunder night from day with fire
Dividing my delight and my desire,
   The crescent life and love the plenilune,
Love me though dusk begin and dark retire;
   Ah God, ah God, that day should be so soon.

Ah, my heart fails, my blood draws back; I know,
When life runs over, life is near to go;
   And with the slain of love love's ways are strewn,
And with their blood, if love will have it so;
   Ah God, ah God, that day should be so soon.

Ah, do thy will now; slay me if thou wilt;
There is no building now the walls are built,
   No quarrying now the corner-stone is hewn,
No drinking now the vine's whole blood is spilt;
   Ah God, ah God, that day should be so soon.

Nay, slay me now; nay, for I will be slain;
Pluck thy red pleasure from the teeth of pain,
   Break down thy vine ere yet grape-gatherers prune,
Slay me ere day can slay desire again;
   Ah God, ah God, that day should be so soon.

Yea, with thy sweet lips, with thy sweet sword; yea
Take life and all, for I will die, I say;
   Love, I gave love, is life a better boon?
For sweet night's sake I will not live till day;
   Ah God, ah God, that day should be so soon.

Nay, I will sleep then only; nay, but go.
Ah sweet, too sweet to me, my sweet, I know
   Love, sleep, and death go to the sweet same tune;
Hold my hair fast, and kiss me through it soon.
   Ah God, ah God, that day should be so soon.

ALGERNON SWINBURNE

A Painted Turtle

18 May 1955: We took a picnic to Duck Pond. Beautiful bright clear day with a little wind. Later on I always feel that the crystalline Cape Cod air is being polluted by the summer people, and the alcohol gets into the sunlight. Elena sat on the clean white sand – which she loves and which sets her off – with long slim bare legs stretched out a little apart and no panties on; blue skirt and black bathing suit. We drank some domestic *vin rosé*. She said that the domestic wines were getting more and more 'fruity', they sold them as soon as they made them, so that they tasted like simple grape juice gone a little sour. This is the kind of thing I never notice. We made love – I was slowed by the wine, and it lasted a long time, but was delightful, in spite of the fact that after a while the sand is rather hard on your knees – I finally put the towel under mine. Airplane overhead that swerved away. Elena said that at one point there was a bird of prey hovering over us. Afterwards, I walked around the pond, feeling perfectly happy – enjoyed the sight of a painted turtle swimming from the shore to the depths. I looked back toward Elena from time to time – she was taking a nap: I loved to see her – her bare legs and blue clothes (skirt and sweater) – and know that she was still with me, that we could still be happy together in the open air on the beach. When, coming back,

I had almost reached her, she sat up, with legs together and knees bent, one on top of the other, pointed in my direction, tapering to her beautiful little feet, one on top of the other. – I drank most of two bottles of wine, yet seemed to remain perfectly clear-headed, but admired perhaps extravagantly the wavy grain of some roots in the path, as we were going back. Further on, Elena stopped to admire some sprouts of oak, of a red that was almost scarlet, in the middle of the path. She says that there are a great many varieties of scrub oak, and that the sprouts are likely to be quite different. – When I got home, I drank some whisky and was out like a light before six – put myself to bed above my study and didn't come to till three in the morning, when I had an awful dream that Elena was dead and went over to the other side of the house to find her. My sexual powers must be definitely flagging. I was sixty ten days ago.

EDMUND WILSON, *The Fifties*

A Paradise in Madrid

From the building plots on the Plaza de Toros, the uncomfortable refuge of poor couples who accept what comes, like those fierce, utterly honest lovers in the Old Testament, it is possible to hear the tramcars passing not far away, on their run to the sheds. They are cold, decrepit, loose-jointed, with rattling coach-work and harsh, grinding brakes.

The waste plot that is the morning playground of noisy, quarrelsome boys who throw stones at each other all day long, is, from the time that front doors are locked, a rather grubby Garden of Eden where one cannot dance smoothly to the music of a concealed, almost unnoticed radio set; where one cannot smoke a scented, delightful cigarette as a prelude; where no easy, candid endearments may be whispered in security, in complete security. After lunch time the waste ground is the resort of old people who come there to feed on the sunshine like lizards. But after the hour when the children and the middle-aged couples go to bed, to sleep and dream, it is an uninhibited paradise with no room for evasion or subterfuge, where all know what they are after, where they make love nobly, almost harshly, on the soft ground which still retains the lines scratched in by the little girl who spent the morning playing hop-scotch, and the neat, perfectly round holes dug by the boy who greedily used all his spare time to play at marbles.

CAMILO JOSÉ CELA, *The Hive*

Proletarians on Hampstead Heath

I remember walking with Mr H. G. Wells on Hampstead Heath on the afternoon of King Edward's funeral when no police were present. The proletarians were taking advantage of the situation and he wanted to provide them with cubicles on the Heath. Both he and Lord Olivier were true Fabians in wanting to interfere with mankind, if not on exactly the same lines. To mutilate Hampstead Heath seems to me at least as undesirable as to interfere with human pleasure.

E. S. P. HAYNES, *A Lawyer's Notebook*

A Ramble in St James's Park

Much wine had passed, with grave discourse
Of who fucks who, and who does worse
(Such as you usually do hear
From those that diet at the Bear),
When I, who still take care to see
Drunkenness relieved by lechery,
Went out into St James's Park
To cool my head and fire my heart.
But though St James has th' honor on 't,
'Tis consecrate to prick and cunt.
There, by a most incestuous birth,
Strange woods spring from the teeming earth;
For they relate how heretofore,

When ancient Pict began to whore,
Deluded of his assignation
(Jilting, it seems, was then in fashion),
Poor pensive lover, in this place
Would frig upon his mother's face;
Whence rows of mandrakes tall did rise
Whose lewd tops fucked the very skies.

Each imitative branch does twine
In some loved fold of Aretine,
And nightly now beneath their shade
Are buggeries, rapes, and incests made.
Unto this all-sin-sheltering grove
Whores of the bulk and the alcove,
Great ladies, chambermaids, and drudges,
The ragpicker, and heiress trudges.
Carmen, divines, great lords, and tailors,
Prentices, poets, pimps, and jailers,
Footmen, fine fops do here arrive,
And here promiscuously they swive …

EARL OF ROCHESTER

Sir Walter Raleigh

He loved a wench well; and one time getting one of the Maids of
Honour up against a tree in a wood ('twas his first lady) who seemed at
first boarding to be something fearful of her honour, and modest, she
cried, 'Sweet Sir Walter, what do you me ask? Will you undo me? Nay,
sweet Sir Walter! Sweet Sir Walter! Sir Walter!' At last, as the danger and
the pleasure at the same time grew higher, she cried in the ecstasy,
'Swisser Swatter, Swisser Swatter!' She proved with child, and I doubt not
but this hero took care of them both, as also that the product was more
than an ordinary mortal.

JOHN AUBREY, *Brief Lives*

Cruelty

Cowardice is the mother of cruelty.

MICHEL DE MONTAIGNE

It is a grosse flattering of tired cruelty, to honest it with the title of clemency.

SIR THOMAS OVERBURY

An over-scrupulous man is always inclined to be a trifle cruel, for it is not easy for virtue to subsist with an even temper.

SEIGNEUR DE SAINT EVREMOND

Bull-fighting

Lincoln's Inn Fields are neither so large, nor spacious, as this place of public resort at Madrid, which is exactly square; being surrounded with houses, uniform all along in their dimensions, erected to the altitude of five pairs of stairs, with a great many most curious windows, and balconies overlaid with the purest gold. Moreover, the square is level; to the end, that the foaming bulls, and prancing horses, may run their courses with the greater easiness and celerity. From the ground to the first pair of stairs, are reared up theatres made of timber for the people. The thirty balconies, set apart for the king and court, are sumptuously furnished with the richest tapestry, and choicest velvet, that money or art can purchase ...

We told you, that the bull was shut up in a large room; therefore the person, whose undaunted courage or boldness sets him a work to encounter with this raging creature, stands to his posture at the door of the said house, with a long and sharp-pointed lance in his hand, having one of his knees set to the ground. Immediately after the sound of a trumpet, a constable runs with all possible speed, and sets the door of the room, where the furious animal is enclosed, wide open. Way being thus made, and all persons attentively looking on, the man is, by-and-by, assaulted with great violence; which onset, if by dexterity, or good luck, he can evade, there is a fair occasion presented him, for killing or wounding the bull to purpose; which if he miss to do, his life or members are in jeopardy. It is a thirsting desire after some imaginary honour, that sets such bold fellows upon the exposing of themselves to those dangerous circumstances, rather than the advantage of getting the beasts which they have killed, or wounded to purpose.

That the next bull may be rendered the more furious, they set up a quantity of wool, in figure representing a man, with a considerable weight at his legs; which while the beast pusheth in a most formidable manner, the weight keeps it in a straight position, by which means the bull is wonderfully enraged. Sometimes a very despicable peasant is set upon a lean deformed horse, and exposed very often to a violent death, because of his antagonist's strength and rage. For dragging out the bulls once killed, six mules of divers colours are appointed, which, by the conduct of four men, accomplish this work with all possible velocity and artifice. Six footmen are ordained to encounter with the four beasts yet remaining, to whom no other weapon is granted, but a dagger with some few rexones in a bag, which in length exceed not six or seven inches; having hafts well ordered with bunches of garlands, and points exceeding sharp, for the more ready carrying on of the intendment. Such as be thus stated, are commonly most dextrous, whom it behoves to fight with the bull face to face: he who doth otherwise, will undoubtedly incur the risk of imprisonment, with most abashing reproaches, and the loss of a considerable prize. Some men are so nimble, that by a gentle motion they can easily evade the bull's fury, and attain their design. Thus matters go on until such time as the trumpet sounds: then butchers-dogs, and men armed with broad swords, quickly dispatch the strength and violence of those formidable animals.

JAMES SALGADO, *An Impartial and Brief Description of the Plaza, or Sumptuous Market-Place of Madrid, and the Bull-Baiting there* (1683)

Trimmer Halifax's Views

There is an accumulative cruelty in a number of men, though none in particular are ill-natured.

More men hurt others they do not know why than for any reason.

State business is a cruel trade; good-nature is a bungler in it.

Weak Men are apt to be cruel, because they stick at nothing that may repair the ill Effect of their Mistakes.

MARQUIS OF HALIFAX

The Delicate Prey

A good while before he arrived at the camp he heard singing. This surprised him. He halted and listened: the voice was too far away to be identified, but Driss felt certain it was the Moungari's. He continued around the side of the hill to a spot in full view of the camels. The singing stopped, leaving silence. Some of the packs had been loaded back on to the beasts, preparatory to setting out. The sun had sunk low, and the shadows of the rocks were stretched out along the earth. There was no sign that they had caught any game. He called out, ready to dismount. Almost at the same instant there was a shot from very nearby, and he heard the small rushing sound of a bullet go past his head. He seized his gun. There was another shot, a sharp pain in his arm, and his gun slipped to the ground.

For a moment he sat there holding his arm, dazed. Then swiftly he leapt down and remained crouching among the stones, reaching out with his good arm for the gun. As he touched it, there was a third shot, and the rifle moved along the ground a few inches toward him in a small cloud of dust. He drew back his hand and looked at it: it was dark and blood dripped from it. At that moment the Moungari bounded across the open space between them. Before Driss could rise the man was upon him, had pushed him back down to the ground with the barrel of his rifle. The untroubled sky lay above; the Moungari glanced up at it defiantly. He straddled the supine youth, thrusting the gun into his neck just below the chin, and under his breath he said: 'Filali dog!'

Driss stared up at him with a certain curiosity. The Moungari had the upper hand; Driss could only wait. He looked at the face in the sun's light, and discovered a peculiar intensity there. He knew the expression: it comes from hashish. Carried along on its hot fumes, a man can escape very far from the world of meaning. To avoid the malevolent face he rolled his eyes from side to side. There was only the fading sky. The gun was choking him a little. He whispered: 'Where are my uncles?'

The Moungari pushed harder against his throat with the gun, leaned partially over and with one hand ripped away his *serouelle*, so that he lay naked from the waist down, squirming a little as he felt the cold stones beneath him.

Then the Moungari drew forth rope and bound his feet. Taking two steps to his head, he abruptly faced in the other direction, and thrust the gun into his navel. Still with one hand, he slipped the remaining garments off over the youth's head and lashed his wrists together. With an old barber's razor he cut off the superfluous rope. During this time Driss called his uncles by name, loudly, first one and then the other.

The man moved and surveyed the young body lying on the stones. He ran his finger along the razor's blade; a pleasant excitement took possession of him. He stepped over, looked down, and saw the sex that sprouted from the base of the belly. Not entirely conscious of what he was doing, he took it in one hand and brought his other arm down with the motion of a reaper wielding a sickle. It was swiftly severed. A round, dark hole was left, flush with the skin; he stared a moment, blankly. Driss was screaming. The muscles all over his body stood out, moved.

Slowly the Moungari smiled, showing his teeth. He put his hand on the hard belly and smoothed the skin. Then he made a small vertical incision there, and using both hands, studiously stuffed the loose organ in until it disappeared.

As he was cleaning his hands in the sand, one of the camels uttered a sudden growling gurgle. The Moungari leapt up and wheeled about savagely, holding his razor high in the air. Then, ashamed of his nervousness, feeling that Driss was watching and mocking him (although the youth's eyes were unseeing with pain), he kicked him over onto his stomach where he lay making small spasmodic movements. And as the Moungari followed these with his eyes, a new idea came to him. It would be pleasant to inflict an ultimate indignity upon the young Filali. He threw himself down; this time he was vociferous and leisurely in his enjoyment. Eventually he slept.

At dawn he awoke and reached for his razor, lying on the ground nearby. Driss moaned faintly. The Moungari turned him over and pushed the blade back and forth with a sawing motion into his neck, until he was certain he had severed the windpipe. Then he rose, walked away, and finished the loading of the camels he had started the day before. When this was done he spent a good while dragging the body over to the base of the hill and concealing it there among the rocks.

In order to transport the Filala's merchandise to Tessalit (for in Taoudeni there would be no buyers), it was necessary to take their *mehara* [camels] with him. It was nearly fifty days later when he arrived. Tessalit is a small town. When the Moungari began to show the leather around, an old Filali living there, whom the people called Ech Chibani, got wind of his presence. As a prospective buyer he came to examine the hides, and the Moungari was unwise enough to let him see them. Filali leather is unmistakable, and only the Filala buy and sell it in quantity. Ech Chibani knew the Moungari had come by it illicitly, but he said nothing.

When a few days later another caravan arrived from Tabelbala with friends of the three Filala who asked after them, and showed great distress on hearing that they never had arrived, the old man went to the Tribunal. After some difficulty, he found a Frenchman who was willing to listen to him. The next day the Commandant and two subordinates paid the Moungari a visit. They asked him how he happened to have the three extra *mehara*, which still carried some of their Filali trappings; his replies took a devious turn. The Frenchmen listened seriously, thanked him, and left. He did not see the Commandant wink at the others as they went out into the street. And so he remained sitting in his courtyard, not knowing that he had been judged and found guilty.

The three Frenchmen went back to the Tribunal where the newly arrived Filali merchants were sitting with Ech Chibani. The story had an old pattern; there was no doubt at all about the Moungari's guilt. 'He is yours,' said the Commandant. 'Do what you like with him.'

The Filala thanked him profusely, held a short conference with the aged Chibani, and strode out in a group. When they arrived at the Moungari's dwelling he was making tea. He looked up, and a chill moved along his spine. He began to scream his innocence at them; they said nothing, but at the point of a rifle bound him and tossed him into a corner, where he continued to babble and sob. Quietly, they drank the tea he had been brewing, made some more, and went out at twilight. They tied him to one of the *mehara*, and mounting their own, moved in a silent procession (silent save for the Moungari) out through the town gate into the infinite wasteland beyond.

Half the night they continued, until they were in a completely unfrequented region of the desert. While he lay raving, bound to the camel, they dug a well-like pit, and when they had finished they lifted him off, still trussed tightly, and stood him in it. Then they filled all the space around his body with sand and stones, until only his head remained above the earth's surface. In the faint light of the new moon his shaved pate without its turban looked rather like a rock. And still he pleaded with them, calling upon Allah and Sidi Ahmed ben Moussa to witness his innocence. But he might have been singing a song for all the attention they paid to his words. Presently they set off for Tessalit; in no time they were out of hearing.

When they had gone the Moungari fell silent, to wait through the cold hours for the sun that would bring first warmth, then heat, thirst, fire, visions. The next night he did not know where he was, did not feel the cold. The wind blew dust along the ground into his mouth as he sang.

PAUL BOWLES, *Pages from Cold Point*

A London Fête

All night fell hammers, shock on shock,
With echoes Newgate's granite clanged:
The scaffold built, at eight o'clock
They brought the man out to be hanged.
Then came from all the people there
A single cry, that shook the air;
Mothers held up their babies to see,
Who spread their hands, and crowed with glee;
Here a girl from her vesture tore
A rag to wave with, and joined the roar;
There a man, with yelling tired,
Stopped, and the culprit's crime inquired;
A sot, below the doomed man dumb,
Bawled his health in the world to come;
These blasphemed and fought for places;
These, half-crushed, with frantic faces,
To windows, where, in freedom sweet,
Others enjoyed the wicked treat.
At last, the show's black crisis pended;
Struggles for better standings ended;
The rabble's lips no longer cursed,
But stood agape with horrid thirst;
Thousands of breasts beat horrid hope;
Thousands of eyeballs, lit with hell,
Burnt one way all, to see the rope

Unslacken as the platform fell.
The rope flew tight; and then the roar
Burst forth afresh; less loud, but more
Confused and affrighting than before.

A few harsh tongues for ever led
The common din, the chaos of noises,
But ear could not catch what they said.
As when the realm of the damned rejoices
At winning a soul to its will,
That clatter and clangour of hateful voices
Sickened and stunned the air, until
The dangling corpse hung straight and still.
The show complete, the pleasure past,
The solid masses loosened fast;
A thief slunk off, with ample spoil,
To ply elsewhere his daily toil;
A baby strung its doll to a stick;
A mother praised the pretty trick;
Two children caught and hanged a cat;
Two friends walked on, in lively chat;
And two, who had disputed places,
Went forth to fight, with murderous faces.

COVENTRY PATMORE

Mr Potts

29 January 1899: Constance Fletcher came to supper and Mr Potts [Mayfair chemist and bibliophile]. The account Potts gave of his war with the cats who used to haunt the leads and ledges of S. Audley Street was most amusing. He used, when much disturbed, to rise at night, with a small syringe filled with prussic acid, and to go down to the window opening on the roof and wait till one of the screaming cats drew near.

Puss-puss he called, and the innocent approached. Then he discharged the acid into the eye of the beast, and with a loud shriek the unfortunate crossed the Styx.

REV. STOPFORD BROOKE

Obsessed by Gladiators

Alypius did not indeed abandon the earthly career of whose prizes his parents had sung to him. He had arrived in Rome before I did to study law. There he had been seized by an incredible obsession for gladiatorial spectacles and to an unbelievable degree. He held such spectacles in aversion and detestation; but some of his friends and fellow-pupils on their way back from a dinner happened to meet him in the street and, despite his energetic refusal and resistance, used friendly violence to take him into the amphitheatre during the days of the cruel and murderous games. He said: 'If you drag my body to that place and sit me down there, do not imagine you can turn my mind and my eyes to those spectacles. I shall be as one not there, and so I shall overcome both you and the games.' They heard him, but none the less took him with them, wanting perhaps to discover whether he could actually carry it off. When they arrived and had found seats where they could, the entire place seethed with the most monstrous delight in the cruelty. He kept his eyes shut and forbade his mind to think about such fearful evils. Would that he had blocked his ears as well! A man fell in combat. A great roar from the entire crowd struck him with such vehemence that he was overcome by curiosity. Supposing himself strong enough to despise whatever he saw and to conquer it, he opened his eyes. He was struck in the soul by a wound graver than the gladiator in his body, whose fall had caused the roar. The shouting entered by his ears and forced open his eyes. Thereby it was the means of wounding and striking to the ground a mind still more bold than strong, and the weaker for the reason that he presumed on himself when he ought to have relied on you. As soon as he saw the blood, he at once drank in savagery and did not turn away. His eyes were riveted. He imbibed madness. Without any awareness of what was happening to him, he found delight in the murderous contest and was inebriated by bloodthirsty pleasure. He was not now the person who had come in, but just one of the crowd which he had joined, and a true member of the group which had brought him. What should I add? He looked, he yelled, he was on fire, he took the madness home with him so that it urged him to return not only with those by whom he had originally been drawn there, but even more than them, taking others with him.

ST AUGUSTINE, Confessions

Rabbit Shooting

30 June 1826: It is now two years since, as I was walking in the woods of Copy near Norwich with my Friend Hawkes, who carried his gun to amuse himself with, whatever pain it might inflict on others, equally susceptible of pain & pleasure as himself. It was a delicious June evening, the Sun was setting, slowly, & in a glow! The Trees were still, brown, & massy; the birds were singing in long throbbing warbles as if their little throats were in extasy at the calmness & peace around them, and all nature conspired to fill the soul with sympathy, deep feeling, & those mysterious emotions which crowd the fancy at such moments of majestic blessedness & angelic quiet.

It was so silent that the very hares & rabbits, as the sun declined, forgot their habitual apprehension and danced out & gamboled about us! For my part it appeared sacrilege to disturb for the sake of *amusement* the innocent pleasure of these innocent & timid inhabitants of this leafy solitude; not so my Friend; in him the Sportsman predominated, & the singing of the birds, the beauty of the evening, the leaping of the hares, the glow of the sunset, or the approach of night, calm, balmy, & serene, were lost, in the hope of shooting a rabbit for dinner, as his Party must not be disappointed. I lagged behind in sorrowful & quiet meditation, & watched the form of my Friend, now lighted up by a golden beam, now flickered by the golden shadow of a golden tree, as he darted in & out to get a good place to shoot rabbits, who were squatting on their haunches, pricking up their ears, now nibbling the grass, now jumping with their little tails in the air, and then unconscious of the enemy frisked in inno-cence near each other.

My Friend had his hat off. His back was bent, his gun cocked, his neck stretched, and like an assassin he was creeping to his innocent victims. I stood & watched. At that moment the sun shone forth as upon a heated mist, the birds warbled out with ten times more ecstasy than before. I could not help feeling a sort of Communion with my God at this deli-cious scene of harmony & peace. I had forgotten my Friend, when I accidentally saw him dart up his deadly gun; in one instant I saw the little creatures in gamboling happiness, in the next the blank crash of the fowling piece scattered death among them; they were gone as if by magic & left one of their young companions, bloody, struggling, & wounded!

I ran up. My Friend Hawkes did the same. The smile of Triumph was on his face, as he wiped the perspiration from his heated forehead, on which Victory sat plumed & boasting. 'I knew I should have him,' said he. I made no reply, but looked at this poor innocent white bellied vic-tim, as he strained & struggled & bled (for he was young & vigorous). The sun was nearly descended, & in one last deadly leap forwards side-long on the bloody grass, the little creature breathed forth existence & lay without motion!

BENJAMIN ROBERT HAYDON, Diary

The Runnable Stag

When the pods went pop on the broom, green broom,
   And apples began to be golden-skinned,
We harboured a stag in the Priory coomb,
   And we feathered his trail up-wind, up-wind,
   We feathered his trail up-wind –
      A stag of warrant, a stag, a stag,
      A runnable stag, a kingly crop,
      Brow, bay and tray and three on top,
      A stag, a runnable stag.

Then the huntsman's horn rang yap, yap, yap,
 And 'Forwards' we heard the harbourer shout;
But 'twas only a brocket that broke a gap
 In the beechen underwood, driven out,
 From the underwood antlered out
  By warrant and might of the stag, the stag,
  The runnable stag, whose lordly mind
  Was bent on sleep, though beamed and tined
  He stood, a runnable stag.

So we tufted the covert till afternoon
 With Tinkerman's Pup and Bell-of-the-North;
And hunters were sulky and hounds out of tune
 Before we tufted the right stag forth,
 Before we tufted him forth,
  The stag of warrant, the wily stag,
  The runnable stag with his kingly crop,
  Brow, bay and tray and three on top,
  The royal and runnable stag.

It was Bell-of-the-North and Tinkerman's Pup
 That stuck to the scent till the copse was drawn.
'Tally ho! tally ho!' and the hunt was up,
 The tufters whipped and the pack laid on,
 The resolute pack laid on,
  And the stag of warrant away at last,
  The runnable stag, the same, the same,
  His hoofs on fire, his horns like flame,
  A stag, a runnable stag.

'Let your gelding be: if you check or chide
 He stumbles at once and you're out of the hunt;
For three hundred gentlemen, able to ride,
 On hunters accustomed to bear the brunt,
 Accustomed to bear the brunt,
  Are after the runnable stag, the stag,

The runnable stag with his kingly crop,
Brow, bay and tray and three on top,
The right, the runnable stag.'

By perilous paths in coomb and dell,
    The heather, the rocks, and the river-bed,
The pace grew hot, for the scent lay well,
    And a runnable stag goes right ahead,
    The quarry went right ahead –
        Ahead, ahead, and fast and far;
        His antlered crest, his cloven hoof,
        Brow, bay and tray and three aloof,
        The stag, the runnable stag.

For a matter of twenty miles and more,
    By the densest hedge and the highest wall,
Through herds of bullocks he baffled the lore
    Of harbourer, huntsman, hounds and all,
    Of harbourer, hounds and all –
        The stag of warrant, the wily stag,
        For twenty miles, and five and five,
        He ran, and he never was caught alive,
        This stag, this runnable stag.

When he turned at bay in the leafy gloom,
    In the emerald gloom where the brook ran deep,
He heard in the distance the rollers boom,
    And he saw in a vision of peaceful sleep,
    In a wonderful vision of sleep,
        A stag of warrant, a stag, a stag,
        A runnable stag in a jewelled bed,
        Under the sheltering ocean dead,
        A stag, a runnable stag.

So a fateful hope lit up his eye,
    And he opened his nostrils wide again,
And he tossed his branching antlers high
    As he headed the hunt down the Charlock glen,

As he raced down the echoing glen
   For five miles more, the stag, the stag,
   For twenty miles, and five and five,
   Not to be caught now, dead or alive,
   The stag, the runnable stag.

Three hundred gentlemen, able to ride,
   Three hundred horses as gallant and free,
Beheld him escape on the evening tide,
   Far out till he sank in the Severn Sea,
   Till he sank in the depths of the sea —
   The stag, the buoyant stag, the stag
   That slept at last in a jewelled bed
   Under the sheltering ocean spread,
   The stag, the runnable stag.

JOHN DAVIDSON

The Toreador's Eye

The first bull, the one whose balls Simone looked forward to having served raw on a plate, was a kind of black monster, who shot out of the pen so quickly that despite all efforts and all shouts, he disembowelled three horses in a row before an orderly fight could take place; one horse and rider were hurled aloft together, loudly crashing down behind the horns. But when Granero faced the bull, the combat was launched with brio, proceeding amid a frenzy of cheers. The young man sent the furious beast racing around him in his pink cape; each time, his body was lifted by a sort of spiralling jet, and he just barely eluded a frightful impact. In the end, the death of the solar monster was performed cleanly, with the beast blinded by the scrap of red cloth, the sword deep in the blood-smeared body. An incredible ovation resounded as the bull staggered to its knees with the uncertainty of a drunkard, collapsed with its legs sticking up, and died.

Simone, who sat between Sir Edmund and myself, witnessed the killing with an exhilaration at least equal to mine, and she refused to sit down again when the interminable acclamation for the young man was over. She took my hand wordlessly and led me to an outer courtyard of the filthy arena, where the stench of equine and human urine was suffocating because of the great heat. I grabbed Simone's cunt, and she seized my furious cock through my trousers. We stepped into a stinking shithouse, where sordid flies whirled about in a sunbeam. Standing here, I exposed Simone's cunt, and into her blood-red, slobbery flesh I stuck my fingers, then my penis, which entered that cavern of blood while I tossed off her arse, thrusting my bony middle finger deep inside. At the same time, the roofs of our mouths cleaved together in a storm of saliva.

A bull's orgasm is not more powerful than the one that wrenched through our loins to tear us to shreds, though without shaking my thick penis out of that stuffed vulva, which was gorged with come.

Our hearts were still booming in our chests, which were equally burning and equally lusting to press stark naked against wet unslaked hands, and Simone's cunt was still as greedy as before and my cock stubbornly rigid, as we returned to the first row of the arena. But when we arrived at our places next to Sir Edmund, there, in broad sunlight, on Simone's seat, lay a white dish containing two peeled balls, glands the size and shape of eggs, and of a pearly whiteness, faintly bloodshot, like the globe of an eye: they had just been removed from the first bull, a black-haired creature, into whose body Granero had plunged his sword.

'Here are the raw balls,' Sir Edmund said to Simone in his British accent.

Simone was already kneeling before the plate, peering at it in absorbed interest, but in something of a quandary. It seemed she wanted to do something but didn't know how to go about it, which exasperated her. I picked up the dish to let her sit down, but she grabbed it away from me with a categorical 'no' and returned it to the stone seat.

Sir Edmund and I were growing annoyed at being the focus of our neighbours' attention just when the bullfight was slackening. I leaned over and whispered to Simone, asking what had got into her.

'Idiot!' she replied. 'Can't you see I want to sit on the plate, and all these people watching!'

'That's absolutely out of the question,' I rejoined, 'sit down.'

At the same time, I took away the dish and made her sit, and I stared at her to let her know that I understood, that I remembered the dish of milk, and that this renewed desire was unsettling me. From that moment on, neither of us could keep from fidgeting, and this state of malaise was contagious enough to affect Sir Edmund. I ought to say that the fight had become boring, unpugnacious bulls were facing matadors who didn't know what to do next; and to top it off, since Simone had demanded seats in the sun, we were trapped in something like an immense vapour of light and muggy heat, which parched our throats as it bore down upon us.

It really was totally out of the question for Simone to lift her dress and place her bare behind in the dish of raw balls. All she could do was hold the dish in her lap. I told her I would like to fuck her again before Granero returned to fight the fourth bull, but she refused, and she sat there, keenly involved, despite everything, in the disembowelments of horses, followed, as she childishly put it, by 'death and destruction', namely the cataract of bowels.

Little by little, the sun's radiance sucked us into an unreality that fitted our malaise – the wordless and powerless desire to explode and get up off our behinds. We grimaced, because our eyes were blinded and because we were thirsty, our senses ruffled, and there was no possibility of quenching our desires. We three had managed to share in the morose dissolution that leaves no harmony between the various spasms of the body. We were so far gone that even Granero's return could not pull us out of that stupefying absorption. Besides, the bull opposite him was distrustful and seemed unresponsive; the combat went on just as drearily as before.

The events that followed were without transition or connection, not because they weren't actually related, but because my attention was so absent as to remain absolutely dissociated. In just a few seconds: first, Simone bit into one of the raw balls, to my dismay; then Granero advanced towards the bull, waving his scarlet cloth; finally, almost at once, Simone, with a blood-red face and a suffocating lewdness, uncovered her long white thighs up to her moist vulva, into which she slowly and surely fitted the second pale globule – Granero was thrown back by the bull and wedged against the balustrade; the horns struck the balustrade three times at full speed; at the third blow, one horn plunged into the right eye and through the head. A shriek of unmeasured horror coincided with a brief orgasm for Simone, who was lifted up from the stone seat only to be flung back with a bleeding nose, under a blinding sun; men instantly rushed over to haul away Granero's body, the right eye dangling from the head.

GEORGES BATAILLE, *Story of the Eye, by Lord Auch*

Dancing

No sober man dances, unless he is mad.

CICERO

As in all Feasts and pastimes, dauncing is the last, so it is the extream of all other vice.

PHILIP STUBBES

Ballrooms

All is show, and varnish and hypocrisy and coquetry; they dress up their moral character for the evening at the same toilet where they manufacture their shapes and faces. Ill-temper lies buried under a studied accumulation of smiles. Envy, hatred and malice retreat from the countenance, to entrench themselves more deeply in the heart. Treachery lurks under the flowers of courtesy. Ignorance and folly take refuge in that unmeaning gabble which it would be profanation to call language …

A ballroom is an epitome of all that is most worthless and unamiable in the great sphere of human life.

THOMAS LOVE PEACOCK, *Headlong Hall*

Concord and Nobility

A man in his naturall perfection is fiers, hardy, stronge in opinion, covaitous of glorie, desirous of knowlege, appetiting by generation to brynge forthe his semblable. The good nature of a woman is to be milde, timerouse, tractable, benigne, of sure remembrance, and shamfast, divers other qualities of eche of them mought be founde out, but these be moste apparaunt, and for this time sufficient.

Wherfore whan we beholde a man and a woman daunsinge to gether, let us suppose there to be a concorde of all the saide qualities, beinge joyned to gether, as I have set them in ordre. And the meving of the man wolde be more vehement, of the woman more delicate, and with lasse advauncing of the body, signifienge the courage & strengthe that oughte to be in a man, and the pleasant sobrenesse that shulde be in a woman. And in this wise *fiersenesse*, joyned with *mildenesse*, maketh *Severitie*: *Audacitie* with *timerositie* maketh *Magnanimitie*: wilfull opinion and *Tractabilitie* (which is to be shortly persuaded and meved) makethe *Constance* a vertue: *Covaitise of glorie* adourned with *benignitie*, causeth honour: *desire of knowlege*, with *sure remembrance*, procureth *Sapience*: *Shamfastnes* joyned to *Appetite of generation* maketh *Continence*: whiche is a meane betwene *Chastitie* and *inordinate luste*. These qualities, in this wise being knitte to gether, and signified in the personages of man and woman daunsinge, do expresse or sette out the figure of very nobilitie: whiche in the higher astate it is contained, the more excellent is the vertue in estimation.

SIR THOMAS ELYOT, *The boke named the Governour* (1531)

Dance

Wild crap-shooters with a whoop and a call
Danced the juba in their gambling hall
And laughed fit to kill, and shook the town,
And guyed the policemen and laughed them down
With a boomlay, boomlay, boomlay, Boom.
Then I saw the Congo, creeping through the black,
Cutting through the forest with a golden track.
A negro fairyland swung into view,
A minstrel river
Where dreams come true.
The ebony palace soared on high
Through the blossoming trees to the evening sky.
The inlaid porches and casements shone
With gold and ivory and elephant-bone.
And the black crowd laughed till their sides were sore
At the baboon butler in the agate door,
And the well-known tunes of the parrot band
That trilled on the bushes of that magic land.

A troupe of skull-faced witch-men came
Through the agate doorway in suits of flame,
Yea, long-tailed coats with a gold-leaf crust
And hats that were covered with diamond-dust.
And the crowd in the court gave a whoop and a call
And danced the juba from wall to wall.
But the witch-men suddenly stilled the throng
With a stern cold glare, and a stern old song:
'Mumbo-Jumbo will hoo-doo you' …
Just then from the doorway, as fat as shotes,
Came the cake-walk princes in their long red coats,
Canes with a brilliant lacquer shine,
And tall silk hats that were red as wine.

And they pranced with their butterfly partners there,
Coal-black maidens with pearls in their hair,
Knee-skirts trimmed with the jassamine sweet,
And bells on their ankles and little black feet.
And the couples railed at the chant and the frown
Of the witch-men lean, and laughed them down.
(Oh, rare was the revel, and well worth while
That made those glowering witch-men smile.)

VACHEL LINDSAY

The Dancing Cabman

Alone on the lawn
    The cabman dances:
In the dew of dawn
    He kicks and prances.
His bowler is set
    On his bullet-head.
For his boots are wet,
    And his aunt is dead.
There on the lawn,
    As the light advances,
On the tide of the dawn,
    The cabman dances.
Swift and strong
    As a garden roller,
He dances along
    In his little bowler,
Skimming the lawn
    With royal grace,
The dew of the dawn
    On his great red face.

To fairy flutes,
   As the light advances,
In square black boots
   The cabman dances.

J. B. MORTON ('BEACHCOMBER')

Dancing Leads to Vice

What godly eye can it delight,
   what pleasure in it dwell,
Which is the line that leads to vice,
   and hedlong unto hell?
While men with maides in wanton daunce
   unseemly oft doo turn,
Their hartes blinde Cupid oft doth cause
   with Venus games to burn.
Thus flames of love incensed are;
   theffecte is yet behinde,
Which to obtaine by secret meanes,
   they showe eche others minde.
If that his mate doo seeme to like
   the game that he would have,
He trips her toe, and clicks her cheek,
   to shewe what he doth crave.
Such jests they use, and jumps unchaste,
   that make immodest meane,
Such filthy woords that they may seeme
   chaste harts to ravish cleane ...

THOMAS LOVELL

But, say they, it induceth loove: so I say also: but what loove? Truely, a lustful love, a venerous loove, a concupiscencious, baudie, & bestiall loove, such as proceedeth from the stinking pump and lothsome sink of carnall affection and fleshly appetite, and not such as distilleth from the bowels of the hart ingenerat by the spirit of God.

PHILIP STUBBES

Dancing is in itself a very trifling, silly thing; but is one of those established follies to which people of sense are sometimes obliged to conform; and then they should be able to do it well.

EARL OF CHESTERFIELD

The greater the fool, the better the dancer.

THEODORE HOOK

Everything Sparkles

January 1933: Poisson d'Or. Tziganes. Three aristocratic Russian women, beautiful, with two wealthy men. Seven bottles of champagne. Ordering gypsy singer to sing for them at their table. Russian painter seated in front of me. Stares at me. When I dance with my escort, we collide and he kisses my neck. Orgy of singing and dancing. The three Russian women weep, quietly, with enjoyment, voluptuous satisfaction. The painter and the host almost fight because a man breaks lumps of sugar while the gypsy sings. Musicians sing and dance for the angry man as if to soothe him. The painter smiles subtly at me. Lady in white also begins to dance in front of him. The painter is whisked away by his partner who makes a scene. Irony, with the deep emotional music going on. The feeling that when I handed my coat at the check room, I handed over my identity. I become dissolved in the atmosphere, into red curtains, champagne, ice, music, singing, the weeping which the Russians love to do, the caress of the painter's eyes. Everything sparkles and exudes a warmth and a flowering. I am not like Jeanne, fragmented into a thousand pieces. I am at one with a sea of sensations, glitter, silk, skin, eyes, mouths, desire.

ANAIS NIN, *Journals*

A Marriage Mart

These panting damsels, dancing for their lives,
Are only maidens waltzing into wives.
Those smiling matrons are appraisers sly,
Who regulate the dance, the squeeze, the sigh,
And each base cheapening buyer having chid,
Knock down their daughters to the noblest bid!

ANONYMOUS

Outside the Ballroom

Behold the ball-room flashing on the sight,
From step to cornice one grand glare of light;
The noise of mirth and revelry resounds,
Like fairy melody on haunted grounds.
But who demands this profuse, wanton glee,
These shouts prolonged and wild festivity –
Not sure our city – web, more woe than bliss,
In any hour, requiring aught but this!

Deaf is the ear of all that jewelled crowd
To sorrow's sob, although its call be loud.
Better than waste long nights in idle show,
To help the indigent and raise the low –

To train the wicked to forsake his way,
And find th' industrious work from day to day!
Better to charity those hours afford,
Which now are wasted at the festal board!

And ye, O high-born beauties! in whose soul
Virtue resides, and Vice has no control;
Ye whom prosperity forbids to sin,
So fair without – so chaste, so pure within –
Whose honour Want ne'er threatened to betray,
Whose eyes are joyous, and whose heart is gay;
Around whose modesty a hundred arms,
Aided by pride, protect a thousand charms;
For you this ball is pregnant with delight;
As glitt'ring planets cheer the gloomy night: –
But, O, ye wist not, while your souls are glad,
How millions wander, homeless, sick and sad!
Hazard has placed you in a happy sphere,
And like your own to you all lots appear;
For blinded by the sun of bliss your eyes
Can see no dark horizon to the skies.

Such is the chance of life! Each gallant thane,
Prince, peer, and noble, follow in your train; –
They praise your loveliness, and in your ear
They whisper pleasing things, but insincere;
Thus, as the moths enamoured of the light,
Ye seek these realms of revelry each night.
But as ye travel thither, did ye know
What wretches walk the streets through which you go.
Sisters, whose gewgaws glitter in the glare
Of your great lustre, all expectant there,
Watching the passing crowd with avid eye,
Till one their love, or lust, or shame may buy;
Or, with commingling jealousy and rage,

They mark the progress of your equipage;
And their deceitful life essays the while
To mask their woe beneath a sickly smile!

VICTOR HUGO

Rules and Regulations for Public Dance Halls

1. No shadow or spotlight dances allowed.
2. Moonlight dances not allowed where a single light is used to illuminate the Hall. Lights may be shaded to give Hall dimmed illuminated effect.
3. All unnecessary shoulder or body movement or gratusque dances positively prohibited.
4. Pivot reverse and running on the floor prohibited.
5. All unnecessary hesitation, rocking from one foot to the other and see-sawing back and forth of the dancers will be prohibited.
6. No loud talking, undue familiarity or suggestive remarks unbecoming any lady or gentleman will be tolerated.

POSITION OF DANCERS

1. Right hand of gentleman must not be placed below the waist nor over the shoulder nor around the lady's neck, nor lady's left arm around gentleman's neck. Lady's right hand and gentleman's left hand clasped and extended at least six inches from the body, and must not be folded and lay across the chest of dancers.
2. Heads of dancers must not touch.

MUSIC

No beating of drum to produce Jazz effect will be allowed.
Any and all persons violating any of these rules will be subject to expulsion from the hall, also arrest for disorderly conduct.

By Order of

CHIEF OF POLICE

Regulations posted in the dance halls of Lansing, Michigan, c. 1920

Sad Strains of a Gay Waltz

The truth is that there comes a time
When we can mourn no more over music
That is so much motionless sound.

There comes a time when the waltz
Is no longer a mode of desire, a mode
Of revealing desire and is empty of shadows.

Too many waltzes have ended. And then
There's that mountain-minded Hoon,
For whom desire was never that of the waltz,

Who found all form and order in solitude,
For whom the shapes were never the figures of men.
Now, for him, his forms have vanished.

There is order in neither sea nor sun.
The shapes have lost their glistening.
There are these sudden mobs of men,

These sudden clouds of faces and arms,
An immense suppression, freed,
These voices crying without knowing for what,

Except to be happy, without knowing how,
Imposing forms they cannot describe,
Requiring order beyond their speech.

Too many waltzes have ended. Yet the shapes
For which the voices cry, these, too, may be
Modes of desire, modes of revealing desire.

Too many waltzes – The epic of disbelief
Blares oftener and soon, will soon be constant.
Some harmonious sceptic soon in a sceptical music

Will unite these figures of men and their shapes
Will glisten again with motion, the music
Will be motion and full of shadows.

WALLACE STEVENS

A Sergeants' Mess Song

With our arms round the waists of the charming girls,
Through the galop-sweeps and the swift waltz-whirls,
While our beards are brushed by their dancing curls,

Dance, boys, dance!

With the old black pipe and the steaming glass,
And a toast to the health of each sonsie lass,
And a right jolly set the toast to pass,

Drink, boys, drink!

For we have our hold of the world today,
And must snatch our share of it while we may,
Before they bury us out of the way:

Dance, boys, dance!

So we'll smoke our pipe, and we'll drink our glass,
And we'll play our game, and we'll hug our lass;
And as for the rest – why the devil's an ass:

Drink, boys, drink!

JAMES THOMSON

A Transvestite Ball

In those days there was a sort of masquerade at court every Tuesday, which was indeed not to everyone's taste, but it pleased me and my fifteen years very much. The Empress [Elizabeth, who ruled Russia from

1741 to 1762] had decreed that at these masquerades, to which only those persons had access who had been selected by her, all the men had to be dressed as women and all the women as men. I must say there could have been nothing more ugly and at the same time more laughable than most of the men so disguised, and nothing more miserable than the women in men's clothing. The Empress alone, who was best suited to men's clothing, looked really well; thus costumed, she was in fact very beautiful. As a rule, the men were in a churlish humour at these masquerades, and the women were in constant danger of being knocked over by some frightful Colossus, for the men moved about most clumsily in their gigantic hoop-skirts. One was being constantly struck against, for however cleverly one managed, one was always getting between them again, for custom required that the ladies should approach the hoop-shirts.

At one of these balls I once saw a very funny sight. The very tall Monsieur Sievers, in those days Chamberlain, wearing a hoop-skirt which the Empress had given him, was dancing a polonaise with me. Countess Hendrikov, who was dancing behind me, was over-thrown by the hoop-skirt of Monsieur Sievers as he gave me his hand in turning. In falling she struck me in such a way that I fell beneath the hoop-skirt of Monsieur Sievers which had sprung upright beside me. Monsieur Sievers entangled himself in his long skirts, which were in great disorder, and all three of us lay on the ground with me entirely covered by his skirt. I was dying of laughter and trying to get up; but they had to come and lift us up because the three of us were so tangled in Monsieur Sievers' clothing that no one could rise without causing the other two to fall.

CATHARINE THE GREAT, EMPRESS OF RUSSIA, *Memoirs*

Whiskit and Friskit

1 July 1818: We are this morning at Carlisle. After Skiddaw, we walked to Ireby, the oldest market town in Cumberland – where we were greatly amused by a country dancing-school holden at the Inn, it was indeed 'no new cotillon fresh from France'. No, they kickit and jumpit with mettle extraordinary, and whiskit, and friskit, and toed it, and go'd it, and twirl'd it, and wheel'd it, and stamped it, and sweated it, tattooing the floor like mad; The difference between our country dances and these Scottish figures is about the same as leisurely stirring a cup o' Tea and beating up a batter-pudding. I was extremely gratified to think, that if I had pleasures they knew nothing of, they had also some into which I could not possibly enter.

JOHN KEATS, *Letters*

Dressing

This Arsnecke of Pride.

PHILIP STUBBES

Singularity in dress shows something wrong in the mind.

SAMUEL RICHARDSON

Savages are fops and fripples more than any other man.

WILLIAM BLAKE

Fashion is the abortive issue of vain ostentation and exclusive egotism: it is haughty, trifling, affected, servile, despotic, mean and ambitious, precise and fantastical, all in a breath – tied to no rule, and bound to conform to every whim of the minute.

WILLIAM HAZLITT

Black Fops

There is a class of fops not usually designated by that epithet – men clothed in profound black, with large canes, and strange amorphous hats – of big speech, and imperative presence – talkers about Plato – great affecters of senility – despisers of women, and all the graces of life – fierce foes to common sense – abusive of the living, and approving no one who has not been dead for at least a century. Such fops, as vain, and as shallow as their fraternity in Bond Street, differ from these only as Gorgonius differed from Rufillus.

REV. SYDNEY SMITH, *Essays*

Boot Blacking

One day a youthful beau approached Brummell and said, 'Permit me to ask you where you get your blacking?' 'Ah!' replied Brummell, gazing complacently at his boots, 'my blacking positively ruins me. I will tell you in confidence; it is made with the finest champagne!'

REES HOWELL GRONOW, *Reminiscences*

A Codpiece

For his codpiece were used sixteen ells and a quarter of the same cloth, and it was fashioned on the top like unto a triumphant arch most gallantly fastened with two enamelled clasps, in each of which was set a great emerald, as big as an orange; for, as says Orpheus, *lib. de lapidibus*, and Plinius, *libro ultimo*, it hath an erective virtue and comfort and comfortative of the natural member. The exiture, out-jecting or out-standing of his codpiece, was of the length of a yard, jagged and pinked, and withal bagging, and strutting out with the blue damask lining, after the manner of his breeches. But had you seen the fair embroidery of the small needle-work pearl, and the curiously interlaced knots, by the goldsmith's art set out and trimmed with rich diamonds, precious rubies, fine torquoises, costly emeralds, and Persian pearls, you would have compared it to a fair Cornucopia, or horn of abundance, such as you see in antiques, or as Rhea gave to the two nymphs, Amalthea and Ida, the nurses of Jupiter.

And, like to that horn of abundance, it was still gallant, succulent, droppy, sappy, pithy, lively, always flourishing, always fructifying, full of juice, full of flower, full of fruit, and all manner of delight. I avow God, it would have done one good to have seen him, but I will tell you more of him in the book which I have made of the dignity of codpieces. One thing I will tell you, that, as it was both long and large, so was it well furnished and victualled within, nothing like unto the hypocritical codpieces of some fond wooers, and wench-courters, which are stuffed only with wind, to the great prejudice of the female sex.

FRANÇOIS RABELAIS, *Gargantua*

Dandies

How unspeakably odious – with a few brilliant exceptions, such as [Lord] Alvanley and others – were the dandies of forty years ago. They were a motley crew, with nothing remarkable about them but their insolence. They were generally not high-born, nor rich, nor very good-looking, nor clever, nor agreeable; and why they arrogated to themselves the right of setting up their own fancied superiority on a self-raised pedestal, and despising their betters, Heaven only knows. They were generally middle-aged, some even elderly men, had large appetites and weak digestions, gambled freely, and had no luck. They hated everybody, and abused everybody, and would sit together in White's bay window, or the pit boxes at the Opera, weaving tremendous crammers. They swore a good deal, never laughed, had their own particular slang, looked hazy after dinner, and had most of them been patronised at one time or other by Brummel and the Prince Regent.

These gentlemen were very fond of having a butt. Many years ago Tom Raikes filled this capacity; though he did kick out sometimes, and to some purpose. They gloried in their shame, and believed in nothing good, or noble, or elevated. Thank Heaven, that miserable race of used-up dandies has long been extinct!

REES HOWELL GRONOW, *Reminiscences*

Dandyism

It is, unfortunately, quite true that without leisure and money love can be nothing but a plebeian orgy or the fulfilment of a conjugal duty. Instead of being a burning or fantastical caprice, it becomes a loathsome *utility*.

My reason for speaking of love in connection with dandyism is that love is the natural occupation of the leisured; but the dandy does not make love his special aim. Similarly, my reason for mentioning money is that money is indispensable to people who make a cult of their desires; but the dandy does not wish to have money for its own sake; he would be content to be allowed to live indefinitely on credit; he leaves the coarse desire for money to baser mortals.

Dandyism is not even, as many unthinking people seem to suppose, an immoderate interest in personal appearance and material elegance. For the true dandy these things are only a symbol of the aristocratic superiority of his personality. In his eyes, therefore, which seek, above all, distinction, the perfection of personal appearance consists in complete simplicity – this being, in fact, the best means of achieving distinction.

What, then, is this ruling passion that has turned into a creed and created its own skilled tyrants? What is this unwritten constitution that has created so haughty a caste? It is, above all, a burning need to acquire originality, within the apparent bounds of convention. It is a sort of cult of oneself, which can dispense even with what are commonly called illusions. It is the delight in causing astonishment, and the proud satisfaction of never oneself being astonished. A dandy may be indifferent, or he may be unhappy; but in the latter case he will smile like the Spartan under the teeth of the fox.

It will be seen that, in certain aspects, dandyism borders on spirituality and stoicism. But a dandy can never indulge in anything vulgar. If he committed a crime, he would perhaps not be too upset about it; but if this crime had some trivial cause, his disgrace would be irreparable ...

Whether the name they win for themselves be Corinthians, swells, bucks, lions or dandies, their origin is the same. They all have the same characteristics of opposition and revolt. They all represent the best element in human pride – that need, which nowadays is too uncommon, to combat and destroy triviality. This is what gives the dandy his haughty attitude, the attitude of a caste whose very reserve is a provocation.

Dandyism arises especially in periods of transition, when democracy is not yet all-powerful and aristocracy is only partially tottering or brought low. In the disturbance of such periods a certain number of men, detached from their own class, disappointed and disorientated, but still rich in native energy, may form a project of founding a new sort of aristocracy, which will be all the more difficult to break because it will be based on the most precious and indestructible of human powers – on those celestial gifts that neither toil nor money can bestow.

Dandyism is the last gleam of heroism in times of decadence. The fact that a type of dandy was discovered by a traveller in North America does not invalidate this statement; for there is nothing to prevent us from supposing that what we call the 'savage' tribes are the debris of great vanished civilisations. Dandyism is a setting sun. Like the great sinking star, it is superb, cold and melancholy.

CHARLES BAUDELAIRE, *The Dandy*

Doom of Fops in the Next World

I saw some there with collars of gold about their necks, and some of silver, and some men I saw with gay girdles of silver and gold, and harneist horns about their necks, some with more jagges on their clothes than whole cloth, some had their clothes full of gingles and belles of silver all overset, and some with long pokes [bags] on their sleeves, and women with gowns trayling behind them a great space, and some others with gay chaplets on their heads of gold and pearls, and other precious stones. And then I looked on him that I saw first in payn, and saw the collars, and the gay girdles, and bawdricks, burning, and the fiends dragging him; and two fingers deep and more within their flesh was all burning; and I saw the jagges that men were clothed in turn all to adders, to dragons, and to toads, and many other horrible beasts, sucking them, and biting them, and stinging them with all their might; and through every gingle I saw fiends drive burning nails of fire into their flesh. I also saw fiends drawing down the skin of their shoulders like to pokes, and cutting these off, and drawing them over the heads of those they cut them from, all burning as fire. And then I saw the women that had side trails behind them, and these side trails were cut off by fiends, and burnt on their heads; and some took off these cuttings all burning, and stopped therewith their mouthes, their noses, and their eyes. I saw also their gay chaplets of gold, of pearls, and of other precious stones, turned into nails of iron, burning, and fiendes with burning hammers smiting them into their heads.

WILLIAM STAUNTON, *Visions of Patrick's Purgatory* (1409)

A Dressmaker

Here? Yes, we have a hole here, yes, obviously, a hole ... Think of a stone torn from a wall, huh? The couturier looks in my direction for a nod of approval. Shall I bow to this image, this bold new image? I feel detached. I slip him my best confraternal smile. He scares me a little – but less than he scares my friend Valentine, standing fervently before him. But then, I'm not the one he's dressing. I have no reason to assume that anxious and abandoned look, the look of the voluptuous victim ...

My friend Valentine appals me. She dangles her bare arms, and when the 'master's' despotic forefinger points at her, she imperceptibly tightens her elbows against her sides. I feel like telling my friend, 'Come now, pull yourself together, he's your dressmaker!' But she would answer back, still more vanquished, 'Exactly!'

Moreover, the master shows an almost exaggerated, I was going to write: squeamish, discretion. It is with a distant, seemingly magnetic, index finger that he commands his client's revolutions. She turns, takes a step forward, and stops, mesmerised – he does not even graze the material of the dress. Perhaps this extreme reserve is not an affectation at all. Around us I hear an exclusively feminine hum; in the warm, dry air I breathe in mixed perfumes, and that of my friend Valentine, décolleté, is fresh and strong – and I think of a confession from my corset maker, who flees her apartment at night and goes out, sick to her stomach, to have her dinner in a restaurant. 'After all those fittings, Madame, I can't bear to eat at home. It smells too strongly of women at the end of the day, it ruins my appetite.'

This is the first time I've come here with my friend Valentine, who, of course, has her dresses made by a 'master couturier'. I study the 'master', who returns the compliment. He busies himself with Valentine, but I am the one he wants to impress. He takes his time with her, he ignores his other impatient subjects – he poses, not quite knowing whether what I am making of him is a flattering portrait or a caricature ...

He's a rather small man, well dressed, neither young nor old. His jacket is dark, his tie severe. Nothing aggressive about his clothes or his shoes, no jewellery. One doesn't think of looking for what there's too much of, but rather for what's missing. He's missing ... a little of everything: three inches in height, as much in width, and then one would like more decisiveness in the nose, a more adventurous chin. He's arrogant without being authoritative, and his ferrety gaze deliberately loses all its expression when it fixes on something. I wonder why it is he seems disguised, from head to foot: his face looks as if it doesn't belong to him.

'A hole,' repeats Valentine devoutly, 'yes, a hole ...'

She nervously fingers the small lace fichu pinned to her shoulders, crumpling it in her hand over the by-now-famous 'hole', high on the waist, beneath the breast. The rest of the dress is a close-fitting shift, in a singular shade of mauve, which turns blue when the folds of transparent silk are gathered. There is also a small sprinkling of long pearls at the bottom of the tunic, and some sort of ragged piece of material, without any definite purpose, which trails off to the side onto the carpet. It is an 'important' dinner dress.

'Wait! Why didn't I think of it sooner?'

The master steals off with a malicious little hop and reappears, preciously cradling what he needed to fill in the hole: a green flower, made of knitted wool, from which hangs a ludicrous cluster of blue cherries, made of knitted wool, topped by three black leaves – made of knitted wool.

'There!'

He plants the thing in the hollow of the décolleté bodice, and quickly pulls away his hand, like a cat that has burned its paw, and laughs an odious, theatrical laugh.

I look in the triple mirror at my friend Valentine. She has not batted an eyelash and, with the tips of her fingers, pushes up the knitted object, the horror, which is a disgrace to the mauve dress. Without hiding the sickness I feel, I also look at the master, who winks and leans his head to the side like a satisfied painter: I detest fools ...

Very calmly, and in my honour, the master begins his recitation on the needlework so dear to our grandmothers, he sings the praises of naïve Tunisian crocheting and touchingly old-fashioned macramé – for these unsophisticated ornaments he claims a place of honour on our dresses of woven air and flowing water. Predictably, he uses words like 'innovation', 'amusing attempts' ...

'We are a "young house" but we are prepared to attack everything routine. No respect for our elders. You, Madame, who are an artist, don't you like this youthful enthusiasm which laughs while trampling on the established customs of austere couture – and which some-times makes mistakes, heaven knows – but who else will jump into the breach and forge ahead?'

He slips away again, without waiting for an answer. And while silent young girls bustle about to get my passive and charmed friend dressed again, he calls out the procession of models for us – for me!

One after the other, in the dreary elegance of the white salon, the models dance the steps to the 'mermaid on her tail fin' and the 'upright serpent'. They progress with difficulty, knees joined and bound, and cut through the air as though it were heavy water, helping themselves along with their hands, which paddle the air at hip level. These are lovely creatures, whose every deformity has its grace: they no longer have any rumps – the curve is gone from the small of their backs accentuating their length: where does the stomach begin? Where are the breasts hiding?

A sign from the master hurries them on or holds them back. Now and then I move involuntarily toward a particular dress, pink and alive like a glittering skin, toward this one, in a savage blue colour which blots out everything around it, toward that one made of black velvet, deep and thick as a pelt.

But something holds my arm back and dampens my pleasure: every dress has its ludicrous flaw, the imbecilic and bizarre detail, the toad thrown there like a signature by the despotic and wicked dress-maker. I see knitted flowers on moonlight gauze and unseemly little white horsehair fringe on royal Alençon lace. A delicate train hangs from a tapestry cabbage: a sheath of black plush, slender, curvacious, with a satanic elegance, tapers off, prisoner of the heaviest founda-tion of white cloth, twisted into a double skirt; a Greek tunic, pure white, moves forward, barred at the knees by a row of little taffeta flounces with chenille borders; finally, a spiral skirt of green Empire faille, tied up in all directions with Tom Thumb trimmings, unleashes my indignation.

'Monsieur,' I say to the dressmaker, 'Monsieur, will you please just look at that! Surely you must know how ugly that is. It's not simply a matter of bad taste; in every one of these dresses there is an *intention*:

take any one of them, take this one here, which wipes the floor with this little square tail of gold linen embroidered with thick white cotton! Why, *why* do you do it?'

My unexpected vehemence makes the master stop short, and his beady eyes meet mine for a long moment. He hesitates; he lets me catch his true and mediocre face, the face of a small shopkeeper who had a hard time starting out – he hesitates between his urge to deceive me and a sudden need for confession, for cynicism ...

'Would you please tell me, Monsieur, just me, why you do this?'

He smiles a loathsome, confidential smile, he looks around him, as if he wished we were alone: will he betray his appetite for domination, claim revenge for his past as an impoverished clerk, confess the disgusted misogyny that comes from dealing with too many females, the pleasure he takes in making them ugly, in humiliating them, in subjecting them to his half-crazed fantasies, in 'branding' them ...

He hesitates, he doesn't dare, and, finally, turning his eyes away from mine: 'Just to see ...' he says.

COLETTE, *The Master*

Nothing els is garish apparraile, but Prydes ulcer broken forth.

THOMAS NASHE

[Of Disraeli] No man would go on in that odd manner, wear green velvet trowsers and ruffles, without having odd feelings. He ought to be kicked.

BENJAMIN ROBERT HAYDON

Crime committed in evening dress is what most appeals to popular imagination.

ANATOLE FRANCE

A Duchess Dresses

'Give me a wrap, Button. You can start doing my hair. Sebastian, give me the plan of the dinner-table. On the table there. No, silly boy. Button, give it to his Grace. Now, Sebastian, read it out to me while I have my hair done. Oh, George Roehampton takes me in, does he? *Must* he? Such a bore that man is. And Sir Adam the other side. Don't pull my hair like that, Button; really, I never knew such a clumsy woman; now you have given me a headache for the rest of the evening. Do be more careful. Well, I am not going to enjoy myself very much, I can see: Sir Adam and George Roehampton. However, it's inevitable. Or no, let me see for myself. That Miss Wace is such a fool that she may quite well have made a muddle of the whole thing. Come and hold the plan for me to see, Sebastian. Button! you pulled my hair again. How many times must I tell you to be careful? Once more, and I give you notice, I declare I will. Tilt it up, Sebastian; I can't see.'

Sebastian stood beside his mother holding the red leather pad, with slits into which cards bearing the names of the guests were inserted. As he stood holding it, he watched his mother's reflection in the mirror. With her fair hair and lively little crumpled face, she looked extraordinarily young for her age as a rule, but now she was busily applying cream and wiping the cosmetics from her face with a hand-kerchief, at the same time as Button removed the pads from under her hair and laid them on the dressing-table. 'Rats,' her children called them. They were unappetising objects, like last year's bird's-nests, hot and stuffy to the head, but they could not be dispensed with, since they provided the foundation on which the coiffure was to be swathed and piled, and into which the innumerable hairpins were to be stuck. It was always a source of great preoccupation with the ladies that no bit of the pad should show through the natural hair. Often they put up a tentative hand to feel, even in the midst of the most absorbing conversation; and then their faces wore the expression which is seen only on the faces of women whose fingers investigate the back of their heads. Sebastian had watched this hair-dressing process a hundred times, but now seeing it take place in the mirror, he observed it with a new eye. He stared at his mother's reflection, with the pool of rubies in the foreground, and the uncomely 'rats', as though she were a stranger to him, realising that behind the glitter and animation in which they lived he had absolutely no knowledge of her. If he had been asked to describe his mother, he must have said, 'She is a famous hostess, with a talent for mimicry and a genius for making parties a success. She is charming and vivacious. In private life she is often irritable and sometimes unkind. She likes bridge and racing. She never opens a book, and she cannot bear to be alone. I have not the faintest idea of what she is really like.' He would not have added, because he did not know, that she was ruthless and predatory.

'Why are you staring like that, Sebastian? You make me quite shy.' Her hair was about her shoulders now, and Button was busy with the curling-tongs. She heated them first on the spirit lamp, and then held them carefully to her own cheek to feel if they were hot enough. 'Bless the boy, one would think he had never watched me dress before. Now about that dinner-table, yes, it's all wrong; I thought it would be. She has clean forgotten the ambassador. Button, you must call Miss Wace – no, Sebastian, you fetch her. No, ring the bell; I don't want you to go away. Why on earth can't people do their own jobs properly? What do I pay Wacey a hundred and fifty a year for, I should like to know? Oh dear, and look at the time; I shall be late for dinner. I declare the trouble of entertaining is enough to spoil all one's pleasure. It's a little hard, I do think, that one should never have any undiluted pleasure in life. Who's that at the door? Button, go and see. And Miss Wace must come at once.'

'Lady Viola would like to know if she may come and say good night to your Grace.'

'Oh, bother the child – well, yes, I suppose she must if she wants to. Now, Button, haven't you nearly finished? Don't drag my hair back like that, woman. Give me the tail comb. Don't you see, it wants more fullness at the side. Really, Button, I thought you were supposed to be an expert hairdresser. You may think yourself lucky, Sebastian, that you were born a boy. This eternal hair, these eternal clothes! they wear a woman out before her time. Oh there you are, Miss Wace. This plan is all wrong – perfectly hopeless. I don't go in with Lord Roehampton at all. What about the ambassador? You must alter it. Do it in here, as quick as you can. Sebastian will help you. And Viola. Come in, Viola; don't look so scared, child; I can't bear people who look scared. Now I must leave you all while I wash. No, I don't want you now, Button; you get on my nerves. I'll call you when I want you. Get my dress ready. Children, help Miss Wace – yes, you too, Viola; it's high time you took a little trouble to help your poor mother – and do, all three of you, try to show a little intelligence.'

The duchess retired into her dressing-room, from where she kept up a flow of comments.

'Viola, you must really take a little more trouble about your appearance. You looked a perfect fright at luncheon to-day; I was ashamed of you. And you really must talk more, instead of sitting there like a stuffed doll. You had that nice Mr Anquetil, who is perfectly easy to get on with. You might be ten, instead of seventeen. I have a good mind to start you coming down to dinner, except that you would cast a blight over everything. Girls are such a bore – poor things, they can't help it, but really they are a problem. They ruin conversation; one has to be so careful. Women ought to be married, or at any rate widowed. I don't mean you, of course, Wacey. I'm ready for you, Button.'

Button vanished into the dressing-room, and for a while there was silence, broken only by irritable exclamations from within. These inner mysteries of his mother's toilet were unknown to Sebastian, but Viola knew well enough what was going on: her mother was seated, poking at her hair meanwhile with fretful but experienced fingers, while Button knelt before her, carefully drawing the silk stockings on to her feet and smoothing them nicely up the leg. Then her mother would rise, and, standing in her chemise, would allow the maid to fit the long stays of pink coutil, heavily boned, round her hips and slender figure, fastening the busk down the front, after many adjustments; then the suspenders would be clipped to the stockings; then the lacing would follow, beginning at the waist and travelling gradually up and down, until the necessary proportions had been achieved. The silk laces and their tags would fly out, under the maid's deft fingers, with the flick of a skilled worker mending a net. Then the pads of pink satin would be brought, and fastened into place on the hips and under the arms, still further to accentuate the smallness of the waist. Then the drawers; and then the petticoat would be spread into a ring on the floor, and Lucy would step into it on her high-heeled shoes, allowing Button to draw it up and tie the tapes. Then Button would throw the dressing-gown round her shoulders again – Viola had followed the process well, for here the door opened, and the duchess emerged. 'Well, have you done that table? Read it out. Louder. I can't hear. Yes, that's better. I'm sorry, Sebastian, you'll have to take in old Octavia Hull again. Nonsense, she's very amusing when she's not too fuddled with drugs. She'll be all right to-night because she'll be afraid of losing too much money to Sir Adam after dinner. Now, Wacey, off you go and rearrange the cards on the table. And you too, Viola. There are too many people in this room. Oh, all right, you can stop till I'm dressed if you like. Button, I'm ready for my dress. Now be careful. Don't catch the hooks in my hair. Sebastian, you must turn round while I take off my dressing-gown. Now, Button.'

Button, gathering up the lovely mass of taffeta and tulle, held the bodice open while the duchess flung off her wrap and dived gingerly into the billows of her dress. Viola watched enraptured the sudden gleam of her mother's white arms and shoulders. Button breathed a sigh of relief as she began doing up the innumerable hooks at the back. But Lucy could not stand still for a moment, and strayed all over the room with Button in pursuit, hooking. 'Haven't you finished *yet*, Button? Nonsense, it isn't tight. You'll say next that I'm getting fat.' Lucy was proud of her waist, which indeed was tiny, and had changed since her girlish days only from eighteen to twenty inches. 'Only when your Grace stoops,' said Button apologetically, for Lucy at the moment was bending forward and peering into her mirror as she puffed the roll of her hair into a rounder shape. '*There*, then,' said the duchess, straightening herself, but reaching down stiffly for the largest of her rubies, which she tried first against her shoulder, but finally pinned into a knot at her waist. Then she encircled her throat with the high dog-collar of rubies and diamonds, tied with a large bow of white tulle at the back. 'You must choose a wife who will do credit to the jewels, Sebastian,' she said as she slipped an ear-ring into its place, 'because, of course, the day will come when your poor old mother has to give up everything to her daughter-in-law, and we shan't like that – eh, Button?' – for she was in a better humour now, again completely adorned and clothed – 'but we'll put up with it for the joy of seeing a bride brought to Chevron – eh, Button? eh, Wacey? oh, no, of course Wacey has gone to do the table – and you and I, Button, will retire to the Dower House and live humbly for the rest of our lives, and perhaps his Grace will ask us to the garden-party – eh, Sebastian, you rogue? – will you, if your wife allows it?' Lucy was herself again, adjusting her frock, clasping her bracelets, dusting her throat with powder – for she was one of those who used powder, to the disapproval of her elders – and everybody except Sebastian was radiant with responsive smiles. She flicked her handkerchief across Sebastian's lips. 'Sulky boy! but Sylvia Roehampton says you are even more attractive when you sulk than when you are amiable, so I suppose I must believe her. Now Viola, my darling, I must run. Kiss me good-night. Go straight to bed. Do I look nice?'

'Oh mother, you look too lovely!'

'That's all right.' Lucy liked as much admiration as she could get. 'Now you'll run away to bed, won't you? Dear me, I quite envy you the quiet of the schoolroom instead of that noisy dinner. Don't you, Sebastian? Good-night, my darling. Come along, Sebastian. I shall want you to wait up for me, Button, of course. You go in front, Sebastian, and open the doors. Dear, dear, how late you children have made me. Sebastian, you must apologise to old Octavia at dinner, and tell her it was all your fault. My fan, Button! good heavens, woman, what are you there for? One has to think of everything for oneself.'

V. SACKVILLE-WEST, *The Edwardians*

An Epicene Sea Captain

Our tyrant having left the ship, and carried his favourite Mackshane along with him, to my inexpressible satisfaction, our new commander came on board in a ten-oar'd barge, overshadowed with a vast umbrella, and appeared in every thing the reverse of Oakhum, being a tall, thin young man, dressed in this manner: a white hat, garnished with a red feather, adorned his head, from whence his hair flowed upon his shoulders, in ringlets tied behind with a ribbon. His coat consisting of pink-coloured silk, lined with white, by the elegance of the cut retired backwards as it were, to discover a white satin waistcoat embroidered with gold, unbuttoned at the upper part to display a broch set with garnets, that glittered in the breast of his shirt, which was of the finest cambric, edged with right Mechline; the knees of his crimson velvet breeches scarce descended so low as to meet his silk stockings, which rose without spot or wrinkle on his meagre legs, from shoes of blue Meroquin, studded with diamond buckles that flamed forth rivals to the sun! A steel-hilted sword, inlaid with gold, and decked with a knot of ribbon which fell down in a rich tassle, equipped his side; and an amber-headed cane hung dangling from his wrist: But the most remarkable parts of his furniture were a mask on his face, and white gloves on his hands, which did not seem to be put on with an intention to be pulled off occasionally, but were fixed with a curious ring on the little finger of each hand. In this garb, captain Whiffle, for that was his name, took possession of the ship, surrounded with a crowd of attendants, all of whom, in their different degrees, seemed to be of their patron's disposition; and the air was so impregnated with perfumes, that one may venture to affirm the clime of Arabia Fœlix was not half so sweet scented.

TOBIAS SMOLLETT, *Roderick Random*

Hats that defy virtue

Sometimes they use them sharp on the crowne, peaking up like a sphere, or shafte of a steeple, standing a quarter of a yard above the crowne of their heades; some more, some lesse, as please the phantasies of their mindes. Othersome be flat and broad on the crowne, like the battlements of a house. An other sort have round crownes, sometime with one kinde of bande, sometime with an other; nowe blacke, now white, now russet, now red, now greene, now yellowe, now this, nowe that, never content with one colour or fashion two dayes to an ende. And thus in vanitie they spende the Lorde his treasure, consuming their golden yeares and silver dayes in wickednes & sin. And as the fashions bee rare and straunge, so are the thinges whereof their Hattes be made, diverse also; for some are of silke, some of velvet, some of taffetie, some of carcanet, some of wooll: & which is more curious, some of a certaine kind of fine haire, far fetched and deare bought, you maye bee sure; And so common a thing it is, that everie Servingman, Countreyman, and other, even all indifferently, do weare of these hattes …

An other sort (as phantasticall as the rest) are content with no kind of Hatt without a great bunche of feathers of diverse and sundrie colours, peaking on toppe of their heades, not unlyke (I dare not say) Cockcombes, but as sternes of pride and ensigns of vanitie; and these fluttering sayles are fethered flags of defiance to vertue (for so they are) and so advanced in *Ailgna*, that every Childe hath them in his hat or cap.

PHILIP STUBBES, *Anatomie of Abuses* (1583)

Madrid in the 1760s

In order to adopt the distinguished air of a dandy, one must start by wearing two watches, and chained to them, all sorts of pendants. There you can find in miniature, watering cans, almanacs, lamp-posts, acorns, violins, harps, diaries, hooks, keys, guitars, seals, clarinets, cages, drums, fishes, and all sorts of odds and ends.

J. CLAVIJO Y FAJARDO, El Pensador

Martyrs to Fashion

Who hath not heard of her at Paris, which only to get a fresher hew of a new skin, endured to have her face flead all over? There are some who, being sound, and in perfit health, have had some teeth puld-out, thereby to frame a daintier or more pleasing voyce, or to set them in better order? How many examples of paine or smarte have we of that kind and sex? What can they not doe? What will they not doe? What feare they to doe? So they may but hope for some amendment of their beautie?

> Who take great care to root out their gray haire,
> And skin flead-off a new face to repaire.

I have seene some swallow gravell, ashes, coales, dust, tallow, candles and for the-nonce, labour and toyle themselves to spoile their stomacke, only to get a pale-bleake colour. To become slender in wast, and to have a straight spagnolized body what pinching, what girding, what cingling will they not indure; Yea sometimes with yron-plates, with whale-bones, and other such trash, that their very skin, and quicke flesh is eaten in and consumed to the bones; Whereby they sometimes worke their owne death.

MICHEL DE MONTAIGNE, The Taste of Goods or Evils

The New Vestments

> There lived an old man in the Kingdom of Tess,
> Who invented a purely original dress;
> And when it was perfectly made and complete,
> He opened the door, and walked into the street.

By way of a hat, he'd a loaf of Brown Bread,
In the middle of which he inserted his head;
His Shirt was made up of no end of dead Mice,
The warmth of whose skins was quite fluffy and nice;
His Drawers were of Rabbit-skins; so were his Shoes;
His Stockings were skins, but it is not known whose;
His Waistcoat and Trowsers were made of Pork Chops;
His Buttons were Jujubes, and Chocolate Drops;
His Coat was all Pancakes with Jam for a border,
And a girdle of Biscuits to keep it in order;
And he wore over all, as a screen from bad weather,
A Cloak of green Cabbage-leaves stitched all together.

He had walked a short way, when he heard a great noise,
Of all sorts of Beasticles, Birdlings, and Boys;
And from every long street and dark lane in the town
Beasts, Birdles, and Boys in a tumult rushed down.
Two Cows and a half ate his Cabbage-leaved Cloak;
Four Apes seized his Girdle, which vanished like smoke;
Three Kids ate up half of his Pancaky Coat,
And the tails were devour'd by an ancient He Goat;
An army of Dogs in a twinkling tore *up* his
Pork Waistcoat and Trowsers to give to their Puppies;
And while they were growling, and mumbling the Chops,
Ten Boys prigged the Jujubes and Chocolate Drops.
He tried to run back to his house, but in vain,
For Scores of fat Pigs came again and again;
They rushed out of stables and hovels and doors,
They tore off his stockings, his shoes, and his drawers;
And now from the housetops with screechings descend,
Striped, spotted, white, black, and gray Cats without end,
They jumped on his shoulders and knocked off his hat,
When Crows, Ducks, and Hens made a mincemeat of that;
They speedily flew at his sleeves in a trice,
And utterly tore up his Shirt of dead Mice;

They swallowed the last of his Shirt with a squall,
Whereon he ran home with no clothes on at all.

And he said to himself as he bolted the door,
'I will not wear a similar dress any more,
'Any more, any more, any more, never more!'

EDWARD LEAR

The Picture of a Fine Gentleman

See Florio in his *vis-à-vis* —
No comet shines more bright than he;
The spectacle attracts the eye,
And captive fair ones round him die;
Or if, exalted in his seat,
On phaeton he shakes the street,
Trembling with wonder, we behold
A Macaroni grown so bold;
He lashes on his prancing steeds,
And looks disdainful o'er our heads;
But should he to the Opera come,
Elate with pride in beauty's bloom,
There guard your hearts, ye tender misses!
For Florio there the sex bewitches.

He comes in all the pomp of dress,
And lovely spite of haughtiness;
A *broche* is on his jabot placed,
His finger with a diamond graced,
And to complete the finished Beau,
A giant buckle hides his shoe;
A muff as vast as Ajax' shield,
Behold this modern Paris wield;
A sword is dangling at his side,

Of tempered steel, but never tried;
A feather, white as Celia's breast,
Adorns his *chapeau bras*; his vest,
Enriched with spangles, foils, and lace,
Is deemed the finest in the place.

A golden snuff-box he displays,
Takes snuff, and talks in foreign phrase;
Looks at his watch, whose brilliant chain
A hundred trinkets does sustain,
Games, swears, and acts the man of *ton*,
By self-importance only known;
Makes love, and rhymes, *coquets*, and sings,
Whilst with his praise th' assembly rings.
But could we follow Florio home,
And view him in his dressing-room,
Without the aid of powerful art,
How would the pretty misses start,
To see him void of the disguise,
Which fashionable dress supplies!
Florio no longer could be known
The gay Lothario of the town;
But all your sex would spurn the creature,
Nor recollect a single feature
Of him who, not an hour before,
Each was ambitious to adore.

LADY SOPHIA BURRELL

A Regal Wardrobe

Queen Elizabeth left behind her a wardrobe containing three thousand dresses. Three years before her death, her wardrobe, *exclusive* of her coronation, mourning, parliament robes, and those of the Order of the Garter, consisted of

99	Robes.	31	Cloakes and saufegardes.
102	French gownes.	13	Saufegardes.
67	Rounde gownes.	43	Saufegardes and juppes.
100	Loose gownes.	85	Dublettes.
126	Kirtells.	18	Lappe mantles.
136	Forepartes (*stomachers*)	27	Fannes.
125	Petticoates.	9	Pantobles.
96	Cloakes.		

ELIZABETH STONE, *Chronicles of Fashion*

Riding Garb

12 June 1666: Walking in the galleries at White Hall, I find the Ladies of Honour dressed in their riding garbs, with coats and doublets with deep skirts, just, for all the world, like mine; and buttoned their doublets up the breast, with perriwigs and with hats; so that, only for a long petticoat dragging under their men's coats, nobody could take them for women in any point whatever; which was an odde sight, and a sight did not please me. It was Mrs Wells and another fine lady that I saw thus.

SAMUEL PEPYS, *Diary*

Such a Sweet Girl

Her head-dress was a Brussels lace mob, peculiarly adapted to the charming air and turn of her features. The sky-blue ribbon illustrated that. But although the weather was somewhat sharp, she had not on either hat or hood; for, besides that she loves to use herself hardily (by which means, and by a temperance truly exemplary, she is allowed to have given high health and vigour to an originally tender constitution), she seems to have intended to show me that she was determined not to stand to her appointment. O Jack! that such a sweet girl should be a rogue!

Her morning gown was a pale primrose-coloured paduasoy: the cuffs and robings curiously embroidered by the fingers of this ever-charming Arachne, in a running pattern of violets and their leaves; the light in the flowers silver; gold in the leaves. A pair of diamond snaps in her ears. A white handkerchief, wrought by the same inimitable fingers, concealed – O Bedford! what still more inimitable beauties did not conceal! (by its throbbing motions I saw it!) dancing beneath the charming umbrage.

Her ruffles were the same as her mob. Her apron a flowered lawn. Her coat white satin, quilted: blue satin her shoes, braided with the same colour, without lace; for what need has the prettiest foot in the world of ornament? Neat buckles in them: and on her charming arms a pair of black velvet glove-like muffs of her own invention; for she makes and gives fashions as she pleases. Her hands, velvet of themselves, thus uncovered the freer to be grasped by those of her adorer.

SAMUEL RICHARDSON, *Clarissa*

Tea Gowns

It is not so very long ago that the appearance in the drawing-room or in any other place where she was visible to the naked eye of the male sex, of a lady loosely wrapped in her dressing gown, would have been an impossibility. But the world moves rapidly in this last quarter of the nineteenth century; and ladies, who a few years ago would have considered the idea appalling, calmly array themselves in the glorified dressing robe known as a 'tea gown', and proceed to display themselves to the eyes of their admirers ... It is absolutely useless and utterly ridiculous; but this is not the worst that may be said about it. It is, to all intents and purposes, a *déshabillé*; and so great is the force of association, that the conversation is exceedingly apt, nay almost certain, to become *déshabillé* as well. The gentlemen, in houses where tea gowns prevail, relieve themselves of their shooting attire, and reappear very frequently in gorgeous smoking suits; there is an ease and *sans façon* about the whole proceeding that favours laxity of discourse, and advantage is generally taken of the latitude afforded. It is easier to take three strides forward than half a step backwards; consequently, when the company reassembles at dinner, the point of departure for the conversation is several degrees nearer to the doubtful borderland of *hasardé* allusions and *double entendres* than it would have been without the antecedent symposium *en négligé* ... Old-fashioned prudery has long been thrown aside in the eager desire for more admirers of such becoming raiment; the tea gowns have descended to the drawing-room and the hall, and have become more marvellous and more *voyant* in the transit. With the graceful *négligé* toilet there has come in a habit of lounging, which is certainly of most doubtful grace. Hands are not unfrequently to be seen clasped above or behind the head, thus often liberally exhibiting the arm by the falling back of the loose sleeve; feet and ankles are lavishly displayed as dainty slippers are rested on the fender; more ardent spirits recline in ostentatious repose on various sofas. It is considered the thing to suit the action to the attire, and exhibit in it the supremacy of ease. Any quiet spirits in the party generally disappear; they feel themselves as out of place among the stray remarks and *hasardé* stories, as their quiet morning dresses are among the pink and blue and other rainbow-hued tea gowns, with their lavish cascades of lace and bewitching caps to match. They disappear; and when they again meet their friends at dinner-time, are apt to be somewhat astonished to find how much ceremony has been thrown to the winds in their brief absence, and on how much more familiar a footing their friends are than when they parted from them two or three hours before.

Royal Exchange, 9 November 1878

A Thousand Singularities

The fancy took, one day, the Comte *de Guiche*, and Monsieur *de la Vallière*, to draw the eyes of the spectators after them: to put which noble design in execution, they both resolv'd that their Dress should have all the magnificence which this part of the world was able to afford, and, at the same time, discover the nicety of their inventions. The Count distinguish'd himself by a thousand singularities: he had a tuft of feathers in his hat, which was button'd up by a buckle of Diamonds, that he could have wish'd to have been larger, for this occasion. He wore about his neck some Point de Venise, which was neither a Cravat nor a Band; but a small Ruff, that might gratify the secret inclination he had contracted for the *Golilla*, when he liv'd at Madrid. After this, Madam, you would expect to find him in a Doublet, after the Spanish manner; but, to your surprize, I must tell you, it was an Hungarian Vest. Next, the ghost of Antiquity haunted his memory; so he cover'd his legs with Buskins, but infinitely sprucer and genteeler than those the antient Romans used to wear; and on which he had order'd his Mistress's name to be written in letters that were extremely well design'd, upon an embroidery of pearls ... As for *la Vallière*, he had apparell'd himself after as extraordinary a manner as he possibly could, but he follow'd too much the French way, and could not raise himself to the perfection of fantasticalness.

This was the equipage of our Gentlemen, when they made their appearance in the Voorhout, which is the place where Persons of Quality use to take the air at the Hague. They had scarce enter'd it, when multitudes ran from all hands to gaze and stare at them; and as every body was surpriz'd at the novelty of the thing, they were at first puzzled, whether to admire it as extraordinary, or to laugh at it as extravagant. In this short uncertainty of thought, Monsieur *de Louvigny* arriv'd in the place, and put a stop to their grave contemplation. He wore a plain black suit, and clean linnen made up the rest: but then he had the finest head of hair, the most agreeable face, and the genteelest air that can be imagin'd. His modest deportment silently insinuated the merits of all his excellent Qualities: the Ladies were touch'd, and the Men were infinitely pleas'd.

SEIGNEUR DE SAINT EVREMOND, *Letters*

What Fashions Have Been and Will Be

Daisy and Lily,
Lazy and silly,
Walk by the shore of the wan grassy sea,

Talking once more 'neath a swan-bosomed tree.
Rose castles,
Tourelles,
Those bustles
Where swells
Each foam-bell of ermine,
They roam and determine
What fashions have been and what fashions will be,
What tartan leaves born,
What crinolines worn.
By Queen Thetis,
Pelisses
Of tarlatine blue,
Like the thin plaided leaves that the castle crags grew;
Or velours d'Afrande:
On the water-gods' land
Her hair seemed gold trees on the honey-cell sand
When the thickest gold spangles, on deep water seen,
Were like twanging guitar and like cold mandoline,
And the nymphs of great caves,
With hair like gold waves,
Of Venus, wore tarlatine.
Louise and Charlottine
(Boreas' daughters)
And the nymphs of deep waters,
The nymph Taglioni, Grisi the ondine,
Wear plaided Victoria and thin Clementine
Like the crinolined waterfalls;
Wood-nymphs wear bonnets, shawls,
Elegant parasols
Floating are seen.
The Amazons wear balzarine of jonquille
Beside the blond lace of a deep-falling rill;
Through glades like a nun
They run from and shun
The enormous and gold-rayed rustling sun;

And the nymphs of the fountains
Descend from the mountains
Like elegant willows
On their deep barouche pillows,
In cashmere Alvandar, barège Isabelle,
Like bells of bright water from clearest wood-well.
Our élégantes favouring bonnets of blond,
The stars in their apiaries,
Sylphs in their aviaries,
Seeing them, spangle these, and the sylphs fond
From their aviaries fanned
With each long fluid hand
The manteaux espagnols,
Mimic the waterfalls
Over the long and the light summer land.

So Daisy and Lily,
Lazy and silly,
Walk by the shore of the wan grassy sea,
Talking once more 'neath a swan-bosomed tree.
Rose castles,
Tourelles,
Those bustles!
Mourelles
Of the shade in their train follow.
Ladies, how vain, hollow,
Gone is the sweet swallow,
Gone, Philomel!

DAME EDITH SITWELL

Drink

It is to wine that humankind is indebted for being the only creatures that drink without being thirsty.

PLINY

When the strength of wine has hit, our limbs become heavy, we lurch and trip over our legs, our speech slurs, our mind becomes sodden, our eyes glazed. Then comes the din, hiccoughs and fights.

LUCRETIUS

What is said when drunk has been thought out beforehand.

Flemish proverb

Give a scholler wine, going to his booke, or being about to invent, it sets a new poynt on his wit, it glazeth it, it scowres it, it gives him *acumen*.

THOMAS NASHE

Lechery, sir, it provokes and unprovokes; it provokes the desire, but it takes away the performance. Therefore much drink may be said to be an equivocator with lechery: it makes him and it mars him; it sets him on and it takes him off; it persuades him and it disheartens him; makes him stand to and not stand to; in conclusion, equivocates him in a sleep, and, giving him the lie, leaves him.

WILLIAM SHAKESPEARE, *Macbeth*

An Alcoholic

Relief drinking occasional then constant, increase in alcohol tolerance, first blackouts, surreptitious drinking, growing dependence, urgency of *first* drinks, guilt spreading, unable to bear discussion of the problem, blackout crescendo, failure of ability to stop along with others (the evening really begins after you leave the party, 'my soul ran in the night, and ceased not: my soul refused to be comforted'), support-excuses, grandiose and aggressive behaviour, remorse without respite, controls fail, resolutions fail, decline of other interests, avoidance of wife and friends and colleagues, work troubles, irrational resentments, inability to eat, erosion of the ordinary will, tremor and sweating, out-of-bed-in-the-morning drinks, *decrease* in alcohol tolerance, physical deterioration, long drunks, injuries, moral deterioration, impaired and deluded thinking, low bars and witless cronies, indefinable fears (terror of the telephone, for me – never mind *who*, menace, out of the house!), formless plans along with incapacity to initiate action, obsession with drinking, conformance to it of the entire life-style, *beyond* the alibi-system, despair, hallucinations – ah! he knew every abyss of it.

JOHN BERRYMAN, *Recovery*

An Aphrodisiac Drink

Put together in a glass: two lumps of sugar and eight drops of Curaçao. Fill up the glass with port. Put it in a receptacle and boil it. When just boiling take it off the fire and serve hot with a slice of lemon and nutmeg sprinkled over it.

NORMAN DOUGLAS, *Venus in the Kitchen*

A Binge

The people who told you about my health, when you were last in London were *all* correct, & at the same time. I was roaringly well, then, some minutes after, a little mewling ruin. I would very nearly run down one street, to cringe, very nearly on my belly, up the next. In Finch's I was a lion; in the Duke of York's a piece of cold lamb with vomit sauce. Now I am back in ordinary middle health again, headachy, queasy, feverish, of a nice kind of normal crimson & bilious. I think that I am nearly well enough not to have to go out this morning in order to feel well enough to work this afternoon: a preposterous process, as it means I go to sleep with my face in the pudding & wake up sticky & fretful & bite my nails to the shoulder-bone. I hope, very much, that you are well too.

DYLAN THOMAS, letter of 1 March 1947

Bottles

The Consul dropped his eyes at last. How many bottles since then? In how many glasses, how many bottles had he hidden himself, since then alone? Suddenly he saw them, the bottles of aguardiente, of anis, of jerez, of Highland Queen, the glasses, a babel of glasses – towering, like the smoke from the train that day – built to the sky, then falling, the glasses toppling and crashing, falling downhill from the Generalife Gardens, the bottles breaking, bottles of Oporto, tinto, blanco, bottles of Pernod, Oxygénée, absinthe, bottles smashing, bottles cast aside, falling with a thud on the ground in parks, under benches, beds, cinema seats, hidden in drawers at Consulates, bottles of Calvados dropped and broken, or bursting into smithereens, tossed into garbage heaps, flung into the sea, the Mediterranean, the Caspian, the Caribbean, bottles floating in the ocean, dead Scotchmen on the Atlantic highlands – and now he saw them, smelt them, all, from the very beginning – bottles, bottles, bottles, and glasses, glasses, glasses, of bitter, of Dubonnet, of Falstaff, Rye, Johnny Walker, Vieux Whisky, *blanc Canadien*, the apéritifs, the digestifs, the demis, the dobles, the *noch ein* Herr Obers, the *et glas* Araks, the *tusen taks*, the bottles, the bottles, the beautiful bottles of tequila, and the gourds, gourds, gourds, the millions of gourds of beautiful mescal ... The Consul sat very still. His conscience sounded muffled with the roar of water. It whacked and whined round the wooden frame house with the spasmodic breeze, massed, with the thunderclouds over the trees, seen through the windows, its factions. How indeed could he hope to find himself to begin again when, somewhere, perhaps in one of these lost or broken bottles, in one of those glasses, lay, for ever, the solitary clue to his identity? How could he go back and look now, scrabble among the broken glass, under the eternal bars, under the oceans?

MALCOLM LOWRY, *Under the Volcano*

Cursed Fiend

Gin, cursed fiend, with fury fraught,
Makes human race a prey;
It enters by a deadly draught,
And steals our life away.
Virtue and truth driven to despair,
Its rage compels to flee;
But cherishes, with hellish care,
Theft murder perjury.

Damned cup, that on the vitals preys,
That liquid fire contains;
Which madness to the heart conveys,
And rolls it through the veins.

JAMES TOWNLEY

In great Cities men are often in Drink before they goe to Bed which makes the Children they get prove soe foolish.

SAMUEL BUTLER I

Wine, though it begins like a friend, goes on like a fool, and most commonly ends, like a devil, in a fury.

DUCHESS OF NEWCASTLE

Wine: give a man none and he cannot find truth; give him too much, and the same happens.

BLAISE PASCAL

It is a piece of arrogance to dare to be drunk, because a man showeth himself without a veil.

MARQUIS OF HALIFAX

Wine is credited only with the misdeeds it induces: the hundreds of good deeds which it causes are forgotten. Wine excites action: good actions in the good, bad in the bad.

GEORG LICHTENBERG

Drinking

The thirsty *Earth* soaks up the *Rain*,
And drinks, and gapes for drink again.
The *Plants* suck in the *Earth*, and are
With constant drinking fresh and fair.
The *Sea* it self, which one would think
Should have but little need of *Drink*,
Drinks ten thousand *Rivers* up,
So fill'd that they or'eflow the *Cup*.
The busie *Sun* (and one would guess
By's drunken fiery face no less)
Drinks up the *Sea*, and when h'as done,
The *Moon* and *Stars* drink up the *Sun*.
They drink and dance by their own light,
They drink and revel all the night.
Nothing in *Nature*'s *Sober* found,
But an eternal *Health* goes round.
Fill up the *Bowl* then, fill it high,
Fill all the *Glasses* there, for why
Should every creature drink but *I*,
Why, *Man* of *Morals*, tell me why?

ABRAHAM COWLEY

Drunk Song

Johnny are you there, are you there, are you there,
   Johnny are you there lovely Johnny?
      I can see the Demon Rum
      bouncing on its little bum
      at the bar of Kingdom Come
and hear the thunder of the Crown and Anchor money.

Whiskey are you there, are you there, are you there,
   Whiskey are you there, whiskey honey?
      O I've rolled the sweet potheen
      in her beds among the green
      hills of Blarney and I've been
Counted out like the Crown and Anchor money.

      I've seen diamonds and pearls
      in the temporary curls
      of the bar and tender girls
        like Godivas,
      and I've seen the chicadees
      with the bottles on their knees
      snoring underneath big trees
        of lovely fivers.

Whiskey are you there, are you there, are you there,
   Whiskey are you there, O my honey?
      When I begged you for a spot
      that you hadn't even got
      why, you gave me all the lot
      every goddam precious jot
      in a Crown and Anchor pot
and we whistled up the wind for the money.

GEORGE BARKER

Eight Kinds of Drunkenness

Nor have we one or two kinde of drunkards onely, but eight kindes. The
first is Ape drunke, and he leaps, and sings, and hollowes, and daunceth
for the heavens: the second is Lion drunke, and he flings the pots about
the house, calls his Hostesse whore, breakes the glass windowes with his
dagger, and is apt to quarrell with any man that speaks to him: the third
is Swine drunke, heavy, lumpish, and sleepie, and cries for a little more

drinke, and a fewe more cloathes: the fourth is Sheepe drunke, wise in his owne conceipt, when he cannot bring foorth a right word: the fifth is Mawdlen drunke when a fellowe will weepe for kindnes in the midst of his Ale, and kisse you, saying; By God, Captaine, I love thee; goe thy waies, thou dost not thinke so often of me as I do of thee, I would (if it pleased GOD) I could not love thee so well as I doo; and then he puts his finger in his eie, and cries: the sixt is Martin drunke, when a man is drunke, and drinkes himselfe sober ere he stirre: the seventh is Goate drunke, when, in his drunkennes, he hath no minde but on Lechery: the eighth is Foxe drunke, when he is craftie drunke, as many of the Dutch men bee, that will never bargaine but when they are drunke. All these *species*, and more, I have seene practised in one Company at one sitting, when I have beene permitted to remaine sober amongst them, onely to note their severall humors. Hee that plies any one of them harde, it will make him to write admirable verses, and to have a deepe casting head, though hee were never so verie a Dunce before.

THOMAS NASHE, *Pierce Penilesse*

The Gin Shop; or, A Peep into Prison

Behold that shivering female there,
    Who plies her woeful trade!
'Tis ten to one you'll find that Gin
    That hopeless wretch has made.

Look down these steps, and view below
    Yon cellar under ground;
There every want and every woe,
    And every sin is found.

Those little wretches, trembling there
    With hunger and with cold,
Were by their parents' love of Gin
    To sin and misery sold ...

To prison dire misfortune oft
   The guiltless debtor brings;
Yet oftener far it will be found
   From Gin the misery springs.

See the pale manufacturer there,
   How lank and lean he lies!
How haggard is his sickly cheek!
   How dim his hollow eyes!

He plied the loom with good success,
   His wages still were high;
Twice what the village-labourer gains
   His master did supply.

No book-debts kept him from his cash,
   All paid as soon as due;
His wages on the Saturday
   To fail he never knew.

How amply had his gains sufficed,
   On wife and children spent!
But all must for his pleasures go;
   All to the Gin-Shop went.

See that apprentice, young in years,
   But hackneyed long in sin;
What made him rob his master's till?
   Alas! 'twas love of Gin.

That serving-man – I knew him once,
   So jaunty, spruce and smart!
Why did he steal, then pawn the plate?
   'Twas Gin ensnared his heart.

But hark! what dismal sound is that?
   'Tis Saint Sepulchre's bell!
It tolls, alas! for human guilt,
   Some malefactor's knell.

O! woeful sound, O! what could cause
   Such punishment and sin?
Hark! hear his words, he owns the cause –
   Bad Company and Gin.

And when the future lot is fixed
   Of darkness, fire and chains,
How can the drunkard hope to 'scape
   Those everlasting pains?

For if the murderer's doomed to woe,
   As holy writ declares,
The drunkard with Self-murderers
   That dreadful portion shares.

HANNAH MORE

Gob Music

I do not have a fiddle so
   I get myself a stick,
And then I beat upon a can,
   Or pound upon a brick;
And if the meter needs a change
   I give the cat a kick.

   Ooomph dah doodle dah
   Ooomph dah doodle dah
   Ooomph dah doodle dah do.

Whenever I feel it coming on
   I need a morning drink,
I get a stool and sit and stare
   In the slop-pail by the sink;
I lean my head near the brimming edge
   And do not mind the stink.

Oh, the slop-pail is the place to think
On the perils of too early drink,
Too early drink, too early drink,
Can bring a good man down.

I went fishing with a pin
    In the dark of an ould spittoon;
Me handkerchee had fallen in
    With more than half a crown.
I stared into the dented hole
    And what do you think I saw?
A color pure, O pure as gold,
    A color without flaw,
A color without flaw, flaw, flaw,
    A color without flaw.
I stared and stared, and what do you think?
    My thirst came on, and I had to drink.

Indeed I saw a shimmering lake
    Of slime and shining spit,
And I kneeled down and did partake
    A bit of the likes of it.
And it reminded me – But Oh!
    I'll keep my big mouth shut.

It happened O, in Bofin Town,
    The color, my dears, was Guinness brown,
But it had a flavor all its own,
    As I gulped it down, as I gulped it down.
There on my knees, a man of renown,
    I did partake of it, I did partake of it.

Oh, the slop-pail is the place to think
On the perils of too early drink,
Too early drink, too early drink
Will bring a good man down.

THEODORE ROETHKE

Tea is not a Cossack drink.

ALEXANDER PUSHKIN

A Drunkard would not give money to sober people. He said they would only eat it, and buy clothes and send their children to school with it.

SAMUEL BUTLER II

The sway of alcohol over mankind is unquestionably due to its power to stimulate the mystical faculties of human nature, usually crushed to earth by the cold facts and dry criticisms of the sober hour. Sobriety diminishes, discriminates, and says no; drunkenness expands, unites and says yes. It is in fact the great votary of the *Yes* function in man. It brings its votary from the chill periphery of things to the radiant core. It makes him for the moment one with truth. Not through mere perversity do men run after it. To the poor and unlettered it stands in the place of symphony concerts and of literature; and it is part of the deeper mystery of life that whiffs and gleams of something that we immediately recognise as excellent should be vouchsafed to so many of us only in the fleeting earlier phases of what is in its totality so degrading a poisoning.

WILLIAM JAMES

Port – still the milk of donhood.

GEORGE SAINTSBURY

Champagne: bottled sunlight.

LORD THOMSON OF CARDINGTON

If de river was whisky,
An' if I was a duck,
I'd go down and never come up.

Alabaman folksong, *circa* 1915

I Feel No Pain

I feel no pain, dear mother, now,
But oh, I am so dry!
Oh take me to a brewery
And leave me there to die.

Marching song of North Lancashire regiment

A Man Who Boozes

It was an evening in November,
As I very well remember,
I was strolling down the street in drunken pride,
But my knees were all a-flutter,
And I landed in the gutter
And a pig came up and landed by my side.

Yes I lay there in the gutter
Thinking thoughts I could not utter,
When a colleen passing by did softly say
'You can tell a man who boozes
By the company he chooses.'
Then the pig got up and walked away.

Irish song

The Mouth Organ

The Duke entered his dining-room, where in a recess of the wall, a cupboard was contrived, containing a row of small barrels, ranged side by side, resting on miniature stocks of sandal wood and each pierced underneath by a silver spigot.

This collection of casks he called his *mouth organ.*

A small rod connected the spigots together, and enabled them to be all turned in the same movement, so that it was possible by touching a knob concealed in the panelling to open each conduit simultaneously and so fill with alcohol the tiny cups suspended beneath each tap.

The organ was then open. The stops, labelled 'flute', 'horn', 'vox humana' were pulled out, ready for use. Des Esseintes would take a drop here, another there, another further along, thus playing symphonies on his internal economy, producing on his palate a series of sensations analogous to those with which music gratifies the ear.

Indeed, each liquor corresponded in taste, he fancied, with the sound of a particular instrument. Dry curaçao, for example, resembled the clarinet in its shrill, velvety tone; kümmel was like the oboe, whose timbre is sonorous and nasal; crème de menthe and anisette were like the flute, both sweet and poignant, whining and soft. Then to complete the orchestra came kirsch, blowing a wild trumpet blast; gin and whisky, deafening the palate with their harsh eruptions of cornets and trombones; liqueur brandy, blaring with the overwhelming crash of tubas, while the thundering of cymbals and the big drum, beaten hard, evoked the rakis of Chios and the mastics.

He held that this analogy might be pushed yet further, that a quartet of stringed instruments might be contrived to play upon the palate, with the violin represented by old brandy, delicate yet heady, biting and clean-toned; with the alto, simulated by rum, more robust, rumbling, heavier in tone; with vespetro, long-drawn, pathetic, as sad and tender as a violoncello; with the double bass, full-bodied, as solid and black as a strong old bitter beer. One might even, if pressed to make a quintet, add another instrument: the harp, closely enough mimicked by the keen savour and silvery note, clear and self-sufficing, of dry cumin.

JORIS KARL HUYSMANS, *À Rebours*

No Pink Elephants

Well, Lou was true to his word. I didn't see him for some time, not even on weekends, and meanwhile I was going through a kind of personal hell. I was very jumpy, nerves gone – a little noise and I'd jump out of my skin. I was afraid to go to sleep: nightmare after nightmare, each more terrible than the one which preceded it. You were all right if you went to sleep totally drunk, that was all right, but if you went to sleep half-drunk or, worse, sober, then the dreams began, only you were never sure whether you were sleeping or whether the action was taking place in the room, for when you slept you dreamed the entire room, the dirty dishes, the mice, the folding walls, the pair of shit-in pants some whore had left on the floor, the dripping faucet, the moon like a bullet out there, cars full of the sober and well-fed, shining headlights through your window, everything, everything, you were in some sort of dark corner, dark dark, no help, no reason, no no reason at all, dark sweating corner, darkness and filth, the stench of reality, the stink of everything: spiders, eyes, land-ladies, sidewalks, bars, buildings, grass, no grass, light, no light, nothing belonging to you. The pink elephants never showed up but plenty of little men with savage tricks or a looming big man to strangle you or sink his teeth into the back of your neck, lay on your back and you sweating, unable to move, this black stinking hairy thing laying there on you on you on you.

CHARLES BUKOWSKI, *South of No North*

I got out my office bottle and took the drink and let my self-respect ride its own race.

RAYMOND CHANDLER

Chronic and inescapable sobriety is a most horrible affliction.

ALDOUS HUXLEY

[Definition of an alcoholic] When he buys his ties he has to ask if gin will make them run.

F. SCOTT FITZGERALD

Connoisseurs who like martinis very dry suggest simply allowing a ray of sunlight to shine through a bottle of Noilly Prat before it hits the bottle of gin.

LUIS BUÑUEL

There is a terrible sameness to the euphoria of alcohol and the euphoria of metaphor – the sense that the imagination is boundless.

JOHN CHEEVER

[A toast] Champagne for my real friends and real pain for my sham friends.

FRANCIS BACON

After a month's sobriety my faculties became unbearably acute and I found myself unhealthily clairvoyant, having insights into places I'd as soon not journey to. Unlike some men, I had never drunk for boldness

129

or charm or wit; I had used alcohol for precisely what it was, a depressant to check the mental exhilaration produced by extended sobriety.

FREDERICK EXLEY

A Slur on the Divine

I've spent whole summers at Neauphle alone except for drink. People used to come at the weekends. But during the week I was alone in that huge house, and that was how alcohol took on its full significance. It lends resonance to loneliness, and ends up making you prefer it to everything else. Drinking isn't necessarily the same as wanting to die. But you can't drink without thinking you're killing yourself. Living with alcohol is living with death close at hand. What stops you killing yourself when you're intoxicated out of your mind is the thought that once you're dead you won't be able to drink any more. I started drinking at parties and political meetings – glasses of wine at first, then whisky. And then, when I was forty-one, I met someone who really loved alcohol and drank every day, though sensibly. I soon outstripped him. That went on for ten years, until I got cirrhosis of the liver and started vomiting blood. Then I gave up drinking for ten years. That was the first time. Then I started again, and gave it up again, I forget why. Then I stopped smoking, but I could only do that by drinking again. This is the third time I've given it up. I've never smoked opium or hash. I 'doped' myself with aspirin every day for fifteen years, but I've never taken drugs. At first I drank whisky and Calvados – what I call the pale kinds of alcohol. And beer, and vervain from Velay – they say that's the worst for the liver. Lastly I started to drink wine, and I never stopped.

I became an alcoholic as soon as I started to drink. I drank like one straight away, and left everyone else behind. I began by drinking in the evening, then at midday, then in the morning, and then I began to drink at night. First once a night, then every two hours. I've never drugged myself any other way. I've always known that if I took to heroin it would soon get out of control. I've always drunk with men. Alcohol is linked to the memory of sexual violence – it makes it glow, it's inseparable from it. But only in the mind. Alcohol is a substitute for pleasure though it doesn't replace it. People obsessed with sex aren't usually alcoholics. Alcoholics, even those in the gutter, tend to be intellectuals. The proletariat, a class far more intellectual now than the bourgeoisie, has a propensity for alcohol, as can be seen all over the world. Of all human occupations, manual work is probably the kind that leads most directly to thought, and therefore to drink. Just look at the history of ideas. Alcohol makes people talk. It's spirituality carried to the point where logic becomes lunacy; it's reason going mad trying to understand why this kind of society, this Reign of Injustice, exists. And it always ends in despair. A drunk is often coarse, but rarely obscene. Sometimes he loses his temper and kills. When you've had too much to drink you're back at the start of the infernal cycle of life. People talk about happiness, and say it's impossible. But they know what the word means.

What they lack is a god. The void you discover one day in your teens – nothing can ever undo that discovery. But alcohol was invented to help us bear the void in the universe – the motion of the planets, their imperturbable wheeling through space, their silent indifference to the place of our pain. A man who drinks is interplanetary. He moves through interstellar space. It's from there he looks down. Alcohol doesn't console, it doesn't fill up anyone's psychological gaps, all it replaces is the lack of God. It doesn't comfort man. On the contrary, it encourages him in his folly, it transports him to the supreme regions where he is master of his own destiny. No other human being, no woman, no poem or music, book or painting can replace alcohol in its power to give man the illusion of real creation. Alcohol's job is to replace creation. And that's what it does do for a lot of people who ought to have believed in God and don't any more. But alcohol is barren. The words a man speaks in the night of drunkenness fade like the darkness itself at the coming of day. Drunkenness doesn't create anything, it doesn't enter into the words, it dims and slackens the mind instead of stimulating it. I've spoken under its influence. The illusion's perfect: you're sure what you're saying has never been said before. But alcohol can't produce anything that lasts. It's just wind. I've written under its influence too – I had the knack of keeping tipsiness at bay, probably because I have such a horror of it. I never drank in order to get drunk. I never drank fast. I drank all the time and I was never drunk. I was withdrawn from the world – inaccessible but not intoxicated.

When a woman drinks it's as if an animal were drinking, or a child. Alcoholism is scandalous in a woman, and a female alcoholic is rare, a serious matter. It's a slur on the divine in our nature. I realised the scandal I was causing around me. But in my day, in order to have the strength to confront it publicly – for example, to go into a bar on one's own at night – you needed to have had something to drink already.

It's always too late when people tell someone they drink too much. 'You drink too much.' But it's a shocking thing to say whenever you say it. You never know yourself that you're an alcoholic. In a hundred per cent of cases it's taken as an insult. The person concerned says, 'You're only saying that to get at me.' In my own case the disease had already taken hold by the time I was told about it. We live in a world paralysed with principles. We just let other people die. I don't think this kind of thing happens with drugs. Drugs cut the addict off completely from the rest of humanity. But they don't throw him to the winds or into the street; they don't turn him into a vagabond. But alcohol means the gutter, the dosshouse, other alcoholics. With drugs it's very quick: death comes fast – speechlessness, darkness, closed shutters, helplessness. Nor is there any consolation for stopping drinking. Since I've stopped I feel for the alcoholic I once was. I really did drink a lot. Then help came – but now I'm telling my own story instead of talking about alcohol in general. It's incredibly simple – for real alcoholics there's probably the simplest possible explanation. They're in a place where suffering can't hurt them. *Clochards* aren't unhappy, it's silly to say that when they're drunk from morn till night, twenty-four hours a day. They couldn't lead the life they lead anywhere else but in the street. During the winter of 1986–7 they preferred to risk dying of cold rather than go into a hostel and give up their litre of *rouge*. Everyone tried to work out why they wouldn't go into the dosshouse. That was the reason.

The night hours aren't the worst. But of course that's the most dangerous time if you suffer from insomnia. You mustn't have a drop of alcohol in the house. I'm one of those alcoholics who can be set off again by drinking just one glass of wine. I don't know the medical term for it.

An alcoholic's body is like a telephone exchange, like a set of different compartments all linked together. It's the brain that's affected first. The mind. First comes happiness through the mind. Then through the body. It's lapped around, saturated, then borne along – yes, that's the word for it, borne along. And after a time you have the choice – whether to keep drinking until you're senseless and lose your identity, or to go no further than the beginnings of happiness. To die, so to speak, every day, or to go on living.

MARGUERITE DURAS, *Practicalities*

The Tale of Lord Lovell

Lord Lovell he stood at his own front door,
    Seeking the hole for the key;
His hat was wrecked, and his trousers bore
    A rent across either knee,
When down came the beauteous Lady Jane
    In fair white draperie.

'Oh, where have you been, Lord Lovell?' she said,
    'Oh, where have you been?' said she;
'I have not closed an eye in bed,
    And the clock has just struck three.
Who has been standing you on your head
    In the ash-barrel, pardie?'

'I am not drunk, Lad' Shane,' he said:
    'And so late it cannot be;
The clock struck one as I enterèd –
    I heard it two times or three;
It must be the salmon on which I fed
    Has been too many for me.'

'Go tell your tale, Lord Lovell,' she said,
   'To the maritime cavalree,
To your grandmother of the hoary head –
   To any one but me:
The door is not used to be openèd
   With a cigarette for a key.'

ANONYMOUS

This Vice So Foul

Some men are drunke, and being drunke will fight;
Some men are drunke, and being drunke are merrie;
Some men are drunke, and secrets bring to light;
Some men are drunke, and being drunke are sorie:
   Thus may we see that drunken men have passions,
   And drunkennesse hath many foolish fashions.

Fishes that in the sea doe drinke their fill,
Teach men by nature to shun drunkennesse.
What bird is there, that with his chirping bill
Of any liquor ever tooke excesse?
   Thus beastes on earth, fish in seas, birds in skie,
   Teach men to shun all superfluitie.

Would any heare the discommodities
That doe arise from our excesse of drinke?
It duls the braine, it hurts the memorie,
It blinds the sight, it makes men bleare-eyd blinke;
   It kils the bodie, and it wounds the soule;
   Leave, therefore, leave, O leave this vice so foul!

JOHN LANE

The Toper's Rant

Give me an old crone of a fellow
  Who loves to drink ale in a horn,
And sing racy songs when he's mellow,
  Which topers sung ere he was born.
For such a friend fate shall be thankèd,
  And, line but our pockets with brass,
We'd sooner suck ale through a blanket
  Than thimbles of wine from a glass.

Away with your proud thimble-glasses
  Of wine foreign nations supply,
A toper ne'er drinks to the lasses
  O'er a draught scarce enough for a fly.
Club me with the hedger and ditcher
  Or beggar that makes his own horn,
To join o'er an old gallon pitcher
  Foaming o'er with the essence of corn.

I care not with whom I get tipsy
  Or where with brown stout I regale,
I'll weather the storm with a gipsy
  If he be a lover of ale.
I'll weather the toughest storm weary
  Altho' I get wet to the skin,
For my outside I never need fear me
  While warm with real stingo within.

We'll sit till the bushes are dropping
  Like the spout of a watering pan,
And till the cag's drained there's no stopping,
  We'll keep up the ring to a man.

We'll sit till Dame Nature is feeling
   The breath of our stingo so warm,
And bushes and trees begin reeling
   In our eyes like to ships in a storm.

We'll start it three hours before seven,
   When larks wake the morning to dance,
And we'll stand it till night's black eleven,
   When witches ride over to France;
And we'll sit it in spite of the weather
   Till we tumble dead drunk on the plain,
When the morning shall find us together,
   All willing to stand it again.

JOHN CLARE

Used to Claret

I was now in the Strand, and, glancing about, I perceived that I was close by an hotel, which bore over the door the somewhat remarkable name of Holy Lands. Without a moment's hesitation I entered a well-lighted passage, and, turning to the left, I found myself in a well-lighted coffee-room, with a well-dressed and frizzled waiter before me. 'Bring me some claret,' said I, for I was rather faint than hungry, and I felt ashamed to give a humbler order to so well-dressed an individual. The waiter looked at me for a moment, then, making a low bow, he bustled off, and I sat myself down in the box nearest to the window. Presently the waiter returned, bearing beneath his left arm a long bottle, and between the fingers of his right hand two large purple glasses; placing the latter on the table, he produced a corkscrew, drew the cork in a twinkling, set the bottle down before me with a bang, and then, standing still, appeared to watch my movements. You think I don't know how to drink a glass of claret, thought I to myself. I'll soon show you how we drink claret where I come from; and, filling one of the glasses to the brim, I flickered it for a moment between my eyes and the lustre, and then held it to my nose;

having given that organ full time to test the bouquet of the wine, I applied the glass to my lips, taking a large mouthful of the wine, which I swallowed slowly and by degrees, that the palate might likewise have an opportunity of performing its functions. A second mouthful I disposed of more summarily; then, placing the empty glass upon the table, I fixed my eyes upon the bottle, and said – nothing; whereupon the waiter, who had been observing the whole process with considerable attention, made me a bow yet more low than before, and, turning on his heel, retired with a smart chuck of his head, as much as to say It is all right; the young man is used to claret.

GEORGE BORROW, *Lavengro*

Wages of Death

To be an object of compassion to friends, of derision to foes; to be suspected by strangers, stared at by fools; to be esteemed dull when you cannot be witty, to be applauded for witty when you know that you have been dull; to be called upon for the extemporaneous exercise of that faculty which no premeditation can give; to be spurred on to efforts which end in contempt; to be set on to provoke mirth which procures the procurer hatred; to give pleasure and be paid with squinting malice; to swallow draughts of life-destroying wine which are to be distilled into airy breath to tickle vain auditors; to mortgage miserable morrows for nights of madness; to waste whole seas of time upon those who pay it back in little inconsiderable drops of grudging applause, are the wages of buffoonery and death.

CHARLES LAMB, *Confessions of a Drunkard*

Water Is Best

A man who drinks whisky may feel awhile frisky
   And paint the town brilliantly red,
But soon in the gutter, with misery utter,
   Will curse and wish himself dead.

A man who drinks brandy may feel like a dandy
   As long as the smell's on his breath,
But soon in the tremens, snakes, bogies, and demons,
   Will chase him and snare him to death.

A man who drinks wine may feel very fine
   And play funny antics and shout,
But for it he'll pay with a headache next day
   And die when he's young from the gout.

A man who drinks gin with pleasure will grin
   And have what he calls a good time,
Till with a red nose and dirty old clothes
   He homeless will be for a dime.

A man who drinks beer may feel good for a year
   And think it don't hurt him a bit,
Till bloated and red he goes to his bed,
   Or falls in the street in a fit.

But the man who drinks water, as everyone *orter*,
   Enjoys to the utmost his life,
He's happy and healthy, respected and wealthy,
   And loved by his children and wife.

ANONYMOUS

We Live by Quaffing

We – Bee and I – live by the quaffing –
'Tisn't *all Hock* – with us –
Life has its *Ale* –
But it's many a lay of the Dim Burgundy –
We chant – for cheer – when the Wines – fail –

Do we 'get drunk'?
Ask the jolly Clovers!
Do we 'beat' our 'Wife'?
I – never wed –
Bee – pledges *his* – in minute flagons –
Dainty – as the tress – on her deft Head –

While runs the Rhine –
He and I – revel –
First – at the vat – and latest at the Vine –
Noon – our last Cup –
'Found dead' – 'of Nectar' –
By a humming Coroner –
In a By-Thyme!

EMILY DICKINSON

Drugs

The only good which we discover in life, is something which produces an oblivion of existence.

MADAME DE STAËL

The majority of humankind only enjoy life by forgetting that they are alive.

COUNT MAURICE MAETERLINCK

The Addict

Sleepmonger,
deathmonger,
with capsules in my palms each night,
eight at a time from sweet pharmaceutical bottles
I make arrangements for a pint-sized journey.
I'm the queen of this condition.
I'm an expert on making the trip

and now they say I'm an addict.
Now they ask why.
Why!

Don't they know
that I promised to die!
I'm keeping in practice.
I'm merely staying in shape.
The pills are a mother, but better,
every color and as good as sour balls.
I'm on a diet from death.

Yes, I admit
it has gotten to be a bit of a habit —
blows eight at a time, socked in the eye,
hauled away by the pink, the orange,
the green and the white goodnights.
I'm becoming something of a chemical
mixture.
That's it!

My supply
of tablets
has got to last for years and years.
I like them more than I like me.
Stubborn as hell, they won't let go.
It's a kind of marriage.
It's a kind of war
where I plant bombs inside
of myself.

Yes
I try
to kill myself in small amounts,
an innocuous occupation.
Actually I'm hung up on it.
But remember I don't make too much noise.
And frankly no one has to lug me out

and I don't stand there in my winding sheet.
I'm a little buttercup in my yellow nightie
eating my eight loaves in a row
and in a certain order as in
the laying on of hands
or the black sacrament.

It's a ceremony
but like any other sport
it's full of rules.
It's like a musical tennis match where
my mouth keeps catching the ball.
Then I lie on my altar
elevated by the eight chemical kisses.

What a lay me down this is
with two pink, two orange,
two green, two white goodnights.
Fee-fi-fo-fum –
Now I'm borrowed.
Now I'm numb.

ANNE SEXTON

A Bad Trip

I was stared at, hooted at, grinned at, chattered at, by monkeys, by cock-
atoos. I ran into pagodas, and was fixed for centuries at the summit or in
secret rooms; I was the idol; I was the priest; I was worshipped; I was
sacrificed. I fled from the wrath of Brahman through all the forests
of Asia; Vishnu hated me; Sceva lay in wait for me. I came suddenly
upon Isis and Osiris; I had done a deed, they said, which the ibis and the
crocodile trembled at. Thousands of years I was buried in stone coffins,
with mummies and sphinxes, in narrow chambers at the heart of eternal

pyramids. I was kissed, with cancerous kisses, by crocodiles, and was laid, confounded with all unalterable abortions, amongst reeds and Nilotic mud.

THOMAS DE QUINCEY, *Confessions of an English Opium Eater*

The Burning of the Pipes
[*Bangkok, 1 July 1959*]

Who had imagined they were government property? –
Wooden cylinders with collars of silver, coming
From China, brown and shiny with sweat and age.
Inside them were banks of dreams, shiny with
Newness, though doubtless of time-honoured stock.
They were easy to draw on: you pursed your lips
As if to suckle and sucked your breath as if to
Sigh: two skills which most of us have mastered.

The dreams themselves weren't government property.
Rather, the religion of the people. While the state
Took its tithes and the compliance of sleepers.
Now a strong government dispenses with compliance,
A government with rich friends has no need of tithes.

What acrid jinn was it that entered their flesh?
For some, a magic saucer, over green enamelled
Parks and lofty flat-faced city offices, to
Some new Tamerlane in his ticker-tape triumph –
Romantics! They had been reading books.
Others found the one dream left them: dreamless sleep.

As for us, perhaps we had eaten too much to dream,
To need to dream, I mean, or have to sleep.
For us, a moment of thinking our thoughts were viable,
And hope not a hopeless pipe-dream; for us

The gift of forgiveness for the hole in the road,
The dog we ran over on our way to bed.
Wasn't that something? The Chinese invented so much.

A surprise to find they were government property
– Sweat-brown bamboo with dull silver inlay –
As they blaze in thousands on a government bonfire,
In the government park, by government order!
The rice crop is expected to show an increase,
More volunteers for the army, and navy, and
Government service, and a decrease in petty crime.

Not the first time that fire destroys a dream.
Coca-cola sellers slither through the crowd; bats
Agitate among the rain-trees; flash-bulbs pop.
A holocaust of wooden legs – a miracle constated!
Rubbing his hands, the Marshal steps back from
The smoke, lost in a dream of strong government.
Sad, but they couldn't be beaten into TV sets;
As tourist souvenirs no self-respecting state
Could sponsor them, even at thirty dollars each.

D. J. ENRIGHT

Cocaine

He had a job as a waiter in the international dining car of a German fast train. His name was Aleksey Lvovich Luzhin.

He had left Russia five years before, in 1919, and since then, as he made his way from city to city, had tried a good number of trades and occupations: he had worked as a farm laborer in Turkey, a messenger in Vienna, a housepainter, a sales clerk, and so forth. Now, on either side of the diner, the meadows, the hills overgrown with heather, the pine groves flowed on and on, and the bouillon steamed and splashed in the thick cups on the tray that he nimbly carried along the narrow aisle between the window tables. He waited with masterful dispatch, forking up from the dish he carried slices of beef or ham, depositing them on the plates, and in the process rapidly dipping his close-cropped head, with its tensed forehead and black, bushy eyebrows.

The car would arrive in Berlin at five p.m., and at seven it would depart in the opposite direction, toward the French border. Luzhin lived on a kind of steel seesaw: he had time to think and reminisce only at night, in a narrow nook that smelled of fish and dirty socks. His most frequent recollections were of a house in St Petersburg, of his study there, with those leather buttons on the curves of overstuffed furniture, and of his wife Lena, of whom he had had no news for five years. At present, he felt his life wasting away. Too-frequent sniffs of cocaine had ravaged his mind; the little sores on the inside of his nostrils were eating into the septum.

When he smiled, his large teeth would flash with an especially clean luster, and this Russian ivory smile somehow endeared him to the other two waiters – Hugo, a thickset, fair-haired Berliner who made out the checks, and quick, red-haired, sharp-nosed Max, who resembled a fox, and whose job it was to take coffee and beer to the compartments. Lately, however, Luzhin smiled less often.

During the leisure hours when the crystal-bright waves of the drug beat at him, penetrating his thoughts with their radiance and transforming the least trifle into an ethereal miracle, he painstakingly noted on a sheet of paper all the various steps he intended to take in order to trace his wife. As he scribbled, with all those sensations still blissfully taut, his jottings seemed exceedingly important and correct to him. In the morning, however, when his head ached and his shirt felt clammy and sticky, he looked with bored disgust at the jerky, blurry lines. Recently, though, another idea had begun to occupy his thoughts. He began, with the same diligence, to elaborate a plan for his own death; he would draw a kind of graph indicating the rise and fall of his sense of fear; and, finally, so as to simplify matters, he set himself a definite date – the night between the first and second of August. His interest was aroused not so much by death itself as by all the details preceding it, and he would get so involved with these details that death itself would be forgotten. But as soon as he sobered up, the picturesque setting of this or that fanciful method of self-destruction would pale, and only one thing remained clear: his life had wasted away to nothing and there was no use continuing it …

A telegraph pole, black against the sunset, flew past, interrupting the smooth ascent of the wires. They dropped as a flag drops when the wind stops blowing. Then furtively they began rising again. The express was traveling swiftly between the airy walls of a spacious fire-bright evening. From somewhere in the ceilings of the compartments a slight crackling kept coming, as if rain were falling on the steel roofs. The German cars swayed violently. The international one, its interior upholstered in blue cloth, rode more smoothly and silently than the others. Three waiters were laying the tables in the diner. One of them, with close-cropped hair and beetling brows, was thinking about the little vial in his breast pocket. He kept licking his lips and sniffling. The vial contained a crystalline powder and bore the brand name Kramm. He was distributing knives and forks and inserting sealed bottles into rings on the tables, when suddenly he could stand it no longer. He flashed a flustered smile toward Max Fuchs, who was lowering the thick blinds, and darted across the unsteady connecting platform into the next car. He locked himself in the toilet. Carefully calculating the jolts of the train, he poured a small mound of the powder on his thumbnail; greedily applied it to one nostril, then to the other; inhaled; with a flip of his tongue licked the sparkling dust off his nail; blinked hard a couple of times from the rubbery bitterness, and left the toilet, boozy and buoyant, his head filling with icy delicious air. As he crossed the diaphragm on his way back into the diner, he thought: how simple it would be to die right now! He smiled. He had best wait till nightfall. It would be a pity to cut short the effect of the enchanting poison.

VLADIMIR NABOKOV, A Matter of Chance

Cocaine Lil and Morphine Sue

Did you ever hear tell about Cocaine Lil?
She lived in Cocaine town on Cocaine hill,
She had a cocaine dog and a cocaine cat,
They fought all night with a cocaine rat.

She had cocaine hair on her cocaine head.
She had a cocaine dress that was poppy red:
She wore a snowbird hat and sleigh-riding clothes,
On her coat she wore a crimson, cocaine rose.

Big gold chariots on the Milky Way,
Snakes and elephants silver and gray.
Oh the cocaine blues they make me sad,
Oh the cocaine blues make me feel bad.

Lil went to a snow party one cold night.
And the way she sniffed was sure a fright.
There was Hophead Mag with Dopey Slim,
Kankakee Liz and Yen Shee Jim.

There was Morphine Sue and the Poppy Face Kid,
Climbed up snow ladders and down they skid;
There was the Stepladder Kid, a good six feet,
And the Sleigh-riding Sister who were hard to beat.

Along in the morning about half past three
They were all lit up like a Christmas tree;
Lil got home and started for bed,
Took another sniff and it knocked her dead.

They laid her out in her cocaine clothes:
She wore a snowbird hat with a crimson rose;
On her headstone you'll find this refrain:
'She died as she lived, sniffing cocaine.'

ANONYMOUS

That mighty Prince with the moth's eyes and the feathered feet, one of whose names is Chloral.

VIRGINIA WOOLF

From ashes to ashes
And from dust to dust;
If de whiskey don't kill me
De morphine must.

Alabaman black folksong, *circa* 1915

10 May 1927: Many opium smokers and cocaine addicts in Zurich. Some of them, Rychner tells me, began to inject themselves during their last year at the Gymnasium; that is, when aged sixteen or seventeen. He knows one whom the professors caught using a syringe in a final examination. Cornered, he confessed he had got his habit in class. 'Do you think anyone could endure the dullness of X's teaching without shooting up?' he asked.

ANDRÉ GIDE

An Egyptian Cigarette

The box contained six cigarettes, evidently hand-made. The wrappers were of pale-yellow paper, and the tobacco was almost the same color. It was of finer cut than the Turkish or ordinary Egyptian, and threads of it stuck out at either end.

'Will you try one now, Madam?' asked the Architect, offering to strike a match.

'Not now and not here,' I replied, 'after the coffee, if you will permit me to slip into your smoking-den. Some of the women here detest the odor of cigarettes.'

The smoking-room lay at the end of a short, curved passage. Its appointments were exclusively oriental. A broad, low window opened out upon a balcony that overhung the garden. From the divan upon which I reclined, only the swaying tree-tops could be seen. The maple leaves glistened in the afternoon sun. Beside the divan was a low stand which contained the complete paraphernalia of a smoker. I was feeling quite comfortable, and congratulated myself upon having escaped for a while the incessant chatter of the women that reached me faintly.

I took a cigarette and lit it, placing the box upon the stand just as the tiny clock, which was there, chimed in silvery strokes the hour of five.

I took one long inspiration of the Egyptian cigarette. The grey-green smoke arose in a small puffy column that spread and broadened, that seemed to fill the room. I could see the maple leaves dimly, as if they were veiled in a shimmer of moonlight. A subtle, disturbing current passed through my whole body and went to my head like the fumes of disturbing wine. I took another deep inhalation of the cigarette.

'Ah! the sand has blistered my cheek! I have lain here all day with my face in the sand. Tonight, when the everlasting stars are burning, I shall drag myself to the river.'

He will never come back.

Thus far I followed him; with flying feet; with stumbling feet; with hands and knees, crawling; and outstretched arms, and here I have fallen in the sand.

The sand has blistered my cheek; it has blistered all my body, and the sun is crushing me with hot torture. There is shade beneath yonder cluster of palms.

I shall stay here in the sand till the hour and the night comes.

I laughed at the oracles and scoffed at the stars when they told that after the rapture of life I would open my arms inviting death, and the waters would envelop me.

Oh! how the sand blisters my cheek! and I have no tears to quench the fire. The river is cool and the night is not far distant.

I turned from the gods and said: 'There is but one; Bardja is my god.' That was when I decked myself with lilies and wove flowers into a garland and held him close in the frail, sweet fetters.

He will never come back. He turned upon his camel as he rode away. He turned and looked at me crouching here and laughed, showing his gleaming white teeth.

Whenever he kissed me and went away he always came back again. Whenever he flamed with fierce anger and left me with stinging words, he always came back. But today he neither kissed me nor was he angry. He only said:

'Oh! I am tired of fetters, and kisses, and you. I am going away. You will never see me again. I am going to the great city where men swarm like bees. I am going beyond, where the monster stones are rising heavenward in a monument for the unborn ages. Oh! I am tired. You will see me no more.'

And he rode away on his camel. He smiled and showed his cruel white teeth as he turned to look at me crouching here.

How slow the hours drag! It seems to me that I have lain here for days in the sand, feeding upon despair. Despair is bitter and it nourishes resolve.

I hear the wings of a bird flapping above my head, flying low, in circles.

The sun is gone.

The sand has crept between my lips and teeth and under my parched tongue.

If I raise my head, perhaps I shall see the evening star.

Oh! the pain in my arms and legs! My body is sore and bruised as if broken. Why can I not rise and run as I did this morning? Why must I drag myself thus like a wounded serpent, twisting and writhing?

The river is near at hand. I hear it – I see it – Oh! the sand! Oh! the shine! How cool! how cold!

The water! the water! In my eyes, my ears, my throat! It strangles me! Help! will the gods not help me?

Oh! the sweet rapture of rest! There is music in the Temple. And here is fruit to taste. Bardja came with the music – The moon shines and the breeze is soft – A garland of flowers – let us go into the King's garden and look at the blue lily, Bardja.

The maple leaves looked as if a silvery shimmer enveloped them. The gray-green smoke no longer filled the room. I could hardly lift the lids of my eyes. The weight of centuries seemed to suffocate my soul that struggled to escape, to free itself and breathe.

I had tasted the depths of human despair.

The little clock upon the stand pointed to a quarter past five. The cigarettes still reposed in the yellow box. Only the stub of the one I had smoked remained. I had laid it in the ash tray.

As I looked at the cigarettes in their pale wrappers, I wondered what other visions they might hold for me; what might I not find in their mystic fumes? Perhaps a vision of celestial peace; a dream of hopes fulfilled; a taste of rapture, such as had not entered into my mind to conceive.

I took the cigarettes and crumpled them between my hands. I walked to the window and spread my palms wide. The light breeze caught up the golden threads and bore them writhing and dancing far out among the maple leaves.

My friend, the Architect, lifted the curtain and entered, bringing me a second cup of coffee.

'How pale you are!' he exclaimed, solicitously. 'Are you not feeling well?'

'A little the worse for a dream,' I told him.

KATE CHOPIN, *An Egyptian Cigarette*

The Hair Tonic Bottle

How dear to my heart is the old village drugstore,
　　When tired and thirsty it comes to my view.
The wide-spreading sign that asks you to 'Try it',
　　Vim, Vaseline, Vermifuge, Hop Bitters, too.
The old rusty stove and the cuspidor by it,
　　That little back room. Oh! you've been there yourself,
And ofttimes have gone for the doctor's prescription,
　　But tackled the bottle that stood on the shelf.
　　　　The friendly old bottle,
　　　　The plain-labeled bottle,
The 'Hair-Tonic' bottle that stood on the shelf.

How oft have I seized it with hands that were glowing,
　　And guzzled awhile ere I set off for home;
I owned the whole earth all that night, but next morning

My head felt as big as the Capitol's dome.
And then how I hurried away to receive it,
   The druggist would smile o'er his poisonous pelf,
And laugh as he poured out his unlicensed bitters,
   And filled up the bottle that stood on the shelf.
     The unlicensed bottle,
     The plain-labeled bottle,
That 'Hair-Tonic' bottle that stood on the shelf.

BEN KING

Hashish in Marseilles

One of the first signs that hashish is beginning to take effect 'is a dull feeling of foreboding; something strange, ineluctable is approaching ... images and chains of images, long-submerged memories appear, whole scenes and situations are experienced; at first they arouse interest, now and then enjoyment, and finally, when there is no turning away from them, weariness and torment. By everything that happens, and by what he says and does, the subject is surprised and overwhelmed. His laughter, all his utterances happen to him like outward events. He also attains experiences that approach inspiration, illumination ... Space can expand, the ground tilt steeply, atmospheric sensations occur: vapour, an opaque heaviness of the air; colours grow brighter, more luminous; objects more beautiful, or else lumpy and threatening ... All this does not occur in a continuous development; rather, it is typified by a continual alternation of dreaming and waking states, a constant and finally exhausting oscillation between totally different worlds of consciousness; in the middle of a sentence these transitions can take place ... All this the subject reports in a form that usually diverges very widely from the norm. Connections become difficult to perceive, owing to the frequently sudden rupture of all memory of past events, thought is not formed into words, the situation can become so compulsively hilarious that the hashish eater for minutes on end is capable of nothing except laughing' ...

Now the hashish eater's demands on time and space come into force.

As is known, these are absolutely regal. Versailles, for one who has taken hashish, is not too large, or eternity too long. Against the background of these immense dimensions of inner experience, of absolute duration and immeasurable space, a wonderful, beatific humour dwells all the more fondly on the contingencies of the world of space and time ...

On the way to the Vieux Port I already had this wonderful lightness and sureness of step that transformed the stony, unarticulated earth of the great square that I was crossing into the surface of a country road along which I strode at night like an energetic hiker. For at this time I was still avoiding the Cannebière, not yet quite sure of my regulatory functions. In that little harbour bar the hashish then began to exert its canonical magic with a primitive sharpness that I had scarcely felt until then. For it made me into a physiognomist, or at least a contemplator of physiognomies, and I underwent something unique in my experience: I positively fixed my gaze on the faces that I had around me, which were, in part, of remarkable coarseness or ugliness. Faces that I would normally have avoided for a twofold reason: I should neither have wished to attract their gaze nor endured their brutality. It was a very advanced post, this harbour tavern. (I believe it was the farthest accessible to me without danger, a circumstance I had gauged, in the trance, with the same accuracy with which, when utterly weary, one is able to fill a glass exactly to the brim without spilling a drop, as one can never do with sharp senses.) It was still sufficiently far from rue Bouterie, yet no bourgeois sat there; at the most, besides the true port proletariat, a few petty-bourgeois families from the neighbourhood. I now suddenly understood how, to a painter – had it not happened to Rembrandt and many others? – ugliness could appear as the true reservoir of beauty, better than any treasure cask, a jagged mountain with all the inner gold of beauty gleaming from the wrinkles, glances, features. I especially remember a boundlessly animal and vulgar male face in which the 'line of renunciation' struck me with sudden violence. It was above all men's faces that had begun to interest me. Now began the game, to be long maintained, of recognizing someone I knew in every face; often I knew the name, often not; the deception vanished as deceptions vanish in dreams: not in shame and compromised, but peacefully and amiably, like a being who has performed his service. Under these circumstances there was no question of loneliness. Was I my own company? Surely not so undisguisedly. I doubt whether they would have made me so happy. More likely this: I became my own skilful, fond, shameless procurer, gratifying myself with the ambiguous assurance of one who knows from profound study the wishes of his employer. Then it began to take half an eternity until the waiter reappeared. Or, rather, I could not wait for him to appear. I went into the bar-room and paid at the counter. Whether tips are usual in such taverns I do not know. But under other circumstances I should have given something in any case. Under hashish yesterday, however, I was on the stingy side; for fear of attracting attention by extravagance, I succeeded in making myself really conspicuous …

A deeply submerged feeling of happiness that came over me afterward, on a square off the Cannebière where rue Paradis opens onto a park, is more difficult to recall than everything that went before. Fortunately I find on my newspaper the sentence 'One should scoop sameness from reality with a spoon.' Several weeks earlier I had noted another, by Johannes V. Jensen, which appeared to say something similar: 'Richard was a young man with understanding for everything in the world that was of the same kind.' This sentence had pleased me very much. It enabled me now to confront the political, rational sense it had had for me earlier with the individual magical meaning of my experience the day before. Whereas Jensen's sentence amounted, as I had understood it, to saying that things are as we know them to be, thoroughly mechanized and rationalised, the particular being confined today solely to nuances, my new insight was entirely different. For I saw only nuances, yet these were the same. I immersed myself in contemplation of the sidewalk before me, which, through a kind of unguent with which I covered it, could have been, precisely as these very stones, also the sidewalk of Paris. One often speaks of stones instead of bread. These stones were the bread of my imagination, which was suddenly seized by a ravenous hunger to taste what is the same in all places and countries. And yet I thought with immense pride of sitting here in Marseilles in a hashish trance; of who else might be sharing my intoxication this evening, how few. Of how I was incapable of fearing future misfortune, future solitude, for hashish would always remain …

The trance abated when I crossed the Cannebière and at last turned the corner to have a final ice cream at the little Café des Cours Belsunce. It was not far from the first café of the evening, in which, suddenly, the amorous joy dispensed by the contemplation of some fringes blown by the wind had convinced me that the hashish had begun its work. And when I recall this state I should like to believe that hashish persuades nature to permit us – for less egoistic purposes – that squandering of our own existence that we know in love. For if, when we love, our existence runs through nature's fingers like golden coins that she cannot hold and lets fall to purchase new birth thereby, she now throws us, without hoping or expecting anything, in ample handfuls to existence.

WALTER BENJAMIN, *One-Way Street and Other Writings*

He Wears Badly

23 September 1931: Yesterday Fernande Cabanel and her companion Sacha Xanaris, took me into Toulon for the afternoon. On the way Fernande said to me: 'I have some very urgent shopping to do. I'm completely out of something which I have to have. It is making me ill. Yesterday I tried to use some of Sacha's drug but it's too heavy, too strong for me. It upset me dreadfully. Jean Cocteau is here, we'll look him up and he's sure to be able to give me an address.' – 'Fine,' I said. 'Jean is an old friend of mine and I'd like to see him again.' She took me down to the port, near the Arsenal, and led me along a horrible street with reeking gutters which ran parallel with the quay. It was lined on either side with the most frightful shady-looking hotels. She said: 'Oh God – Jean is living in one of these.' We went into a foul slum called Hôtel du Port et des Négociants. She asked for Jean; the proprietor was smiling and eager, all amiability and complicity. He sent for Liou, the Annamite boy – a prince's son, it seems – who serves Jean. Fernande scribbled a note. Liou took it away, then reappeared with three words of answer: 'In an hour.' We left the hotel by another door, through a fairly clean little bistro opening onto the quay. There was an antique shop next door. Sacha and I went in and began bargaining for all kinds of things. Fernande kept watch by the door. While we were looking at ornaments in the back of the shop Sacha told me: 'Two cops followed us down that street and saw us go in. They are over there now – look. This hotel is often raided because of drugs and pederasty. The proprietor procures little sailor-boys and it's not expensive.' Five minutes later we were sitting at table before some excellent coffee, croissants, butter and jam – four-o'clock tea is always when they eat their first meal. They sleep late in the mornings because they go to bed late. When they saw us sitting down the policemen came back to the hotel, suspecting something. Sacha was paler than usual, Fernande very nervy and agitated. We went back into the antique shop and Sacha gave me a Louis-Philippe glass, a blue one. We saw Liou go by, looking for us. He led us away along the quay and said: 'Jean is expecting the two ladies. Will Monsieur be kind enough to have a drink in the hotel restaurant. The ladies should follow me.' All this went on while the policemen were watching the house. On our way upstairs we passed two little sailor-boys running down very fast, their heads hanging. Liou opened the door of a sordid room, letting out a strong whiff of the drug. It was sinister – what an extraordinary pleasure it is! Jean was lying on the floor covered with a disgusting bedspread, behind a horribly filthy bed. His voice was deathly, dull, dry, hoarse. He said: 'What are you doing, Liou? Shut the door. Don't let anyone in. I'm very ill.' I backed out onto the narrow landing, but Fernande went in: 'Jean, for pity's sake give me an address. Liane is here with me.' What can he have thought? That I too have started to smoke? He answered almost inaudibly: 'Liou, give her some of my special supply: three francs a gramme. Forgive me, if you knew how ill I am! Lock the door, Liou.'

I got a glimpse of Jean, thin, pale, drawn, a shadow of himself and he was already a shadow. He had a three-day beard and his clothes were in disorder, dirty and crumpled. We went into Liou's room, even more sordid. On the wall a drawing of Jean's, signed and inscribed 'To my dear Liou,' and a page of poetry in his handwriting: 'To my dear Liou.' 'How Jean squanders himself,' whispered Fernande while Liou opened a mould-smelling cupboard. Liou: 'Here are 700 grammes, Madame, that will be 2,100 francs.' Fernande: 'That's too much for me. I'm afraid of overdoing it if I have that big a supply.' He went back to the cupboard and took out a smaller pot. 'Here are 150 grammes for 450 francs.' – 'That will do,' said Fernande. 'That will keep me going for two months.'

She paid and we left. Xanaris, very nervous, was waiting downstairs. 'The cops are still there, complete with their revolvers,' he said. 'Let's leave by the other door. Have you got it?' 'Yes,' said Fernande, happy and appeased. He took the box, looked at it. 'The princess had better look after it. She has a big handbag.' I understood that they were afraid of being picked up. Opium smokers are not brave. I didn't want to make a fuss because I'm fond of all of them, Jean and these two – I'm sorry for them, too – so I slid the drug into my bag as inconspicuously as possible. Whereupon they began to run – to run much more nimbly than I would ever have expected; I had a hard time keeping up. They hailed a taxi, plunged into it. I caught up, they pulled me in, the taxi drove off. 'Ouf!' went Fernande. 'Ouf!' went Sacha. We drove past the cops who didn't notice us. Perhaps they never had. 'Quick, Liane, hand over my box.' She snatched it, looked at it lovingly, squeezed it between her hands with a tender delight that I have sometimes seen in lovers. She explained: 'Jean's stuff is very good, light, quite old. The older the better, with opium. In China princes and emperors use an opium covered with mould that's hundreds of years old, and it's beyond compare.' – 'Oh poor Jean, poor Jean,' I said, obsessed by that painful image of decay and intoxication. Emaciated, tormented little Jean, whom I used to know when he was twenty. His talent, a gift from heaven; his poor mother, so beautiful with her white hair; he was trampling all that under foot, and for what! When Mayol spoke about him the other day he told me: 'Cocteau comes to my open-air theatre on Sunday evenings. *He wears badly.*' With those words he was trying to say it all.

LIANE DE POUGY, *My Blue Notebooks*

In Time of Plague

My thoughts are crowded with death
and it draws so oddly on the sexual
that I am confused
confused to be attracted
by, in effect, my own annihilation.

Who are these two, these fiercely attractive men
who want me to stick their needle in my arm?
They tell me they are called Brad and John,
one from here, one from Denver, sitting the same
on the bench as they talk to me,
their legs spread apart, their eyes attentive.
I love their daring, their looks, their jargon,
and what they have in mind.

Their mind is the mind of death.
They know it, and do not know it,
and they are like me in that
(I know it, and do not know it)
and like the flow of people through this bar.
Brad and John thirst heroically together
for euphoria – for a state of ardent life
in which we could all stretch ourselves
and lose our differences. I seek
to enter their minds: am I a fool,
and they direct and right, properly
testing themselves against risk,
as a human must, and does,
or are they the fools, their alert faces
mere death's heads lighted glamorously?

I weigh possibilities
till I am afraid of the strength
of my own health
and of their evident health.

They get restless at last with my indecisiveness
and so, first one, and then the other,
move off into the moving concourse of people
who are boisterous and bright
carrying in their faces and throughout their bodies
the news of life and death.

THOM GUNN

Mescaline

Have I not understood then? Have I not understood what? That it is not so much the vision that counts, but the trance, the treacherous trance come to carry me off, the trance which grows and grows and grows, pushing me forward precipitously into pleasure, pleasure within me, which cannot be localised, which is not physical, essential pleasure at my very core, dragging me down like a jailer to the centre of my being, inebriating me in this cell, overthrowing me, corrupting me, dissolving me in a delirium of delight, without check, without counterweight, devoid of censure and of all possibility, an all-devouring and symphonic concupiscence whose lewd panoramas are but the corroboration and illustration of the multiple, outrageous and cerebral orgasm in whose relentless grip I am held.

trance increasing erotic trance

catapulted into world of eros

foraging fluids within me bore down upon my soul

metaphysical orgasm

The entire world seems to be in the throes of an extraordinary pleasure. Eyes drown, limbs drown, beings drown. Great gushes of bodies stream past me, interlinked, interlocked, astraddle, adrift, trunks intertwined, holding on to each other, lost like me in the schism of delight.

tidal swell and break of delights careering down upon me

Creepers in giant straddlings intertwine and uncurl, creepers unlike any to be seen on earth, ecstasies and groanings, vines, creepers, lianas. Earth, waters, mountains, trees, writhe in riots of debauchery. All is fashioned by delight, for delight, but delight of a superhuman variety, ranging from the most excited rapture to a kind of half-death where searing pleasure yet seeps in. In a cataclysm of delight this mass of animal humanity is seized with convulsions and by these spasms it becomes one with the ecstatic disorder of my mind ...

cataclysm of delights

Profusion of profanities, displayed. Sprouting buds or limbs, undistinguishable, unimportant the distinction, respond with exuberance to the monstrous call of pleasure from beneath the surface of the skin; all things are compelled to participate; each image of the mind is enlisted to give its support to this extraordinary flight of rhetoric, this grammar of animal heat.

Water-lilies, roses, antique columns, exaggeratedly obese morulae, Ottoman cupolas, naves, vaults, minarets, basins, pillars, a multitude of forms of every kind now speak unmistakably and no longer in hushed tones. The features of perversity emerge clearly from monuments, from ornaments, overladen as they are. How did one avoid seeing them, how did they pass unrecognised?

HENRI MICHAUX, *Infinite Turbulence*

A Miraculous Elixir

Behold this little Viol, which contains in its narrow Bounds what the whole Universe cannot purchase, if sold to its true Value; this admirable, this miraculous Elixir, drawn from the Hearts of Mandrakes, Phenix Livers, and Tongues of Maremaids, and distill'd by contracted Sun-Beams, has besides the unknown Virtue of curing all Distempers both of Mind and Body, that divine one of animating the Heart of Man to that Degree, that, however remiss, cold and cowardly by Nature, he shall become vigorous and brave. Oh stupid and insensible Man, when Honour and secure Renown invites you, to treat it with Neglect, even when you need but passive Valour, to become the Heroes of the Age; receive a thousand Wounds, each of which wou'd let out fleeting Life: Here's that can snatch the parting Soul in its full Career, and bring it back to its native Mansion; baffles grim Death, and disappoints even Fate.

APHRA BEHN, *The Banish'd Cavaliers*

Mother's Habit

'I went back to my pharmacist friend who said he couldn't do anything more for me but if I really needed help, I might try le Docteur Joyeu. Remember? He came to this house once. I went to see him, he lives in what looks like a half empty house – no apparent wife, just a creepy little servant who opens the door – in that pine-wood behind the tennis court. I told him, *Docteur, mon mari me trompe* – pure French farce – my husband is unfaithful, I can't take it and make scenes day and night. He made no comment except saying that he could give me something that might save my marriage. He produced a syringe and asked me to pull up my sleeve, and gave me a hypodermic injection. It took just a few seconds. I was to go home and report next day.'

......

'In no time at all I had an extraordinary sense of lightness, I felt like floating in body and even more so in mind – lucid, serene, aloof. I could

161

think about Alessandro and Doris and it seemed small and remote, everything was easy – one would just love everyone and be good and it would be all right. The universe is *All Right*. It's the most wonderful feeling – one is no longer vulnerable or human: all sorrow dissolved, filled with an extraordinary sensation of well-being.'

......

'Perhaps that's what the saints mean when they are talking of ecstasy.'

......

'No, it does not last.'

......

'Next day I went back to Docteur Joyeu. I told him about the effect. He seemed pleased – if that man can ever look pleased – he said I was a very good subject and did I think that with this treatment I would be able to keep the peace? I could stop a world war, I told him. He gave me another injection, and wrote out a prescription to last a week. One in the morning, one in the late afternoon. Would I be able to do it? Give myself a hypodermic injection: with a needle? Of course not! It's quite easy, he said. I daresay. Nor did I fancy coming to the Villa Joyeu morning, noon and night. Perhaps my husband could do it? He will, I told him, he's very good with his hands. Tell him he must sterilize the syringe. Each time, he said.'

......

'So Alessandro gives it to me. You had better learn how to do it, in case Alessandro isn't here. Because I have to have it three times a day now. Sometimes four. But the good doctor is getting stingy with the pre-scriptions, he tells me I must try to manage not to take the treatment more than three times a day maximum.'

......

'Now? That wonderful feeling? No, not like the first times; it's not as intense any longer, and it fades away more quickly. You can feel it leaving ...'

......

'What happens then? when the effect wears off? I become raging and frightened again, and very very nasty to Alessandro. You see, I am two people now. And I don't want to be the other one, I want to be as you find me now. That's why I must go on with the treatment.'

Very gently I said, 'Mummy, what is it … this thing that helps … this thing Alessandro gives you?'

'Morphine.'

. . . .

What frightened me was the increasing dosage. Five in any twenty-four hours by now was not unusual. There was the perpetual worry of getting the stuff in time; far too often we were near running out. It seemed I was always en route to Joyeu or trying to find a complacent chemist. The routine at Joyeu's consisted of my stammering out something about *ma mère* and another attack in the night, his looking at me bleakly from his opaque and shadowed eyes, heaving a sigh and after a pause, a long pause, slowly writing out a prescription. Once in a while he would say, '*Dites lui de faire attention*', mostly he would say nothing. I would utter the customary formula (French patients pay on the nail at the door), '*Combien je vous dois, Docteur?*' He would name the unvarying modest sum. I had it ready. '*Merci.*' '*Bonsoir, Docteur.*' '*Bonsoir, Mademoiselle.*'

I was losing my nerve about going to the pharmacies and so exercised perhaps unnecessary care, hesitating, saying a prayer on the doorstep, asking for toothpaste and aspirin along with the prescription. I was never turned down (intense relief each time) nor was I ever asked to produce the rigmarole about heart asthma.

There was one brutish occasion at home when I dropped the syringe, a glass syringe already primed with the precious contents of an ampoule, on the tiled floor. It shattered. My mother crouched down trying to retrieve fragments with her fingers. Then she flew at me, pulling my hair. I did the most sensible thing I could, ran out of the house, started the car and drove down to the chemist, our friendly chemist. Fortunately it was neither siesta hours nor night. From then on we kept two syringes in the house.

SYBILLE BEDFORD, *Jigsaw*

An Opium Den

An ancient English Cathedral Tower? How can the ancient English Cathedral tower be here! The well-known massive grey square tower of its old Cathedral? How can that be here! There is no spike of rusty iron in the air, between the eye and it, from any point of the real prospect. What is the spike that intervenes, and who has set it up? Maybe it is set up by the Sultan's orders for the impaling of a horde of Turkish robbers, one by one. It is so, for cymbals clash, and the Sultan goes by to his palace in long procession. Ten thousand scimitars flash in the sunlight, and thrice ten thousand dancing-girls strew flowers. Then, follow white elephants caparisoned in countless gorgeous colours, and infinite in number and attendants. Still the Cathedral Tower rises in the background, where it cannot be, and still no writhing figure is on the grim spike. Stay! Is the spike so low a thing as the rusty spike on the top of a post of an old bedstead that has tumbled all awry? Some vague period of drowsy laughter must be devoted to the consideration of this possibility.

Shaking from head to foot, the man whose scattered consciousness has thus fantastically pieced itself together, at length rises, supports his trembling frame upon his arms, and looks around. He is in the meanest and closest of small rooms. Through the ragged window-curtain, the light of early day steals in from a miserable court. He lies, dressed, across a large unseemly bed, upon a bedstead that has indeed given way under the weight upon it. Lying, also dressed and also across the bed, not long-wise, are a Chinaman, a Lascar, and a haggard woman. The two first are in a sleep or stupor; the last is blowing at a kind of pipe, to kindle it. And as she blows, and shading it with her lean hand, concentrates its red spark of light, it serves in the dim morning as a lamp to show him what he sees of her.

'Another?' says this woman, in a querulous, rattling whisper. 'Have another?'

He looks about him, with his hand to his forehead.

'Ye've smoked as many as five since ye come in at midnight,' the woman goes on, as she chronically complains. 'Poor me, poor me, my head is so bad. Them two come in after ye. Ah, poor me, the business is slack, is slack! Few Chinamen about the Docks, and fewer Lascars, and no ships coming in, these say! Here's another ready for ye, deary. Ye'll remember like a good soul, won't ye, that the market price is dreffle high just now? More nor three shillings and sixpence for a thimbleful! And ye'll remember that nobody but me (and Jack Chinaman t'other side the court; but he can't do it as well as me) has the true secret of mixing it? Ye'll pay up according, deary, won't ye?'

She blows at the pipe as she speaks, and, occasionally bubbling at it, inhales much of its contents.

'O me, O me, my lungs is weak, my lungs is bad! It's nearly ready for ye, deary. Ah, poor me, poor me, my poor hand shakes like to drop off! I see ye coming-to, and I ses to my poor self, "I'll have another ready for him, and he'll bear in mind the market price of opium, and pay according." O my poor head! I makes my pipes of old penny ink-bottles, ye see, deary – this is one – and I fits-in a mouthpiece, this way, and I takes my mixter out of this thimble with this little horn spoon; and so I fills, deary. Ah, my poor nerves! I got Heavens-hard drunk for sixteen year afore I took to this; but this don't hurt me, not to speak of. And it takes away the hunger as well as wittles, deary.'

She hands him the nearly-emptied pipe, and sinks back, turning over on her face.

He rises unsteadily from the bed, lays the pipe upon the hearthstone, draws back the ragged curtain, and looks with repugnance at his three companions. He notices that the woman has opium-smoked herself into a strange likeness of the Chinaman. His form of cheek, eye, and temple, and his colour, are repeated in her. Said Chinaman convulsively wrestles with one of his many Gods or Devils, perhaps, and snarls horribly. The Lascar laughs and dribbles at the mouth. The hostess is still.

'What visions can *she* have?' the waking man muses, as he turns her face towards him, and stands looking down at it. 'Visions of many butchers' shops, and public-houses, and much credit? Of an increase of hideous customers, and this horrible bedstead set upright again, and this horrible court swept clean? What can she rise to, under any quantity of opium, higher than that! – Eh?'

He bends down his ear, to listen to her mutterings.

'Unintelligible!'

As he watches the spasmodic shoots and darts that break out of her face and limbs, like fitful lightning out of a dark sky, some contagion in them seizes upon him: insomuch that he has to withdraw himself to a lean arm-chair by the hearth – placed there, perhaps, for such emergencies – and to sit in it, holding tight, until he has got the better of this unclean spirit of imitation.

Then he comes back, pounces on the Chinaman, and seizing him with both hands by the throat, turns him violently on the bed. The Chinaman clutches the aggressive hands, resists, gasps, and protests.

'What do you say?'

A watchful pause.

'Unintelligible!'

Slowly loosening his grasp as he listens to the incoherent jargon with an attentive frown, he turns to the Lascar and fairly drags him forth upon the floor. As he falls, the Lascar starts into a half-risen attitude, glares with his eyes, lashes about him fiercely with his arms, and draws a phantom knife. It then becomes apparent that the woman has taken possession of this knife, for safety's sake; for, she too starting up, and restraining and expostulating with him, the knife is visible in her dress, not in his, when they drowsily drop back, side by side.

There has been chattering and clattering enough between them, but to no purpose. When any distinct word has been flung into the air, it has had no sense or sequence. Wherefore 'unintelligible!' is again the comment of the watcher, made with some reassured nodding of his head, and a gloomy smile. He then lays certain silver money on the table, finds his hat, gropes his way down the broken stairs, gives a good morning to some rat-ridden doorkeeper, in bed in a black hutch beneath the stairs, and passes out.

CHARLES DICKENS, *The Mystery of Edwin Drood*

Peyote

Peyote is a small cactus and only the top part that appears above the ground is eaten. This is called a button. The buttons are prepared by peeling off the bark and fuzz and running the button through a grater until it looks like avocado salad. Four buttons is the average dose for a beginner.

We washed down the peyote with tea. I came near gagging on it several times. Finally I got it all down and sat there waiting for something to happen. The herb dealer brought out some bark he claimed was like opium. Johnny rolled a cigarette of the stuff and passed it around. Pete and Johnny said, 'Crazy! This is the greatest.'

I smoked some and felt a little dizzy and my throat hurt. But Johnny bought some of that awful-smelling bark with the intention of selling it to desperate hipsters in the U.S.

After ten minutes I began to feel sick from the peyote. Everyone told me, 'Keep it down, man.' I held out ten minutes more, then headed for the W.C. ready to throw in the towel, but I couldn't vomit. My whole body contracted in a convulsive spasm, but the peyote wouldn't come up. It wouldn't stay down either.

Finally, the peyote came up solid like a ball of hair, solid all the way up, clogging my throat. As horrible a sensation as I ever stood still for. After that, the high came on slow.

Peyote high is something like benzedrine high. You can't sleep and your pupils are dilated. Everything looks like a peyote plant. I was driving in the car with the Whites and Cash and Pete. We were going out to Cash's place in the Lomas. Johnny said, 'Look at the bank along the road. It looks like a peyote plant.'

I turned around to look, and was thinking, 'What a damn silly idea. People can talk themselves into anything.' But it did look like a peyote plant. Everything I saw looked like a peyote plant.

Our faces swelled under the eyes and our lips got thicker through some glandular action of the drug. We actually looked like Indians. The others claimed they felt primitive and were laying around on the grass and acting the way they figured Indians act. I didn't feel any different from ordinary except high like on benny.

We sat up all night talking and listening to Cash's records. Cash told me about several cats from 'Frisco who had kicked junk habits with peyote. 'It seems like they didn't want junk when they started using peyote.' One of these junkies came down to Mexico and started taking peyote with the Indians. He was using it all the time in large quantities: up to twelve buttons in one dose. He died of a condition that was diagnosed as polio. I understand, however, that the symptoms of peyote poisoning and polio are identical.

I couldn't sleep until the next morning at dawn, and then I had a nightmare every time I dozed off. In one dream, I was coming down with rabies. I looked in the mirror and my face changed and I began howling. In another dream, I had a chlorophyll habit. Me and about five other chlorophyll addicts are waiting to score on the landing of a cheap Mexican hotel. We turn green and no one can kick a chlorophyll habit. One shot and you're hung for life. We are turning into plants.

WILLIAM BURROUGHS, *Junky*

Sinbad the Sailor – a Dealer

Franz did not disturb him whilst he absorbed his favourite sweetmeat, but when he had finished, he inquired, 'What, then, is this precious stuff?'

'Did you ever hear,' he replied, 'of the Old Man of the Mountain, who attempted to assassinate Philip Augustus?' – 'Of course I have.' – 'Well, you know he reigned over a rich valley which was overhung by the mountain whence he derived his picturesque name. In this valley were magnificent gardens planted by Hassen-ben-Sabah, and in these gardens isolated pavilions. Into these pavilions he admitted the elect; and there, says Marco Polo, gave them to eat a certain herb, which transported them to Paradise, in the midst of ever-blooming shrubs, ever-ripe fruit, and ever-lovely virgins. What these happy persons took for reality was but a dream: but it was a dream so soft, so voluptuous, so enthralling, that they sold themselves body and soul to him who gave it to them, and obedient to his orders as to those of a deity, struck down the designated victim, died in torture without a murmur, believing that the death they underwent was but a quick transition to that life of delights of which the holy herb, now before you, had given them a slight foretaste.'

'Then,' cried Franz, 'it is hashish! I know that – by name at least.'

'That is it precisely, Signor Aladdin; it is hashish – the purest and most unadulterated hashish of Alexandria, the hashish of Abon-Gor, the celebrated maker, the only man, the man to whom there should be built a palace, inscribed with these words, "*A grateful world to the dealer in happiness.*"'

'Do you know,' said Franz, 'I have a very great inclination to judge for myself of the truth or exaggeration of your eulogies.'

'Judge for yourself, Signor Aladdin – judge, but do not confine yourself to one trial. Like everything else, we must habituate the senses to a fresh impression, gentle or violent, sad or joyous. There is a struggle in nature against this divine substance, in nature which is not made for joy and clings to pain. Nature subdued must yield in the combat, the dream must succeed to reality, and then the dream reigns supreme, then the dream becomes life, and life becomes the dream. But what changes occur! It is only by comparing the pains of actual being with the joys of the assumed existence, that you would desire to live no longer, but to dream thus forever. When you return to this mundane sphere from your visionary world, you would seem to leave a Neapolitan spring for a Lapland winter – to quit paradise for earth – heaven for hell! Taste the hashish, guest of mine – taste the hashish.'

Franz's only reply was to take a teaspoonful of the marvellous preparation, about as much in quantity as his host had eaten, and lift it to his mouth. '*Diable!*' he said, after having swallowed the divine preserve. 'I do not know if the result will be as agreeable as you describe, but the thing does not appear to me as palatable as you say.'

'Because your palate has not yet been attuned to the sublimity of the substances it flavours. Tell me, the first time you tasted oysters, tea, porter, truffles, and sundry other dainties which you now adore, did you like them? Could you comprehend how the Romans stuffed their pheasants with assafœtida, and the Chinese eat swallows' nests? Eh? no! Well, it is the same with hashish; only eat for a week, and nothing in the world will seem to you to equal the delicacy of its flavour, which now appears to you flat and distasteful. Let us now go into the adjoining chamber, which is your apartment, and Ali will bring us coffee and pipes.' They both arose, and while he who called himself Sinbad – and whom we have occasionally named so, that we might, like his guest, have some title by which to distinguish him – gave some orders to the servant, Franz entered still another apartment. It was simply yet richly furnished. It was round, and a large divan completely encircled it. Divan, walls, ceiling, floor, were all covered with magnificent skins as soft and downy as the richest carpets; there were heavy-maned lion-skins from Atlas, striped tiger-skins from Bengal; panther-skins from the Cape, spotted beautiful-ly, like those that appeared to Dante; bear-skins from Siberia, fox-skins from Norway, and so on; and all these skins were strewn in profusion one on the other, so that it seemed like walking over the most mossy turf, or reclining on the most luxurious bed. Both laid themselves down on the divan; chibouques with jasmine tubes and amber mouthpieces were within reach, and all prepared so that there was no need to smoke the same pipe twice. Each of them took one, which Ali lighted and then retired to prepare the coffee. There was a moment's silence, during which Sinbad gave himself up to the thoughts that seemed to occupy him incessantly, even in the midst of his conversation; and Franz aban-doned himself to that mute reverie, into which we always sink when smoking excellent tobacco, which seems to remove with its fume all the troubles of the mind, and to give the smoker in exchange all the visions of the soul. Ali brought in the coffee. 'How do you take it?' inquired the unknown; 'in the French or Turkish style, strong or weak, sugar or none, cool or boiling? As you please; it is ready in all ways.' – 'I will take it in the Turkish style,' replied Franz.

'And you are right,' said his host; 'it shows you have a tendency for an Oriental life. Ah, those Orientals: they are the only men who know how to live. As for me,' he added, with one of those singular smiles which did not escape the young man, 'when I have completed my affairs in Paris, I shall go and die in the East; and should you wish to see me again, you must seek me at Cairo, Bagdad, or Ispahan.'

'*Ma foi*,' said Franz, 'it would be the easiest thing in the world; for I feel eagle's wings springing out at my shoulders, and with these wings I could make a tour of the world in four and twenty hours.'

'Ah, yes, the hashish is beginning its work. Well, unfurl your wings, and fly into superhuman regions; fear nothing, there is a watch over you; and if your wings, like those of Icarus, melt before the sun, we are here to ease your fall.' He then said something in Arabic to Ali, who made a sign of obedience and withdrew, but not to any distance. As to Franz, a strange transformation had taken place in him. All the bodily fatigue of the day, all the preoccupation of mind which the events of the evening had brought on, disappeared as they do at the first approach of sleep, when we are still sufficiently conscious to be aware of the coming of slumber. His body seemed to acquire an airy lightness, his perception brightened in a remarkable manner, his senses seemed to redouble their power, the horizon continued to expand; but it was not the gloomy horizon of vague alarms, and which he had seen before he slept, but a blue, transparent, unbounded horizon, with all the blue of the ocean, all the spangles of the sun, all the perfumes of the summer breeze; then, in the midst of the songs of his sailors — songs so clear and sonorous, that they would have made a divine harmony had their notes been taken down — he saw the Island of Monte Cristo, no longer as a threatening rock in the midst of the waves, but as an oasis in the desert; then, as his boat drew nearer, the songs became louder, for an enchanting and mysterious harmony rose to heaven, as if some Loreley had decreed to attract a soul thither, or Amphion, the enchanter, intended there to build a city.

At length the boat touched the shore, but without effort, without shock, as lips touch lips; and he entered the grotto amidst continued strains of most delicious melody. He descended, or rather seemed to descend, several steps, inhaling the fresh and balmy air, like that which may be supposed to reign around the grotto of Circe, formed from such perfumes as set the mind a dreaming, and such fires as burn the very senses; and he saw again all he had seen before his sleep, from Sinbad, his singular host, to Ali, the mute attendant; then all seemed to fade away and become confused before his eyes, like the last shadows of the magic lantern before it is extinguished, and he was again in the chamber of statues, lighted only by one of those pale and antique lamps which watch in the dead of the night over the sleep of pleasure. They were the same statues, rich in form, in attraction, and poesy, with eyes of fascination, smiles of love, and bright and flowing hair. They were Phryne, Cleopatra, Messalina, those three celebrated courtesans. Then among them glided like a pure ray, like a Christian angel in the midst of Olympus, one of those chaste figures, those calm shadows, those soft visions, which seemed to veil its virgin brow before these marble wantons. Then the three statues advanced towards him with looks of love, and approached the couch on which he was reposing, their feet hidden in their long white tunics, their throats bare, hair flowing like waves, and assuming attitudes which the gods could not resist, but which saints withstood, and looks inflexible and ardent like those with which the serpent charms the bird; and then he gave way before looks that held him in a torturing grasp and delighted his senses as with a voluptuous kiss. It seemed to Franz that he closed his eyes, and in a last look about him saw the vision of modesty completely veiled; and then followed a dream of passion like that promised by the Prophet to the elect. Lips of stone turned to flame, breasts of ice became like heated lava, so that to Franz, yielding for the first time to the sway of the drug, love was a sorrow and voluptuousness a torture, as burning mouths were pressed to his thirsty lips, and he was held in cool serpent-like embraces. The more he strove against this unhallowed passion the more his senses yielded to its thrall, and at length, weary of a struggle that taxed his very soul, he gave way and sank back breathless and exhausted beneath the kisses of these marble goddesses, and the enchantment of his marvellous dream.

ALEXANDRE DUMAS, *The Count of Monte Cristo*

Smack

I was curled up in her king-size bed
reading Eco's *Travels In Hypereality*.
'You look awful,' she said, and smiled
a most sympathetic of smiles:
I felt as if I hadn't slept
for the best part of a week.

I woke up with a start
to discover her packing a suitcase.
When I asked where she was going
she mumbled something about krugerrands
and how this must have been
the coldest Christmas since 1962.

'The streets are paved with gold
and silver and purest platinum,'
she'd shrieked as she stumbled downstairs.
The next instant she was in a taxi
speeding up the Airport Road
to catch the 8am flight for London.

On The Feast of Saint Bridget
she posted me one gramme of heroin –
Compliments of a gold-digger of 1986.
As Montale said, 'The step between
the horrific and the ridiculous is nothing.'
I assumed she'd be dead within the year.

'An irresponsible and undeveloped nature'
was her own opinion of herself
when she arrived at my door
out of a cold and wet St Valentine's Day.
I implored her not to bother me:
she shivered and fell into my arms.

I woke out of that dream
of a dream of a visitation
just as she turned the last page for me.
Where do you come from? I asked.
'From here, from this bed,' she replied
without the slightest hint of mystery.

She laughed? I laughed, we laughed together.
But where do you come from?
From Black Narcissus or Audley's Acre?
I asked as my vision blurred
and I began to die the death again
in the arms of a complete stranger.

                                        JOHN HUGHES

Sonnet to the Poppy

While summer roses all their glory yield
   To crown the votary of love and joy,
   Misfortune's victim hails, with many a sigh,
   Thee, scarlet Poppy of the pathless field,
Gaudy, yet wild and lone; no leaf to shield
   Thy flaccid vest that, as the gale blows high,
   Flaps, and alternate folds around thy head.
   So stands in the long grass a love-crazed maid,
Smiling aghast; while stream to every wind
   Her garish ribbons, smeared with dust and rain;
   But brain-sick visions cheat her tortured mind,
And bring false peace. Thus, lulling grief and pain,
   Kind dreams oblivious from thy juice proceed,
   Thou flimsy, showy, melancholy weed.

ANNA SEWARD

Stoned

Many of those who are being initiated complain at first of the tedium; they wait with futile impatience, and if the drug does not act swiftly enough, they give sardonic satisfaction to Initiates by boasting that they are impervious to the effects of Hashish. The first signs of an approaching storm appear and multiply. In the early moments of getting stoned you are seized by an outrageous hilarity, irresistible and ludicrous. These motiveless fits of hilarity, of which you feel ashamed, recur and destroy the placidity of your stupor. The most simple words and most trivial ideas assume bizarre and fantastic shapes; you feel astonished not to have realised their simplicity before. Incongruous affinities, unexpected reconciliations, interminable jests, comical absurdities, rush continually from your brain ...

This hilarity, languishing and poignant, this uneasy joy, this insecurity, this sick indecision, seldom endure. Soon your ideas become so vague, your mental conceptions so strained, that only your accomplices can understand you ... At the same time, wisdom and sagacity, the measured thoughts of the unintoxicated, divert and amuse you with their inanity. It is all inverted.

CHARLES BAUDELAIRE

The Yellow Peril

We took a rickisha, and our 'Tshia, tshia'-yelling coolie quickly perambulated his light cart through a maze of foul-smelling passages and by-streets of Shanghai. We stopped at a dimly lighted house in a side street and entered a dismal building. At the door we were assailed by a heavy, nauseating odour that filled the air. The affable headman, the Chinese owner of the den – for den it was – received us, and invited us, with many smiles, to sit on one of the numerous dirty stools that were placed around the dingy apartment. It was a real opium den.

A basin, containing a small quantity of foul-smelling oil, fed the wick of a flickering light that only helped to heighten the sordidness of the surroundings in this den of malignity – nay, of death.

The Chinaman, with the evil grin of one of the imps of darkness, twisted himself into many suave bows; he fawned on us, his depraved countenance beaming with knowing smiles. He asked what the desire of his visitors was? Lady? Or opium? Or both ... eh?

Being enlightened on the subject, and some dollars having found their way to his greasy palm, we ascended the rickety staircase, and, to the tune of the creaking boards, landed in a dark, narrow passage on the top floor.

The foul opium-smoke-charged air almost stifled us.

Opening one of the doors in the passage he led us on to a broad ledge along the side of the house, which served as a means of access to an adjoining building: the real opium den.

Cautiously we entered; the Chinaman, placing his finger warningly on his lips, motioned us to follow.

A large and comfortable room received us. Soft velvet couches and settees, heavy carpets of the softest texture suggested an atmosphere of luxury I certainly had not expected in this vile corner.

We seated ourselves on one of the couches, while the son of the Celestial Empire spoke in a subdued voice to a hard-faced hag who had entered from a side door. She immediately took her departure, returning with two young, almond-eyed creatures dressed in the flimsiest of garments.

My companion drew one of them towards him and put his arm around the slender waist of the girl – or rather child – and then invited me to follow his example and have a try at the opium pipe. He was going to smoke, he said. He told me he only did so to get to know the drug; he could then judge of its effects better and experiment with his 'cure'.

The sickly smell that had been so noticeable on entering the house was quite sufficient to destroy any desire on my part for such experiments.

My companion made himself comfortable on one of the settees, the girl smoothing the pillows on his couch. He, for some reason or other, seemed a favoured patron; probably he paid handsomely for his indulgences.

The pipe, lamp, and usual paraphernalia which form the opium-smoker's outfit were soon forthcoming.

The girl sat on the edge of the couch and tended the pipe, while my friend, with his arm tightly encircling her waist, soon proved by his stertorous breathing to have fallen into a heavy sleep.

The girl dried the perspiration from his heated brow and loosened his collar, while his powerful arm still held her in a firm embrace.

The old woman now shuffled from the room unobserved, and, at a sign from her, the girl, with a weary sigh, placed her head on my companion's pillow, while she threw her arms around him. A terrible picture to contemplate! A soul in the grasp of the Lord of Hells! Now I knew my companion's hypocrisy.

The horrid drug and vice had taken possession of his brain and his manhood, and my companion, a fine specimen of nature's handiwork, was now in the grip of the vice he had wooed. He was sinking into those depths where life is meaningless beyond the desires created by the drug.

While I was thus gazing at the pitiful sight before me, the old hag's hand touched me on the shoulder, and motioned me to follow her.

I left the room. She grinned and said, 'He no makee go; he stop top-side. Suppose to-mollow he makee go. Ha, ha, ha!' she grinned; 'ha, ha, ha!'

So, I thought, this is evidently the custom – to spend the whole night under the influence of opium, and then stagger home, like a drunken man, whilst the early rays of the rising sun were dispelling the dense vapours that hovered over the waters of the Yangtze River at beautiful Shanghai!

What I had seen was sufficient to give me a good idea of the iron grip in which the cursed opium pipe holds its victims.

The old woman came to me with the information that, for 'kum sia' (a present), she would show me the house and how others smoked the drug.

Though, as I said, I was really quite sated and sick with the sight before me, yet I wanted to see the *natives* indulging in their favourite vice.

I followed the old woman, and she led me through a maze of passages until we reached a carved door. She then gently tapped, and a grinning Chinese boy of some sixteen years of age opened the door.

They had a few hurried words in whispers, and then the old hag motioned me to follow her. On entering I noticed that the room was as well fitted as the one in which I had left my friend – the same display of costly furniture, except that the general arrangement plainly showed a woman's hand.

We passed into the inner room, and – almighty Heaven! on the couch, with the cursed pipe in the grasp of her slender fingers, and nude, save for a scanty *négligé*, lay my beautiful companion of the hotel table; and, to add to the horror of it, she was attended by a Chinaman!

The beautiful creature, who had been crossing my mind all day long, lay here in an opium den, open to the gaze of every Chinaman who cared to pay for the privilege of feasting his eyes on the form of a white woman, drugged and unconscious. The sight was pitiable, most pitiable.

To see her there, unconsciously one of the main attractions of the opium hell of an unscrupulous, slant-eyed heathen, fairly unnerved me. I turned round, and with a kick sent the Chinaman flying through the door. True the woman was not British, but she was a lovely, white Christian – and to see her so fallen, so near to hell! She must immediately leave this den – and yet the horror of shame, once she could realise that I had seen her under those terrible conditions, might kill her!

I drew back. I would leave her. Probably she would be carried out unconscious when the patrons of the house had left.

I turned towards the door – when a voice seemed to say to me:

'Coward! how dare you desert a white girl in such a place and with such devils around her?'

The woman's position struck me to the heart.

I lifted the poor creature in my arms, while the frightened Chinese hag assisted me to place a cloak around the drugged form and a cloth over the pallid features.

Then I carried the unconscious girl downstairs, placed her in the rickisha, and we sped rapidly away from that disgusting den.

The girl was placed in a sheltering home, away from her tempters, but whether she stayed there or not I do not know ...

Can nothing be done in England – in Germany – in France – in America – to stop the devil filling up the bottomless pit of hell with the victims of the white slave traffic in the East?

Surely it is time to act! In God's name let the answer be: Yea – though the heavens fall!

MRS ARCHIBALD MACKIRDY (OLIVE CHRISTIAN MALVERY)
and W. N. WILLIS, *The White Slave Market*

Junk is the ultimate merchandise. The junk merchant does not sell his product to the consumer, he sells the consumer to the product.

WILLIAM BURROUGHS

I'll die young, but it's like kissing God.

LENNY BRUCE

Flirting

Make love to the most impertinent beauty of condition that you meet with, and be gallant with all the rest.

EARL OF CHESTERFIELD

Glances are the heavy artillery of the flirt: everything can be conveyed in a look, yet that look can always be denied, for it cannot be quoted word for word.

STENDHAL

Unless you love someone nothing makes any sense.

e e cummings

The only way of knowing a person is to love them without hope.

WALTER BENJAMIN

The Art of Coquetry

First form your artful looks with studious care,
From mild to grave, from tender to severe.
Oft on the careless youth your glances dart,
A tender meaning let each glance impart.
Whene'er he meet your looks, with modest pride
And soft confusion turn your eyes aside,
Let a soft sigh steal out, as if by chance,
Then cautious turn, and steal another glance.
Caught by these arts, with pride and hope elate,
The destined victim rushes on his fate:
Pleased, his imagined victory pursues,
And the kind maid with soft attention views,
Contemplates now her shape, her air, her face,
And thinks each feature wears an added grace;

Till gratitude, which first his bosom proves,
By slow degrees sublimed, at length he loves.
'Tis harder still to fix than gain a heart;
What's won by beauty must be kept by art.
Too kind a treatment the blest lover cloys,
And oft despair the growing flame destroys:
Sometimes with smiles receive him, sometimes tears,
And wisely balance both his hopes and fears.
Perhaps he mourns his ill-requited pains,
Condemns your sway, and strives to break his chains;
Behaves as if he now your scorn defied,
And thinks at least he shall alarm your pride:
But with indifference view the seeming change,
And let your eyes to seek new conquests range;

While his torn breast with jealous fury burns,
He hopes, despairs, adores and hates by turns;
With anguish now repents the weak deceit,
And powerful passion bears him to your feet.

CHARLOTTE LENNOX

The Cold Coquette

There's also nightly, to the uninitiated,
    A peril – not indeed like love or marriage,
But not the less for this to be depreciated:
    It is – I meant and mean not to disparage
The show of virtue even in the vitiated –
    It adds an outward grace unto their carriage –
But to denounce the amphibious sort of harlot,
Couleur de rose, who's neither white nor scarlet.

Such is your cold coquette, who can't say 'no',
    And won't say 'yes', and keeps you on- and off-ing
On a lee shore, till it begins to blow –
    Then sees your heart wreck'd with an inward scoffing.
This works a world of sentimental woe,
    And sends new Werters yearly to their coffin;
But yet is merely innocent flirtation,
Not quite adultery, but adulteration.

LORD BYRON

Epitaph

[on Frances, Countess of Jersey, mistress of King George IV]

Had she possessed more Prudence, with less Vivacity; more Affection, with less Inconstancy; more Sincerity, with less Insinuation;
She would have lived a Pattern to the Wives and Daughters of Great Britain.
Her Ladyship died in the —th Year of her Age of the Spleen, after having been long indisposed with the incurable Malady of Coquetry.

SIR HERBERT CROFT, *The Abbey of Kilkhampton*

A Love Scene

She was sitting as nearly upright as she ever did, and he had brought a chair close to the sofa, so that there was only the corner of the table between him and her. It so happened that as she spoke her hand lay upon the table, and as Mr Slope answered her he put his hand upon hers. 'No heart!' said he. 'That is a heavy charge which you bring against yourself, and one of which I cannot find you guilty.'

She withdrew her hand, not quickly and angrily as though insulted by his touch, but gently and slowly. 'You are in no condition to give a verdict on the matter,' said she, 'as you have not tried me. No; don't say that you intend doing so, for you know you have no intention of the kind. Nor indeed have I either. As for you, you will take your vows where they will result in something more substantial than the pursuit of such a ghostlike, ghastly love as mine –'

'Your love should be sufficient to satisfy the dream of a monarch,' said Mr Slope, not quite clear as to the meaning of his words.

'Say an archbishop, Mr Slope,' said she. Poor fellow! she was very cruel to him. He went round again upon his cork on this allusion to his profession. He tried, however, to smile, and gently accused her of joking on a matter, which was, he said, to him of such vital moment.

'Why – what gulls do you men make of us,' she replied. 'How you fool us to the top of our bent; and of all men you clergymen are the most fluent of your honeyed caressing words. Now look me in the face, Mr Slope, boldly and openly.'

Mr Slope did look at her with a languishing loving eye, and as he did so, he again put forth his hand to get hold of hers.

'I told you to look at me boldly, Mr Slope; but confine your boldness to your eyes.'

'Oh, Madeline!' he sighed.

'Well, my name is Madeline,' said she; 'but none except my own family usually call me so. Now look me in the face, Mr Slope. Am I to understand that you say you love me?'

Mr Slope never had said so. If he had come there with any formed plan at all, his intention was to make love to the lady without uttering any such declaration. It was, however, quite impossible that he should now deny his love. He had, therefore, nothing for it, but to go down on his knees distractedly against the sofa, and swear that he did love her with a love passing the love of man.

The Signora received the assurance with very little palpitation or appearance of surprise. 'And now answer me another question,' said she; 'when are you to be married to my dear friend Eleanor Bold?'

Poor Mr Slope went round and round in mortal agony. In such a condition as his it was really very hard for him to know what answer to give. And yet no answer would be his surest condemnation. He might as well at once plead guilty to the charge brought against him. 'Why do you accuse me of such dissimulation?' said he.

'Dissimulation! I said nothing of dissimulation. I made no charge against you, and make none. Pray don't defend yourself to me. You swear that you are devoted to my beauty, and yet you are on the eve of matrimony with another. I feel this to be rather a compliment. It is to Mrs Bold that you must defend yourself. That you may find difficult; unless, indeed, you can keep her in the dark. You clergymen are cleverer than other men.'

'Signora, I have told you that I loved you, and now you rail at me?'

'Rail at you! God bless the man; what would he have? Come, answer me this at your leisure, not without thinking now, but leisurely and with consideration; are you not going to be married to Mrs Bold?'

'I am not,' said he. And as he said it, he almost hated, with an exquisite hatred, the woman whom he could not help loving with an exquisite love.

'But surely you are a worshipper of hers?'

'I am not,' said Mr Slope, to whom the word worshipper was peculiarly distasteful. The Signora had conceived that it would be so.

'I wonder at that,' she said. 'Do you not admire her? To my eye she is the perfection of English beauty. And then she is rich too. I should have thought she was just the person to attract you. Come, Mr Slope, let me give you advice on this matter. Marry the charming widow. She will be a good mother to your children, and an excellent mistress of a clergyman's household.'

'Oh, Signora, how can you be so cruel?'

'Cruel,' said she, changing the voice of banter which she had been using for one which was expressively earnest in its tone; 'is that cruelty?'

'How can I love another, while my heart is entirely your own?'

'If that were cruelty, Mr Slope, what might you say of me if I were to declare that I returned your passion? What would you think if I bound you even by a lover's oath to do daily penance at this couch of mine? What can I give in return for a man's love? Ah, dear friend, you have not realised the conditions of my fate.'

Mr Slope was not on his knees all this time. After his declaration of love he had risen from them as quickly as he thought consistent with the new position which he now filled, and as he stood was leaning on the back of his chair. This outburst of tenderness on the Signora's part quite overcame him, and made him feel for the moment that he could sacrifice everything to be assured of the love of the beautiful creature before him, maimed, lame, and already married as she was.

'And can I not sympathise with your lot?' said he, now seating himself on her sofa, and pushing away the table with his foot.

'Sympathy is so near to pity!' said she. 'If you pity me, cripple as I am, I shall spurn you from me.'

'Oh, Madeline, I will only love you,' and again he caught her hand and devoured it with kisses. Now she did not draw it from him, but sat there as he kissed it, looking at him with her great eyes, just as a great spider would look at a great fly that was quite securely caught.

'Suppose Signor Neroni were to come to Barchester,' said she, 'would you make his acquaintance?'

'Signor Neroni!' said he.

'Would you introduce him to the bishop, and Mrs Proudie, and the young ladies?' said she, again having recourse to that horrid quizzing voice which Mr Slope so particularly hated.

'Why do you ask such a question?' said he.

'Because it is necessary that you should know that there is a Signor Neroni. I think you had forgotten it.'

'If I thought that you retained for that wretch one particle of the love of which he was never worthy, I would die before I would distract you by telling you what I feel. No! were your husband the master of your heart, I might perhaps love you; but you should never know it.'

'My heart again! how you talk. And you consider then, that if a husband be not master of his wife's heart, he has no right to her fealty. If a wife ceases to love, she may cease to be true. Is that your doctrine on this matter, as a minister of the Church of England?'

Mr Slope tried hard within himself to cast off the pollution with which he felt that he was defiling his soul. He strove to tear himself away from the noxious siren that had bewitched him. But he could not do it.

ANTHONY TROLLOPE, Barchester Towers

Love, You've Been a Villain

Lovers who are young indeed, and wish to know the sort of life
That in this world you're like to lead, ere you can say you've caught a
    wife,
Listen to the lay of one who's had with Cupid much to do,
And love-sick once, is love-sick still, but in another point of view.
Woman, though so kind she seems, will take your heart and tantalise it,
Were it made of Portland stone, she'd manage to McAdamise it.
      Dairy-maid or duchess,
        Keep it from her clutches,
If you'd ever wish to know a quiet moment more.

> Wooing, cooing,
> Seeming, scheming,
> Smiling, wiling,
> Pleasing, teasing,
> Taking, breaking,
> Clutching, touching
> Bosoms to the core.
Oh love you've been a villain since the days of Troy and Helen,
When you caused the fall of Paris and of very many more.
Sighing like a furnace, in the hope that you may win her still,
And losing health and appetite, and growing thin and thinner still;
Walking in the wet before her window or her door o'nights,
And catching nothing but a cold with waiting there a score o'nights.
Spoiling paper by the ream with rhymes devoid of reasoning,
As silly and insipid as a goose without the seasoning.
> Running bills with tailors,
> Locking up by jailers,
Bread and water diet then, your senses to restore.
> Sighing, crying,
> Losing, musing,
> Walking, stalking,
> Hatching, catching,
> Spoiling, toiling,
> Rhyming, chiming,
> Running up a score.

JAMES PLANCHÉ

Only Trying to Please

But to try to please others; to be sad with the gloomy, gay with the thoughtless, crafty with the politic; to listen with feigned attention to chatterers; to fight battles with soldiers, and grow passionate for the good of the country with philanthropists; to give to each his little dose of flattery — why, this seems to me as necessary as to wear flowers in my hair, or diamonds, or gloves, or clothes. Such things are the mental and moral part of dress, and we put them on or off with our feathers. Surely you do not call that coquetry?

HONORÉ DE BALZAC, *La Duchesse de Langeais*

The Resolve

Whilst thirst of praise, and vain desire of fame,
In every age, is every woman's aim;
With courtship pleased, of silly toasters proud;
Fond of a train, and happy in a crowd;
On each poor fool bestowing some kind glance;
Each conquest owing to some loose advance;
Whilst vain coquets affect to be pursued,
And think they're virtuous, if not grossly lewd;
Let this great maxim be my virtue's guide:
In part she is to blame, who has been tried,
He comes too near, that comes to be denied.

LADY MARY WORTLEY MONTAGU

Sweet Language of Fans

The fan, indeed, has its own particular language, more eloquent than that of flowers – the Spanish *novia* (lady-love) communicates her thoughts by code to her *novio* (sweetheart) ...

A few examples will probably suffice as an indication of the method:

1. *You have won my love.* Place the shut fan near the heart.
2. *When may I be allowed to see you?* The shut fan resting upon the right eye.
3. *At what hour?* The number of the sticks of the fan indicate the hour.

4. *I long always to be near thee.* Touch the unfolded fan in the act of waving.
5. *Do not be so imprudent.* Threaten with the shut fan.
6. *Why do you misunderstand me?* Gaze pensively at the unfolded fan.
7. *You may kiss me.* Press the half-opened fan to the lips.
8. *Forgive me, I pray you.* Clasp the hands under the open fan.
9. *Do not betray our secret.* Cover the left ear with the open fan.
10. *I promise to marry you.* Shut the full-opened fan very slowly.

And so on, through the whole gamut of the language of love.

GEORGE WOOLLISCROFT RHEAD, *A History of the Fan*

Food

O for a plump, fat leg of mutton!
Veal, lamb, capon, pig and coney!
None is happy but a glutton,
None an ass but who wants money.

Wines, indeed, and girls are good;
But brave vituals feast the blood;
For wenches, wine and lusty cheer
Jove would come down to surfeit here.

THOMAS MIDDLETON

Hunger is the cheapest sawce.

SIR THOMAS OVERBURY

'Tis not the meat, but 'tis the appetite
Makes eating a delight;
And if I like one dish
More than another, that a pheasant is.

SIR JOHN SUCKLING

At Paris in popular commotions even the most inflamed are reluctant to miss a meal.

CARDINAL DE RETZ

Breakfast

The breakfast is the *prosopon* of the great work of the day. Chocolate, coffee, tea, cream, eggs, ham, tongue, cold fowl – all these are good, and bespeak good knowledge in him who sets them forth: but the touchstone is fish: anchovy is the first step, prawns and shrimps the second; and I laud him who reaches even to these: potted char and lampreys are the third, and a fine stretch of progression; but lobster is, indeed, matter for a May morning, and demands a rare combination of knowledge and virtue in him who sets it forth.

THOMAS LOVE PEACOCK, Crotchet Castle

Breakfast for the Clergy

The breakfast service on the table was equally costly and equally plain; the apparent object had been to spend money without obtaining brilliancy or splendour. The urn was of thick and solid silver, as were also the tea-pot, coffee-pot, cream-ewer, and sugar-bowl; the cups were old, dim dragon china, worth about a pound a piece, but very despicable in the eyes of the uninitiated. The silver forks were so heavy as to be disagreeable to the hand, and the bread-basket was of a weight really formidable to any but robust persons. The tea consumed was the very best, the coffee the very blackest, the cream the very thickest; there was dry toast and buttered toast, muffins and crumpets; hot bread and cold bread, white bread and brown bread, home-made bread and baker's bread, wheaten bread and oaten bread, and if there be other breads than these, they were there; there were eggs in napkins, and crispy bits of bacon under silver covers; and there were little fishes in a little box, and devilled kidneys fizzling on a hot-water dish; which, by-the-by, were placed closely contiguous to the plate of the worthy archdeacon himself. Over and above this, on a snow white napkin, spread upon the sideboard, was a huge ham and a huge sirloin; the latter having laden the dinner table on the previous evening. Such was the ordinary fare at Plumstead Episcopi.

ANTHONY TROLLOPE, *The Warden*

Breakfast in an Edwardian Country House

The smell of last night's port had given place to the smell of this morning's spirits of wine. Rows of little spirit lamps warmed rows of large silver dishes. On a table to the right between the windows were grouped Hams, Tongues, Galantines, Cold Grouse, ditto Pheasant, ditto Partridge, ditto Ptarmigan. No Edwardian meal was complete without Ptarmigan. Hot or cold. Just Ptarmigan. There would also be a little delicate rectangle of pressed beef from the shop of M. Benoist. On a further table, to the left between the doors, stood fruits of different calibre, and jugs of cold water, and jugs of lemonade. A fourth table contained porridge utensils. A fifth coffee, and pots of Indian and China tea. The latter were differentiated from each other by little ribbons of yellow (indicating China) and of red (indicating, without *arrière pensée*, our Indian Empire). The centre table, which was prepared for twenty-three people, would be bright with Malmaisons and toast-racks. No newspapers were, at that stage, allowed ...

Edwardian breakfasts were in no sense a hurried proceeding. The porridge was disposed of negligently, people walking about and watching the rain descend upon the Italian garden. Then would come whiting and omelette and devilled kidneys and little fishy messes in shells. And then tongue and ham and a slice of Ptarmigan. And then scones and honey and marmalade. And then a little melon, and a nectarine or two, and just one or two of those delicious raspberries. The men at that stage would drift (I employ the accepted term) to the smoking room. The women would idle in the saloon watching the rain descend upon the Italian garden. It was then 10.30.

SIR HAROLD NICOLSON, *Small Talk*

Breakfasts of an Irish Baronet

The man who intends to study all the morning, should take a cup or two of coffee, a little well-executed toast, and the wing of a partridge or grouse, when in season; at other times of the year, a small slice of cold chicken, with plenty of pepper and mustard; this light diet prepares him for the elastic exercise of his intellectual powers. On the other hand, if you are going to the fox-chase, or to the moors, or to any sphere of violent bodily exertion whatever, in this case your breakfast will be good and praiseworthy, exactly in proportion as it approaches to the character of a good and praiseworthy dinner. Hot potatoes, chops, beefsteaks, a pint of Burgundy, a quart of good old beer – these are the sort of materials a sportman's dejeune should consist of. Fried fish is an excellent thing also – particularly the herring. If you have been tipsy overnight, and feel squeamish, settle your heart with half a glass of old cogniac, ere you assume the knife and fork; but on no account indulge the whimsies of your stomach, so as to go without a real breakfast ...

Of tea, I have on various occasions hinted my total scorn. It is a weak, nervous affair, adapted for the digestion of boarding-school misses, whose occupation is painting roses from the life, practising quadrilles, strumming on the instrument, and so forth. Old people of sedentary habits may take chocolate if they like it; I, for my part, stick to coffee when I am studious ...

I agree with Falstaff, in his contempt for the prevalent absurdity of eating eggs, eggs, eggs at breakfast. 'No pullet-sperm in my brewage,' say I. I prefer the chicken to the egg, and the hen, when she is really a fine bird, and well roasted or grilled, to the chicken.

Cold pig's face is one of the best things in the world for breakfast, but it should not be taken unless you are to be active shortly after, for it is so good that one can scarcely help taking a great deal when one begins to it.

Eat it with shallot vinegar and French mustard. Fruit at breakfast is what I cannot recommend; but if you will take it, be sure not to omit another dram after it, for if you do, you will certainly feel heavyish all the morning.

The best breakfast-dram is whisky, when it is really very old and fine, but brandy is more commonly to be had in perfection among the majority of my readers. Cherry brandy is not the thing at breakfast; it is too sweet, and not strong enough.

WILLIAM MAGINN, Maxims of Sir Morgan O'Doherty

Cannibalism

There were three sailors of Bristol city
Who took a boat and went to sea,
But first with beef and captain's biscuits
And pickled pork they loaded she.

There was gorging Jack and guzzling Jimmy
And the youngest he was little Billee.
Now when they had got as far as the Equator
They'd nothing left but one split pea.

Says gorging Jack to guzzling Jimmy,
'I am extremely hungaree.'
To gorging Jack says guzzling Jimmy,
'We've nothing left, us must eat we.'

Says gorging Jack to guzzling Jimmy,
'With one another we shouldn't agree!
There's little Bill, he's young and tender,
We're old and tough, so let's eat he.'

'Oh! Billee, we're going to kill and eat you
So undo the button of your chemie.'
When Bill received this information
He used his pocket handkerchie.

'First let me say my catechism,
Which my poor mammy taught to me.'
'Make haste, make haste,' says guzzling Jimmy,
While Jack pulled out his snickersnee.

So Billee went up to the main top gallant mast,
And down he fell on his bended knee.
He scarce had come to the twelfth commandment
When up he jumps, ' There's land I see:

'Jerusalem and Madagascar,
And North and South Amerikee:
There's a British flag a-riding at anchor,
With Admiral Napier, K.C.B.'

So when they got aboard of the Admiral's,
He hanged fat Jack and flogged Jimmee:
But as for little Bill he made him
The Captain of a Seventy-three.

W. M. THACKERAY

Carving

Have you learned to carve? for it is ridiculous not to carve well. A man who tells you gravely that he cannot carve, may as well tell you that he cannot blow his nose; it is both as necessary and as easy.

EARL OF CHESTERFIELD, Letters

A College Luncheon

The lunch on this occasion began with soles, sunk in a deep dish, over which the college cook had spread a counterpane of the whitest cream, save that it was branded here and there with brown spots like the spots on the flanks of a doe. After that came the partridges, but if this suggests a couple of bald, brown birds on a plate you are mistaken. The partridges, many and various, came with all their retinue of sauces and salads, the sharp and the sweet, each in its order; their potatoes, thin as coins but not so hard; their sprouts, foliated as rosebuds but more succulent. And no sooner had the roast and its retinue been done with than the silent serving-man, the Beadle himself perhaps in a milder manifestation, set before us, wreathed in napkins, a confection which rose all sugar from the waves. To call it pudding and so relate it to rice and tapioca would be an insult. Meanwhile the wineglasses had flushed yellow and flushed crimson; had been emptied; had been filled. And thus by degrees was lit, halfway down the spine, which is the seat of the soul, not that hard little electric light which we call brilliance, as it pops in and out upon our lips, but the more profound, subtle and subterranean glow which is the rich yellow flame of rational intercourse. No need to hurry. No need to sparkle. No need to be anybody but oneself. We are all going to heaven and Vandyck is of the company – in other words, how good life seemed, how sweet its rewards, how trivial this grudge or that grievance, how admirable friendship and the society of one's kind, as, lighting a good cigarette, one sunk among the cushions in the window-seat.

VIRGINIA WOOLF, *A Room of One's Own*

A Cook

The kitchen is his hell, and he the devil in it, where his meat and he fry together. His revenues are showered down from the fat of the land, and he interlards his own grease among, to help the drippings. Choleric he is not by nature so much as his art, and it is a shrewd temptation that the chopping-knife is so near. His weapons ofter offensive are a mess of hot broth and scalding water, and woe be to him that comes in his way. In the kitchen he will domineer and rule the roast in spite of his master, and curses in the very dialect of his calling. His labour is mere blustering and fury, and his speech like that of sailors in a storm, a thousand businesses at once; yet, in all this tumult, he does not love combustion, but will be the first man that shall go and quench it. He is never a good Christian till a hissing pot of ale has slacked him, like water cast on a firebrand, and for that time he is tame and dispossessed. His cunning is not small in architecture, for he builds strange fabrics in paste, towers and castles, which are offered to the assault of valiant teeth, and like Darius' palace in one banquet demolished. He is a pitiless murderer of innocents, and he mangles poor fowls with unheard-of tortures; and it is thought the martyrs' persecutions were devised from hence: sure we are, St Lawrence's gridiron came out of his kitchen. His best faculty is at the dresser, where he seems to have great skill in the tactics, ranging his dishes in order military, and placing with great discretion in the fore-front meats more strong and hardy, and the more cold and cowardly in the rear; as quaking tarts and quivering custards, and such milk-sop dishes, which scape many times the fury of the encounter. But now the second course is gone up and he down in the cellar, where he drinks and sleeps till four o'clock in the afternoon, and then returns again to his regiment.

JOHN EARLE, *Microcosmographie*

Le Dîner

Come along, 'tis the time, ten or more minutes past,
And he who came first had to wait for the last;
The oysters ere this had been in and been out;
Whilst I have been sitting and thinking about
    How pleasant it is to have money, heigh-ho!
    How pleasant it is to have money.

A clear soup with eggs; *voilà tout*; of the fish
The *filets de sole* are a moderate dish
A la Orly, but you're for red mullet, you say:
By the gods of good fare, who can question to-day
    How pleasant it is to have money, heigh-ho!
    How pleasant it is to have money.

After oysters, sauterne; then sherry; champagne,
Ere one bottle goes, comes another again;
Fly up, thou bold cork, to the ceiling above,
And tell to our ears in the sound that they love
    How pleasant it is to have money, heigh-ho!
    How pleasant it is to have money.

I've the simplest of palates; absurd it may be,
But I almost could dine on a *poulet-au-riz*,
Fish and soup and omelette and that – but the deuce –
There were to be woodcocks, and not *Charlotte Russe!*
    So pleasant it is to have money, heigh-ho!
    So pleasant it is to have money.

Your Chablis is acid, away with the Hock,
Give me the pure juice of the purple Médoc:
St Peray is exquisite; but, if you please,
Some Burgundy just before tasting the cheese.
    So pleasant it is to have money, heigh-ho!
    So pleasant it is to have money.

As for that, pass the bottle, and damn the expense,
I've seen it observed by a writer of sense,
That the labouring classes could scarce live a day,
If people like us didn't eat, drink, and pay.
    So useful it is to have money, heigh-ho!
    So useful it is to have money.

One ought to be grateful, I quite apprehend,
Having dinner and supper and plenty to spend,
And so suppose now, while the things go away,
By way of a grace we all stand up and say
    How pleasant it is to have money, heigh-ho!
    How pleasant it is to have money.

ARTHUR HUGH CLOUGH

A Duke's Banquet

He won a great reputation as an eccentric – a reputation he crowned by adopting a costume of black velvet worn with a gold-fringed waistcoat and sticking by way of cravat a bunch of Parma violets in the opening of a very low-necked shirt. Then he would invite parties of literary friends to dinners that set all the world talking. In one instance in particular, modelling the entertainment on a banquet of the eighteenth century, he had organised a funeral feast in celebration of the most unmentionable of minor personal calamities. The dining-room was hung with black and looked out on a strangely metamorphosed garden, the walks being strewn with charcoal, the little basin in the middle of the lawn bordered with a rim of black basalt and filled with ink; and the ordinary shrubs superseded by cypresses and pines. The dinner itself was served on a black cloth, decorated with baskets of violets and scabiosæ and illuminated by candelabra in which tall tapers flared.

While a concealed orchestra played funeral marches, the guests were waited on by naked negresses wearing shoes and stockings of cloth of silver besprinkled with tears.

The viands were served on black-bordered plates – turtle soup, Russian black bread, ripe olives from Turkey, caviar, mule steaks, Frankfurt smoked sausages, game dished up in sauces coloured to resemble liquorice water and boot-blacking, truffles in jelly, chocolate-tinted creams, puddings, nectarines, fruit preserves, mulberries and cherries. The wines were drunk from dark-tinted glasses – wines of the Limagne and Roussillon vintages, wines of Tenedos, the Val de Peñas and Oporto. After the coffee and walnuts came other unusual beverages, kwas, porter and stout.

The invitations, which purported to be for a dinner in pious memory of the host's (temporarily) lost virility, were couched in the regulation phraseology of letters summoning relatives to attend the obsequies of a defunct kinsman.

JORIS KARL HUYSMANS, *À Rebours*

Dyspeptic Vision

23 January 1826: I dined yesterday with Kearsey, a man wallowing in the comforts of life & luxuries, and from ill health in consequence of too great a relish for them, rendered totally insensible & indifferent to their value or their enjoyment. There he lay, on a down sofa, with a Turkey carpet, a roaring fire, a beautiful garden, a nice house, a copious dinner, rich wines, tarts, confectionery, a carriage, horses, servants, & money, blasting every thing, cursing the gardeners, damning the frost, sneering at his cabbages, ridiculing the soil of his ground, groaning over his hay, scolding his wife, abusing his nephews, and saying if there was not another world, he had not been fairly used in this! – and why? Because he, being too fond of eating, had by an improper indulgence, brought on a diseased vision, which rendered his life a burthen. 'Christ Jesus, Lord Jesus, God Almighty,' said he, as he lay surrounded with comforts, 'what I suffer!'

BENJAMIN ROBERT HAYDON, Diary

An Epicurean Diet

We'll therefore go withal, my girl, and live
In a free state, where we will eat our mullets,
Soused in high-country wines, sup pheasant's eggs,
And have our cockles boil'd in silver shells;
Our shrimps to swim again, as when they liv'd,
In a rare butter made of dolphin's milk,
Whose cream does look like opals; and with these
Delicate meats set our selves high for pleasure,
And take us down again, and then renew
Our youth and strength with drinking the elixir,
And so enjoy a perpetuity
Of life and lust!

BEN JONSON, The Alchemist

A Heavy Meal

11 November 1791, Friday: We had for Dinner today at Weston House some fresh Salmon and Whitings, White-Soup, boiled Chicken and Pigg's Face, a Leg Mutton rosted, Pork Stakes, Goose-Giblets and Garden-Stuff. 2 Course, a brace of Pheasants and a brace of Partridges rosted, Trifle, Jelly, Blamange, Rammerkins, and some baked kind of Cakes. Desert, Pears and Apples, Almonds and Raisins, some India sweetmeats, Olives. Claret, Teneriffe, and Port Wines to drink. Mr Willm. Beauchamp slept and snored a good deal after Dinner and the Ladies were retired.

REV. JAMES WOODFORDE, *Diary of a Country Parson*

The Hour of Dinner

An excellent and well-arranged dinner is a most pleasing occurrence, and a great triumph of civilised life. It is not only the descending morsel, and the enveloping sauce – but the rank, wealth, wit, and beauty which surround the meats – the learned management of light and heat – the silent and rapid services of the attendants – the smiling and sedulous host, proffering gusts and relishes – the exotic bottles – the embossed plate – the pleasant remarks – the handsome dresses – the cunning artifices in fruit and farina! The hour of dinner, in short, includes everything of sensual and intellectual gratification which a great nation glories in producing.

In the midst of all this, who knows that the kitchen chimney caught fire half an hour before dinner! – and that a poor little wretch, of six or seven years old, was sent up in the midst of the flames to put it out.

REV. SYDNEY SMITH, *Chimney Sweepers*

In the old days I knew another kind of ruin that turned up regularly in the month of September. Figs, Melons, Peaches, Grapes, Quails, Partridges controlled our appetites, and our appetites our sobriety; so that when September came round, we used to say: *Now it is time to ruin our selves.*

SEIGNEUR DE SAINT EVREMONDE

Health that is purchased by a rigorous watching of the diet is but a tedious disease.

BARON DE MONTESQUIEU

When you heard him say the word ' succulent' you felt you were biting a ripe peach.

GEORG LICHTENBERG

If you are ever at a loss to support a flagging conversation, introduce the subject of eating.

JAMES LEIGH HUNT

A woman should never be seen eating or drinking, unless it be *lobster salad* and *champagne.*

LORD BYRON

A Hunger Artist

The longest period of fasting was fixed by his impresario at forty days, beyond that term he was not allowed to go, not even in great cities, and there was good reason for it, too. Experience had proved that for about forty days the interest of the public could be stimulated by a steadily increasing pressure of advertisement, but after that the town began to lose interest, sympathetic support began notably to fall off; there were of course local variations as between one town and another or one country and another, but as a general rule forty days marked the limit. So on the fortieth day the flower-bedecked cage was opened, enthusiastic spectators filled the hall, a military band played, two doctors entered the cage to measure the results of the fast, which were announced through a megaphone, and finally two young ladies appeared, blissful at having been selected for the honour, to help the hunger artist down the few steps leading to a small table on which was spread a carefully chosen invalid repast. And at this very moment the artist always turned stubborn. True, he would entrust his bony arms to the outstretched helping hands of the ladies bending over him, but stand up he would not. Why stop fasting at this particular moment, after forty days of it? He had held out for a long time, an illimitably long time; why stop now, when he was in his best fasting form, or rather, not yet quite in his best fasting form? Why should he be cheated of the fame he would get for fasting longer, for being not only the record hunger artist of all time, which presumably he was already, but for beating his own record by a performance beyond human imagination, since he felt that there were no limits to his capacity for fasting? His public pretended to admire him so much, why should it have so little patience with him; if he could endure fasting longer, why shouldn't the public endure it? Besides, he was tired, he was comfortable sitting in the straw, and now he was supposed to lift himself to his full height and go down to a meal the very thought of which gave him a nausea that only the presence of the ladies kept him from betraying, and even that with an effort. And he looked up into the eyes of the ladies who were apparently so friendly and in reality so cruel, and shook his head, which felt too heavy on its strengthless neck. But then there happened yet again what always happened. The impresario came forward, without a word – for the band made speech impossible – lifted his arms in the air above the artist, as if inviting Heaven to look down upon its creature here in the straw, this suffering martyr, which indeed he was, although in quite another sense; grasped him around the emaciated waist, with exaggerated caution, so that the frail condition he was in might be appreciated; and committed him to the care of the blenching ladies, not without secretly giving him a shaking so that his legs and body tottered and swayed. The artist now submitted completely; his head lolled on his breast as if it had landed there by chance; his body was hollowed out; his legs in a spasm of self-preservation clung close to each other at the knees, yet scraped on the ground as if it were not really solid ground, as if they were only trying to find solid ground; and the whole weight of his body, a featherweight after all, relapsed onto one of the ladies, who, looking around for help and panting a little – this post of honour was not at all what she had expected it to be – first stretched her neck as far as she could to keep her face at least free from contact with the artist, then finding this impossible, and her more fortunate companion not coming to her aid but merely holding extended in her own trembling hand the little bunch of knucklebones that was the artist's, to the great delight of the spectators burst into tears and had to be replaced by an attendant who had long been stationed in readiness. Then came the food, a little of which the impresario managed to get between the artist's lips, while he sat in a kind of half-fainting trance, to the accompaniment of cheerful patter designed to distract the public's attention from the artist's condition; after that, a toast was drunk to the public, supposedly prompted by a whisper from the artist in the impresario's ear; the band confirmed it with a mighty flourish, the spectators melted away, and no one had any cause to be dissatisfied with the proceedings, no one except the hunger artist himself, he only, as always.

FRANZ KAFKA, *Collected Short Stories*

Indigestion

I feel as if a nest of rats were nibbling my bowels, while a horrible dwarf, a hooded goblin, wearing a red tunic, and shoes, had gone down into my stomach, and was attacking it with a pick-axe, and making a deep hole.

ANATOLE FRANCE, *King Christophe*

Marrow-Bone Pye

After you have mixt the crusts of the best sort for pasts, and raised the coffin in such a manner as you please; you shall first in the bottome thereof lay a course of marrow of beef, mixt with currants; then upon it a lay of the soals of artichokes, after they have been boyled and are divided from the thistle; then cover them with marrow, currants, and great raisins, the stones pickt out; then lay a course of potatoes cut in thick slices, after they have been boiled soft, and are clean pilled; then cover them with marrow, currants, great raisins, sugar and cinnamon; then lay a layer of candied eringo roots mixt very thick with the slices of dates; then cover it with marrow, currants, great raisins, sugar, cinnamon, and dates, with a few Damask prunes, and so bake it; and after it is bak't, pour into it, as long as it will receive it, white wine, rosewater, sugar and cinnamon and vinegar mixt together, and candy all the cover with rosewater and sugar only, and so set it into the oven a little, and serve it forth.

GERVASE MARKHAM, *The English House-Wife, containing the inward and outward Vertues which ought to be in a Compleat Woman* (1611)

The Most Nourishing Diet

To eat much at other men's cost, and little at his owne, is the wholesomest and most nourishing diet, both in court and country.

SIR THOMAS OVERBURY, *Characters*

Oysters

'Oysters,' I read on the notice.

A strange word. I had lived in the world already eight years and three months, and had never heard this word. What did it mean? Was it the proprietor's surname? No, for signboards with innkeepers' names hang outside the doors, and not on the walls inside.

'Father, what are oysters?' I asked hoarsely, trying to turn my face towards his.

My father did not hear me. He was looking at the flow of the crowd, and following every passer-by with his eyes. From his face I judged that he dearly longed to speak to the passers, but the fatal, leaden words hung on his trembling lips, and would not tear themselves off. One passer-by he even stopped and touched on the sleeve, but when the man turned to him my father stammered, 'I beg your pardon,' and fell back in confusion.

'Papa, what does "oysters" mean?' I repeated.

'It is a kind of animal ... It lives in the sea ...'

And in a wink I visualised this mysterious animal. Something between a fish and a crab, it must be, I concluded; and as it came from the sea, of course it made up into delightful dishes, hot *bouillabaisse* with fragrant peppercorns and bay leaves, or sour *solianka* with gristle, crab-sauce, or cold with horseradish ... I vividly pictured to myself how this fish is brought from the market, cleaned, and thrust quickly into a pot ... quickly, quickly, because every one is hungry ... frightfully hungry. From the restaurant kitchen came the smell of boiled fish and crab soup.

This smell began to tickle my palate and nostrils; I felt it permeating my whole body. The restaurant, my father, the white notice, my sleeve, all exhaled it so strongly that I began to chew. I chewed and swallowed as if my mouth were really full of the strange animal that lives in the sea ...

The pleasure was too much for my strength, and to prevent myself falling I caught my father's cuff, and leaned against his wet summer overcoat. My father shuddered. He was cold ...

'Father, can you eat oysters on fast days?' I asked.

'You eat them alive ...' he answered. 'They are in shells ... like tortoises, only in double shells.'

The seductive smell suddenly ceased to tickle my nostrils, and the illusion faded. Now I understood!

'How horrible!' I exclaimed. ' How hideous!'

So that was the meaning of oysters! However, hideous as they were, my imagination could paint them. I imagined an animal like a frog. The frog sat in the shell, looked out with big, bright eyes, and moved its disgusting jaws. What on earth could be more horrible to a boy who had lived in the world just eight years and three months? Frenchmen, they said, ate frogs. But children – never! And I saw this fish being carried from market in its shell, with claws, bright eyes, and shiny tail ... The children all hide themselves, and the cook, blinking squeamishly, takes the animal by the claws, puts it on a dish, and carries it to the dining-room. The grown-ups take it, and eat ... eat it alive, eyes, teeth, claws. And it hisses, and tries to bite their lips.

I frowned disgustedly. But why did my teeth begin to chew? An animal, disgusting, detestable, frightful, but still I ate it, ate it greedily, fearing to notice its taste and smell. I ate in imagination, and my nerves seemed braced, and my heart beat stronger ... One animal was finished, already I saw the bright eyes of a second, a third ... I ate these also. At last I ate the table-napkin, the plate, my father's goloshes, the white notice ... I ate everything before me, because I felt that only eating would cure my complaint. The oysters glared frightfully from their bright eyes, they made me sick, I shuddered at the thought of them, but I wanted to eat. To eat!

'Give me some oysters! Give me some oysters.' The cry burst from my lips, and I stretched out my hands.

'Give me a kopeck, gentlemen!' I heard suddenly my father's dulled, choked voice. 'I am ashamed to ask, but, my God, I can bear it no longer!'

'Give me some oysters!' I cried, seizing my father's coat-tails.

'And so you eat oysters! Such a little whipper-snapper!' I heard a voice beside me.

Before me stood two men in silk hats, and looked at me with a laugh.

'Do you mean to say that this little manikin eats oysters? Really! This is too delightful! How does he eat them?'

I remember a strong hand dragged me into the glaring restaurant. In a minute a crowd had gathered, and looked at me with curiosity and amusement. I sat at a table, and ate something slippy, damp, and mouldy. I ate greedily, not chewing, not daring to look, not even knowing what I ate. It seemed to me that if I opened my eyes, I should see at once the bright eyes, the claws, the sharp teeth.

I began to chew something hard. There was a crunching sound.

'Good heavens, he's eating the shells!' laughed the crowd. 'Donkey, who ever heard of eating oyster shells?'

After this, I remember only my terrible thirst. I lay on my bed, kept awake by repletion, and by a strange taste in my hot mouth. My father walked up and down the room and gesticulated.

'I have caught cold, I think!' he said. 'I feel something queer in my head ... As if there is something inside it ... But perhaps it is only... because I had no food to-day. I have been strange altogether ... stupid. I saw those gentlemen paying ten roubles for oysters; why didn't I go and ask them for something ... in loan? I am sure they would have given it.'

Towards morning I fell asleep, and dreamed of a frog sitting in a shell and twitching its eyes. At midday thirst awoke me. I sought my father; he still walked up and down the room and gesticulated.

ANTON CHEKHOV, *Oysters*

The pleasures of Paris soon destroy a man, whereas provincial debauch pushes him gently into obesity.

EDMOND ABOUT

Man is a cooking animal.

Cornhill Magazine, 1862

Love and gluttony justify everything.

OSCAR WILDE

There is no love sincerer than the love of food.

GEORGE BERNARD SHAW

The rich have cooks who rob and poison them. The greatest cooks are those that rob and poison the most.

ANATOLE FRANCE

I hate with a bitter hatred the name of lentils and haricots – those pretentious cheats of the appetite, those tabulated humbugs, those certificated avidities calling themselves human food.

GEORGE GISSING

People Dig Their Graves With Their Teeth

'You see, Sir Harry,' he would say, 'it's all done by eating. More people dig their graves with their teeth than we imagine. Not that I would deny you the good things of this world, but I would recommend a few at a time, and no mixing. No side dishes. No liqueurs – only two or three wines. Whatever your stomach fancies, give it. Begin now, tomorrow, with the waters. A pint before breakfast – half an hour after, tea, fried ham, and eggs, brown bread, and a walk. Luncheon – another pint – a roast pigeon and fried potatoes, then a ride. Dinner at six, not later, mind; gravy soup, glass of sherry, nice fresh turbot and lobster sauce – wouldn't recommend salmon – another glass of sherry – then a good cut out of the middle of a well-browned saddle of mutton, wash it over with a few glasses of iced champagne; and if you like a little light pastry to wind up with, well and good. A pint of old port and a devilled biscuit can hurt no man. Mind, no salads, or cucumbers, or celery, at dinner, or fruit after. Turtle soup is very wholesome, so is venison. Don't let the punch be too acid though. Drink the water, live on a regimen, and you'll be well in no time.'

208

With these and suchlike comfortable assurances, he pocketed his guineas and bowed his patients out by the dozen.

ROBERT SURTEES, *Handley Cross*

Pig and Plumb Sauce

Do but recollect how many hard-featured fellows there are in the world that frown in the midst of enjoyment, chew with unthankfulness, and seem to swallow with pain instead of pleasure; now anyone who sees you eat pig and plumb sauce, immediately *feels that pleasure* which a plump morsel, smoothly gliding through a narrow glib passage into the regions of bliss and moistened with the dew of imagination, naturally creates.

THOMAS GAINSBOROUGH, letter of 18 July 1773

Rôti Sans Pareil

Take a large olive, stone it and stuff it with a paste made of anchovy, capers and oil.

Put the olive inside a trussed and boned bec-figue (garden warbler).
Put the bec-figue inside a fat ortolan.
Put the ortolan inside a boned lark.
Put the stuffed lark inside a boned thrush.
Put the thrush inside a fat quail.
Put the quail, wrapped in vine-leaves, inside a boned lapwing.
Put the lapwing inside a boned golden plover.
Put the plover inside a fat, boned, red-legged partridge.
Put the partridge inside a young, boned, and well-hung woodcock.
Put the woodcock, rolled in bread-crumbs, inside a boned teal.
Put the teal inside a boned guinea-fowl.
Put the guinea-fowl, well larded, inside a young and boned tame duck.
Put the duck inside a boned and fat fowl.

Put the fowl inside a well-hung pheasant.

Put the pheasant inside a boned and fat wild goose.

Put the goose inside a fine turkey.

Put the turkey inside a boned bustard.

Having arranged your roast after this fashion, place it in a saucepan of proper size with onions stuffed with cloves, carrots, small squares of ham, celery, mignonette, several strips of bacon well seasoned, pepper, salt, spice, coriander seeds, and two cloves of garlic.

Seal the saucepan hermetically by closing it with pastry. Then put it for ten hours over a gentle fire, and arrange it so that the heat penetrates evenly. An oven moderately heated would suit better than the hearth.

Before serving, remove the pastry, put your roast on a hot dish after having removed the grease, if there is any, and serve.

NORMAN DOUGLAS, *Venus in the Kitchen*

Russian Cuisine

If one is to judge from the restaurants at Moscow there is no better place in the world to come to in order to try the temper. The best of them is dear and bad beyond comparison, and the only things good are the wine and the bread. It must be admitted that the latter is excellent, light, sweet, white, and wholesome, and our London bakers would do well if they came to Moscow for an apprenticeship in the art of making bread. It is very hard to have to pay £1 for cabbage soup, *filet du cheval*, a bit of bad fish, one stewed pear, and a bottle of light French wine; but it is harder still to wait for twenty minutes between every dish, while leaden-eyed waiters are staring at you with a mixture of contempt and compassion because of your ignorance of the Russian tongue. Tired, cross, and dyspeptic, the stranger seeks a Russian dining room where the arts of French cookery have never been employed to render bad meat still worse. There, amid the odours of tobacco – for a Russian not being able to smoke in the streets makes up for it *chez lui* – you resign yourself to an unknown bill of fare and the caprices of your bearded attendant. It is fair to say of the said waiter, that he is clad in a milk-white and scrupulously clean robe, which descends in easy folds from his neck to his heels, so that he looks like a very high priest of the deity of gastronomy, and that you need not be as uneasy about his fingers and hands as you have good cause to be in the Russo-French restaurants. First you will be presented with a huge bowl of cabbage soup, a kind of *pot-au-feu*, which must be eaten, however, with several odd adjuncts, such as cakes stuffed with chopped vegetables, a dish of guelots, chopped fat, fried brown and crisp, and lastly a large ewer full of sour milk. Then comes a *vol-au-vent* of fowl and toadstools. Next, if you are alive, *porosenok*, or a boiled sucking pig, with tart sauce; then a very nasty little fish, much prized in Moscow, and called sterlet; a fid of roast beef and a dish of birds about the size of pigeons, called guillemots; a compote of fruit closes the meal. I have forgotten to say how it begins. Before dinner a tray is laid out with caviare, raw salt herrings, raw ham and sardines, bottles of brandy, vodka, anisette, and doppel kümmel, a sweet spirit with a flavour of mint. It is *de rigueur* to eat some of this, and as the caviare is generally good, it is the best part of the dinner.

PETER LUND SIMMONDS, The Curiosities of Food (1859)

A Sybarite's Pampered Wishes

The dinner made about a hundred dishes;
  Lamb and pistachio nuts – in short, all meats,
And saffron soups, and sweetbreads; and the fishes
  Were of the finest that e'er flounced in nets,
Drest to a Sybarite's most pamper'd wishes;
  The beverage was various sherbets
Of raisin, orange, and pomegranate juice,
Squeezed through the rind, which makes it best for use.

These were ranged round, each in its crystal ewer,
  And fruits, and date-bread loaves closed the repast,
And Mocha's berry, from Arabia pure,
  In small fine China cups, came in at last;

> Gold cups of filigree made to secure
>   The hand from burning underneath them placed,
> Cloves, cinnamon, and saffron too were boil'd
> Up with the coffee, which (I think) they spoil'd.

LORD BYRON

Theft in a Cake Shop

Baby pulled himself up on the smooth wall like a monkey, pushed in the cardboard without a sound, and stuck his head through. It was then that he became aware of the smell; he took a deep breath and up through his nostrils wafted an aroma of freshly baked cakes. It gave him a feeling of shy excitement, of remote tenderness, rather than of actual greed.

'Oh, what a lot of cakes there must be in here,' he thought. It was years since he had eaten a proper bit of cake, not since before the war perhaps. He decided to search around till he found them. He jumped down into the darkness, kicked against a telephone, got a broomstick up his trouser-leg, and then hit the ground. The smell of cakes was stronger than ever, but he couldn't tell where it was coming from.

'Yes, there must be a lot of cakes in here,' thought Baby.

He reached out a hand, trying to feel his way in the dark, so as to reach the door and open it for Dritto. Quickly he recoiled in horror; he must be face to face with some animal, some soft, slimy sea-thing, perhaps. He stood there with his hand in the air, a hand that had suddenly become damp and sticky, as if covered with leprosy. Between the fingers had sprouted something round and soft, an excrescence, a tumour perhaps. He strained his eyes in the dark but could see nothing, not even when he put his hand under his nose. But he could smell, even though he could not see; and he burst out laughing. He realised he had touched a tart and was holding a blob of cream and a crystallised cherry.

At once he began licking the hand, and groping around with the other at the same time. It touched something solid but soft, with a thin covering of fine sugar; a doughnut! Still groping, he popped the whole of it into his mouth and gave a little cry of pleasure on discovering it had jam inside. It really was the most wonderful place; whatever way he stretched his hand out in the darkness, it found new kinds of cakes.

He was suddenly aware of an impatient knocking on a door nearby; it was Dritto waiting to be let in. Baby moved towards the sound and his hands bumped first into a meringue and then into an almond cake. He opened the door and Dritto's torch lit up his little face with its moustaches already white with cream.

'It's full of cakes, here!' exclaimed Baby, as if the other did not know.

'This isn't a time for cakes,' said Dritto, pushing him aside. 'We've got to hurry.' And he went ahead twisting the beam of his torch round in the dark. Everywhere it touched it lit up rows of shelves, and on the shelves rows of trays, and on the trays rows of cakes of every conceivable shape and colour, tarts filled with cream glittering like candle wax, and piles of sugar-coated buns and castles of almond cakes.

It was then that a terrible worry came over Baby; the worry of not having time to eat all he wanted, of being forced to make his escape before he had sampled all the different kinds of cakes, of having all this land of milk and honey at his disposal only for a few minutes in his whole life. And the more cakes he discovered, the more his anxiety increased, and every new corner and every fresh view of the shop that was lit up by Dritto's torch seemed to be about to shut him off.

He flung himself on the shelves, choking himself with cakes, cramming two or three inside his mouth at a time, without even tasting them; he seemed to be battling with the cakes, as if they were threatening enemies, strange monsters besieging him, a crisp and sticky siege which he must break through by the force of his jaw. The slit halves of the big sugared buns seemed to be opening yellow throats and eyes at him, the cream-horns to be blossoming like flowers of carnivorous plants; for a horrible moment Baby had the feeling that it was he who was being devoured by the cakes.

Dritto pulled him by the arm. 'The till,' he said. 'We've got to open the till.'

At the same time, as he passed, he stuffed a piece of multi-coloured sponge into his mouth, a cherry off a tart and then a brioche, hurriedly as if anxious not to be distracted from the job on hand. He had switched off his torch.

'From outside they could see us quite clearly,' he said.

They had now reached the front of the cakeshop with its showcases and marbled top counters. Through the grilled shutters the lights from the street came in streaks, and could be seen outside casting strange shadows on the trees and houses.

Now the moment had come to force the till.

'Hold this,' said Dritto, handing the torch to Baby with the beam pointing downwards so that it could not be seen from outside.

But Baby was holding the torch with one hand and groping around with the other. He seized an entire plum cake, and while Dritto was busy at the lock with his tools, began chewing it as if it were a loaf of bread. But he soon tired of it and left it half eaten on the marble slab.

'Get away from there! Look what a filthy mess you're making,' hissed Dritto through clenched teeth; in spite of his trade he had a strange respect for tidy work. Then he, too, couldn't resist the temptation and stuffed two biscuits, the kind that were half sponge and half chocolate, into his mouth, without interrupting his work though.

Now Baby, in order to have both hands free, had constructed a kind of lampshade from tray cloths and pieces of nougat. He then espied some large cakes with 'Happy Birthday' written on them. He moved round them, studying the plan of attack; first he reviewed them with a finger and licked off a bit of chocolate cream, then he buried his face inside and began biting them from the middle one by one.

But he still felt a kind of frenzy which he did not know how to satisfy; he could not discover any way of enjoying everything completely. Now he was crouching on all fours over a table laden with tarts; he would have liked to lie down in those tarts, cover himself with them and never have to leave them. But five or ten minutes from now it would be all over; for the rest of his life cakeshops would be out of bounds to him again, for ever, like when he was a child squashing his nose against the window-pane. If only, at least, he could stay there three or four hours ...

'Dritto,' he exclaimed. 'Suppose we hide here till dawn, who'll see us?'

'Don't be a fool,' said Dritto, who had now succeeded in forcing the till and was searching round among the notes. 'We've got to get out of here before the cops arrive.'

Just at that moment they heard a knock on the window In the dim moonlight Uora-Uora could be seen knocking on the blind and making signs to them. The two in the shop gave a jump, but Uora-Uora motioned for them to keep calm and for Baby to come out and take his place, so that he could come in. The other two shook their fists and showed their teeth at him and made signs for him to get away from the front of the shop, if he didn't want his brains blown out.

Dritto, however, had found only a few thousand *lire* in the till, and was cursing and blaming Baby for not trying to help him. But Baby seemed beside himself; he was biting into doughnuts, picking up raisins, licking syrups, plastering himself all over and leaving sticky marks on the show-cases and counters. He found that he no longer had any desire for cakes, in fact a feeling of nausea was beginning to creep up from the pit of his stomach, but he refused to believe it, he simply could not give up yet. And the doughnuts began to turn into soggy pieces of sponge, the tarts to flypaper and the cakes to asphalt. Now he saw only the corpses of cakes lying putrifying on their marble slabs, or felt them disintegrating like turgid glue inside his stomach.

Dritto was now cursing and swearing at the lock on another till, forgetful of cakes and hunger. Suddenly from the back of the shop appeared Uora-Uora swearing in his Sicilian dialect, which was quite unintelligible to either of them.

'The cops?' they asked, already pale.

'Change of guard! Change of guard!' Uora-Uora was croaking in his dialect, trying hard to explain how unjust it was to leave him starving out in the cold while they guzzled cakes inside.

'Go back and keep guard, go and keep guard!' shouted Baby angrily, the nausea from having eaten too much making him feel savage and selfish.

Dritto knew that it was only fair to Uora-Uora to make the change, but he also knew that Baby would not be convinced so easily, and without someone on guard they couldn't stay. So he pulled out his revolver and pointed it at Uora-Uora.

'Back to your post at once, Uora-Uora,' he said.

Desperately, Uora-Uora thought of getting some supplies before leaving, and gathered a small pile of little almond cakes with nuts on them in his big hands.

'And suppose they catch you with your hands full of cakes, you fool, what'll you tell them?' Dritto swore at him. 'Leave them all there and get out.'

Uora-Uora burst into tears. Baby felt he hated him. He picked up a cake with 'Happy Birthday' written on it and flung it in his face. Uora-Uora could easily have avoided it, instead of which he stuck his face out to get the full force, then burst out laughing, as his face, hat and tie were all covered in cream cake. Off he went, licking himself right up to his nose and cheeks.

At last Dritto succeeded in forcing the till and was stuffing all the notes he could find into his pocket, cursing because they stuck to his jammy fingers.

'Come on, Baby, time to go,' he said.

But Baby could not leave just like that; this was a feast to be talked over for years to come with his cronies and with Tuscan Mary. Tuscan Mary was Baby's girl-friend; she had long smooth legs and a face and body that were almost horse-like. Baby liked her because he could curl himself up and wind round her like a cat.

Uora-Uora's second entry interrupted the course of these thoughts. Dritto quickly pulled out his revolver, but Uora-Uora shouted 'The cops!' and rushed off, flapping the ends of his raincoat. Dritto gathered up the last few notes and was at the door in a couple of leaps; and Baby behind.

Baby was still thinking of Tuscan Mary and it was then that he remembered he might have taken her some cakes; he never gave her a present and she might make a scene about it. He went back, snatched up some cream-rolls, thrust them under his shirt, then quickly thinking that he had chosen the most fragile ones, looked around for something more solid and stuffed those into his bosom too. At that moment he saw the shadows of policemen moving on the window, waving their arms and pointing at something at the end of the street; and one of them aimed a revolver in that direction and fired.

Baby squatted down behind a counter. The shot did not seem to have hit its target; now they were making angry gestures and peering inside the shop. Shortly after he heard them finding the little door open, and then coming in. Now the shop was teeming with armed policemen. Baby remained crouched there, but meanwhile he found some candied fruit within arm's reach and chewed at slivers of citron and bergamot to calm his nerves.

The police had now discovered the theft and also found the remains of half-eaten cakes on the shelves. And so, distractedly, they, too, began to nibble little cakes that were lying about, taking care, though, to leave the traces of the thieves. After a few moments, becoming more enthusiastic in their search for evidence, they were all eating away heartily.

Baby was chewing, but the others were chewing even more loudly and drowned the sound. All of a sudden he felt a thick liquid oozing up from between his skin and his shirt, and a mounting nausea from his stomach. He was so dizzy with candied fruit that it was some time before he realised that the way to the door was free. The police described later how they had seen a monkey with its nose plastered with cream swing across the shop, overturning trays and tarts; and how by the time that they had recovered from their amazement and cleared the tarts from under their feet, he had escaped.

When Baby got to Tuscan Mary's and opened his shirt, he found his whole chest covered with a strange sticky paste. And they stayed till morning, he and she, lying on the bed licking and picking at each other till they had finished the last crumb of cake and blob of cream.

ITALO CALVINO, *Adam, One Afternoon*

A Wonderful Closet

Above it, a portrait of Handel in a flowing wig beamed down at the spectator, with a knowing air of being up to the contents of the closet, and a musical air of intending to combine all its harmonies in one delicious fugue. No common closet with a vulgar door on hinges, openable all at once, and leaving nothing to be disclosed by degrees, this rare closet had a lock in mid-air, where two perpendicular slides met; the one falling down, and the other pushing up. The upper slide, on being pulled down (leaving the lower a double mystery), revealed deep shelves of pickle-jars, jam-pots, tin canisters, spice-boxes, and agreeably outlandish vessels of blue and white, the luscious lodgings of preserved tamarinds and ginger. Every benevolent inhabitant of this retreat had his name inscribed upon his stomach. The pickles, in a uniform of rich brown double-breasted buttoned coat, and yellow or sombre drab continuations, announced their portly forms, in printed capitals, as Walnut, Gherkin, Onion, Cabbage, Cauliflower, Mixed, and other members of that noble family. The jams, as being of a less masculine temperament, and as wearing curlpapers, announced themselves in feminine caligraphy, like a soft whisper, to be Raspberry, Gooseberry, Apricot, Plum, Damson, Apple, and Peach. The scene closing on these charmers, and the lower slide ascending, oranges were revealed, attended by a mighty japanned sugar-box, to temper their acerbity if unripe. Home-made biscuits waited at the Court of these Powers, accompanied by a goodly fragment of plum-cake, and various slender ladies' fingers, to be dipped into sweet wine and kissed. Lowest of all, a compact leaden vault enshrined the sweet wine and a stock of cordials: whence issued whispers of Seville Orange, Lemon, Almond, and Caraway-seed. There was a crowning air upon this closet of closets, of having been for ages hummed through by the Cathedral bell and organ, until those venerable bees had made sublimated honey of everything in store; and it was always observed that every dipper among the shelves (deep, as has been noticed, and swallowing up head, shoulders, and elbows) came forth again mellow-faced, and seeming to have undergone a saccharine transfiguration.

CHARLES DICKENS, *The Mystery of Edwin Drood*

Gambling

Nothing brings a man sooner into fashion and increases his importance more than gambling; it is almost as good as getting drunk.

JEAN DE LA BRUYÈRE

Death and dice level all distinctions.

SAMUEL FOOTE

It is the child of avarice, the brother of iniquity and the father of mischief.

GEORGE WASHINGTON

There is no pleasure in winning money from a man who doesn't feel it.

MARQUESS OF HERTFORD

Gamblers are as happy as most people, being always *excited*; women – wine – fame – the table – even Ambition – *sate* now & then – but every turn of the card – & cast of the dice – keeps the Gambler alive – besides one can Game ten times longer than one can do anything else.

LORD BYRON

Adamant Cruel and Terrible

Gamblers play just as lovers make love and drunkards drink – blindly and of necessity, under domination of an irresistible force. There are beings vowed to play, as there are others vowed to love. I wonder who invented the story of the two sailors who were so possessed by the lust of gambling? They were shipwrecked, and only escaped a watery grave, after experiencing the most appalling vicissitudes, by climbing on the back of a whale. The instant they were installed there, they lugged out of their pockets dice and dice-boxes and settled themselves down to play. The story is truer than truth. Every gambler is like those sailors. And in every deed there is something in play that does terribly stir the fibres of daring hearts. Is it an insignificant delight to tempt fortune? Is it a pleasure devoid of intoxication to taste in one second months, years, a whole lifetime of fears and hopes?

What is play, I should like to know, but the art of producing in a second the changes that Destiny ordinarily effects only in the course of many hours or even many years, the art of collecting into a single instant the emotions dispersed throughout the slow-moving existence of ordinary men, the secret of living a whole lifetime in a few minutes? Play is a hand-to-hand encounter with Fate. It is the wrestling of Jacob with the Angel, the pact of Doctor Faustus with the Devil. The stake is money – in other words immediate, infinite possibilities of pleasure. Perhaps the next card turned, the ball now rolling, will give the player parks and gardens, fields and forests, castles and manors lifting heavenward their pointed turrets and fretted roofs. Yes, that little dancing ball holds within it acres of good land and roofs of slate with sculptured chimneys reflected in the broad bosom of the Loire; it contains treasures of art, marvels of taste, jewels of price, the most exquisite bodies in all the world, nay! even souls – souls none ever dreamt were venal, all the decorations, all the distinctions, all the elegance, and all the puissance of the world. What do I say? It contains better than that; it embraces the dream and vision of it all. And you would have me give up play? Nay; if play only availed to give endless hopes, if our only vision of it were the smile of its green eyes, it would be loved less fanatically. But it has nails of adamant, it is cruel and terrible, at its caprice it gives poverty and wretchedness and shame; that is why its votaries adore it.

The fascination of danger is at the bottom of all great passions. There is no fullness of pleasure unless the precipice is near. It is the mingling of terror with delight that intoxicates. And what more terrifying than play? It gives and takes away; its logic is not our logic. It is dumb and blind and deaf. It is almighty. It is a God.

Yes, a God; it has its votaries and its saints, who love it for itself, not for what it promises, and who fall down in adoration when its blow strikes them. It strips them ruthlessly, and they lay the blame on themselves, not on their deity.

'I played a bad game,' they say.

They find fault with themselves; they do not blaspheme their God.

ANATOLE FRANCE, *The Garden of Epicurus*

Backgammon

One day a Dutch frigate came into the harbour. The officers invited us to dinner. We drank copiously of all sorts of wines; and when the cloth was removed, not knowing what to do, for our hosts spoke very bad French, we began to play. The Dutchmen seemed to have plenty of money; and their first lieutenant especially wanted to play for such high stakes that none of us cared to take him on. But Roger, who did not play as a rule, felt it incumbent on him on this occasion to uphold the honour of his country. So he played for the stakes that the Dutch lieutenant proposed. At first he won, then he lost, and after several changes of fortune they separated without any decisive result. We returned this dinner, and invited the Dutch officers. Again we played, and Roger and the lieutenant got to grips once more. In short, they played for several days, meeting either in cafés or on board ship; they tried all sorts of games, especially backgammon, steadily increasing their stakes until they came to the point of playing for twenty-five napoleons a game. This was an enormous sum for poverty-stricken officers like us – more than two months' pay! At the end of a week Roger had lost every penny he possessed, and more than three or four thousand francs which he had borrowed right and left.

As you may imagine, Roger and Gabrielle had ended up by sharing bed and purse; that is to say that Roger, who had just received a large payment in the way of prize-money, had contributed ten or twenty times more than the actress. However, he still considered that this sum belonged chiefly to his mistress, and he had only kept back for his own expenses about fifty napoleons. All the same, he had been obliged to draw on this reserve to go on playing, and Gabrielle did not raise the slightest objection.

The housekeeping money went the same way as his pocket-money. Soon Roger was reduced to playing his last twenty-five napoleons. He concentrated all his attention on the game, so it was lengthy and hotly contested. The moment came when Roger, who held the dice-box, had only one chance left to win; I think he had to get a six and a four. The night was far advanced, and an officer who had been watching them play for a long time, had ended up by falling asleep in an arm-chair. The Dutchman was tired and drowsy; moreover, he had drunk a great deal of punch. Roger alone was wide awake and a prey to the most violent despair. He trembled as he threw the dice. He threw them so roughly on to the board that the shock knocked a candle over on to the floor. The Dutchman turned his head first towards the candle, which had just spattered his new trousers with wax, and then looked at the dice. They showed six and four. Roger, who was as pale as death, received the twenty-five napoleons, and they went on playing. Chance began to favour my unlucky friend, for all that he made blunder after blunder and secured points as if he had wanted to lose. The Dutch lieutenant refused to give in, and doubled and quadrupled his stakes; he lost every time. I can see him now – a tall, fair, phlegmatic fellow, whose face seemed to be made of wax. At last he got up, having lost forty thousand francs, and paid them over without his features betraying the least trace of emotion.

'We won't count tonight,' Roger said to him. 'You were half asleep. I don't want your money.'

'You are joking,' replied the phlegmatic Dutchman; 'I played very well, but the dice were against me. I am sure I can easily beat you another time. Good night!'

And he went out.

We learnt the next day that, driven to despair by his losses, he had blown out his brains in his room, after drinking a bowl of punch.

PROSPER MÉRIMÉE, The Game of Backgammon

Bakers and Butchers

Even one's fellow passengers on this line seemed often unusual; intriguingly criminal or suggestively odd. One Sunday in December, some card sharpers got into my carriage. Their leader, a scarlet-faced man in a check cap, opened the conversation by exclaiming heartily: 'Well, Christmas is here!' He offered all of us his cigarettes; stretched himself, gave a large theatrical yawn: 'Been at the club, all night,' he told his two friends, 'playing with a Yankee.' 'What were you playing?' one of the friends asked. The red-faced man didn't answer directly; he smiled round at us, knowingly, tantalisingly: 'We played for a turkey a point.' 'What were you playing – cards?' '*Cards?*' (with great scorn) '*No!* We were playing – and I beat him every round.' 'You were boxing, perhaps?' the accomplice suggested; winking at us, as if to say that this was a lunatic who must be humoured. The man in the check cap laughed out loud: '*Boxing?* That's good! *No!* We played two into four, four into six, six into eight, eight into ten, ten into nothing …' 'Come on, now,' interrupted the other accomplice, 'we don't want to hear all that. We want to know what you were playing. Was it billiards?' '*Billiards?* Ha, ha!' Deliberately, timing his effect, check-cap produced from his pocket three greasy cards, and laid them, as carefully as if they had been banknotes, on a piece of newspaper unfolded on his lap: 'Just take a look at these.' We all stared, unwillingly fascinated – an elderly farmer in leggings, with his wife, a bullet-headed young man and his girl, a mild gold-spectacled bank clerk in the corner, who had been reading *Our Mutual Friend*. 'This morning there's a match between the Bakers and the Butchers: who do you say'll win, sir?' The red-faced man addressed me: ' The Butchers have got more beef, but the Bakers have got more dough.' He began to run the cards through his fingers, picking them up, showing them, throwing them down, over and over again, with a mechanical regularity which was, perhaps intentionally, hypnotic. At first, only the two accomplices betted. Three or four times, they lost. Then one of them, winking at the company, turned up the corner of a card. After this, he won, again and again. Check-cap kept trying to draw us into the game: we were all shy, except the bank clerk, who said that he didn't want to bet, but he thought he could spot the ace. He did spot it, needless to say; and check-cap tried to force him to accept a shilling. Within five minutes, the bank clerk was betting; within ten, he had lost five shillings. He was indignant. The two accomplices soothed him by taking his side; and check-cap, as he pocketed the money, said kindly but reproachfully: 'You're not a cry-baby, are you, sir?' They all three got out at Maryland Point. Check-cap shook hands with the farmer and his wife: 'Always shake hands with the old folks,' he told us. 'Good morning, ladies and gentlemen. Happy Christmas!' When he had gone, there was a general outburst of conversation and mutual sympathy in the carriage. We all congratulated ourselves on our shrewdness and consoled the bank clerk for his loss. 'We thought you was one of them, see?' the bullet-headed young man explained; and his girl confided: 'We'd been warned, you know – only last night. Just fancy!' 'Ah well,' sighed the bank clerk, philosophically, 'they say it takes all sorts to make a world.' He adjusted his spectacles and reopened *Our Mutual Friend*. The farmer and his wife said nothing. They just sat there, with their oblique sparkling little eyes, smiling fatly and seeming pleased.

CHRISTOPHER ISHERWOOD, *Lions and Shadows*

Childish, Reprehensible, Superstitious

Childish, he thought; reprehensible, superstitious; the game that could become too important; and nobody who hadn't the virus in his blood could understand what you meant when you said 'the game'. To the non-addict, roulette was simply a wheel that spun and sent a ball by chance into a socket with a number. The chances against your chosen number were thirty-five to one; and that was all; and it was idiocy.

To David and his kind, roulette was not only the most beguiling of all battles between oneself and the gods, it was a mystical experience.

Like other mystical experiences, it was largely unshareable; not to be communicated. Any attempt to communicate with those who did not know turned you into something one degree sillier than the golf bore. Your talk was gibberish, 'I had a *mille* on the *quatre premier*; two came up and I doubled, and, damn it, three came up twice running. After that, of course, I had to cover the twenty-six, but I *didn't* forget my darling twenty-one, which, in simple arithmetic, was pretty obvious, coming after the three.' Only a fellow-mystic would see the beauty of it. (Only a fellow-mystic knew that you could fall in love with a certain number and remain faithful; or find suddenly that your ardour had cooled and that this year you loved the seventeen instead.) Linda, like other sane persons, would ask, 'How much did you win?' Or, should she know what had happened next, 'You ought to have stopped there.'

David drank his brandy at leisure. He was in a mood of luminous tranquillity. The novel, for better or worse, was inching its way forward on paper. He had given eight hours to it every day, for a week. He had drunk nothing stronger than *rosé* and he had kept out of the Casino for what seemed a lifetime and was in fact eleven days.

Last time, Linda had been with him, staying away from his table, never asking how it went, ready to drink with him when he took time out from the enjoyable warfare, demonstrably content to wander and watch the play; the gambler's wife wearing her psychological approach on her sleeve. Nor had she asked him about his losses. 'Because,' she had said before this, 'you'd only lie. You're pedantically honest. Outside a Casino, you're the most truthful person I know. The moment you connect with this imbecile game, you become the biggest liar in five continents.'

He set down his glass. The hot room, with the windows open to the Mediterranean night, shimmered for him with the magic of Tom Tiddler's ground. He lingered, lighting a cigarette. This was his last chance of detachment from the crowd before he went down and in and was one of them; the murmurous devotees, solemn and savage with concentration, held at each table by the invisible threads of their faith. Really, he thought, they were extremely funny. And the tables themselves were funny too; each one a point of heavy significance in the room, as though surgical operations were taking place on them. They looked a little like operating-tables, with the lamps above them hanging low.

Supposing, after all, he decided not to play tonight? That was an idea: to drink and stroll around the tables, in glorious freedom from the drug, pitying the addicts ... Think, he said to himself, of the nervous energy that you will save; think of the agonies you will be spared; think of the utter peace that comes from not caring what the wheel is doing; and think (since you're thinking) of how it will feel to leave this place with the same amount of money you had when you came in. To say nothing of leaving it without a sense of guilt. How would *that* be for fun? Magnificent ...

He went down the three shallow steps from the bar.

As he joined the thinnest of the crowds at the five-hundred-franc table, he saw that Anne's forbidden friends were sitting beside the window; René in his white dinner-jacket and cummerbund, van Merren with his crew-cut and red satin tie, Mrs van Merren, aged twenty-two; the little Austrian girl with the gentian-coloured eyes and her beau, the Spaniard who drove the racing-car. Enamelled children, chattering round a bottle of champagne, not playing, though René had a pile of chips in front of him. Just as well, David reflected, that Linda wasn't here.

And now the insane magic began. The wheel was still; they were paying out on the last spin. The ball lay in the socket below the number twenty; the pink woman with the mysteriously rectangular bosom had covered the twenty with eight separate *mille* plaques. She was a fellow-mystic and she acknowledged David's congratulatory grin with the only sort of smile that the mystics allowed themselves when in full play; a fleeting, precarious signal; no more, lest the gods should see and reverse the luck.

After the twenty, David said to himself, the twenty-one; simple arithmetic; and, to juggle with higher mathematics, the three and the twelve; naturally, the *quatre premier* because of one's old friend Zero, and the *dix-douze* because it was a habit.

The first three spins, in David's superstition, foreshadowed the evening's play. If none of his numbers came up in the first three spins, he could look out for trouble; any sort of win on the first three augured a painless evening; and a *plein* on the first spin of all meant honey and jam hereafter.

He did not mean to play in *milles* until he saw which way prophecy pointed. He would begin small with the five-hundreds. He had been careful to put his five-hundreds in one pocket and his *mille* plaques in the other. Unfortunately, while giving his bets to the croupier, he put his hand in the wrong pocket. He found himself playing *milles* on the first shot. This often happened. He decided to take it as an omen. One of the amiable aspects of roulette was that you could make an omen out of anything.

Now for the wait; the low-voiced, painstaking instructions, the ranging of the bets. The heads and the hands kept coming, the black rakes went forward, the coloured chips moved into their places on the green cloth. The wheel turned slowly under the croupier's hand. '*Vos jeux, Messieurs, Mesdames.*'

It was the moment for invocation. Those who kept track of the numbers on printed cards bent their heads over them as though the cards were prayer-books. Those who stared upward in fixed suppliance, stared. Those who watched the wheel turned to it like pointers, rigid from head to foot. David, who never watched the wheel, began his automatic pacing, away from the table to the left (always keep on the left side for luck) halting at the ash-tray, turning the chips in his pocket, gazing through the windows at the sea, pacing back, but not to look at the wheel, lighting another cigarette, striding to the window again.

'*Plus rien, Messieurs, Mesdames!*'

He kept his back to the table. Now the hush came down and he could hear the ball rattling around the wheel, rattling around its range of thirty-seven chances, taking its pick. He could hear the slower rattle; now was the moment that it came. The one out of the thirty-seven. His Twenty-One. *Vingt-et-Un-rouge-impair-et-passe*. He was entirely certain. The ball clicked.

'*Vingt-et-Un! Rouge, Impair et Passe. Carré , cheval et plein.*'

He never knew how he could be so certain in forecast and still dazed with astonishment by the fact. It was always going to happen and always impossible that it should have happened. The warm sizzle of gratification, the triumphant shout in his head, never varied. He allowed himself, with the control of the mystic, to smile guardedly at the pink woman, who had the *carré* and the *cheval*. This was as good as you could wish. A *plein* with the first spin. Honey and jam. The four *mille* lost on the other numbers didn't count. Not with thirty-five to come, they didn't. (And if there had been twenty of them, they still wouldn't ... As all mystics understood.)

As the rake slid the neat castle of chips towards David, René's voice beside his shoulder said, '*A la bonheur!*' In looks, René had a harlequin slickness that David found a little repulsive, but his youth, his smile, were disarming. He added in English, 'Jolly good show!' and when David told the croupier to double the stake, René leaned over and placed a *mille* of his own on Twenty-One. '*Vous allez encore toucher, j'en suis sûr, Monsieur Neilson.*' Unable to reconcile this comradeship of lunacy with the things that he said to René on the telephone ten days ago, David covered the Three and the Twelve again. René followed him. The croupier, who knew David's game, invited further stakes. '*Et le Quatre Premier? Et le Dix-Douze? Mais, Monsieur, vous n'avez pas joué le Vingt-et-Un Vingt-Quatre.*' Grinning, he took another *mille* from David and flipped it on the *cheval* between Twenty-One and Twenty-Four.

René stood, pallid and tense, watching the wheel.

'It is,' David reminded him, 'highly improbable that Twenty-One will come up twice. Not the sort of thing it does. Mark you, other numbers do. Four, for example, and that monster, Twenty-Five.'

René was apparently praying. He did not reply.

This time, the wait was longer. And from the slowly turning wheel, the inimical Nineteen was shimmering and leering at him. 'Shall I? Shan't I?' David said to himself. He didn't really approve of placating the Nineteen.

Dix-Neuf Vingt-Deux perhaps; *Vingt-Deux* was something of a chum. No. Be firm … the hell with it. He put the *mille* back in his pocket, congratulating himself on his strong-mindedness.

He quickened his pacing on the left side. Superstition made him do all the same things a second time, even to the dropping of his half-smoked cigarette in the ash-tray, the pacing back, the lighting of another cigarette. Rigidly he kept his back to the table as the whirring rattle of the ball began. He looked at the sea, drew a deep breath because tension could wreck everything, and thought simply, trustfully, 'Now!'

'*Vingt-et-Un! Rouge, impair et passe.*'

The thing that couldn't happen, had. Twice running, with the stake doubled and, thanks to the croupier, the *cheval* added to the *plein*. Carillons in your head. Standing, like Colossus, while they paid the lesser winnings, warm and pious and in love with the whole world.

René, obviously no mystic, had lost control. He had summoned his gang with a yell; about him the gang leaped and applauded. All the truly faithful looked at them with cold, hostile eyes. Not even the young could be excused for such behaviour in the sacred edifice. The young did not care. René's hands shook so much when he grabbed his thirty-five *mille* that some of the chips spilled off into the bosom of the pink woman. She salvaged them, unsmiling, returned them to René and took her recurrent twenty-three *mille* complacently, ranging it beside the last.

Eighty-seven *mille* slid down the cloth towards David.

PAMELA FRANKAU, *The Bridge*

Crockford's Club

In the reign of George IV, a new star rose upon the horizon in the person of Mr William Crockford; and the old-fashioned games of faro, macao, and lansquenet gave place to the all-devouring thirst for the game of hazard. Crockey, when still a young man, had relinquished the peaceful trade of a fishmonger for a share in a 'hell', where, with his partner Gye, he managed to win, after a sitting of twenty-four hours, the enormous sum of one hundred thousand pounds from Lords Thanet and

Granville, Mr Ball Hughes, and two other gentlemen whose names I do not now remember. With this capital added to his former gains, he built the well-known palace in St James's Street, where a club was established and play organised on a scale of magnificence and liberality hitherto unknown in Europe.

One may safely say, without exaggeration, that Crockford won the whole of the ready money of the then existing generation. As is often the case at Lords' Cricket-ground, the great match of the gentlemen of England against the professional players was won by the latter. It was a very hollow thing, and in a few years twelve hundred thousand pounds were swept away by the fortunate fishmonger. He did not, however, die worth more than a sixth part of this vast sum; the difference being swallowed up in various unlucky speculations.

No one can describe the splendour and excitement of the early days of Crockey. A supper of the most exquisite kind, prepared by the famous Ude, and accompanied by the best wines in the world, together with every luxury of the season, was furnished gratis. The members of the club included all the celebrities of England, from the Duke of Wellington to the youngest Ensign of the Guards; and at the gay and festive board, which was constantly replenished from midnight to early dawn, the most brilliant sallies of wit, the most agreeable conversation, the most interest-ing anecdotes, interspersed with grave political discussions and acute logical reasoning on every conceivable subject, proceeded from the soldiers, scholars, statesmen, poets, and men of pleasure, who, when the 'house was up' and balls and parties at an end, delighted to finish their evening with a little supper and a good deal of hazard at old Crockey's. The tone of the club was excellent. A most gentlemanlike feeling pre-vailed, and none of the rudeness, familiarity, and ill-breeding which disgrace some of the minor clubs of the present day, would have been tolerated for a moment.

Though not many years have elapsed since the time of which I write, the supper-table had a very different appearance from what it would pre-sent did the club now exist. Beards were completely unknown, and the rare mustachios were only worn by officers of the Household Brigade or hussar regiments. Stiff white neckcloths, blue coats and brass buttons, rather short-waisted white waistcoats and tremendously embroidered shirt-fronts with gorgeous studs of great value, were considered the right thing. A late deservedly popular Colonel in the Guards used to give Storr and Mortimer £25 a year to furnish him with a new set of studs every Saturday night during the London season.

The great foreign diplomatists, Prince Talleyrand, Count Pozzo di Borgo, General Alava, the Duke of Palmella, Prince Esterhazy, the French, Russian, Spanish, Portuguese, and Austrian ambassadors, and all persons of distinction and eminence who arrived in England, belonged to Crockford's as a matter of course; but many rued the day when they became members of that fascinating but dangerous coterie. The great Duke himself, always rather a friend of the dandies, did not disdain to appear now and then at this charming club; whilst the late Lord Raglan, Lord Anglesey, Sir Hussey Vivian, and many more of our Peninsula and Waterloo heroes, were constant visitors. The two great novelists of the day, who have since become great statesmen, Disraeli and Bulwer Lytton, displayed at that brilliant supper-table the one his sable, the other his auburn curls; there Horace Twiss made proof of an appetite, and Edward Montague of a thirst, which astonished all beholders; whilst the bitter jests of Sir Joseph Copley, Colonel Armstrong, and John Wilson Croker, and the brilliant wit of Alvanley, were the delight of all present, and their *bons mots* were the next day retailed all over England.

In the play-room might be heard the clear ringing voice of that agreeable reprobate, Tom Duncombe, as he cheerfully called 'Seven', and the powerful hand of the vigorous Sefton in throwing for a ten. There might be noted the scientific dribbling of a four by 'King' Allen, the tremendous backing of nines and fives by Ball Hughes and Auriol, the enormous stakes played for by Lords Lichfield and Chesterfield, George Payne, Sir St Vincent Cotton, D'Orsay, and George Anson, and, above all, the gentlemanly bearing and calm and unmoved demeanour, under losses or gains, of all the men of that generation.

The old fishmonger himself, seated snug and sly at his desk in the corner of the room, watchful as the dragon that guarded the golden apples of the Hesperides, would only give credit to sure and approved signatures. Who that ever entered that dangerous little room can ever forget the large green table with the croupiers, Page, Darking, and Bacon, with their suave manners, sleek appearance, stiff white neckcloths, and the almost miraculous quickness and dexterity with which they swept away the money of the unfortunate punters when the fatal cry of 'Deuce ace', 'Aces', or 'Sixes out', was heard in answer to the caster's bold cry of 'Seven', or 'Nine', or 'Five's the main'.

O noctes cœnœque deum! but the brightest medal has its reverse, and after all the wit and gaiety and excitement of the night, how disagreeable the waking up, and how very unpleasant the sight of the little card, with its numerous figures marked down on the debtor side in the fine bold hand of Mr Page. Alas, poor Crockey's! shorn of its former glory, has become a sort of refuge for the destitute, a cheap dining-house. How are the mighty fallen! Irish buckeens, spring captains, 'welchers' from Newmarket, and suspicious-looking foreigners, may be seen swaggering, after dinner, through the marble halls and up that gorgeous staircase where once the chivalry of England loved to congregate; and those who remember Crockford's in all its glory, cast, as they pass, a look of unavailing regret at its dingy walls, with many a sigh to the memory of the pleasant days they passed there, and the gay companions and noble gentlemen who have long since gone to their last home.

REES HOWELL GRONOW, *Reminiscences*

The Derby

'Will any one do anything about Hybiscus?' sang out a gentleman in the ring at Epsom. It was full of eager groups; round the betting post a swarming cluster, while the magic circle itself was surrounded by a host of horsemen shouting from their saddles the odds they were ready to receive or give, and the names of the horses they were prepared to back or to oppose.

'Will any one do anything about Hybiscus?'

'I'll bet you five to one,' said a tall, stiff Saxon peer, in a white great-coat. 'No; I'll take six.'

The tall, stiff peer in the white great-coat mused for a moment with his pencil at his lip, and then said, 'Well, I'll bet you six. What do you say about Mango?'

'Eleven to two against Mango,' called out a little hump-backed man in a shrill voice, but with the air of one who was master of his work.

'I should like to do a little business with you, Mr Chippendale,' said Lord Milford, in a coaxing tone, 'but I must have six to one.'

'Eleven to two, and no mistake,' said this keeper of a second-rate gaming-house, who, known by the flattering appellation of Hump Chippendale, now turned with malignant abruptness from the heir-apparent of an English earldom.

'You shall have six to one, my Lord,' said Captain Spruce, a debonair personage, with a well-turned silk hat arranged a little aside, his coloured cravat tied with precision, his whiskers trimmed like a quickset hedge. Spruce, who had earned his title of Captain on the plains of Newmarket, which had witnessed for many a year his successful exploits, had a weakness for the aristocracy, who, knowing his graceful infirmity, patronised him with condescending dexterity, acknowledged his existence in Pall-Mall as well as at Tattersall's, and thus occasionally got a point more than the betting out of him. Hump Chippendale had none of these gentle failings; he was a democratic leg, who loved to fleece a noble, and thought all men were born equal – a consoling creed that was a hedge for his hump.

'Seven to four against the favourite; seven to two against Caravan; eleven to two against Mango. What about Benedict? Will any one do anything about Pocket Hercules? Thirty to one against Dardanelles.'

'Done.'

'Five-and-thirty ponies to one against Phosphorus,' shouted a little man vociferously and repeatedly.

'I will bet forty,' said Lord Milford. No answer – nothing done.

'Forty to one!' murmured Egremont, who stood against Phosphorus. A little nervous, he said to the peer in the white great-coat, 'Don't you think that Phosphorus may, after all, have some chance?'

'I should be cursed sorry to be deep against him,' said the peer.

Egremont with a quivering lip walked away. He consulted his book; he meditated anxiously. Should he hedge? It was scarcely worth while to mar the symmetry of his winnings; he stood 'so well' by all the favourites; and for a horse at forty to one. No; he would trust his star, he would not hedge.

'Mr Chippendale,' whispered the peer in the white great-coat, 'go and press Mr Egremont about Phosphorus. I should not be surprised if you got a good thing.'

At this moment, a huge, broad-faced, rosy-gilled fellow, with one of those good-humoured yet cunning countenances that we meet occasionally on the northern side of the Trent, rode up to the ring on a square cob, and, dismounting, entered the circle. He was a carcass-butcher famous in Carnaby-market, and the prime counsellor of a distinguished nobleman, for whom privately he betted on commission. His secret service today was to bet against his noble employer's own horse, and so he at once sung out, 'Twenty to one against Man-trap.'

A young gentleman just launched into the world, and who, proud of his ancient and spreading acres, was now making his first book, seeing Man-trap marked eighteen to one on the cards, jumped eagerly at this bargain, while Lord Fitzheron and Mr Berners, who were at hand, and who in their days had found their names in the book of the carcass-butcher, and grown wise by it, interchanged a smile.

'Mr Egremont will not take,' said Hump Chippendale to the peer in the white great-coat.

'You must have been too eager,' said his noble friend.

The ring is up; the last odds declared; all gallop away to the Warren. A few minutes, only a few minutes, and the event that for twelve months has been the pivot of so much calculation, of such subtle combinations, of such deep conspiracies, round which the thought and passion of the sporting world have hung like eagles, will be recorded in the fleeting tablets of the past. But what minutes! Count them by sensation, and not by calendars, and each moment is a day and the race a life ...

They are saddling the horses; Caravan looks in great condition; and a scornful smile seems to play upon the handsome features of Pavis, as, in the becoming colours of his employer, he gracefully gallops his horse before his admiring supporters. Egremont, in the delight of an English patrician, scarcely saw Mango, and never even thought of Phosphorus – Phosphorus, who, by the by, was the first horse that showed, with both his forelegs bandaged.

They are off!

As soon as they are well away, Chifney makes the running with Pocket

Hercules. Up to the Rubbing House he is leading; this is the only point the eye can select. Higher up the hill, Caravan, Hybiscus, Benedict, Mahometan, Phosphorus, Michel Fell, and Rat-trap are with the grey, forming a front rank, and at the new ground the pace has told its tale, for half a dozen are already out of the race.

The summit is gained; the tactics alter: here Pavis brings up Caravan, with extraordinary severity – the pace round Tattenham corner terrific; Caravan leading, then Phosphorus a little above him, Mahometan next, Hybiscus fourth, Rat-trap looking badly, Wisdom, Benedict, and another handy. By this time Pocket Hercules has enough, and at the road the tailing grows at every stride. Here the favourite himself is *hors de combat*, as well as Dardanelles, and a crowd of lesser celebrities.

There are now but four left in the race, and of these, two, Hybiscus and Mahometan, are some lengths behind. Now it is neck and neck between Caravan and Phosphorus. At the stand, Caravan has decidedly the best; but just at the post, Edwards, on Phosphorus, lifts the gallant little horse, and with an extraordinary effort contrives to shove him in by half a length.

'You look a little low, Charley,' said Lord Fitzheron, as, taking their lunch in their drag, he poured the champagne into the glass of Egremont.

'By Jove!' said Lord Milford, 'only think of Cockie Graves having gone and done it!'

BENJAMIN DISRAELI, Sybil

The Nicker Nicked

Gaming is an enchanting witchery, begot betwixt idleness and avarice; which has this ill property above all other vices, that it renders a man incapable of prosecuting any serious action, and makes him unsatisfied with his own condition: he is either lifted up to the top of mad joy with success, or plunged to the bottom of despair by misfortune; always in extremes, always in a storm …

Betwixt twelve and one of the clock, a good dinner is prepared by way of ordinary, and some gentlemen of civility and condition oftentimes eat there, and play a while for recreation after dinner, both moderately, and most commonly without deserving reproof.

Towards night, when ravenous beasts usually seek their prey, there come in shoals of hectors, trepanners, gilts, pads, biters, prigs, divers, lifters, kidnappers, vouchers, mill-kens, piemen, decoys, shop-lifters, foil-ers, bulkers, droppers, gamblers, donnakers, crossbiters, &c. under the general appellation of rooks; and in this particular it serves as a nursery for Tyburn, for every year some of this gang march thither! One Millard was hanged in April, 1664, for burglary; and others since.

When a young gentleman or apprentice comes into this school of virtue, unskilled in the quibbles and devices there practised, they call him a lamb; then a rook (who is properly the wolf) follows him close, and engages him in advantageous bets, and at length worries him, that is, gets all his money, and then they smile and say, 'The lamb is bitten.'

Of these rooks, some will be very importunate to borrow money of you, without any intention of repaying, or to go with you seven to twelve, half a crown, and take it ill if they are refused; others watch, if, when you are serious at game, your sword hang loose behind, and lift that away; others will not scruple, if they espy an opportunity, directly to pick your pocket; yet, if all fail, some will nim off the gold buttons of your cloak, or steal the cloak itself, if it lie loose; others will throw at a sum of money with a 'dry fist', as they call it; that is, if they nick you, it is theirs; if they lose, they owe you so much, with many other quillets: or, if you chance to nick them, it is odds they wait your coming out at night, and beat you as one Cock was served in June, 1664.

Blaspheming, drunkenness, and swearing, are here so familiar, that civility is, by the rule of contrarieties, accounted a vice. I do not mean swearing, when there is occasion to attest a truth, but upon no occasion; as, 'God damn me, how dost? What a clock is it, by God?' &c. Then, before two hours are at an end, some one who has been heated with wine, or made choleric with loss of his money, raises a quarrel, swords are drawn, and perhaps the boxes and candlesticks thrown at one another; and all the house in a garboil, forming a perfect type of hell.

Would you imagine it to be true? That a grave gentleman, well stricken in years, insomuch as he cannot see the pips of the dice, is so infatuated with this witchery, as to play here with others' eyes; of whom this quibble was raised, 'That Mr — such a one plays at dice by the ear.' Another gentleman, stark blind, I have seen play at Hazard, and sure that must be by the ear too.

Late at night, when the company grows thin, and your eyes dim with watching, false dice are often put upon the ignorant, or they are otherwise cozened with topping, or slurring, &c. And, if you be not vigilant, the box-keeper shall score you up double or treble boxes, and, though you have lost your money, dun you as severely for it, as if it were the justest debt in the world.

There are yet some genteeler and more subtle rooks, whom you shall not distinguish by their outward demeanour from persons of condition; and who will sit by, a whole evening, and observe who wins; and then, if the winner be bubbleable, they will insinuate themselves into his acquaintance, and civilly invite him to drink a glass of wine; wheedle him into play, and win all his money, either by false dice, as high fullams, low fullams, 5, 4, 2, s. &c.; or by palming, topping, knapping, or slurring; or, in case he be past that classis of ignoramusses, then by crossbiting, or some other dexterity, of which they have variety unimaginable. Note by the way, that when they have you at the tavern, and think you a sure bubble, they will many times purposely lose some small sum to you the first time, to engage you more freely to *bleed* (as they call it) at the second meeting, to which they will be sure to invite you.

A gentleman, whom ill fortune had hurried into passion, took a box and dice to a side-table, and there fell to throwing by himself; at length swears with an emphasis, 'Damme, now I throw for nothing, I can win a thousand pounds; but when I play for money, I lose my arse.'

LEATHERMORE, *The Nicker Nicked: or, The Cheats of Gaming Discovered*

On the Cardes, and Dice

Beefore the sixt day of the next new year,
Strange wonders in this kingdome shall appear.
Foure Kinges shalbe assemblied in this Ile,
Whear they shall keepe great tumult for a while.
Many men then shall have an end of Crosses,
And many like wise shall susteyne great losses.
Many that now full joyfull are and gladd,
Shall at that time be sorrowfull and sadd.
Full many a Christians heart shall quake for fear,
The dreadfull sound of trumpe when he shall hear.
Dead bones shall then be tumbled up and downe,
In every citty, and in every towne.
By day or night this tumult shall not cease,
Untill an Heralld shall proclaime a peace.
An Herauld strange, the like was never borne
Whose very beard is flesh, and mouth is horne.

SIR WALTER RALEIGH

The Passion of Play

12 June 1819: I have been at Oatlands for the Ascot party, and lost about 300 gs. at Whist; one night I lost 420. On the course I did nothing. Ever since the Derby ill fortune has pursued me, and I cannot win anywhere. I played last night and the night before at Brooks's, and had won 300 one night and near 600 the other, but I only brought off 200 by the two nights. This was my own fault, for playing with a very small capital I ought to be contented with very small winnings. I probably shall have no other opportunity of putting this rule in practice, but if I should have I am resolved to leave off when I have won a little. It is dreadful to depend upon the chance of the dice for almost one's existence. The life it makes me lead is too agitating for I have too much at stake and amusement is the last object I have in view in playing. Play is a detestable occupation; it absorbs all our thoughts and renders us unfit for everything else in life. It is hurtful to the mind and destroys the better feelings; it incapacitates us for study and application of every sort; it makes us thoughtful and nervous; and our cheerfulness depends upon the uncertain event of our nightly occupation. How anyone can play who is not in want of money I cannot comprehend; surely his mind must be strangely framed who requires the stimulus of gambling to heighten his pleasures. Some indeed may have become attached to gaming from habit, and may not wish to throw off the habit from the difficulty of finding fresh employment for the mind at an advanced period of life. Some may be unfitted by nature or taste for society, and these may also be ignorant of the transports of love: for such gaming may have a powerful attraction. The mind is excited; at the gaming-table all men are equal; no superiority of birth, accomplishments, or ability avail here; great noblemen, merchants, orators, jockeys, statesmen, and idlers are here thrown together in levelling confusion; the only pre-eminence is that of success, the only superiority that of temper. But why does a man play who is blessed with fortune, endowed with understanding, and adorned with accomplishments which might ensure his success in any pursuit which taste or fancy might incite him to follow? It is contrary to reason, but we see such instances every day. The passion of play is not artificial; it must have existed in certain minds from the beginning; at least some must have been so constituted that they yield at once to the attraction, and enter with avidity into the pursuit in which other men can never take the least interest.

CHARLES GREVILLE, *Memoirs*

Russian Roulette

An officer who was sitting in a corner of the room stood up, and, coming slowly to the table, surveyed us all with a quiet and solemn glance. He was a native of Servia, as was evident from his name.

The outward appearance of Lieutenant Vulich was quite in keeping with his character. His height, swarthy complexion, black hair, piercing black eyes, large but straight nose – an attribute of his nation – and the cold and melancholy smile which ever hovered around his lips, all seemed to concur in lending him the appearance of a man apart, incapable of reciprocating the thoughts and passions of those whom fate gave him for companions.

He was brave; talked little, but sharply; confided his thoughts and family secrets to no one; drank hardly a drop of wine; and never dangled after the young Cossack girls, whose charm it is difficult to realise without having seen them. It was said, however, that the colonel's wife was not indifferent to those expressive eyes of his; but he was seriously angry if any hint on the subject was made.

There was only one passion which he did not conceal – the passion for gambling. At the green table he would become oblivious of everything. He usually lost, but his constant ill success only aroused his obstinacy. It was related that, on one occasion, during a nocturnal expedition, he was keeping the bank on a pillow, and had a terrific run of luck. Suddenly shots rang out. The alarm was sounded; all but Vulich jumped up and rushed to arms.

'Stake, *va banque!*' he cried to one of the most ardent gamblers.

'Seven,' the latter answered as he hurried off.

Notwithstanding the general confusion, Vulich calmly finished the deal – seven was the card.

By the time he reached the cordon a violent fusillade was in progress. Vulich did not trouble himself about the bullets or the sabres of the Chechenes, but sought for the lucky gambler.

'Seven it was!' he cried out, as at length he perceived him in the cordon of skirmishers who were beginning to dislodge the enemy from the wood; and going up to him, he drew out his purse and pocket-book and handed them to the winner, notwithstanding the latter's objections on the score of the inconvenience of the payment. That unpleasant duty discharged, Vulich dashed forward, carried the soldiers along after him, and, to the very end of the affair, fought the Chechenes with the utmost coolness.

When Lieutenant Vulich came up to the table, we all became silent, expecting to hear, as usual, something original.

'Gentlemen!' he said – and his voice was quiet though lower in tone than usual – 'gentlemen, what is the good of futile discussions? You wish for proofs? I propose that we try the experiment on ourselves: whether a man can of his own accord dispose of his life, or whether the fateful moment is appointed beforehand for each of us. Who is agreeable?'

'Not I. Not I,' came from all sides. 'There's a queer fellow for you! He does get strange ideas into his head!' ...

'I propose a wager,' I said in jest.

'What sort of wager?'

'I maintain that there is no such thing as predestination,' I said, scattering on the table a score or so of ducats – all I had in my pocket.

'Done,' answered Vulich in a hollow voice. 'Major, you will be judge. Here are fifteen ducats, the remaining five you owe me, kindly add them to the others.'

'Very well,' said the major; 'though, indeed, I do not understand what is the question at issue and how you will decide it!'

Without a word Vulich went into the major's bedroom, and we followed him. He went up to the wall on which the major's weapons were hanging, and took down at random one of the pistols – of which there were several of different calibres. We were still in the dark as to what he meant to do. But, when he cocked the pistol and sprinkled powder in the pan, several of the officers, crying out in spite of themselves, seized him by the arms.

'What are you going to do?' they exclaimed. 'This is madness!'

'Gentlemen!' he said slowly, disengaging his arm. 'Who would like to pay twenty ducats for me?'

They were silent and drew away.

Vulich went into the other room and sat by the table; we all followed him. With a sign he invited us to sit round him. We obeyed in silence – at that moment he had acquired a certain mysterious authority over us. I stared fixedly into his face; but he met my scrutinising gaze with a quiet and steady glance, and his pallid lips smiled. But, notwithstanding his composure, it seemed to me that I could read the stamp of death upon his pale countenance. I have noticed – and many old soldiers have corroborated my observation – that a man who is to die in a few hours frequently bears on his face a certain strange stamp of inevitable fate, so that it is difficult for practised eyes to be mistaken.

'You will die today!' I said to Vulich.

He turned towards me rapidly, but answered slowly and quietly :

'May be so, may be not.'

Then, addressing himself to the major, he asked: 'Is the pistol loaded?'

The major, in the confusion, could not quite remember.

'There, that will do, Vulich!' exclaimed somebody. 'Of course it must be loaded, if it was one of those hanging on the wall there over our heads. What a man you are for joking!'

'A silly joke too!' struck in another.

'I wager fifty rubles to five that the pistol is not loaded!' cried a third.

A new bet was made.

I was beginning to get tired of it all.

'Listen,' I said, 'either shoot yourself, or hang up the pistol in its place and let us go to bed.'

'Yes, of course!' many exclaimed. 'Let us go to bed.'

'Gentlemen, I beg of you not to move,' said Vulich, putting the muzzle of the pistol to his forehead.

We were all petrified.

'Mr Pechorin,' he added, 'take a card and throw it up in the air.'

I took, as I remember now, an ace of hearts off the table and threw it into the air. All held their breath. With eyes full of terror and a certain vague curiosity they glanced rapidly from the pistol to the fateful ace, which slowly descended, quivering in the air. At the moment it touched the table Vulich pulled the trigger . . . a flash in the pan!

'Thank God!' many exclaimed. 'It wasn't loaded!'

'Let us see, though,' said Vulich.

He cocked the pistol again, and took aim at a forage-cap which was hanging above the window. A shot rang out. Smoke filled the room; when it cleared away, the forage-cap was taken down. It had been shot right through the centre, and the bullet was deeply embedded in the wall.

For two or three minutes no one was able to utter a word. Very quietly Vulich poured my ducats from the major's purse into his own.

MIKHAIL LERMONTOV, *A Hero of Our Time*

The Seven of Cups

The sun appears over the horizon as the train crosses the last switch in the yards, the last signal, the last marker. At this hour there are no children playing in the outer suburbs. Far off to the south the Cerro de los Angeles stands all by itself. The fields are green and the crops well grown; it is hard to believe they are in the outskirts of Madrid. Between two cultivated fields is a fallow one, a field with poppies gently rippling in the light morning breeze. The train is already running clear along the track when the traveller turns away from the window, sits down, lights a cigarette and lays his head back.

As the train passes the stop at Vallecas, the silent atmosphere of the coach is violently shattered. A man in a lilac-coloured jacket, with a handkerchief at his throat and a gold tooth, is offering at the top of his voice some strips of paper representing playing cards, each with a number on the back.

'Try your luck, ladies and gentlemen; a special package of fine candies or a bag of almonds, as you choose! Five céntimos a card! And then, in honour of my customers, I'll raffle off this Manolita doll, the sensational toy!'

The traveller decides to test his luck. He buys a strip and holds it in his hand a trifle doubtfully. The traveller is unpractised in gambling. He lifts his head and looks out the window. Off toward the north, on the horizon, he can see the Sierra de Guadarrama with some of the peaks – La Maliciosa, Valdermartín, Las Cabezas de Hierro – still covered with snow.

The man with the gold tooth has given the usual spiel about honest hands and uncovered a card.

' The two of swords! Where's the two of swords? Who's the lucky one?'

The traveller didn't win; his few cents' worth was in face cards. The holder of the two of swords is a man who doesn't even smile. He takes the special package of fine candies without looking at anyone, almost scornfully, as if he wanted to give the impression that he is used to receiving important news without a flicker of emotion. Everybody looks at him, and possibly there is someone who admires him as well. What a way he has of carrying it off!

The traveller feels a sort of obligation to be a good fellow. He perceives something like a sudden flash of inspiration and raises his voice: 'Give me all the threes; it's time the threes won.'

Near Vicálvaro, the conductor goes through snipping tickets.

'That's the way to talk! This gentleman is going to take the prize for twenty céntimos! Here go the threes!'

The traveller half-closes his eyes and waits. He fully expects to hear, after a bit, 'The three of —' The traveller intends to answer abruptly, 'Stop right there; I have all four of them.' Toward his right he can see some green hills with red clay cracks running down them. One of his fellow passengers is reading, with great attention, a weekly paper on bullfighting. A wasp is fluttering on the glass, up and then down. The voice of the man in the lilac-coloured jacket resounds throughout the car.

'The seven of cups! Who has the seven of cups?'

The traveller trembles from head to foot, notices his heart beating violently, feels that his mouth is dry, squeezes his eyes shut. The traveller is afraid that all eyes are upon him, fastened like darts, smiling maliciously as if saying, 'What happened to your threes?' The traveller begins to think, he doesn't know why – maybe to distract his attention – of river water flowing under a bridge. When he cautiously opens his eyes a little at a time he sees that no one is watching him.

CAMILO JOSÉ CELA, *Journey to the Alcarria*

Soldiers During the Thirty Years War

We then arose and went over to the gambling place, where tournaments were held with dice and everyone cursed in their hundreds and thousands, gave away galley loads and moats' full of curses. The place was almost as big as the old market square in Cologne, covered everywhere with cloaks and equipped with tables each surrounded by gamblers. Every party had three four-cornered rascal-bones or dice to which they entrusted their fortunes – thus they shared their money, giving it to one and taking it from the other. At every cloak or table, one acted as play-master (who might better be called a flay-master), and he was the adjudicator who had to see that no wrong was done. He supplied cloaks, tables and dice, and kept back from each winning a fee so that he commonly snapped up most of the money. But even to them, the money did no great service as they lost it again in gambling or spent it at the sutler, if not at the surgeon who often enough had to stitch up their heads.

These foolish gamblers all hoped to win, which could only have been possible if they would have played with money from another's pocket. And though they all had this one hope, it could be said 'Many heads, many arguments' as each longed for his own good luck. Some hit, some missed, some gained, some lost. Some cursed and others thundered; some cheated, others were deceived. The winners laughed and the losers ground their teeth; some sold their clothes and everything they treasured, and others gained them. Some asked for honest dice but others wanted loaded ones, smuggling them secretly into the game, until their opponents threw them out, smashed them, bit them with their teeth and tore the play-masters' cloaks into tatters. Some of the loaded dice were Netherlanders which had to be thrown with a slide; they had sharp edges where they carried the fives and sixes, as sharp as the wooden donkeys on which the soldiers had to sit for punishment. Others were called Highlanders which needed a special twist called 'the Bavarian Height' to be thrown effectively. Some were made of stag's horn, light above and heavy underneath; some were lined with quicksilver or lead, and others with chopped hair, tinder, chaff and charcoal. Some had sharp corners; on others the corners were completely ground off, some were long like rifle butts and others broad like turtles. And all these species were solely made for cheating: they fulfilled that for which they were made, whether they were thrown violently or shuffled gently, and no amount of shaking could help, not to speak of those which had two fives and sixes, or on the contrary, two aces and two deuces. With these rascal-bones they snatched, lured and stole each other's money, which in turn they had robbed or looted or gained with bitter trouble and toil, endangering body and life.

HANS JACOB VON GRIMMELSHAUSEN, *Simplicius Simplicissimus*

The Spoiled Child

Was she beautiful or not beautiful? and what was the secret of form or expression which gave the dynamic quality to her glance? Was the good or the evil genius dominant in those beams? Probably the evil; else why was the effect that of unrest rather than of undisturbed charm? Why was the wish to look again felt as coercion and not as a longing in which the whole being consents?

She who raised these questions in Daniel Deronda's mind was occupied in gambling: not in the open air under a southern sky, tossing coppers on a ruined wall, with rags about her limbs; but in one of those splendid resorts which the enlightenment of ages has prepared for the same species of pleasure at a heavy cost of gilt mouldings, dark-toned colour and chubby nullities, all correspondingly heavy – forming a suitable condenser for human breath belonging, in great part, to the highest fashion, and not easily procurable to be breathed in elsewhere in the like proportion, at least by persons of little fashion.

It was near four o'clock on a September day, so that the atmosphere was well-brewed to a visible haze. There was deep stillness, broken only by a light rattle, a light chink, a small sweeping sound, and an occasional monotone in French, such as might be expected to issue from an ingeniously constructed automaton. Round two long tables were gathered two serried crowds of human beings, all save one having their faces and attention bent on the tables. The one exception was a melancholy little boy, with his knees and calves simply in their natural clothing of epidermis, but for the rest of his person in a fancy dress. He alone had his face turned towards the doorway, and fixing on it the blank gaze of a bedizened child stationed as a masquerading advertisement on the platform of an itinerant show, stood close behind a lady deeply engaged at the roulette-table.

About this table fifty or sixty persons were assembled, many in the outer rows, where there was occasionally a deposit of new comers, being mere spectators, only that one of them, usually a woman, might now and then be observed putting down a five franc piece with a simpering air, just to see what the passion of gambling really was. Those who were taking their pleasure at a higher strength, and were absorbed in play, showed very distant varieties of European type: Livonian and Spanish, Græco-Italian and miscellaneous German, English aristocratic and English plebeian. Here certainly was a striking admission of human equality. The white bejewelled fingers of an English countess were very near touching a bony, yellow, crab-like hand stretching a bared wrist to clutch a heap of coin – a hand easy to sort with the square, gaunt face, deep-set eyes, grizzled eyebrows, and ill-combed scanty hair which seemed a slight metamorphosis of the vulture. And where else would her ladyship have graciously consented to sit by that dry-lipped feminine figure prematurely old, withered after short bloom like her artificial flowers, holding a shabby velvet reticule before her, and occasionally putting in her mouth the point with which she pricked her card? There too, very near the fair countess, was a respectable London tradesman, blond and soft-handed, his sleek hair scrupulously parted behind and before, conscious of circulars addressed to the nobility and gentry, whose distinguished patronage enabled him to take his holidays fashionably, and to a certain extent in their distinguished company. Not his the gambler's passion that nullifies appetite, but a well-fed leisure, which in the intervals of winning money in business and spending it showily, sees no better resource than winning money in play and spending it yet more showily – reflecting always that Providence had never manifested any disapprobation of his amusement, and dispassionate enough to leave off if the sweetness of winning much and seeing others lose had turned to the sourness of losing much and seeing others win. For the vice of gambling lay in losing money at it. In his bearing there might be something of the tradesman, but in his pleasures he was fit to rank with the owners of the oldest titles. Standing close to his chair was a handsome Italian, calm, statuesque, reaching across him to place the first pile of napoleons from a new bagful just brought him by an envoy with a scrolled mustache. The pile was in half a minute pushed over to an old bewigged woman with eyeglasses pinching her nose. There was a slight gleam, a faint mumbling smile about the lips of the old woman; but the statuesque Italian remained impassive, and – probably secure in an infallible system which placed his foot on the neck of chance – immediately prepared a new pile. So did a man with the air of an emaciated beau or worn-out libertine, who looked at life through one eyeglass, and held out his hand tremulously when he asked for change. It could surely be no severity of system, but rather some dream of white crows, or the induction that the eighth of the month was lucky, which inspired the fierce yet tottering impulsiveness of his play.

But while every single player differed markedly from every other, there was a certain uniform negativeness of expression which had the effect of a mask – as if they had all eaten of some root that for the time compelled the brains of each to the same narrow monotony of action.

Deronda's first thought when his eyes fell on this scene of dull, gas-poisoned absorption was that the gambling of Spanish shepherd-boys had seemed to him more enviable: so far Rousseau might be justified in maintaining that art and science had done a poor service to mankind. But suddenly he felt the moment become dramatic. His attention was arrested by a young lady who, standing at an angle not far from him, was the last to whom his eyes travelled. She was bending and speaking English to a middle-aged lady seated at play beside her; but the next instant she returned to her play, and showed the full height of a graceful figure, with a face which might possibly be looked at without admiration, but could hardly be passed with indifference.

The inward debate which she raised in Deronda gave to his eyes a growing expression of scrutiny, tending farther and farther away from the glow of mingled undefined sensibilities forming admiration. At one moment they followed the movements of the figure of the arms and hands, as this problematic sylph bent forward to deposit her stake with an air of firm choice; and the next they returned to the face which, at present unaffected by beholders, was directed steadily towards the game. The sylph was a winner; and as her taper fingers, delicately gloved in pale-grey, were adjusting the coins which had been pushed towards her in order to pass them back again to the winning point, she looked round her with a survey too markedly cold and neutral not to have in it a little of that nature which we call art concealing an inward exultation.

But in the course of that survey her eyes met Deronda's, and instead of averting them as she would have desired to do, she was unpleasantly conscious that they were arrested – how long? The darting sense that he was measuring her and looking down on her as an inferior, that he was of different quality from the human dross around her, that he felt himself in a region outside and above her, and was examining her as a specimen of a lower order, roused a tingling resentment which stretched the moment with conflict. It did not bring the blood to her cheeks, but sent it away from her lips. She controlled herself by the help of an inward defiance, and without other sign of emotion than this lip-paleness turned to her play. But Deronda's gaze seemed to have acted as an evil eye. Her stake was gone. No matter; she had been winning ever since she took to roulette with a few napoleons at command, and had a considerable reserve. She had begun to believe in her luck, others had begun to believe in it: she had visions of being followed by a *cortège* who would worship her as a goddess of luck and watch her play as a directing augury. Such things had been known of male gamblers; why should not a woman have a like supremacy? Her friend and chaperon who had not wished her to play at first was beginning to approve, only administering the prudent advice to stop at the right moment and carry money back to England – advice to which Gwendolen had replied that she cared for the excitement of play, not the winnings. On that supposition the present moment ought to have made the flood-tide in her eager experience of gambling. Yet when her next stake was swept away, she felt the orbits of her eyes getting hot, and the certainty she had (without looking) of that man still watching her was something like a pressure which begins to be torturing. The more reason to her why she should not flinch, but go on playing as if she were indifferent to loss or gain. Her friend touched her elbow and proposed that they should quit the table. For reply Gwendolen put ten louis on the same spot: she was in that mood of defiance in which the mind loses sight of any end beyond the satisfaction of enraged resistance; and with the puerile stupidity of a dominant impulse includes luck among its objects of defiance. Since she was not winning strikingly, the next best thing was to lose strikingly. She controlled her muscles, and showed no tremor of mouth or hands. Each time her stake was swept off she doubled it. Many were now watching her, but the sole observation she was conscious of was Deronda's, who, though she never looked towards him, she was sure had not moved away. Such a drama takes no long while to play out: development and catastrophe can often be measured by nothing clumsier than the moment-hand. '*Faites votre jeu, mesdames et messieurs,'* said the automatic voice of destiny from between the mustache and imperial of the croupier; and Gwendolen's arm was stretched to deposit her last poor heap of napoleons. *'Le jeu ne va plus,'* said destiny. And in five seconds Gwendolen turned from the table, but turned resolutely with her face towards Deronda and looked at him. There was a smile of irony in his eyes as their glances met; but it was at least better that he should have kept his attention fixed on her than that he should have disregarded her as one of an insect swarm who had no individual physiognomy.

GEORGE ELIOT, *Daniel Deronda*

Gambling, on the great scale, is not republican. It belongs to two phases of society – a cankered over-civilisation, such as exists in rich aristocracies, and the reckless life of borderers and adventurers, or the semi-barbarism of a civilisation resolved into its primitive elements.

OLIVER WENDELL HOLMES

This cursed Bridge which is like a mill-stone about Society's neck, dragging it down into the depths of this sewer of loathsome filthiness.

FR BERNARD VAUGHAN

You cannot learn poker by playing with chips that cost you nothing.

'CONSTITUTION HILL'

Losing as much money as I can get hold of is an instant solution to my economic problems.

LUCIAN FREUD

A gambler without an excuse is a gambler who can't continue.

CHARLES BUKOWSKI

Success, Victory, Power

The first series of numbers from one to eighteen inclusive is called
'*Manque*': but what was that to me? I was not calculating, I had not even
heard what had been the winning number last, and I did not ask about it
when I began to play – as every player of any prudence would do. I
pulled out all my twenty friedrichs d'or and staked them on '*passe*,' the
word which lay before me.

'*Vingt-deux*,' cried the croupier.

I had won and again staked all: including my winnings.

'*Trente et un*,' cried the croupier.

I had won again. I had in all eighty friedrichs d'or. I staked the whole
of that sum on the twelve middle numbers (my winnings would be three
to one, but the chances were two to one against me). The wheel rotated
and stopped at twenty-four. I was passed three rolls each of fifty
friedrichs d'or in paper and ten gold coins; I had now two hundred
friedrichs d'or.

I was as though in delirium and I moved the whole heap of gold to red
– and suddenly thought better of it. And for the only time that whole
evening, all the time I was playing, I felt chilled with terror and a shudder
made my arms and legs tremble. I felt with horror and instantly realised
what losing would mean for me now! My whole life was at stake.

'*Rouge*,' cried the croupier, and I drew a breath; fiery pins and needles
were tingling all over my body. I was paid in banknotes. It came to four
thousand florins and eight friedrichs d'or (I could still keep count at that
stage).

Then, I remember, I staked two thousand florins on the twelve middle
numbers, and lost: I staked my gold, the eight friedrichs d'or, and lost. I
was seized with fury: I snatched up the two hundred florins I had left
and staked them on the first twelve numbers – haphazard, at random,
without thinking! There was, however, an instant of suspense, like,

perhaps, the feeling experienced by Madame Blanchard when she flew from a balloon in Paris to the earth.

'*Quatre!*' cried the croupier.

Now with my stake I had six thousand florins. I looked triumphant already. I was afraid of nothing – nothing, and staked four thousand florins on black. Nine people followed my example and staked on black. The croupiers exchanged glances and said something to one another. People were talking all round in suspense.

Black one. I don't remember my winnings after, nor what I staked on. I only remember as though in a dream that I won, I believe, sixteen thousand florins; suddenly three unlucky turns took twelve thousand from it; then I staked the last four thousand on '*passe*' (but I scarcely felt anything as I did so; I simply waited in a mechanical, senseless way) – and again I won; then I won four times running. I only remember that I gathered up money in thousands; I remember, too, that the middle twelve won most often and I kept to it. It turned up with a sort of regularity, certainly three or four times in succession, then it did not turn up twice running and then it followed three or four times in succession. Such astonishing regularity is sometimes met with in streaks, and that is what throws inveterate gamblers who calculate with a pencil in their hands out of their reckoning. And what horrible ironies of fate happen sometimes in such cases!

I believe not more than half an hour had passed since I came into the room, when suddenly the croupier informed me that I had won thirty thousand florins, and as the bank did not meet claims for a larger sum at one time the roulette would be closed till next morning. I snatched up all my gold, dropped it into my pockets, snatched up all my notes, and at once went into the other room where there was another roulette table; the whole crowd streamed after me; there at once a place was cleared for me and I fell to staking again haphazard without reckoning. I don't understand what saved me!

At times, however, a glimmer of prudence began to dawn upon my mind. I clung to certain numbers and combinations, but soon abandoned them and staked almost unconsciously. I must have been very absent-minded: I remember the croupiers several times corrected me. I made several gross mistakes. My temples were soaked with sweat and my hands were shaking. The Poles ran up, too, with offers of their services, but I listened to no one. My luck was unbroken! Suddenly there were sounds of loud talk and laughter, and everyone cried 'Bravo, bravo!' Some even clapped their hands. Here, too, I collected three hundred thousand florins, and the bank closed till next day.

'Go away, go away,' a voice whispered on my right.

It was a Frankfurt Jew; he was standing beside me all the time, and I believe sometimes helped me in my play.

'For goodness' sake go,' another voice whispered in my left ear.

I took a hurried glance. It was a lady about thirty, very soberly and quietly dressed, with a tired, pale, sickly face which yet bore traces of having once been beautiful. At that moment I was stuffing my pockets with the notes, which I crumpled up anyhow, and gathering up the gold that lay on the table. Snatching up the last roll of notes, I succeeded in putting it into the pale lady's hands quite without attracting notice; I had an intense desire to do so at the time, and I remember her pale slim fingers pressed my hand warmly in token of gratitude. All that took place in one instant.

Having collected quickly all my winnings I went quickly to the trente et quarante.

Trente et quarante is frequented by the aristocratic public. Unlike roulette, it is a game of cards. Here the bank will pay up to a hundred thousand thalers at once. The largest stake is here also four thousand florins. I knew nothing of the game, and scarcely knew how to bet on it, except the red and the black upon which one can bet in this game too. And I stuck to red and black. The whole Casino crowded round. I don't remember whether I once thought of Polina all this time. I was experiencing an overwhelming enjoyment in scooping up and taking away the notes which grew up in a heap before me.

It seemed as though fate were urging me on. This time, as luck would have it, a circumstance occurred which, however, is fairly frequent in the game. Chance favours red, for instance, ten or even fifteen times in succession. I had heard two days before that in the previous week red had turned up twenty-two times in succession; it was something which had never been remembered in roulette, and it was talked of with amazement. Every one, of course, abandoned red at once, and after the tenth time, for instance, scarcely any one dared to stake on it. But none of the experienced players staked on black either. The experienced gambler knows what is meant by this 'freak of chance'. It would mean that after red had won sixteen times, at the seventeenth time the luck would infallibly fall on black. Novices at play rush to this conclusion in crowds, double and treble their stakes, and lose terribly.

But, noticing that red had turned up seven times running, by strange perversity I staked on it. I am convinced that vanity was half responsible for it; I wanted to impress the spectators by taking a mad risk, and – oh, the strange sensation – I remember distinctly that, quite apart from the promptings of vanity, I was possessed by an intense craving for risk. Perhaps passing through so many sensations my soul was not satisfied but only irritated by them and craved still more sensation – and stronger and stronger ones – till utterly exhausted. And, truly I am not lying, if the regulations had allowed me to stake fifty thousand florins at once, I should certainly have staked them. People around shouted that it was madness – that red had won fourteen times already!

'Monsieur a gagné déjà cent mille florins,' I heard a voice say near me.

I suddenly came to myself. What? I had won during that evening a hundred thousand florins? And what more did I want? I fell on my banknotes, crumpled them up in my pockets without counting them, scooped up all my gold, all my rolls of notes, and ran out of the Casino. Every one was laughing as I went through the room, looking at my bulging pockets and at the way I staggered under the weight of gold. I think it weighed over twenty pounds. Several hands were held out to me; I gave it away in handfuls as I snatched it up. Two Jews stopped me at the outer door.

'You are bold – you are very bold,' they said to me, 'but be sure to go away to-morrow as soon as possible, or else you will lose it all – you will lose it all.'

I didn't listen to them. The avenue was so dark that I could not see my hand before my face. It was half a mile to the hotel. I had never been afraid of thieves or robbers even as a small boy; I did not think of them now either. I don't remember what I thought of on the road; I had no thoughts. I was only aware of an immense enjoyment – success, victory, power.

FEDOR DOSTOEVSKY, *The Gambler*

Gossip

There is no rampart that will hold out against malice.

JEAN BAPTISTE MOLIÈRE

If all men knew what others say of them, there would not be four friends in the world.

BLAISE PASCAL

The man that despiseth slander deserveth it.

MARQUESS OF HALIFAX

Every disclosure of a secret is the fault of him who first confided it.

JEAN DE LA BRUYÈRE

Slander would not stick if it had not always something to lay hold of.

MARQUIS OF HALIFAX

In scandal as in robbery, the receiver is always thought as bad as the thief.

EARL OF CHESTERFIELD

About Bishops

29 July 1667: Among other discourse, my cozen Roger told us as a thing certain, that the Archbishop of Canterbury, that now is, do keep a wench, and that he is as very a wencher as can be: and tells us it is a thing publickly known that Sir Charles Sedley had got away one of the Archbishop's wenches from him, and the Archbishop sent to him to let him know that she was his kinswoman, and did wonder that he would offer any dishonour to one related to him. To which Sir Charles Sedley is said to answer, 'Pray, tell his Grace that I believe he finds himself too old, and is afraid that I should outdo him among his girls, and spoil his trade.' But he makes no more of doubt to say that the Archbishop is a wencher, and known to be so, which is one of the most astonishing things that I have heard of, unless it be, what for certain he says is true, that my Lady Castlemaine hath made a Bishop lately, namely, her uncle, Dr Glenham.

SAMUEL PEPYS, Diary

About a Capitalist

'Mr Merdle is dead.'

'I should wish,' said the Chief Butler, 'to give a month's notice.'

'Mr Merdle has destroyed himself.'

'Sir,' said the Chief Butler, 'that is very unpleasant to the feelings of one in my position, as calculated to awaken prejudice: and I should wish to leave immediate.'

'If you are not shocked, are you not surprised, man?' demanded the Physician, warmly.

The Chief Butler, erect and calm, replied in these memorable words: 'Sir, Mr Merdle never was the gentleman, and no ungentlemanly act on Mr Merdle's part would surprise me. Is there anybody else I can send to you, or any other directions I can give before I leave, respecting what you would wish to be done?' ...

The report that the great man was dead, got about with astonishing rapidity. At first he was dead of all the diseases that ever were known, and of several brand-new maladies invented with the speed of Light to meet the demand of the occasion. He had concealed a dropsy from infancy, he had inherited a large estate of water on the chest from his grandfather, he had had an operation performed upon him every morning of his life for eighteen years, he had been subject to the explosion of important veins in his body after the manner of fireworks, he had had something the matter with his lungs, he had had something the matter with his heart, he had had something the matter with his brain. Five hundred people who sat down to breakfast entirely uninformed on the whole subject, believed before they had done breakfast, that they privately and personally knew Physician to have said to Mr Merdle, 'You must expect to go out, some day, like the snuff of a candle,' and that they knew Mr Merdle to have said to Physician, 'A man can die but once.' By about eleven o'clock in the forenoon, something the matter with the brain, became the favourite theory against the field; and by twelve the something had been distinctly ascertained to be 'Pressure'.

Pressure was so entirely satisfactory to the public mind, and seemed to make everybody so comfortable, that it might have lasted all day but for Bar's having taken the real state of the case into Court at half-past nine. This led to its beginning to be currently whispered all over London by about one, that Mr Merdle had killed himself. Pressure, however, so far from being overthrown by the discovery, became a greater favourite than ever. There was a general moralising upon Pressure, in every street. All the people who had tried to make money and had not been able to do it, said, There you were! You no sooner began to devote yourself to the pursuit of wealth, than you got Pressure. The idle people improved the occasion in a similar manner. See, said they, what you brought yourself to by work, work, work! You persisted in working, you overdid it, Pressure came on, and you were done for! This consideration was very potent in many quarters, but nowhere more so than among the young clerks and partners who had never been in the slightest danger of over-doing it. These one and all declared, quite piously, that they hoped they would never forget the warning as long as they lived, and that their con-duct might be so regulated as to keep off Pressure, and preserve them, a comfort to their friends, for many years.

But, at about the time of High 'Change, Pressure began to wane, and appalling whispers to circulate, east, west, north, and south. At first they were faint, and went no further than a doubt whether Mr Merdle's wealth would be found to be as vast as had been supposed; whether there might not be a temporary difficulty in 'realising' it; whether there might not even be a temporary suspension (say a month or so), on the part of the wonderful Bank. As the whispers became louder, which they did from that time every minute, they became more threatening. He had sprung from nothing, by no natural growth or process that any one could account for; he had been, after all, a low, ignorant fellow; he had been a down-looking man, and no one had ever been able to catch his eye; he had been taken up by all sorts of people, in quite an unaccount-able manner; he had never had any money of his own, his ventures had been utterly reckless, and his expenditure had been most enormous. In steady progression, as the day declined, the talk rose in sound and purpose.

CHARLES DICKENS, *Little Dorrit*

About a Princess

Paris, Monday 15 December 1670

I am going to tell you a thing that is the most astonishing, the most surprising, the most marvellous, the most miraculous, the most supreme, the most confounding, the most unheard, the most singular, the most extraordinary, the most incredible, the most unforeseen, the greatest, the least, the rarest, the most common, the most public, the most private, till to-day; the most brilliant, the most to be envied; in short, a thing of which there has been but one example for ages past, and that not a just one neither; a thing that we cannot believe at Paris; how then will it gain credit at Lyons? A thing which makes everybody cry, Lord have mercy upon us! a thing which causes the greatest joy to Madame de Rohan and Madame de Hauterive; a thing, in fine, which will be done on Sunday next, when those who are present at it will think they see double. A thing which will be done on Sunday, and yet perhaps not finished on Monday. I cannot bring myself to tell it to you: Can't you guess? I give you three times to do it in. What, not a Word to throw at a Dog? Well then, I find I must tell you. Monsieur de Lauzun is to be married next Sunday at the Louvre, to – guess whom! I give you four times to do it in, I give you six, I give you an hundred. Says Madame de Coulanges, it is really very hard to guess. Perhaps it is Madame de la Valière: Indeed, Madam, it is not. It is Mademoiselle de Retz, then: No, nor yet her, you are violently provincial. Lord bless me, say you, what stupid wretches we are; it is Mademoiselle de Colbert all the while. Nay, now you are still further from the mark. Why then it must certainly be Mademoiselle de Créquy: You have it not yet. Well, I find I must tell you at last: He is to be married next Sunday, at the Louvre, with the King's leave, to Mademoiselle, Mademoiselle de ... Mademoiselle – guess her name: He marries Mademoiselle, the great Mademoiselle; Mademoiselle daughter to the late MONSIEUR. Mademoiselle grand-daughter of HENRY the IVth, Mademoiselle d'Eu, Mademoiselle de Dombes, Mademoiselle de Montpensier, Mademoiselle d'Orléans, Mademoiselle the King's cousin-german, Mademoiselle destined to the throne, Mademoiselle, the only match that was worthy of MONSIEUR. Here is glorious matter for talk. If you should cry out, if you are beside yourselves, if you say we have told you a lie, that it's all false, that we are making a jest of you, that it is a very pretty joke indeed! that the invention is dull, flat; in short, if you abuse us, we shall think you are quite in the right; for we have done just the same ourselves. Farewell, you will find from the Letters you receive this post, whether we tell you truth, or not.

Paris, Friday 19 December 1670

What is called falling from the clouds, or from a pinnacle, happened last night at the Thuilleries; but I must take things farther back. You have already shared in the joy, the transport, and ecstacies of the princess and her happy lover. It was just as I told you, the affair was made public on Monday. Tuesday was passed in talking, astonishment, and compliments. Wednesday Mademoiselle made a deed of gift to Monsieur de Lauzun, investing him with certain titles, names, and dignities, necessary to be inserted in the marriage-contract, which was drawn up that day. She gave him then, till she could give him something better, four Duchies; the first was that of Count d'Eu, which entitles him to rank as first peer of France, the Dukedom of Montpensier, which title he bore all that day; the Dukedom de Saint Fargeau, and the Dukedom de Chatellerault, the whole valued at twenty-two millions of livres. The contract was then drawn up, and he took the name of Montpensier. Thursday morning, which was yesterday, Mademoiselle was in expectation of the King's signing the contract, as he had said he would; but, about seven o'clock in the evening, the Queen, Monsieur, and several old dotards that were about him, had so persuaded his Majesty, that his reputation would suffer in this affair, that after sending for Mademoiselle and Monsieur de Lauzun into his presence, he declared to them, before the Prince, that he absolutely forbad them to think any further about this marriage. Monsieur de Lauzun received this order with all the respect, all the submission, all the firmness, and, at the same time, all the despair, that could be expected in so great a reverse of fortune. As for Mademoiselle, being under no restraint, she gave a loose to herself, and burst forth into tears, cries, lamentations, and the most violent expressions of grief; she keeps her bed all day long, and takes nothing within her lips but a little broth. What a fine dream is here! what a glorious subject for a tragedy, or a romance, but especially for an eternity of talk and reasoning! This is what we do day and night, morning and evening, without end or ceasing.

MARQUISE DE SÉVIGNÉ, *Letters*

Little secrets are commonly told again, but great ones generally kept.

EARL OF CHESTERFIELD

Shy and unready men are great betrayers of secrets; for there are few wants more urgent for the moment than the want of something to say.

SIR HENRY TAYLOR

The peachy-skinned charmers with the skeleton throats.

CHARLES DICKENS

She poured a little social sewage into his ears.

GEORGE MEREDITH

Chin-Deep in Malice

Now calumnies arise, and black Reproach
Triumphant croaks aloud, and joyful claps
Her raven wing! Insinuations vile
And slanderous spring from pestilential breath,
And tongues thrice dipped in hell. Contagion foul
Steams from th' infernal furnace, hot and fierce,
And spreads th' infectious influence o'er his fame!
Then each unworthy, ignominious fool,
Each female basilisk with forky sting,
And outward-seeming, heart-unmeaning tear
(Offspring most loathsome of Hypocrisy,
That vile, detested, double-damning sin:
Confusion and perdition overwhelm
And blast them, execrable, into ruin!),
Chin-deep in malice shoot their bitter darts
Of mockery and derision: adding, sly,
Th' invidious wink, the mean, contemptuous leer,
And flouting grin, 'emphatically scornful'.

Nor less th' insidious knave, supremely dull!
Mixture of monkey, crocodile and mole,
Yet stupid as the ostrich, ass and owl;
In high redundance of Typhonic rage,
With harsh stentorian tone, disdainful, flings
Unmerited reflections, vehement, long,
Nonsensical and noisy. Vain, he struts
With domineering insolence replete,
And, lordly, tramples on distress in anguish.

MARY LATTER

Heard on Unimpeachable Authority

[Rudolph Hess, Hitler's Deputy Führer, had flown to Scotland on 11 May to offer peace terms]

13 May 1941: Gladwyn [Jebb, later Lord Gladwyn], [John] Wilmot [later Lord Wilmot of Selmeston] and I dine together. Gladwyn says he has overheard, but must not repeat to me, who was the 'Scottish personality' whom Hess has said he has come to see. I say, 'Was it Lord Brocket or the Duke of Buccleuch?' Gladwyn says he mustn't answer. I say, 'Very well, I shall put it about that it was the Duke of Buccleuch.' Returning to the Ministry I find [David] Bowes-Lyons and [Malcolm] McCorquodale [later Lord McCorquodale of Newton] outside. The latter says that it was the Duke of Hamilton. He knows this from a man who travelled down by the night train to see Andrew Duncan and who heard it from people who were standing drinks to the ploughman who picked Hess up.

LORD DALTON, *Second World War Diary 1940–45*

Inaccurate

3 July [1815], Wednesday, 6.30 a.m., in bed, Geneva: Among more than sixty English travellers here, there is Lord Byron, who is *cut* by everybody. They tell a strange adventure of his … He is now living at a villa on the Savoy side of the lake with that woman, who it seems proves to be a Mrs Shelley, wife to the man who keeps the Mount Coffee-house.

LORD GLENBERVIE, *Journals*

The Gossipers

The gossipers have lowered their voices,
Willing words to make the rumours certain,
Suspicious hands tug at the neighbouring vices,
Unthinking actions given causes
Stir their old bones behind cupboard and curtain.

Putting two and two together,
Informed by rumour and the register,
The virgins smelt out, three streets up,
A girl whose single bed held two
To make ends meet,
Found managers and widows wanting
In morals and full marriage bunting,
And other virgins in official fathers.

For all the inconvenience they make,
The trouble, devildom, and heartbreak,
The withered women win them bedfellows.
Nightly upon their wrinkled breasts
Press the old lies and the old ghosts.

DYLAN THOMAS

Scandal is gossip made tedious by morality.

OSCAR WILDE

Satan's Tongue-Pie.

ANATOLE FRANCE

Scandal is merely the compassionate allowance which the gay make to the humdrum.

SAKI

Gossip is vice enjoyed vicariously.

ELBERT HUBBARD

Asperse. Maliciously to ascribe to another vicious actions which one has not had the temptation and opportunity to commit.

AMBROSE BIERCE

Defamation and calumny never attack where there is no weak place; they magnify, but they do not create.

EARL OF CHESTERFIELD

Love and scandal are the best sweeteners of tea.

HENRY FIELDING

Whisper only of the insanity of the great.

GEORG LICHTENBERG

The motto on all palace-gates is 'HUSH!'

LADY LOUISA STUART

Throw dirt enough and some will stick.

ARCHBISHOP RICHARD WHATELY

Tattle

A scandal or two
I shall mention to you;
And first, here is one
That's as sure as a gun,
For the person who told me was told it
By some one who knew
That the story was true,
For he heard it one day,
In a casual way,
From a man who's a brother
Of some one or other
Who holds an appointment
In Holloway's ointment
And pill branch at Bow;
But, besides that, I *know*.
Well, the Duchess of Dash,
Being troubled for cash,
Pawned an emerald cluster
And large knuckle-duster
Of brilliants and rubies
At Spoonbill and Booby's;
And now they allege
That the forfeited pledge
Is nothing but paste

Set with very good taste,
Which they found was the fact
When the cluster was cracked
By a fall from the 'kerridge'
Of Mrs Sam Gerridge,
To whom S. and B. had just sold it.
So what do you think of your Duchess of Dash?
With my raggery waggery, alumny calumny, slippery sloppery slash!

You've heard what they say
Of your friend, little K.?
Well, there's a fine mess!
And it can't be much less
Than a thousand he's dropped
In the bank that has stopped;
At a time, I'll be bound,
When he wants every pound;
And I'd not be surprised,
As at present advised,
If we chanced to hear tell
That he'd bolted this minute,
And Johnson as well,
For I know he was in it!
And then there's young Q.,
He'll begin to look blue
When B. and C. find
That there's something behind,
As they're sure before long to discover.
Of course you're aware
Of the Whiffer affair?
I'm an old friend of Whiffer,
And that's why we differ,
And when he was single
I told him my mind
About Emily Bingle,
But he was so blind

That he never could see
She was sweet upon *me*.
Oh! The woman's awake;
Don't make any mistake!
She's a nice-looking girl,
And the niece of an Earl,
But she hadn't a rap
When she married this chap,
And now he begins
To cry 'Needles and pins!'
At least I suppose,
Although nobody knows,
That he must have found out
What his wife is about,
And a certain Lord F. is her lover.
So don't you consider old Whiffer was rash?
With my staggery swaggery, blackery quackery, blundery Grundy-ry
hash!

That's rather a queer
Sort of story I hear
Set about to explain
Why Sir John goes to Spain,
And his family too,
With, of course, little Loo.
Yes, it possibly may
Have been just as you say;
But it does appear strange
They should suddenly change
The tour they had planned,
For I can't understand
Why it suits them to go
Where they're sure not to see
A soul whom they know.
Well, it's nothing to me!

But I hear some odd things
That are told of the Byngs;
And one of 'em is
That they're too fond of 'fiz',
To say nothing of brandy
Or anything handy.
Well, now, don't you think
When a girl takes to drink,
It's all up with her quite
As regards what is right?
There is only one answer I *can* see.
But, talking of that,
Come, I'll bet you a hat
You don't know the reason
Why all through last season
The Byngs gave no ball,
Nor the least thing at all
In the house-warming way.
Oh! I know what you'll say;
They had lost a relation;
But that's mere evasion.
The true cause I know,
But you won't let it go
Any further, I'm sure,
For it's well-known that you're
Not the fellow to chatter
About such a matter;
And so, it's just this,
There was something amiss
That had reached Sir John's ears
To awaken his fears
About Miss Louisa
And John Thomas Coombe.
(I need not say he's a
Mere sort of head-groom.)

And John had declared
That if ever she dared
Show herself at a 'hop',
    He'd be there to say 'stop',
And John would have done it, I fancy.
— Bah! Tattlers, beware of the cudgel or lash,
With your blundery Grundy-ry, blackery quackery, staggery swaggery,
    slippery sloppery, alumny calumny, raggery waggery, uttery guttery
    trash!

GODFREY TURNER

Heavenly Vices

Find out where they sell good wine. Then make a stopper for my bottle from the leaves of a climbing vine ... Buy apricots, melons, artichokes, strawberries and cream. This is what I like in summer, when lying on the bank by the edge of a stream I eat to the trickle of water.

PIERRE DE RONSARD

Give me a haunch of buck to eat, and to drink Madeira old,
And a gentle wife to rest with, and in my arms to fold,
An Arabic book to study, a Norfolk cob to ride,
And a house to live in shaded with trees, and near to a riverside;
Wth such good things around me, and blessed with good health withal,
Though I should live for a hundred years, for death I would not call.

SAMUEL PARR

[Luttrell]'s idea of heaven is eating *pâté de foie gras* to the sound of trumpets.

REV. SYDNEY SMITH

Give me books, fruit, French wine and fine weather and a little music out of doors, played by somebody I do not know.

JOHN KEATS

Sitting in bed on Sunday morning eating hot buttered toast with cunty fingers.

HENRY GREEN

My own idea of heaven is playing Bridge on a summer's afternoon with agreeable companions while drinking *crème de menthe frappée* through a straw.

AUBERON WAUGH

Hedonism

'Tis a great Pleasure to cheat the World. 'Tis Power, as divine Hobbes calls it.

APHRA BEHN

Satiety, perpetual Disgust, and Feverishness of Desire, attend those who passionately study Pleasure. They best enjoy it, who study to regulate their passions.

EARL OF SHAFTESBURY

Life would be quite tolerable were it not for its pleasures.

VISCOUNT PALMERSTON

I should like now to promenade round your Gardens – apple tasting – pear tasting – plum judging – apricot nibbling – peach scrunching – Nectarine sucking and Melon carving. I have also a great feeling for antiquated cherries full of sugar cracks – and a white currant tree kept for company. I admire lolling on a lawn by a water-lilied pond to eat white currants and see gold fish: and go to the Fair of an evening if I'm good.

JOHN KEATS

The aristocratic pleasure of giving offence.

CHARLES BAUDELAIRE

A man must not dream of dying before he has drunk five thousand bottles of champagne and smoked a hundred thousand cigars.

PRINCE OTTO VON BISMARCK

Alma Perdida

Yours, vague yearnings; exhilarations;
After-dinner thoughts; sudden ardours;
The warm glow which follows the satisfaction
Of bodily needs; flashes of genius; restlessness
During digestion; relief
Of digestion accomplished; spontaneous moments of joy;
Circulation problems; memories of love;
Scent of benjamin in the morning bath; reveries of love;
My enormous Castillian sense of humour, my huge
Puritan sadness, my peculiar tastes:
Chocolates, sweets so sweet they burn, iced drinks;
Mind-dulling cigars; you, soporific cigarettes;
The thrill of speed; the comfort of the armchair; the gift
Of sleep in total darkness;
Great poetry of the commonplace: *faits divers*; journeys;
Gypsies; sleigh-rides; rain on the sea;
Lunacy of the feverish night, alone with a handful of books;

Ups and downs of the weather, and the inner weather;
Rediscovered moments of another life; recollections, prophecies;
O splendours of shared existence and the usual routine,
Yours this lost soul.

VALÉRY LARBAUD

The Careless Gallant

Let us drink and be merry, dance, joke, and rejoice,
With claret and sherry, theorbo and voice,
The changeable world to our joy is unjust,
All treasure's uncertain, then down with your dust;
   In frolics dispose your pounds, shillings, and pence,
   For we shall be nothing a hundred years hence.

We'll sport and be free with Frank, Betty, and Dolly,
Have lobsters and oysters to cure melancholy,
Fish dinners will make a man spring like a flea,
Dame Venus, love's lady, was born of the sea.
   With her and with Bacchus we'll tickle the sense,
   For we shall be past it a hundred years hence.

Your beautiful bit, that hath all eyes upon her,
That her honesty sells for a hogo of honour,
Whose lightness and brightness doth cast such a splendour,
That none are thought fit but the stars to attend her;
   Though now she seems pleasant and sweet to the sense,
   Will be damnably mouldy a hundred years hence.

Your usurer that in the hundred takes twenty,
Who wants in his wealth, and pines in his plenty,
Lays up for a season which he shall ne'er see,
The year of one thousand, eight hundred and three,
   Shall have changed all his bags, his houses and rents,
   For a worm-eaten coffin a hundred years hence.

Your Chancery-lawyer who by subtlety thrives,
In spinning a suit to the length of three lives,
A suit which the client doth wear out in slavery,
Whilst pleader makes conscience a cloak for his knavery,
    Can boast of his cunning but i' th' present tense,
    For *non est inventus* a hundred years hence.

Then why should we turmoil in cares and in fears,
And turn our tranquillity to sighs and tears?
Let's eat, drink and play, ere the worms do corrupt us,
For I say that, *post mortem nulla voluptas*;
    Let's deal with our Damsels, that we may from thence
    Have broods to succeed us a hundred years hence.

I never could gain satisfaction upon
Your dreams of a bliss when we're cold as a stone,
The Sages call us Drunkards, Gluttons, and Wenchers,
But we find such morsels, upon their own trenchers:
    For Abigail, Hannah, and sister Prudence,
    Will simper to nothing a hundred years hence.

The butterfly courtier, that pageant of state,
The mouse-trap of honour and May-game of fate,
With all his ambitions, intrigues, and his tricks,
Must die like a clown, and then drop into Styx,
    His plots against death are too slender a fence,
    For he'll be out of place a hundred years hence.

Yea, the poet himself that so loftily sings,
As he scorns any subjects, but heroes or kings,
Must to the capricios of fortune submit,
And often be counted a fool for his wit,
    Thus beauty, wit, wealth, law, learning and sense,
    All comes to nothing a hundred years hence.

THOMAS JORDAN

The Four Best Things

Health is the first good lent to men;
A gentle disposition then:
Next, to be rich by no by-wayes;
Lastly, with friends t'enjoy our dayes.

ROBERT HERRICK

Henry Hastings: born 1551, died 1650

Mr Hastings, by his quality, being the son, brother, and uncle to the Earls of Huntingdon, and his way of living, had the first place amongst us. He was peradventure an original in our age, or rather the copy of our nobility in ancient days in hunting and not warlike times; he was low, very strong and very active, of a reddish flaxen hair, his clothes always green cloth, and never all worth when new five pounds. His house was perfectly of the old fashion, in the midst of a large park well stocked with deer, and near the house rabbits to serve his kitchen, many fish-ponds, and great store of wood and timber; a bowling-green in it, long but narrow, full of high ridges, it being never levelled since it was ploughed; they used round sand bowls, and it had a banqueting-house like a stand, a large one built in a tree. He kept all manner of sport-hounds that ran; buck, fox, hare, otter, and badger, and hawks long and short winged; he had all sorts of nets for fishing: he had a walk in the New Forest and the manor of Christ Church. This last supplied him with red deer, sea and river fish; and indeed all his neighbours' grounds and royalties were free to him, who bestowed all his time in such sports, but what he borrowed to caress his neighbours' wives and daughters, there being not a woman in all his walks of the degree of a yeoman's wife or under, and under the age of forty, but it was extremely her fault if he were not intimately acquainted with her. This made him very popular, always speaking kindly to the husband, brother, or father who was to boot very welcome to his house whenever he came. There he found beef pudding and small beer in great plenty, a house not so neatly kept as to shame him or his dirty shoes, the great hall strewed with marrow bones, full of hawks' perches, hounds, spaniels, and terriers, the upper sides of the hall hung with the fox-skins of this and the last year's skinning, here and there a polecat intermixed, guns and keepers' and huntsmen's poles in abundance. The parlour was a large long room, as properly furnished; on a great hearth paved with brick lay some terriers and the choicest hounds and spaniels; seldom but two of the great chairs had litters of young cats in them, which were not to be disturbed, he having always three or four attending him at dinner, and a little white round stick of fourteen inches long lying by his trencher, that he might defend such meat as he had no mind to part with to them. The windows, which were very large, served for places to lay his arrows, crossbows, stonebows, and other suchlike accoutrements; the corners of the room full of the best chose hunting and hawking poles; an oyster-table at the lower end, which was of constant use twice a day all the year round, for he never failed to eat oysters before dinner and sup-per through all seasons; the neighbouring town of Poole supplied him with them. The upper part of this room had two small tables and a desk, on the one side of which was a church Bible, on the other the Book of Martyrs; on the tables were hawks' hoods, bells, and suchlike, two or three old green hats, with their crowns thrust in so as to hold ten or a dozen eggs, which were of a pheasant kind of poultry he took much care of and fed himself; tables, dice, cards and boxes were not wanting. In the hole of the desk were store of tobacco-pipes that had been used. On one side of this end of the room was the door of a closet, wherein stood the strong beer and the wine, which never came thence but in single glasses, that being the rule of the house exactly observed, for he never exceeded in drink or permitted it. On the other side was a door into an old chapel not used for devotion; the pulpit, as the safest place, was never wanting of a cold chine of beef, pasty of venison, gammon of bacon, or great apple-pie, with thick crust extremely baked. His table cost him not much, though it was very good to eat at, his sports supplying all but beef and mutton, except Friday, when he had the best sea-fish as well as other fish he could get, and was the day that his neighbours of best quality most visited him. He never wanted a London pudding, and always sung it in with my part lies there in-a'. He drank a glass of wine or two at meals, very often syrrup of gilliflower in his sack, and had always a tun glass without feet stood by him holding a pint of small beer, which he often stirred with a great sprig of rosemary. He was well-natured, but soon angry, calling his servants bastard and cuckoldy knaves, in one of which he often spoke truth to his own knowledge, and sometimes in both, though of the same man. He lived to a hundred, never lost his eyesight, but always writ and read without spectacles, and got to horse without help. Until past fourscore he rode to the death of a stag as well as any.

IST EARL OF SHAFTESBURY, autobiographical fragment

A Man of Pleasure

DEAR BOY,

Pleasure is the rock which most young people split upon; they launch out with crowded sails in quest of it, but without a compass to direct their course, or reason sufficient to steer the vessel; for want of which, pain and shame, instead of Pleasure, are the returns of their voyage. Do not think that I mean to snarl at Pleasure, like a Stoic, or to preach against it, like a parson; no, I mean to point it out, and recommend it to you, like an Epicurean: I wish you a great deal; and my only view is to hinder you from mistaking it.

The character which most young men first aim at is, that of a Man of Pleasure; but they generally take it upon trust; and, instead of consulting their own taste and inclinations, they blindly adopt whatever those, with whom they chiefly converse, are pleased to call by the name of Pleasure; and a *Man of Pleasure*, in the vulgar acceptation of that phrase, means only a beastly drunkard, an abandoned whoremaster, and a profligate swearer and curser. As it may be of use to you, I am not unwilling, though at the same time ashamed, to own, that the vices of my youth proceeded much more from my silly resolution of being what I heard called a Man of Pleasure, than from my own inclinations. I always naturally hated drinking; and yet I have often drunk, with disgust at the time, attended by great sickness the next day, only because I then considered drinking as a necessary qualification for a fine gentleman, and a Man of Pleasure.

The same as to gaming. I did not want money, and consequently had no occasion to play for it; but I thought Play another necessary ingredient in the composition of a Man of Pleasure, and accordingly I plunged into it without desire, at first; sacrificed a thousand real pleasures to it; and made myself solidly uneasy by it, for thirty of the best years of my life.

I was even absurd enough, for a little while, to swear, by way of adorning and completing the shining character which I affected; but this folly I soon laid aside, upon finding both the guilt and the indecency of it.

Thus seduced by fashion, and blindly adopting nominal pleasures, I lost real ones; and my fortune impaired, and my constitution shattered, are, I must confess, the just punishment of my errors.

Take warning then by them; choose your pleasures for yourself, and do not let them be imposed upon you. Follow nature, and not fashion; weigh the present enjoyment of your pleasures against the necessary consequences of them, and then let your own common sense determine your choice.

EARL OF CHESTERFIELD, letter of 27 March 1747

A Plain Man's Pleasures

I want no variety. Let things be really good, and I, for one, am in no danger of wearying of them. For example, to rise every day about half after nine – eat a couple of eggs and muffins, and drink some cups of genuine, sound, clear coffee – then to smoke a cigar or so – read the *Chronicle* – skim a few volumes of some first-rate new novel, or perhaps pen a libel or two in a light sketchy vein – then to take a bowl of strong, rich, invigorating soup – then to get on horseback, and ride seven or eight miles, paying a visit to some amiable, well-bred, accomplished young lady, in the course of it, and chattering away an hour with her,

> 'Sporting with Amaryllis in the shade,
> Or with the tangles of Neæra's hair,'

as Milton expresses it – then to take a hot-bath, and dress – then to sit down to a plain substantial dinner, in company with a select party of real good, honest, jolly Tories – and to spend the rest of the evening with them over a pitcher of cool chateau-margout, singing, laughing, speechifying, blending wit and wisdom, and winding up the whole with a devil and a tumbler or two of hot rum-punch. This, repeated day after day, week after week, month after month, and year after year, may perhaps appear, to some people, a picture pregnant with ideas of the most sickening and disgusting monotony. Not so with me, however. I am a plain man. I could lead this dull course of uniform unvaried existence for the whole period of the Millennium. Indeed I mean to do so.

WILLIAM MAGINN, *Maxims of Sir Morgan O'Doherty*

Pleasures of a Property Owner

Would that I had £300,000
    Invested in some strong security;
A Midland Country House with formal grounds,
    A Town House, and a House beside the sea,
And one in Spain, and One in Normandy,
    And Friends innumerable at my call
And youth serene – and underneath it all
    One steadfast, passionate flame to nurture me.

HILAIRE BELLOC

Simple Hopes of Sir Epicurean Mammon

I will have all my beds blown up, not stuft;
Down is too hard : and then, mine oval room
Fill'd with such pictures as Tiberius took
From Elephantis, and dull Aretine
But coldly imitated. Then, my glasses
Cut in more subtle angles, to disperse

And multiply the figures, as I walk
Naked between my succubæ. My mists
I'll have of perfume, vapour'd 'bout the room,
To lose our selves in; and my baths, like pits
To fall into; from whence we will come forth,
And roll us dry in gossamer and roses. –
Is it arrived at ruby? – Where I spy
A wealthy citizen, or a rich lawyer,
Have a sublimed pure wife, unto that fellow
I'll send a thousand pound to be my cuckold ...
I'll have no bawds,
But fathers and mothers: they will do it best,
Best of all others. And my flatterers
Shall be the pure and gravest of divines,
That I can get for money. My mere fools,
Eloquent burgesses, and then my poets
The same that writ so subtly of the fart,
Whom I will entertain still for that subject.
The few that would give out themselves to be
Court and town-stallions, and, each-where, bely
Ladies who are known most innocent, for them;
Those will I beg, to make me eunuchs of:
And they shall fan me with ten estrich tails
A-piece, made in a plume to gather wind.
We will be brave, Puffe, now we have the med'cine.
My meat shall all come in, in Indian shells,
Dishes of agat set in gold, and studded
With emeralds, sapphires, hyacinths, and rubies.
The tongues of carps, dormice, and camels heels,
Boil'd in the spirit of sol, and dissolv'd pearl,
Apicius' diet, 'gainst the epilepsy:
And I will eat these broths with spoons of amber,
Headed with diamond and carbuncle.
My foot-boy shall eat pheasants, calver'd salmons,
Knots, godwits, lampreys: I my self will have
The beards of barbels served, instead of sallads;

Oil'd mushrooms; and the swelling unctuous paps
Of a fat pregnant sow, newly cut off,
Drest with an exquisite, and poignant sauce;
For which, I'll say unto my cook, *There's gold,*
Go forth, and be a knight ...
My shirts
I'll have of taffeta-sarsnet, soft and light
As cobwebs; and for all my other raiment,
It shall be such as might provoke the Persian,
Were he to teach the world riot anew.
My gloves of fishes and birds skins, perfumed
With gums of paradise, and eastern air.

BEN JONSON, The Alchemist

Summer Holiday

23 August 1922: Day follows day, fine, happy, golden within and without. Our friends are beautiful, cheerful, healthy, delicious and pleased with everything, all quite naturally, without effort or strain. At Santec we walked barefoot in the sea and the warm, soft sand. We drove back by the Isle of Sieck and by Saint-Pol, past the Danielou estate with the famous fig tree which spreads over six hundred square metres and is supported on ninety stone pillars. Our friends exclaimed : 'But it's a marvel! People go all the way to India to see giant baobabs or to Africa in order to rave about enormous rubber trees, and this beats the lot!' When we got home they went swimming, with Georges. Wrapped in her white towelling robe, the Duchess is as attractive as ever. No one else has such a majestic walk. For breakfast I give them toast, warm brioches, milk bread with raisins in it, tea, the freshest butter and our famous Plougastel strawberry jam, served on Quimper china. They make short work of it. We never stop laughing, we understand each other, we blend and mingle. In the evenings . . . the plot thickens. The Duchess came to lie on my bed and Nathalie snuggled between us. Caresses, loving kisses. It was charming – perhaps a little nerve-racking. Camille kept her head turned away so that she should see nothing. Georges read poetry aloud. Nathalie remembered something Marguerite Moreno said when she was staying with friends in the country, on a rainy day. Someone had asked 'What shall we do?' In her melodious, beautifully modulated voice Marguerite let fall the one word: 'Fornicate.'

I love my friends. Surely, dear Lord, it can't be a great sin? It is You who sent them to me all open-hearted, it's You who made them so sweetly fond and sensual, it's You who made them lean over me with such tenderness – surely it is?

'The Duchess is flighty,' says Nathalie. 'Elegantly, indolently flighty.' What else should Gladness be? No doubt the tenderness displayed by Harmony is more penetrating. As for me, I am Abandon: joyful, strung-up, with – this morning a headache, a back-ache and my head in a whirl. But still a haze of happiness covers everything brought to me recently by my friendship with these charming beings. It is, in fact, an exquisite occasion in which we are all delighting in our true affection for each other. The sin would be if there were dishonesty or trickery in it, if there were an ulterior motive – snobbery or gross sensuality – or if decisive gestures had been made. Whereas these delicate, tentative caresses, like inhaling the perfume of a flower … ?

LIANE DE POUGY, *My Blue Notebooks*

A Tory Patriot

It is good to have walked by oneself five hundred miles in twenty days and one pair of boots (never needing the cobbler till the very last day) without any training and with a fairly heavy knapsack. It is good to have seen something on this and many other occasions, sometimes alone, sometimes in company, of the secret of the sea and the lessons of the land from Scilly to Skye; from the Land's End to Dover; from the Nore to the Moray Firth; from Dartmoor to Lochaber; and from the Weald of Sussex to those Northumbrian lakes that lie, lonely and rather uncanny, under the Roman Wall. It is good to have attended evening chapel at Oxford, then gone up to town and danced all night (the maximum of dances with the minimum of partners), returning next morning and attending chapel again. It is good to have prevented an editor, some time before Pigott caught the *Times*, from engaging in negotiations with that ingenious person as he had intended to do; and to have actually silenced a Radical canvasser.

GEORGE SAINTSBURY, *Notes on a Cellar-Book*

Lust

Eros shakes my senses like a wind on the mountain shaking the oaks.

SAPPHO

A lustful man is always timorous.

QUEEN MARGARET OF NAVARRE

The wicked fire of lust have melted him in his own grease.

WILLIAM SHAKESPEARE

For that sweet sin of lechery, I would say as the Friar did: A young man and a young woman in a green arbour in a May morning – if God does not forgive it, I would.

SIR JOHN HARINGTON

Bed is the best rendezvous of mankind.

SIR THOMAS OVERBURY

Well hung Men are the greatest Blockheads, and the most stupid of Mankind.

NICHOLAS DE VENETTE

The Choise of Valentines

It was the merie moneth of Februarie
  When yong-men in their iollie roguerie
Rose earelie in the morne fore breake of daie
  To seeke them valentines so trimme and gaie.
With whom they maie consorte in summer sheene,
  And dance the heidegeies on our toune-greene.
As Ale's at Easter or at Pentecost
  Perambulate the fields that flourish most,
And goe to som village abbordring neere
  To taste the creame, and cakes and such good cheere,
Or see a playe of strange moralitie
  Shewen by Bachelrie of Maningtree;
Whereto the Contrie franklins flock-meale swarme,
  And Ihon and Jone com marching arme in arme,
Even on the hallowes of that blessed Saint,
  That doeth true lovers with those ioyes acquaint,
I went poore pilgrim to my ladies shrine
  To see if she would be my valentine.
But woe-alass, she was not to be found,
  For she was shifted to an upper-ground.
Good Iustice Dudgein-haft, and crab-tree face
  With bills and staves had scar'd hir from the place;

And now she was compell'd for Sanctuarie
    To flye unto an house of venerie.
Thither went I, and bouldlie made enquire
    If they had hackneis to lett-out to hire,
And what they crav'd by order of their trade
    To lett one ride a iournie on a iade.
Therwith out stept a foggie three-chinnd dame,
    That us'd to take yong wenches for to tame,
And ask't me, if I ment as I profest,
    Or onelie ask't a question but in iest.
In iest? quoth I; that terme it as you will,
    I com for game, therfore giue me my Jill.
Why, Sir, quoth shee, if that be your demande,
    Com, laye me a Gods-pennie in my hand;
For, in our Oratorie siccarlie,
    None enters heere to doe his nicerie.
But he must paye his offertorie first,
    And then perhaps wee'le ease him of his thirst.
I hearing hir so ernest for the box
    Gave hir hir due, and shee the dore unlocks.
In am I entered: venus be my speede;
    But where's this female, that must doe this deede?
By blinde meanders, and by crankled wayes
    Shee leades me onward (as my Aucthor saies)
Untill we came within a shadie loft
    Where venus bounzing vestalls skirmish oft.
And there shee sett me in a leather chaire,
    And brought me forth of prettie Trulls a paire,
To chuse of them which might content myne eye;
    But hir I sought I could nowhere espie.
I spake them faire, and wisht them well to fare,
    Yett so it is, I must have fresher ware.
Wherfore, dame Bawde, as daintie as yow bee,
    Fetch gentle mistris Francis forth to me.
By Halliedame, quoth she, and Gods oune mother,
    I well perceave yow are a wylie brother.

For, if there be a morsell of more price,
    Yow'l smell it out, though I be ner'e so nice.
As yow desire, so shall yow swive with hir,
    But think your purse-strings shall abye it deare;
For, he that will eate quaile's must lavish crounes;
    And mistris Francis in hir velvet goune's,
And ruffs, and periwigs as fresh as Maye
    Can not be kept with half a croune a daye.
Of price good hostess, we will not debate,
    Though yow assize me at the highest rate;
Onelie conduct me to this bonnie bell,
    And tenne good gobbs I will unto thee tell
Of golde or silver, which shall lyke thee best,
    So much doe I hir companie request.
Awaie she went: So sweete a thing is golde,
    That mauger will invade the strongest holde.
Hey-ho, she coms, that hath my heart in keepe,
    Sing lullabie my cares, and falle a-sleepe.
Sweeping she coms, as she would brush the ground,
    Hir ratling silke's my sences doe confound.
Oh, I am ravish't; voide the chamber streight,
    For, I must neede's upon hir with my weight.
My Tomalin, quoth shee, and then she smilde,
    I, I, quoth I; so more men are beguilde
With smiles, with flatt'ring worde's, and fained cheere,
    When in their deede's their falsehood doeth appeere.
As how my lambkin ? (blushing, she replide)
    Because I in this dancing-schoole abide ?
If that be it, that breede's this discontent,
    We will remove the camp incontinent.
For shelter onelie, sweete heart came I hither,
    And to avoide the troblous stormie weather.
But now the coaste is cleare, we wilbe gonne,
    Since but thy self, true lover I have none.
With that she sprung full lightlie to my lips,
    And fast about the neck me colle's and clips.

She wanton faint's, and falle's upon hir bed,
    And often tosseth too and fro hir head.
She shutts hir eyes, and waggles with hir tongue:
    Oh, who is able to abstaine so long ?
I com, I com; sweete lyning be thy leave,
    Softlie my fingers, up theis curtaine, heave
And make me happie stealing by degreese.
    First bare hir leggs, then creepe up to hir kneese.
From thence ascend unto hir mannely thigh.
    (A pox on lingring when I am so nighe)
Smock climbe a-pace, that I maie see my ioyes,
    Oh heaven, and paradize are all but toyes,
Compar'd with this sight, I now bchould,
    Which well might keepe a man from being oldc.
A prettie rysing wombe without a weame,
    That shone as bright as anie silver streame;
And bare out lyke the bending of an hill,
    At whose decline a fountaine dwelleth still,
That hath his mouth besett with uglie bryers
    Resembling much a duskie nett of wyres.
A loftie buttock barred with azure veine's,
    Whose comelie swelling, when my hand distreine's,
Or wanton checketh with a harmeless stype,
    It makes the fruites of love eftsoone be rype;
And pleasure pluckt too tymelie from the stemme
    To dye ere it hath seene Icrusalem.
Oh Gods, that cver anie thing so sweete
    So suddenlie should fade awaie and flcete.
Hir arme's are spread, and I am all unarm'd
    Lyke one with Ovids cursed hemlock charm'd,
So are my limm's unwealdie for the fight,
    That spend their strength in thought of hir delight.
What shall I doe to shewe my self a man?
    It will not be for ought that beawtie can.
I kisse, I clap, I feele, I view at will,
    Yett dead he lyes not thinking good or ill.

Unhappie me, quoth shee, and wilt' not stand?
   Com, lett me rubb and chafe it with my hand.
Perhaps the sillie worme is labour'd sore,
   And wearied that it can doe no more.
If it be so (as I am greate a-dread)
   I wish tenne thousand times, that I were dead.
How ere it is ; no meanes shall want in me,
   That maie availe to his recoverie.
Which saide, she tooke and rould it on hir thigh,
   And when she look't on 't, she would weepe and sighe,
And dandled it, and dance't it up and doune,
   Not ceasing, till she rais'd it from his swoune.
And then he flue on hir as he were wood,
   And on hir breeche did thack, and foyne a-good;
He rub'd, and prickt, and pierst hir to the bones,
   Digging as farre as eath he might for stones.
Now high, now lowe, now stryking short and thick;
   Now dyving deepe he toucht hir to the quick.
Now with a gird, he would his course rebate;
   Streite would he take him to a statelie gate,
Plaie while him list; and thrust he neare so hard,
   Poore pacient Grisill lyeth at hir warde,
And give's, and take's as blythe and free as Maye,
   And ere-more meete's him in the midle waye.
On him hir eyes continualy were fixt,
   With hir eye-beames his melting looke's were mixt,
Which lyke the Sunne, that twixt tuo glasses plaies
   From one to th' other cast's rebounding rayes.
He lyke a starre, that to reguild his beames
   Sucks-in the influence of Phebus streames,
Imbathe's the lynes of his descending light
   In the bright fountaines of hir clearest sight.
She faire as fairest Planet in the Skye
   Hir puritie to no man doeth denye.
The verie chamber, that enclowds hir shine,
   Looke's lyke the pallace of that God devine,

Who leade's the daie about the zodiake,
    And everie even discends to th' Oceane lake:
So fierce and fervent is hir radiance,
    Such fyrie stake's she darts at everie glance,
As might enflame the icie limmes of age,
    And make pale death his surquedrie aswage
To stand and gaze upon hir Orient lamps
    Where Cupid all his chiefest ioyes encamps,
And sitts, and playes with everie atomie
    That in hir Sunne-beames swarme aboundantlie.
Thus gazing, and thus striving we persever,
    But what so firme, that maie continue ever?
Oh not so fast, my ravisht Mistriss cryes,
    Leaste my content, that on thy life relyes
Be brought too-soone from his delightfull seate,
    And me unwares of hoped bliss defeate.
Togeather lett our equall motions stirr
    Togeather let us live and dye my deere
Together lett us marche unto content,
    And be consumed with one blandishment.
As she prescrib'd, so kept we crotchet-time,
    And everie stroake in ordre lyke a chyme.
Whilst she, that had preserv'd me by hir pittie,
    Unto our musike fram'd a groaning dittie.
Alass, alass, that love should be a sinne,
    Even now my blisse and sorrow doeth beginne.
I ould wyde thy lap, my lovelie Danae,
    And entretaine the golden shoure so free,
That trilling falles into thy treasurie,
    As Aprill-drops not half so pleasant be,
Nor Nilus overflowe, to Ægipt-plaines,
    As this sweete-streames, that all hir ioints imbaynes;
With Oh, and Oh, she itching moves hir hipps,
    And to and fro, full lightlie starts and skips.
She ierks hir leggs, and sprauleth with hir heels,
    No tongue maie tell the solace that she feeles.

I faint, I yeald; Oh death rock me a-sleepe;
   Sleepe – sleepe desire, entombed in the deepe.
Not so my deare; my dearest Saint replyde;
   For, from us yett thy spirit maie not glide
Untill the sinnowie channels of our blood
   Withould their source from this imprisoned flood;
And then will we (that then will com to soone)
   Dissolved lye as-though our dayes were donne.
The whilst I speake, my soule is fleeting hence,
   And life forsakes his fleshie residence.
Staie, staie sweete ioye, and leave me not forlorne,
   Why shouldst thou fade, that art but newelie borne?
Staie but an houre; an houre is not so much,
   But half an houre; if that thy haste be such:
Naie but a quarter; I will aske no more,
   That thy departure (which torments me sore)
Maie be alightned with a little pause,
   And take awaie this passions sudden cause.
He heare's me not, hard-hearted as he is:
   He is the sonne of Time, and hate's my blisse.
Time ner'e looke's back, the rivers ner'e returne;
   A second spring must help me or I burne.
No, no, the well is drye that should refresh me,
   The glasse is runne of all my destinie.
Nature of winter learneth nigardize,
   Who, as he over-beare's the streame with ice,
That man nor beaste maie of their pleasance taste,
   So shutts she up hir conduit all in haste,
And will not let hir Nectar over-flowe,
   Least mortall men immortall ioyes should knowe.
Adiew unconstant love, to thy disporte,
   Adiew false mirth, and melodie too-short.
Adiew faint-hearted instrument of lust,
   That falselie hast betrayde our equale trust.
Hence-forth no more will I implore thine ayde,
   Or thee, or men of cowardize upbrayde.

My little dilldo shall suplye their kinde:
  A knave, that moves as light as leaves by winde;
That bendeth not, nor fouldeth anie deale,
  But stands as stiff, as he were made of steele,
And playes at peacock twixt my leggs right blythe,
  And doeth my tickling swage with manie a sighe;
For, by Saint Runnion he'le refresh me well,
  And never make my tender bellie swell.
Poore Priapus, whose triumph now must falle,
  Except thow thrust this weakeling to the walle.
Behould how he usurps in bed and bowre,
  And undermine's thy kingdom everie howre.
How slye he creepe's betwixt the barke and tree,
  And sucks the sap, whilst sleepe detaineth thee.
He is my Mistris page at everie stound,
  And soone will tent a deepe intrenched wound.
He wayte's on Courtlie Nimphs, that be so coye,
  And bids them skorne the blynd-alluring boye.
He give's yong guirls their gamesom sustenance,
  And everie gaping mouth his full sufficeance.
He fortifies disdaine with forraine artes,
  And wanton-chaste deludes all loving hearts.
If anie wight a cruell mistris serve's,
  Or in dispaire unhappie pine's and stearv's,
Curse Eunuke dilldo, senceless, counterfet,
  Who sooth maie fill, but never can begett:
But if revenge enraged with dispaire,
  That such a dwarf his wellfare should empaire,
Would faine this womans secretarie knowe,
  Lett him attend the mark's that I shall showe.
He is a youth almost tuo handfulls highe,
  Streight, round, and plumb, yett having but one eye,
Wherin the rhewme so ferventlie doeth raigne,
  That Stigian gulph maie scarce his teares containe;
Attired in white velvet or in silk,
  And nourisht with whott water or with milk;

Arm'd otherwhile in thick congealed glasse,
 When he more glib to hell be lowe would passe,
Upon a charriot of five wheeles he rydes,
 The which an arme strong driver stedfast guide's,
And often alters pace, as wayes growe deepe;
 (For, who in pathe's unknowen, one gate can keepe?)
Sometimes he smoothlie slideth doune the hill;
 Another while the stones his feete doe kill:
In clammie waies he treaddeth by and by,
 And plasheth and sprayeth all that be him nye.
So fares this iollie rider in his race,
 Plunging, and soursing forward in lyke case,
Bedasht, bespurted, and beplodded foule,
 God give thee shame, thow blinde mischapen owle.
Fy – fy for grief; a ladies chamberlaine,
 And canst not thow thy tatling tongue refraine?
I reade thee beardles blab, beware of stripes,
 And be advised what thow vainelie pipes.
Thow wilt be whipt with nettles for this geare
 If Cicelie shewe but of thy knaverie heere.
Saint Denis shield me from such female sprites.
 Regarde not Dames, what Cupids Poete writes.
I pennd this storie onelie for my self,
 Who giving suck unto a childish Elfe,
And quitte discourag'd in my nurserie,
 Since all my store seemes to hir, penurie.
I am not as was Hercules the stout,
 That to the seaventh iournie could hould out.
I want those hearbe's and rootes of Indian soile,
 That strengthen wearie members in their toile;
Druggs and Electuaries of new devise
 Doe shunne my purse; that trembles at the price.
Sufficeth, all I have, I yeald hir hole,
 Which for a poore man is a princelie dole.
I paie our hostess scott and lott at moste,
 And looke as leane and lank as anie ghoste.

What can be added more to my renowne?
   She lyeth breathlesse, I am taken doune,
The waves doe swell, the tydes climbe or'e the banks,
   Iudge gentlemen if I deserve not thanks,
And so good night unto yow eve'rie one,
   For loe, our threed is spunne, our plaie is donne.

THOMAS NASHE

If dreams and wishes had beene all true, there had not beene since poperie, one maide to make a nun of.

SIR THOMAS OVERBURY

Whoever loves, if he do not propose
The right true end of love, he's one that goes
To sea for nothing but to make him sick.

JOHN DONNE

9 October, 1796: Secretary Craggs was very handsome. He was told on coming into life that if he had three requisites besides his looks he would make his way with the fair sex. The requisites were: 'vigour, generosity and secrecy.'

LORD GLENBERVIE

Lust appears to be the most natural companion of wild ambition; and love of human praise, of that dominion erected by cunning.

MARY WOLLSTONECRAFT

Indolent men make the best lovers.

HARRIETTE WILSON

I Hate Fruition

I hate Fruition, now 'tis past,
'Tis all but nastiness at best;
The homeliest thing, that man can do,
Besides, 'tis short and fleeting too:
A squirt of slippery Delight,
That with a moment takes its flight:
A fulsom Bliss, that soon does cloy,
And makes us loath what we enjoy.
Then let us not too eager run,
By Passion blindly hurried on,
Like Beasts, who nothing better know,
That what meer Lust incites them to:
For when in Floods of Love we're drench'd,
The Flames are by enjoyment quench'd:
But thus, let's thus together lie,
And kiss out long Eternity:
Here we dread no conscious spies,
No blushes stain our guiltless Joys:
Here no Faintness dulls Desires,
And Pleasure never flags, nor tires:
This has pleas'd, and pleases now,
And for Ages will do so:
   Enjoyment here is never done,
   But fresh, and always but begun.

JOHN OLDHAM (*translated from Petronius*)

I'm Going To Be Sore

Come back … Come back because I'm back.
Sit on the mattress.
Sit the way I'm sitting. Stretch out your legs on either side of my hips.
Press your eyebrows to my eyebrows.
I'd rather press my hands against the small of your back
I'm entering. At the place where the hair stops.
Let's divide the earth in two.
A place to get tripe. Known to no one. Known to everyone.
We speak otherwise. I'm helping you and our hands are in the way.
The rhythm of life.
Any rhythm at all.
A promising monotony.
My brain is exhausted, it's hanging by a thread.
Banal perfection.
Amazing takeoff. Boy, I loved you from afar.
Bitch, I would kill for you.
Let's get rid of all these words that mean nothing.
You're rocking me and I'm moving.
Street rat, I throw your head into the dust. Too fast.
Too fast?
You're drugging me.
I'm going to be sore!
I'm as soft as velvet.
I'm mad from our ascent.
You're drugging me, you're drugging me.
I'll be torn to shreds!
The city is fogged in. The fog will lift.
A tree … lightning … any minute …
Your face is anxious.
I'm struggling.
You're illuminating me.
I'm flying overhead, I'm soaring, I'm in the galleys.

The many flashes of the midnight sun. Lighted from within. You give me
    light.,
I want that strange light in your shoulders.
I'm opening my eyes. You're in command. How sad.
It's the nature of man.
I'd never forgive you if you stopped.
I'm giving you my last strength.
Embers. I'm being ripped.
Rave, my love.
Exhaust yourself. Not enough ashes on your face.
I can't go on.
Let's sweep aside the barriers. Let us through …
The avalanche!
Roar.
Running water … We're travelling.
What?
Nothing. Hang on, hold tight.
We're passing the rocks.
The palm groves.
The dovecotes.
Be quiet.
Why should I be quiet? You're my love.
Be quiet!
Two mayflies … one on top of the other … in the air … high above the
    summer!
Be quiet. I …
Me to … Me too …

VIOLETTE LEDUC, *The Taxi*

Leander: Delicious Meat

His bodie was as straight as *Circe's* wand,
Jove might have sipt out *Nectar* from his hand.
Even as delicious meat is to the tast,
So was his necke in touching, and surpast
The white of *Pelop's* shoulder, I could tell ye,
How smooth his brest was, & how white his bellie,
And whose immortall fingars did imprint,
That heavenly path, with many a curious dint,
That runs along his backe.

CHRISTOPHER MARLOWE

Love a Woman?

Love a woman? You're an ass!
   'Tis a most insipid passion
To choose out for your happiness
   The silliest part of God's creation.

Let the porter and the groom,
   Things designed for dirty slaves,
Drudge in fair Aurelia's womb
   To get supplies for age and graves.

Farewell, woman! I intend
   Henceforth every night to sit
With my lewd, well-natured friend,
   Drinking to engender wit.

Then give me health, wealth, mirth, and wine,
 And, if busy love entrenches,
There's a sweet, soft page of mine
 Does the trick worth forty wenches.

EARL OF ROCHESTER

Lust in Action

Th' expense of spirit in a waste of shame
Is lust in action, and till action, lust
Is perjured, murd'rous, bloody, full of blame,
Savage, extreme, rude, cruel, not to trust,
Enjoyed no sooner but despised straight,
Past reason hunted, and no sooner had
Past reason hated as a swallowed bait,
On purpose laid to make the taker mad.
Mad in pursuit and in possession so,
Had, having, and in quest to have, extreme,
A bliss in proof and proved, a very woe,
Before a joy proposed, behind a dream.
 All this the world well knows yet none knows well,
 To shun the heaven that leads men to this hell.

WILLIAM SHAKESPEARE

Lust Postponed

In one of the goodly towns of the kingdom of France there dwelt a nobleman of good birth, who attended the schools that he might learn how virtue and honour are to be acquired among virtuous men. But although he was so accomplished that at the age of seventeen or eighteen years he was, as it were, both precept and example to others,

Love failed not to add his lesson to the rest; and, that he might be the better hearkened to and received, concealed himself in the face and the eyes of the fairest lady in the whole country round, who had come to the city in order to advance a suit-at-law. But before Love sought to vanquish the gentleman by means of this lady's beauty, he had first won her heart by letting her see the perfections of this young lord; for in good looks, grace, sense and excellence of speech he was surpassed by none.

You, who know what speedy way is made by the fire of love when once it fastens on the heart and fancy, will readily imagine that between two subjects so perfect as these it knew little pause until it had them at its will, and had so filled them with its clear light, that thought, wish and speech were all aflame with it. Youth, begetting fear in the young lord, led him to urge his suit with all the gentleness imaginable; but she, being conquered by love, had no need of force to win her. Nevertheless, shame, which tarries with ladies as long as it can, for some time restrained her from declaring her mind. But at last the heart's fortress, which is honour's abode, was shattered in such sort that the poor lady consented to that which she had never been minded to refuse.

In order, however, to make trial of her lover's patience, constancy and love, she only granted him what he sought on a very hard condition, assuring him that if he fulfilled it she would love him perfectly for ever; whereas, if he failed in it, he would certainly never win her as long as he lived. And the condition was this: she would be willing to talk with him, both being in bed together, clad in their linen only, but he was to ask nothing more from her than words and kisses.

He, thinking there was no joy to be compared to that which she promised him, agreed to the proposal, and that evening the promise was kept; in such wise that, despite all the caresses she bestowed on him and the temptations that beset him, he would not break his oath. And albeit his torment seemed to him no less than that of Purgatory, yet was his love so great and his hope so strong, sure as he felt of the ceaseless continuance of the love he had thus painfully won, that he preserved his patience and rose from beside her without having done anything contrary to her expressed wish.

The lady was, I think, more astonished than pleased by such virtue;

and giving no heed to the honour, patience and faithfulness her lover had shown in the keeping of his oath, she forthwith suspected that his love was not so great as she had thought, or else that he had found her less pleasing than he had expected.

She therefore resolved, before keeping her promise, to make a further trial of the love he bore her; and to this end she begged him to talk to a girl in her service, who was younger than herself and very beautiful, bidding him make love speeches to her, so that those who saw him come so often to the house might think that it was for the sake of this damsel and not of herself.

The young lord, feeling sure that his own love was returned in equal measure, was wholly obedient to her commands, and for love of her compelled himself to make love to the girl; and she, finding him so handsome and well-spoken, believed his lies more than other truth, and loved him as much as though she herself were greatly loved by him.

The mistress finding that matters were thus well advanced, albeit the young lord did not cease to claim her promise, granted him permission to come and see her at one hour after midnight, saying that after having so fully tested the love and obedience he had shown towards her, it was but just that he should be rewarded for his long patience. Of the lover's joy on hearing this you need have no doubt, and he failed not to arrive at the appointed time.

But the lady, still wishing to try the strength of his love, had said to her beautiful damsel –

'I am well aware of the love a certain nobleman bears to you, and I think you are no less in love with him; and I feel so much pity for you both, that I have resolved to afford you time and place that you may converse together at your ease.'

The damsel was so enchanted that she could not conceal her longings, but answered that she would not fail to be present.

In obedience, therefore, to her mistress's counsel and command, she undressed herself and lay down on a handsome bed, in a room the door of which the lady left half-open, whilst within she set a light so that the maiden's beauty might be clearly seen. Then she herself pretended to go away, but hid herself near to the bed so carefully that she could not be seen.

Her poor lover, thinking to find her according to her promise, failed not to enter the room as softly as he could, at the appointed hour; and after he had shut the door and put off his garments and fur shoes, he got into the bed, where he looked to find what he desired. But no sooner did he put out his arms to embrace her whom he believed to be his mistress, than the poor girl, believing him entirely her own, had her arms round his neck, speaking to him the while in such loving words and with so beautiful a countenance, that there is not a hermit so holy but he would have forgotten his beads for love of her.

But when the gentleman recognised her with both eye and ear, and found he was not with her for whose sake he had so greatly suffered, the love that had made him get so quickly into the bed, made him rise from it still more quickly. And in anger equally with mistress and damsel, he said –

'Neither your folly nor the malice of her who put you there can make me other than I am. But do you try to be an honest woman, for you shall never lose that good name through me.'

So saying he rushed out of the room in the greatest wrath imaginable, and it was long before he returned to see his mistress. However love, which is never without hope, assured him that the greater and more manifest his constancy was proved to be by all these trials, the longer and more delightful would be his bliss.

The lady, who had seen and heard all that passed, was so delighted and amazed at beholding the depth and constancy of his love, that she was impatient to see him again in order to ask his forgiveness for the sorrow that she had caused him to endure. And as soon as she could meet with him, she failed not to address him in such excellent and pleasant words, that he not only forgot all his troubles but even deemed them very fortunate, seeing that their issue was to the glory of his constancy and the perfect assurance of his love, the fruit of which he enjoyed from that time forth as fully as he could desire.

QUEEN MARGARET OF NAVARRE, *The Heptameron*

Please Master

Please master can I touch your cheek
please master can I kneel at your feet
please master can I loosen your blue pants
please master can I gaze at your golden haired belly
please master can I gently take down your shorts
please master can I have your thighs bare to my eyes
please master can I take off my clothes below your chair
please master can I kiss your ankles and soul
please master can I touch lips to your hard muscle hairless thigh
please master can I lay my ear pressed to your stomach
please master can I wrap my arms around your white ass
please master can I lick your groin curled with blond soft fur
please master can I touch my tongue to your rosy asshole
please master may I pass my face to your balls,
please master, please look into my eyes,
please master order me down on the floor,
please master tell me to lick your thick shaft
please master put your rough hands on my bald hairy skull
please master press my mouth to your prick-heart
please master press my face into your belly, pull me slowly strong
     thumbed
till your dumb hardness fills my throat to the base
till I swallow & taste your delicate flesh-hot prick barrel veined Please
Master push my shoulders away and stare in my eye, & make me bend
     over the table
please master grab my thighs and lift my ass to your waist
please master your hand's rough stroke on my neck your palm down my
     backside
please master push me up, my feet on chairs, till my hole feels the breath
     of your spit and your thumb stroke
please master make me say Please Master Fuck me now Please
Master grease my balls and hairmouth with sweet vaselines
please master stroke your shaft with white creams

please master touch your cock head to my wrinkled self-hole
please master push it in gently, your elbows enwrapped round my breast
your arms passing down to my belly, my penis you touch w/ your fingers
please master shove it in me a little, a little, a little,
please master sink your droor thing down my behind
& please master make me wiggle my rear to eat up the prick trunk
till my asshalfs cuddle your thighs, my back bent over,
till I'm alone sticking out, your sword stuck throbbing in me
please master pull out and slowly roll into the bottom
please master lunge it again, and withdraw to the tip
please please master fuck me again with your self, please fuck me Please
Master drive down till it hurts me the softness the
Softness please master make love to my ass, give body to center, & fuck
    me for good like a girl,
tenderly clasp me please master I take me to thee,
& drive in my belly your selfsame sweet heat-rood
you fingered in solitude Denver or Brooklyn or fucked in a maiden in
    Paris carlots
please master drive me thy vehicle, body of love dops, sweat fuck
body of tenderness, Give me your dog fuck faster
please master make me go moan on the table
Go moan O please master do fuck me like that
in your rhythm thrill-plunge & pull-back-bounce & push down
till I loosen my asshole a dog on the table yelping with terror delight to
    be loved
Please master call me a dog, an ass beast, a wet asshole,
& fuck me more violent, my eyes hid with your palms round my skull
& plunge down in a brutal hard lash thru soft drip-fish
& throb thru five seconds to spurt out your semen heat
over & over, bamming it in while I cry out your name I do love you
please Master.

                                                    ALLEN GINSBERG

It is likely *Eve* studied astronomie, which makes the posterity of her sex ever since to lie on their backes.

SIR THOMAS OVERBURY

The more a man cultivates the arts the less he fucks. Fucking is the lyricism of the people.

CHARLES BAUDELAIRE

Eros is the youngest of the Gods. He is also the most tired.

NATALIE BARNEY

[Cora, Countess of Strafford, who died in 1932] thought it would be a good thing to get a little sex-instruction, so she went over to Paris and took a few lessons from a leading cocotte. On her wedding night she began to turn precept into practice when her bridegroom sternly quelled her by saying: 'Cora, *ladies don't* move.'

SIR RUPERT HART-DAVIS

Chastity, a negative condition.

LIANE DE POUGY

[Explaining her pre-marital virginity] I knew I had to keep myself tidy for what lay ahead.

DIANA, PRINCESS OF WALES

The Raging Foam

When Love its utmost vigour does imploy,
Ev'n then, 'tis but a restless wandring joy:
Nor knows the Lover, in that wild excess,
With hands or eyes, what first he wou'd possess:
But strains at all; and fast'ning where he strains,
Too closely presses with his frantique pains:
With biteing kisses hurts the twining fair,
Which shews his joyes imperfect, unsincere:
For stung with inward rage, he flings around,
And strives t' avenge the smart on that which gave the wound.
But love those eager bitings does restrain,
And mingling pleasure mollifies the pain.
For ardent hope still flatters anxious grief,
And sends him to his Foe to seek relief:
Which yet the nature of the thing denies;
For Love, and Love alone of all our joyes
By full possession does but fan the fire,
The more we still enjoy, the more we still desire.
Nature for meat and drink provides a space;
And when receiv'd they fill their certain place;
Hence thirst and hunger may be satisfi'd,
But this repletion is to Love deny'd:
Form, feature, colour, whatsoe're delight
Provokes the Lover's endless appetite,
These fill no space, nor can we thence remove
With lips, or hands, or all our instruments of love:
In our deluded grasp we nothing find,
But thin aerial shapes, that fleet before the mind.
As he who in a dream with drought is curst,
And finds no real drink to quench his thirst,
Runs to imagin'd Lakes his heat to steep,
And vainly swills and labours in his sleep;

So Love with fantomes cheats our longing eyes,
Which hourly seeing never satisfies;
Our hands pull nothing from the parts they strain,
But wander o'er the lovely limbs in vain:
Nor when the Youthful pair more clossely joyn,
When hands in hands they lock, and thighs in thighs they twine
Just in the raging foam of full desire,
When both press on, both murmur, both expire,
They gripe, they squeeze, their humid tongues they dart,
As each wou'd force their way to t' other's heart:
In vain; they only cruze about the coast,
For bodies cannot pierce, nor be in bodies lost:
As sure they strive to be, when both engage,
In that tumultuous momentary rage,
So 'tangled in the Nets of Love they lie,
Till Man dissolves in that excess of joy.
Then, when the gather'd bag has burst its way,
And ebbing tydes the slacken'd nerves betray,
A pause ensues; and Nature nods a while,
Till with recruited rage new Spirits boil;
And then the same vain violence returns,
With flames renew'd th' erected furnace burns.
Agen they in each other wou'd be lost,
But still by adamantine bars are crost;
All wayes they try, successeless all they prove,
To cure the secret sore of lingring love.

JOHN DRYDEN

Whenas the Rye Reach to the Chin

Whenas the rye reach to the chin,
And chopcherry, chopcherry ripe within,
Strawberries swimming in the cream,
And schoolboys playing in the stream;
   Then O, then O, then O my true love said,
    Till that time come again,
   She could not live a maid.

GEORGE PEELE

Motoring

After the Crash

When he came to he knew
Time must have passed because
The asphalt was high with hemlock
Through which he crawled to his crash
Helmet and found it no more
Than his wrinkled hand what it was.

Yet life seemed still going on:
He could hear the signals bounce
Back from the moon and the hens
Fire themselves black in the batteries
And the silence of small blind cats
Debating whether to pounce.

Then he looked up and marked
The gigantic scales in the sky,
The pan on the left dead empty
And the pan on the right dead empty,
And knew in the dead, dead calm
It was too late to die.

LOUIS MACNEICE

The Back Seat

Where I had come from, seducing a 'nice' girl was hard work. In the back seat of wintry cars one chewed on lower lips for longer periods of time than starlets cohabit with producers. One moved lower then, leaving a trail of perfumed saliva on ears and necks along the way, coming to plant already swollen lips on wool-sweatered nipples, inhaling there, as though trying to draw juice from earmuffed oranges. One huffed and puffed, struggling out of fur-collared greatcoats, meeting convulsive, furious hands all the way. The back seat of the car now reeked of love's odors, so that the entire car was like a Great Northern Womb, and if one was not too drunk or hadn't developed 'blue balls' (like a fierce hand squeezing the genitalia purple), one went miraculously on, touching a thigh and working up to the hot silken flimsiness of underthings where, more often than not, it ended with the beast – what admirable will power! – clamping her vicelike thighs about one's hand and hysterically screaming, 'I'll tell my brother Ed!' Even if one did make it, if the thighs did not break one's furtive hand, the girl felt duty-bound to pass out, so that confronting one in Trigonometry on Monday morning she could give him that sweetly virginal I-don't-remember-nothin' look. There was very little to remember. By the time of contact it was getting light, very cold, with that glacial, white world spread all about one on the lonely road; and one didn't dare look down in fear of seeing a half-dressed, broken-bra'ed, bedraggled, pimply, snot-nosed, shivery-assed creature feigning her conscience-inducing sleep, trying not to moan, as if indeed a scarcely erect, zipper-scraped, partially raw instrument could induce even tremors.

FREDERICK EXLEY, *A Fan's Notes*

A Crash Near Naples

Such is the power of certain calamities on the mind that, once freed of the initial shock, one is able to view with bright clarity all the events leading up to the actual blow. The tone, the mood, the character of whatever transpired before, takes on the gray hue, itself, of disaster and is embalmed in memory with an awful sense of predestination. It is in such a way that I remember the road out of Formia, through Naples and beyond. Leaving the sea, the highway became wide and straight again. But it was Saturday, market day, and the road was swarming with traffic – wagons and carts piled high with produce and fodder, towed by donkeys, all moving so leisurely as to appear like sinister, stationary objects in my path. The sun rose higher and higher over the dusty countryside. Its fire settled down upon the hills; close by stood fields of blighted corn and trees in windless, shriveling groves. Up from the highway the heat rose in greasy waves. And through these waves, roaring, balefully glittering, and often straight at me, came a devil's pageant of vehicles – motorscooters and buses loaded down with vacationers, and caravans of hurtling cars. There were huge trucks, too, carrying gasoline, whipping past me at seventy and leaving a trail of scalding blue vapor on the air. Near Capua, outside of Naples, there was an epidemic of sheep into which I almost skidded, and I had to poke a gingerly path among their sad, expressively wagging behinds. In spite of the sun I put the top down again to get the wind. I also remember turning on the radio again, this time for distraction. By the time I reached the outskirts of Naples the steering wheel was slippery with perspiration. To my disgust I found myself sniveling with tension and with fatigue and murmuring aloud words of courage.

But it was the Alfa Romeo on the Autostrada to Pompeii that led to my downfall. I had passed through Naples by then, for a brief moment calm, thinking that with only an hour more to go Sambuco was in the bag. There was less traffic, it was nearly noon, lunchtime, when most Italians abandon the road to purposeful Anglo-Saxons. It seemed to have turned cooler – though no doubt I was deceived – and I relaxed for the first time, diverted by the outer suburbs of the city, where black smoke was billowing up from a thousand factory chimneys. The noise I heard behind me was abrupt and thunderous, a shocking din which partook both of a salvo of rockets and an airplane in take-off, and above this, pervading it all, a thin, ominous, hurrying whine, as of the approach of a flight of wasps or bees; my eyes sought the mirror, where I saw it bearing down on me in savage haste – the snout of a big black car. With a foretaste of doom and of the fading beauty of life I composed myself to accept a rear-end collision, and a tight, goosey, half-despairing, half-gluttonous feeling swept over me as I watched it become larger and larger, barreling remorselessly on. Five yards from my tail the car swerved, slowed, came abreast: I beheld a fat young Neapolitan, one hand limp and cocky on the wheel, his girl friend all but in his lap, both of them grinning like sharks. We drove side by side for a moment, perilously swaying; then he was off and away with a noise like a string of firecrackers, and with the central finger of one fist raised in ripe phallic tribute. I tore after him for a while, gave up the chase, and fell into aching oppressive woolgathering. My heart was full of murder. I was only dreaming of revenge, doing sixty, when, a little beyond Pompeii, I smashed broadside into the motorscooter ...

Luciano di Lieto: a liquid, resourceful name, one fit for a trapeze artist, or a writer of sonnets, or an explorer of the Antilles, a name certainly deserving more in the way of talents than those of the person who bore it. By turns hod carrier, road worker, peddler of erotic trinkets at the local ruins, a pickpocket so inept as to earn from the police the nickname 'Fessacchiotto' – the Stumblebum – the man di Lieto was a triumph of stunted endowments. One day at the age of twelve he poked a meddlesome hand around in the engine of an automobile, and was shorn of two fingers, clipped off neatly by the fan. A few years later, plunged into some adolescent daydream, he wandered in front of a Naples streetcar, breaking both legs and leaving one elbow impaired forever. Only months after this, barely out of his casts, experimenting with fireworks at a seaside *festa*, he bent his dark, crazy regard down upon the muzzle of a Roman candle, and blew out his right eye. When I slammed into him he was twenty-three and in the fever of early manhood. All of these facts were revealed to me before the ambulance came, and perhaps no more than an hour past that moment when di Lieto came roaring out of a side road on a sputtering Lambretta and into my path, legs akimbo, poised tautly forward like a jockey, hair wild and rampant over his blasted vision, mouth and jaws working with hoots of joy even as I braked frantically on squealing rubber and plowed into him. It seemed as if those joyful cries were one and a part of the collision itself, preceding it for a chilling second before I even saw him and going on and on after the moment of rackety impact, when I sent the motorscooter flying forty feet up the road and kept skidding helplessly on, watching the blur of gray denim overalls and tousled black hair, still hooting, bounce up over the front of the car. Clawing at space, he seemed to suspend there for a moment in mid-air, before gliding with white floundering legs and arms across the hood of the car toward me, shattering the windshield in an icy explosion of glass. Like a collapsed puppet dangling on strings, he floated away past me and was gone. I finally came to a stop on the other side of the road in a shower of flip-flopping tennis balls, the radio undone by the impact and alive with deafening crackles and peeps.

WILLIAM STYRON, *Set This House on Fire*

A Curse

Dark was that day when Diesel
conceived his grim engine that
begot you, vile invention,
more vicious, more criminal
than the camera even,
metallic monstrosity,
bale and bane of our Culture,
chief woe of our Commonweal.

How dare the Law prohibit
hashish and heroin yet
license your use, who inflate
all weak inferior egos?
Their addicts only do harm
to their own lives: you poison
the lungs of the innocent,
your din dithers the peaceful,
and on choked roads hundreds must
daily die by chance-medley.

Nimble technicians, surely
you should hang your heads in shame.
Your wit works mighty wonders,
has landed men on the Moon,
replaced brains by computers,
and can smithy a 'smart' bomb.
It is a crying scandal
that you cannot take the time
or be bothered to build us,
what sanity knows we need,
an odourless and noiseless
staid little electric brougham.

W. H. AUDEN

Driving to Work in 1922

To George F. Babbitt, as to most prosperous citizens of Zenith, his motor-car was poetry and tragedy, love and heroism. The office was his pirate ship but the car his perilous excursion ashore.

Among the tremendous crises of each day none was more dramatic than starting the engine. It was slow on cold mornings; there was the long, anxious whirr of the starter; and sometimes he had to drip ether into the cocks of the cylinders, which was so very interesting that at lunch he would chronicle it drop by drop, and orally calculate how much each drop had cost him.

This morning he was darkly prepared to find something wrong, and he felt belittled when the mixture exploded sweet and strong, and the car didn't even brush the door-jamb, scraped and splintered by many bruisings by fenders, as he backed out of the garage. He was confused. He shouted 'Morning!' to Sam Doppelbrau with more cordiality than he had intended ...

Babbitt fell into a great silence and devoted himself to the game of beating tramway cars to the corner: a spurt, a tail-chase, nervous speeding between the huge yellow side of the tram and the jagged row of parked motors, shooting past just as the tram stopped – a rare game and valiant.

And all the while he was conscious of the loveliness of Zenith. For weeks together he noticed nothing but clients and the vexing To Let signs of rival brokers. To-day, in mysterious malaise, he raged or rejoiced with equal nervous swiftness, and to-day the light of spring was so winsome that he lifted his head and saw.

He admired each district along his familiar route to the office: The bungalows and shrubs and winding irregular drives of Floral Heights. The one-story shops in Smith Street, a glare of plate-glass and new yellow brick; groceries and laundries and chemist shops to supply the more immediate needs of East Side housewives. The market gardens in Dutch Hollow, their shanties patched with corrugated iron and stolen doors. Hoardings with crimson goddesses nine feet tall advertising cinema films, pipe tobacco, and talcum powder. The old 'mansions' along Ninth Street, S.E., like aged dandies in filthy linen; wooden castles turned into boarding-houses, with muddy walks and rusty hedges, jostled by fast-intruding garages, cheap blocks of flats, and fruit-stands conducted by bland, sleek Athenians. Across the belt of railway lines, factories with high-perched water-tanks and tall stacks – factories producing condensed milk, paper boxes, lighting-fixtures, motor-cars. Then the business centre, the thickening darting traffic, the crammed trams unloading, and high doorways of marble and polished granite.

It was big – and Babbitt respected bigness in anything; in mountains, jewels, muscles, wealth, or words. He was, for a spring-enchanted moment, the lyric and almost unselfish lover of Zenith. He thought of the outlying factory suburbs; of the Chaloosa River with its strangely eroded banks; of the orchard-dappled Tonawanda Hills to the North, and all the fat dairy land and big barns and comfortable herds. As he dropped his passenger he cried, 'Gosh, I feel pretty good this morning!'

Epochal as starting the car was the drama of parking it before he entered his office. As he turned from Oberlin Avenue round the corner into Third Street, N.E., he peered ahead for a space in the line of parked cars. He angrily just missed a space as a rival driver slid into it. Ahead, another car was leaving the curb, and Babbitt slowed up, holding out his hand to the cars pressing on him from behind, agitatedly motioning an old woman to go ahead, avoiding a truck which bore down on him from one side. With front wheels scraping the wrought-steel fender of the car in front, he stopped, feverishly cramped his steering-wheel, slid back into the vacant space and, with eighteen inches of room, manoeuvred to bring the car level with the curb. It was a virile adventure masterfully executed. With satisfaction he locked a thief-proof steel wedge on the front wheel, and crossed the street to his real-estate office on the ground floor of the Reeves Building.

SINCLAIR LEWIS, *Babbitt*

Jumping the Lights

We drove from Folkestone in time to join in the great Sunday evening crawl into London. It was so different in France and Italy that after a time we began getting cross. We had meant to be up in time to dine quietly before we parted, and we felt that this would ease the parting a little. But it began to seem that we should not reach London in time for this, or for anything else. Every one had had the idea of starting for home early, so as to miss the crawl, but, since every one had had the idea, no one missed the crawl. People got peevish, they began hooting and cutting in, and I got peevish too, so I took a euphoria pill, which makes you feel as if you would get there in the end. After we were in London the buses all seemed to be rushing on against the lights for about ten seconds after they had gone red. This trick of buses, and of a lot of other drivers, but buses are the worst and the most alarming, has always made me full of rage, it is the height of meanness, stealing their turn from those with the right to cross, it is like pedestrians crossing against the lights and stealing the turn of cars which have been waiting for their chance, but this in England is not actually a legal crime, only caddish, whereas for traffic it is a legal crime as well. The taxi drivers say that when they do it they are run in if seen by the police, but that the buses usually get off, as if a driver is prosecuted the other drivers come out on strike, but this may be only the anti-police malice of taxi drivers.

When Vere was driving, I kept saying, 'Push off the moment they go green. Don't let those cads get away with it,' but Vere said, 'Better let them get away with it and stay alive.' When I took over, I was feeling like an avenging policeman, furious for the cause of legality, buoyed up by my euphoria pill, and all set to show the cads they couldn't get away with it. But they kept at it, and usually I could do nothing about it but hoot, as I was not the front car. Presently I was, and as the lights changed I saw a bus dashing up to crash the red, and I was full of rage and shouted, 'Look at the *lights*,' and started off the moment they were green. I heard Vere say, 'Famous last words,' and that was the last thing I ever heard Vere say. The crash as the bus charged the car and hit it broadside on and smashed us was all I knew for quite a time. When I came to, everything was a mess and a crowd, and I was lying in the mess with someone sponging blood from my face. I tried to turn my head and look for Vere, and saw a figure lying in blankets close by, quite still, and the head was at an odd angle. I think I was only partly conscious, because all I said was, 'that murdering bus crashed the lights,' and went off again.

They kept me in hospital a fortnight, with sprains and cuts and concussion and shock, then aunt Dot drove me down to Troutlands. The bus driver was tried for manslaughter, as so many witnesses had seen him pass the lights, but he was acquitted on the grounds of this being such common form, and only got six months for dangerous driving. He had, after all, driven no more dangerously than buses and many other vehicles drive every day, only this time he had killed someone. I do not think he was even disqualified. No one blamed me, except myself. Only I knew about that surge of rage that had sent me off, the second the lights were with me, to stop the path of that rushing monster, whose driver had thought that no one would dare to oppose him. The rage, the euphoria, the famous last words; only I knew that I and that driver had murdered Vere between us, he in selfish unscrupulousness, I in reckless anger.

I had plenty of time to think about it; no doubt my whole life.

DAME ROSE MACAULAY, *The Towers of Trebizond*

Meditation on the A30

A man on his own in a car
    Is revenging himself on his wife;
He opens the throttle and bubbles with dottle
    And puffs at his pitiful life.

'She's losing her looks very fast,
    She loses her temper all day;
That lorry won't let me get past,
    This Mini is blocking my way.

'Why can't you step on it and shift her!
    I can't go on crawling like this!
At breakfast she said that she wished I was dead –
    Thank heavens we don't have to kiss.

'I'd like a nice blonde on my knee
    And one who won't argue or nag.
Who dares to come hooting at *me*?
    I only give way to a Jag.

'You're barmy or plastered, I'll pass you, you bastard –
    I *will* overtake you. I *will*!'
As he clenches his pipe, his moment is ripe
    And the corner's accepting its kill.

SIR JOHN BETJEMAN

Overtaking

By this time we were out of Rome and driving along the Via Aurelia. Our idea was to go to Santa Marinella, and as it was already getting late I quickened speed. To say I quickened speed, however, is merely a manner of speaking. Along the whole length of the road one car followed another: big cars and little cars, Italian cars and foreign cars, luxurious cars and utility cars. Every now and then there was a milk van, or a big lorry from one of the settlements along the sea driven by a madman who overtook other cars as though he were riding a motor-bicycle. So I settled down to a slow, steady pace, and I might perhaps have gone on like that if those other two, close beside me, had not got on my nerves with their chattering. Somehow or other, I don't know why, the nervousness of jealousy infected my driving and I started to accelerate, with the idea, perhaps, of getting as quickly as possible to Santa Marinella and so interrupting their altogether too confidential conversation. I therefore began overtaking other cars, one after another, like threading pearls on a string. At the insistent sounding of my horn there were some that immediately drew in to the side, well-behaved cars that observed the rules of the road; but there were also cars that wouldn't allow themselves to be overtaken at any price. One thing I noticed: the best-mannered cars were the most powerful ones, the big, luxurious cars driven by people who didn't care a damn about being overtaken, knowing perfectly well that, if they wanted to, they could go faster than anybody; the meanest ones were the small, cheap cars, full of women and children, with the father of the family at the wheel. These unfortunates, having spent the whole week sitting in an armchair, were anxious to prove to their wives and children that they were vigorous, dashing sportsmen; and so, just at the moment when they were being overtaken, instead of slowing down and drawing in to the side, they would accelerate. I could have killed them; all the more so because, while with solemn, set, imperturbable faces they urged on their little hire-purchase cars to the maximum speed, their whole families would be peering at me through the windows with mocking, triumphant expressions, as much as to say: 'We've got the better of you. Papa's a cleverer driver than you are.' I looked back at them and wondered why it was that faces which, if I had seen them in a shop or in the street, would have appeared uninteresting or even, possibly, attractive, seemed to me so completely odious when seen through the windows of a car. Meanwhile we had passed the turning to Fregene and were going towards Ladispoli.

Apart from Ines' and Tullio's chattering and the objectionable faces of the families on their Sunday outing, there was another thing that got on my nerves – the way in which Tullio from time to time interrupted his flirtation with Ines in order to urge me, out of the kindness of his heart, to overtake a car in front. 'Now, Gigi,' he would say, 'do please pass that little car'; or: 'Come on, give it him! Get past him – what are you waiting for?' or again: 'Get on, what are you afraid of? Go into third and overtake him.' Had we been alone, well and good: it's fun, sometimes, to have a race. But Ines was there; and nothing could get it out of my head that Tullio was pressing me to do all this overtaking in order to keep me occupied and distract my attention so that he could have it all his own way with her. And with a touch of ridicule, perhaps, into the bargain. Rather like a pair of lovers in a public garden saying to an importunate child: 'Now come on, be a good boy and go and play ball.' I lost my temper; and instead of slowing down and driving quietly as I should have, I felt myself so carried away by anger that I followed his promptings and overtook one car after another; and the more I did so, the more infuriated I became at the thought that I was thus playing into the hands of Tullio, who looked upon me as a mere trifler who had only to get the wheel of a car between his hands to allow his girl to be pinched from him.

But I kept my eye on them. Tullio was twisted right round in his seat, with one leg bent back on the cushion and his two hands gripping the back of the seat; Ines was bending forward towards him, and she too kept her hand on the back of the seat, although there was no need for it. At a certain moment, without drawing attention to what I was doing, I adjusted the driving-mirror in such a way that I no longer saw the road behind me but could see that part of the seat on which their hands were resting. After a short time I thus saw Tullio's hand sliding very slowly along until it was close to Ines' hand, which soon, at a bend in the road, it covered. At the same moment Tullio said to me: 'Come on, Gigi, do please pass that little car; what are you waiting for?' I looked at the road: the car Tullio was talking about was close in front of me and going fast. It was an old rattletrap with a baby's pram tied on to its roof. Inside it could be seen the usual swarm of women and children; and in the driver's seat the usual *paterfamilias*, fat and square, his big head sunk into his neck, his black, hairy hands gripping the wheel: he looked like a puppet. But when I took my eyes off Tullio's and Ines' hands and looked at the rattletrap in front, the first thing I saw was not the driver, but, at the rear window, the face of a little boy of about six, ugly, pale, with fanlike ears, making rude faces and putting out his tongue at me. The child was making faces at me because he thought I had lost my temper at being outdistanced by his father; but I, for some reason, thought he was making faces in order to mock me about Tullio and Ines. I looked at him and frowned; and he, his mother's arm round his chest and his nose flattened against the glass of the window, looked back at me and again put out his tongue. I raised my eyes again to the driving-mirror and saw that Tullio's hand was now moving from Ines' hand to her wrist and then from her wrist to her arm. Tullio said to me, hypocritically: 'What's the matter, are you dreaming? Why don't you accelerate?' Ines, her voice softened by sensual excitement, supported him. 'We're going too slowly,' she said. 'We shall never get to Santa Marinella at this rate.'

'Oh really?' I replied; 'I'm not going fast enough? Well, now you shall see ...' We were on a straight stretch of road which ended, in the distance, in a hill. On the right there was a hedge along the top of a bank, on the left a row of plane-trees leaning towards the road, their trunks circled with bands of white. I changed into third, pressed hard down on the accelerator, sounded my horn and dashed forward, still hooting, with a powerful roar from the engine. But would you believe it? Instead of moving over to the right, as he should have done, *paterfamilias*, at the sound of my horn, planted himself in the middle of the road and accelerated too. I was thus forced to follow close behind him; and Tullio said: 'What on earth are you doing? Aren't you ashamed?'; then I looked up and saw the little boy putting out his tongue at me. So I threw myself over to the left of the road again and, still sounding my horn, started moving along side by side with the other car. We were almost at the end of the straight stretch where the road started climbing the hill; *paterfamilias* was accelerating, I couldn't get the better of him and I was bursting with rage; then, all of a sudden, I began to gain ground. But lo and behold, just at that very moment there appeared, at a bend in the road, another car coming towards me at a moderate speed but still fast enough to prevent me from finally overtaking the first car. I ought to have given up the attempt and fallen back again; but some devil or other whispered to me to go on. *Paterfamilias* accelerated at the same time, and I had only just time to hurl myself right over to the left, into the ditch, to avoid a collision; I saw the trunk of a plane-tree rushing to meet me. I thought I heard Tullio's voice shouting: 'Brake! brake!'; then I was conscious of nothing more.

ALBERTO MORAVIA, *More Roman Tales*

The Southern Thruway

At first the girl in the Dauphine had insisted on keeping track of the time, but the engineer in the Peugeot 404 didn't care anymore. Anyone could look at his watch, but it was as if that time strapped to your right wrist or the beep beep on the radio were measuring something else – the time of those who haven't made the blunder of trying to return to Paris on the southern thruway on a Sunday afternoon and, just past Fontainebleau, have had to slow down to a crawl, stop, six rows of cars on either side (everyone knows that on Sundays both sides of the thruway are reserved for those returning to the capital), start the engine, move three yards, stop, talk with the two nuns in the 2CV on the right, look in the rear-view mirror at the pale man driving the Caravelle, ironically envy the birdlike contentment of the couple in the Peugeot 203 (behind the girl's Dauphine) playing with their little girl, joking, and eating cheese, or suffer the exasperated outbursts of the two boys in the Simca, in front of the Peugeot 404, and even get out at the stops to explore, not wandering off too far (no one knows when the cars up front will start moving again, and you have to run back so that those behind you won't begin their battle of horn blasts and curses), and thus move up along a Taunus in front of the girl's Dauphine – she is still watching the time – and exchange a few discouraged or mocking words with the two men traveling with the little blond boy, whose great joy at this particular moment is running his toy car over the seats and the rear ledge of the Taunus, or to dare and move up just a bit, since it doesn't seem the cars up ahead will budge very soon, and observe with some pity the elderly couple in the ID Citroën that looks like a big purple bathtub with the little old man and woman swimming around inside, he resting his arms on the wheel with an air of resigned fatigue, she nibbling on an apple, fastidious rather than hungry.

By the fourth time he had seen all that, done all that, the engineer decided not to leave his car again and to just wait for the police to somehow dissolve the bottleneck. The August heat mingled with the tire-level temperature and made immobility increasingly irritating. All was gasoline fumes, screechy screams from the boys in the Simca, the sun's glare bouncing off glass and chrome frames, and to top it off, the contradictory sensation of being trapped in a jungle of cars made to run. The engineer's 404 occupied the second lane on the right, counting from the median, which meant that he had four cars on his right and seven on his left, although, in fact, he could see distinctly only the eight cars surrounding him and their occupants, whom he was already tired of observing. He had chatted with them all, except for the boys in the Simca, whom he disliked. Between stops the situation had been discussed down to the smallest detail, and the general impression was that, up to Corbeil-Essonnes, they would move more or less slowly, but that between Corbeil and Juvisy things would pick up once the helicopters and motorcycle police managed to break up the worst of the bottleneck. No one doubted that a serious accident had taken place in the area, which could be the only explanation for such an incredible delay. And with that, the government, taxes, road conditions, one topic after another, three yards, another commonplace, five yards, a sententious phrase or a restrained curse.

The two little nuns in the 2CV wanted so much to get to Milly-la-Forêt before eight because they were bringing a basket of greens for the cook. The couple in the Peugeot 203 were particularly interested in not missing the games on television at nine-thirty; the girl in the Dauphine had told the engineer that she didn't care if she got to Paris a little late, she was complaining only as a matter of principle because she thought it was a crime to subject thousands of people to the discomforts of a camel caravan. In the last few hours (it must have been around five, but the heat was unbearable) they had moved about fifty yards according to the engineer's calculations, but one of the men from the Taunus who had come to talk, bringing his little boy with him, pointed ironically to the top of a solitary plane tree, and the girl in the Dauphine remembered that this plane (if it wasn't a chestnut) had been in line with her car for such a long time that she would no longer bother looking at her watch, since all calculations were useless.

Night would never come; the sun's vibrations on the highway and cars pushed vertigo to the edge of nausea. Dark glasses, handkerchiefs moistened with cologne pressed against foreheads, the measures improvised to protect oneself from screaming reflections or from the foul breath expelled by exhaust pipes at every start, were being organized, perfected, and were the object of reflection and commentary. The engineer got out again to stretch his legs, exchanged a few words with the couple (who looked like farmers) traveling in the Ariane in front of the nuns' 2CV. Behind the 2CV was a Volkswagen with a soldier and a girl who looked like newlyweds. The third line toward the edge of the road no longer interested him because he would have had to go dangerously far from the 404; he could distinguish colors, shapes, Mercedes Benz, ID, Lancia, Skoda, Morris Minor, the whole catalog. To the left, on the opposite side of the road, an unreachable jungle of Renaults, Anglias, Peugeots, Porsches, Volvos. It was so monotonous that finally, after chatting with the two men in the Taunus and unsuccessfully trying to exchange views with the solitary driver of the Caravelle, there was nothing better to do than to go back to the 404 and pick up the same conversation about the time, distances, and the movies with the girl in the Dauphine.

Sometimes a stranger would appear, someone coming from the opposite side of the road or from the outside lanes on the right, who would slip between cars to bring some news, probably false, relayed from car to car along the hot miles. The stranger would savor the impact of his news, the slamming of doors as passengers rushed back to comment on the events; but after a while a horn, or an engine starting up, would drive the stranger away, zigzagging through the cars, rushing to get into his and away from the justified anger of the others. And so, all afternoon, they heard about the crash of a Floride and a 2CV near Corbeil – three dead and one child wounded; the double collision of a Fiat 1500 and a Renault station wagon, which in turn smashed into an Austin full of English tourists; the overturning of an Orly airport bus, teeming with passengers from the Copenhagen flight. The engineer was sure that almost everything was false, although something awful must have happened near Corbeil or even near Paris itself to have paralysed traffic to such an extent. The farmers in the Ariane, who had a farm near Montereau and knew the region well, told them about another Sunday when traffic had been at a standstill for five hours, but even that much time seemed ludicrous now that the sun, going down on the left side of the road, poured a last avalanche of orange jelly into each car, making metals boil and clouding vision, the treetops behind them never completely disappearing, the shadow barely seen in the distance up ahead never getting near enough so that you could feel the line of cars was moving, even if only a little, even if you had to start and then slam on the brakes and never leave first gear; the dejection of again going from first to neutral, brake, hand brake, stop, and the same thing time and time again.

JULIO CORTÁZAR, *All Fires the Fire*

Sunday Driving

Sunday's weather sent the small cars pouring out of London for the coast even while the papers pinpointed the number of shopping days to Christmas. One side of each of the main roads was occupied by a solid line of family saloons while bigger or faster cars hugged the crown and darted dangerously from one vantage point to the next. Just off the main roads, thousands of other cars stood outside trim villas and trimmer maisonettes while their owners anointed them with water, detergents and polish. It was a glorious late autumn day in the age of the car. Men worshipped the long or short, wide or narrow, high or low metal monsters as they had once worshipped God. Sunday was their day instead of His; they were the means of social introduction and interchange instead of His house; they had become the badge of rank instead of the pew in His church.

MARTYN GOFF, *The Youngest Director*

The Wrong Turn Off

The tide of red taillights flowed on ahead of them, and now they bothered him. In the darkness, amid this red swarm, he couldn't get his bearings. His sense of direction was slipping away. He must be heading north still. The down side of the bridge hadn't curved a great deal. But now there were only signs to go by. His entire stock of landmarks was gone, left behind. At the end of the bridge the expressway split into a Y. MAJOR DEEGAN GEO. WASHINGTON BRIDGE ... BRUCKNER NEW ENGLAND ... Major Deegan went upstate ... No! ... Veer right ... Suddenly another Y ... EAST BRONX NEW ENGLAND ... EAST 138TH BRUCKNER BOULEVARD ... Choose one, you ninny! ... Acey-deucey ... one finger, two fingers ... He veered right again ... EAST 138TH ... a ramp ... All at once there was no more ramp, no more clean cordoned expressway. He was at ground level. It was as if he had fallen into a junkyard. He seemed to be underneath the expressway. In the blackness he could make out a cyclone fence over on the left ... something caught in it ... A woman's head! ... No, it was a chair with three legs and a burnt seat with the charred stuffing hanging out in great wads, rammed halfway through a cyclone fence ... Who on earth would jam a chair into the mesh of a cyclone fence? And why?

'Where are we, Sherman?'

He could tell by the tone of her voice that there weren't going to be any more discussions of Christopher Marlowe or where to have dinner.

'We're in the Bronx.'

'You know how to get outta here?'

'Sure. If I can just find a cross street ... Let's see, let's see, let's see ... 138th Street ...'

They were traveling north underneath the expressway. But what expressway? Two lanes, both heading north ... To the left a retaining wall and cyclone fencing and concrete columns supporting the expressway ... Should head west to find a street back to Manhattan ... turn left ... but he can't turn left because of the wall ... Let's see, let's see ... 138th Street ... Where is it? ... There! The sign – 138th Street ... He keeps to the left, to make the turn ... A big opening in the wall ... 138th Street ... But he can't turn left! To his left are four or five lanes of traffic, down here underneath the expressway, two going north, two going south, and another one beyond them, cars and trucks barreling in both directions – there's no way he can cut across that traffic … So he keeps going … into the Bronx … Another opening in the wall coming up … He hugs the left lane … Same situation! … No way to turn left! … He begins to feel trapped here in the gloom beneath the expressway … But how bad could it be? … Plenty of traffic …

……

Streets converged from odd angles … People were crossing the street in every direction … Dark faces … Over this way a subway entrance … Over there low buildings, shops … Great Taste Chinese Takeout … He couldn't tell which street went due west … *That* one – the likeliest – he turned that way … a wide street … cars parked on both sides … up ahead, double-parked … triple-parked … a crowd … Could he even get through? … So he turned … *that way* … There was a street sign, but the names of the streets were no longer parallel to the streets themselves. East Something seemed to be … in that direction … So he took that street, but it quickly merged with a narrow side street and ran between some low buildings. The buildings appeared to be abandoned. At the next corner he turned – west, he figured – and followed that street a few blocks. There were more low buildings. They might have been garages and they might have been sheds. There were fences with spirals of razor wire on top. The streets were deserted, which was okay, he told himself, and yet he could feel his heart beating with a nervous twang. Then he turned again. A narrow street lined with seven- or eight-storey apartment buildings; no sign of people; not a light in a window. The next block, the same. He turned again, and as he rounded the corner –

– *astonishing.*

TOM WOLFE, *The Bonfire of the Vanities*

Orgies

After a debauch, one always feels more solitary, more abandoned.

CHARLES BAUDELAIRE

Blameless, Shameless

Eroticism's too heavy a burden for human strength. The torment of orgies is inseparable from the agony of war as Jünger pictured it: in the morning you wake up under the table with the litter of the previous evening around you. This is a *given* for orgies, a condition without which they wouldn't exist.

The one I was at (took part in it) last night was as crude as you might imagine. I followed the example of the worst, out of simplicity. In the middle of an uproar, of falling bodies, I'm silent and affectionate, not hostile. To me, the sight's horrible (but more horrible still are the rationalisations and tricks people resort to to protect themselves from such disgusting things, to distance themselves from their inevitable needs).

Blameless, shameless. The more desperate the eroticism, the more hopelessly women show off their heavy breasts, opening their mouths and screaming out, the greater the attraction. In contrast, a promise of light awaits at the limits of the mystical outlook. I find this unbearable and soon return to insolence and erotic vomit – which doesn't respect anybody or anything. How sweet to enter filthy night and proudly wrap myself in it. The whore I went with was as uncomplicated as a child and she hardly talked. There was another one, who came crashing down from a tabletop – sweet, shy, heartbreakingly tender, as I watched her with drunken, unfeeling eyes.

GEORGES BATAILLE, Guilty

Everybody Was Swinging

Georgette whirled digging the scene and everybody was swinging. Even Harry and Lee were making it and the sounds came from the radio and Camille was snapping her fingers (a little too demonstratively if you ask me, but its alright because we're (Vinnie and MS – VINNIE) swinging) and everything fell into its proper place, all words fitted; and Goldie sat beside Malfie and he grinned, *aspet ... una moment;* and Camille felt real bitchy and daring and winked at Sal and he tried to speak but he couldnt stop grinding his teeth and his head just lolled back and forth, droplets of scotch dribbling down his chin, but he was so strong and handsome – O what a marvelous chin – and she giggled thinking of the letter she would write to the pinkteas back home: O honey, do you know from nothing. What a gorgeous way to lose ones virginity! Sal laughed and blurted, I gotit swingin bitch HAARRR; and Malfie emptied his glass, refilled it and followed Goldie into the bedroom and Georgette watched, floating around their heads bopping SALT PEAnuts, SALT PEAnuts – quoth the Diz evermore – Vinnie and MS – VINNie and MS – and Lee moved a few inches and Harry grabbed her by the arm and yanked her back, Where doya think ya goin, queeny, grabbing her wrist and forcing it between his legs. I gotta nice hunka meat forya and Vinnie yelled, Is she tryin ta get fresh witya man? and they both roared and Lee started to panic, trying to free her arm, but Harry squeezed tighter and twisted until she screeched, Stop, Stop! Youre hurting me you vile fairy (wonderful, wonderful. This should teach you a lesson you evil queen. *He* is what you deserve. VINNie and MS – VINNie and MS – cause we're having a

party and the people are nice, and the people are nice ...) and Harrys
eyes bugged even more and he stood up and pulled Lee off the couch,
comon motherfucka. You wanna look like a broad ya gonna get fucked
like one (Camille shoved her fingers in her mouth, rose halfway then fell
back onto the couch and inched her way to the other end (but hes not
like *that* (?))) – Hey Vinnie, comeon. Lets throw a hump intaer. Shit man,
Im down. Letsgo. He grabbed her other arm and they started dragging
her to the bedroom, screaming, screeching, crying, pleading and they
roared and twisted her arms then Harry grabbed her by her hair, her precious golden shoulder length hair, and slapped her face. Comeon ya
cocksucker. Stop theshit. Hey Malfie, open the door. Malfie opened the
door and grinned as they dragged Lee in, and Goldie shrieked and ran
from the room, the door slamming behind her. She listened to Lee
screaming and the guys slapping her and cursing as they ripped her dress
off ... then Goldie swallowed a half dozen bennies; Camille looked at
Georgette, who hadnt moved (No, No! No you fucking bitch. VINNie
VINNie ... VINNIE!!! Not with Lee. I love you Vinnie. I love you. He
will see my red spangled G string. Please Vinnie. Vinnie ...), Camille
looked at Georgette then at Sal as he wobbled across the room toward
her. No room in there. He opened his fly and yanked out his cock (Its so
big. And red. Be careful of your eyes. Put your arms around his ass)
O???? O ... Sal? Sal dont. Sal? Please. Ple – I got a big lob forya. Sa – he
shoved it in her mouth and grabbed her long-shining-wavy-auburn-hair
– Lee stopped squirming as Vinnie and Malfie held her and Harry
mounted her. Vaseline. Vaseline! Please, not without vaseline. Vinnie
handed her the jar, then Lee said alright then closed her eyes and cringed
as Harry lunged viciously then put her arms around him and her legs
around his waist. Vinnie and Malfie leaned against the wall and Harrys
sweat fell on Lees face and she smiled and sucked his neck and groaned,
hoping he would never come, that he would continue to lunge and lunge
and lunge ... – Thats the way Camille. Thats it HAHA OOOOO Hey,
take it easy with yatongue, and Camille clutched at his belt hoping she
was doing it properly; and Goldie took the syrette from her pocket,
calmer now that the screaming had stopped, and though she did not
approve of Camille having public sex like that she had to admit that she
did not have much choice in the matter, and they did so seem to enjoy

each other (I hope Malfie wont be completely useless after this), and turned on. Everything seems to have developed beautifully – He had to help his friends. Of course. Why shouldnt he help Harry fuck her. Cause we're having a party and the people are nice, and the people are nice … – Harry took a slip from a drawer and wiped his cock. I bet yaknow youve been fucked! Harry and Malfie laughed and Lee watched Vinnie as he mounted her then closed her eyes and wrapped her legs around his hips – Goldie went back to the living room and sat on the couch, ignoring Camille and Sal, watched the smoke drift from her mouth and the sound waves from the radio; and Sals legs shook and he bent at the knees and Camille grunted and gurgled, moving her head fantastically, digging her nails into his ass, trying to get every inch of his cock in her mouth – Soon. Soon … (Quaff, oh, quaff this kind nepenthe); and we will hear tugboat whistles blowing high …

HUBERT SELBY, JR, *Last Exit to Brooklyn*

Everything is Acted to the Life

The secret Rites of the *Good Goddess* are now made public, when these Votaries of *Priapus*, provoked by the Music of the Pipe and Horn, and raised by the Vapours of Wine, like distracted Women, toss about their Hair, and make a strange Howling. How their Desires are inflamed! how agitated! what Cries, what Postures? what a Torrent of Filthiness flows all about them? The lewd *Lausella* proposes a Prize among the most infamous Strumpets, and the impure Contention obtains the Victory; but she is all in rapture when *Medullina* acts her Part; the more vile the greater Honour they obtain. Nothing is dissembled in their Sports, every thing is acted to the Life, enough to fire *Priam* frozen with Age, and *Nestor* bursten as he was. Then they are out of all Patience; they shew all the Women undisguised; a general Cry is heard through all the Place. Now is the Time, let in the Men; does the Adulterer sleep still? Then, with her Veil on, she orders the next young Fellow to be brought in; if he is not to be found, she calls eagerly for the Slaves; if there be no hopes of them, a Waterman must be hired and introduced; if, at last, no

Men are to be had, she is impatient of delay, and submits to prostitute herself to an Ass.

JUVENAL, *Satire VI*

Inventiveness of a Roman Caesar

Tiberius built at Capri a private sporting-house where sexual extravagances were played out for his secret pleasure. To furnish it he collected from all over the empire a bevy of girls and youths, selected as adepts in every monstrous kind of libidinous filthiness; called *spintriae*, they performed before him in groups of three, so as to excite his waning lust. He had as well several chambers which he furnished with lascivious pictures, little puppets twisted into wanton postures and erotic manuals from Elephantis in Egypt, so that the *spintriae* would learn exactly what was required of them. He laid out little nooks of lechery in the woods and groves of the island, and had youths and girls dressed as Pan and nymphs frolic in grottoes; the island became generally known as Caprineum, because of his goatish antics.

Some aspects of his infamy may not well be named or heard, still less believed; he trained fine boys, the tenderest and daintiest that might be had (whom he called his little fishes) to chase him while he went swimming, and get between his legs to suck and nibble him.

SUETONIUS, *History of the Twelve Caesars*

A Male Brothel in Victorian London

All rose as we entered, there were ten gentlemen and eight ladies [i.e. transvestites] waiting to receive us. It was a splendid apartment fitted up with mirrors all over the walls, whilst the windows were firmly closed and shuttered, besides the thick curtains which were drawn across them. Here and there were recesses filled by luxurious couches, before each of which stood a small table covered with the most exhilarating refreshments.

Two elderly gentlemen advanced and conducted us to seats.

Presently someone sat down to a piano and struck up a quadrille, and in a few moments we were going through the fascinating evolutions of a dance.

Our partners were particularly attentive to us, mine more especially so – in fact I can speak only for myself. He plied me with refreshments after every dance, and I could see was immensely taken with me. Now and then he would pinch my bottom, and after a little while got one hand up my clothes and groped till he found my prick. His touch added fuel to the flames of lust by which I was already consumed; a very few touches sufficed to make me spend all over his hand, which I perceived gave him great pleasure.

About two o'clock in the morning the lights were suddenly turned out, and we were all in the dark.

'Now, love, I must have you,' he whispered. 'Every one has got a partner; and after I have fucked your delicious bottom, we separate and find another partner in the dark, so there can be no favouritism or neglect of any member.'

He made me lean over the couch on my face, and lifting up my skirts behind he knelt down and kissed my bottom, buggering me with his tongue till the hole was well moistened; then getting up, I felt a fine prick brought up to the charge. It hurt me a little; but he was soon in, then passing his hands round my buttocks he frigged me most deliciously as he worked furiously in my bum.

How I thrust out my arse to meet every lunge! But it did not last long; as we were both too hot, and came almost directly. It was a delightful bottom-fuck; but the rules precluded us from having a second, and we parted with a loving kiss, and went in search of other partners.

Before time was called about 6 a.m., I had had six different gentlemen, besides one of those dressed up as a girl. We sucked; we frigged and gamahuched, and generally finished off by the orthodox buggery.

ANONYMOUS, *The Cities of the Plain, or the Recollections of a Mary Ann* (1881)

An Utter Fiasco

Love gave me, in 1821, a highly comical virtue, chastity.

Despite my efforts, in August 1821, Lussinge, Barot and Poitevin, finding me depressed, arranged a delicious party with girls. Barot, as I have realised since, is one of the leading talents in Paris at arranging this difficult type of pleasure. For him, a woman is a woman only once – the first time. He spends thirty thousand francs of his eighty thousand, and of those, at least twenty thousand on girls.

Barot, then, arranged an evening with one of his former mistresses, Mme Petit, to whom, I believe, he had just lent money to open a brothel in the rue du Cadran, at the corner with rue Montmartre, on the fourth floor.

We had to have Alexandrine – six months later protected by the richest of Englishmen – then only a debutante of two months. We found, at about eight that evening, a charming room, although on the fourth floor, with iced champagne and hot punch. Then Alexandrine appeared, conducted by a maid charged to watch over her. Charged by whom? I have forgotten. But this woman must have had a great reputation, for I saw on the bill of the party that she had been paid twenty francs. Alexandrine surpassed all expectations. She was a well-built girl of seventeen or eighteen, already formed, with black eyes that, since then, I have found again in Titian's portrait of the Duchess of Urbino, in the gallery at Florence. Titian has portrayed her almost to the very tint of her hair. She was gentle, healthy, shy, gay enough, well-behaved. My comrade's eyes goggled at the sight of her. Lussinge offers her a glass of wine, which she refuses, and disappears with her. Mme Petit introduces us to two other girls, not bad; we assert that she is prettier. She had a most shapely foot. Poitevin carried her off. After a frightful interval, Lussinge returns very pale.

'To you, Beyle! Honour to the next one!' was the cry.

I find Alexandrine on a bed, rather tired, in almost the costume, and exactly the position, of the Duchess of Urbino, by Titian.

'Let's just talk for ten minutes,' she said tactfully. 'I'm rather tired, let's have a chat. I shall soon recover the fire of youth.'

She was adorable, I never perhaps saw anything as pretty. There was not too much licence, except in her eyes which gradually became full of excitement again, and if you must, of passion.

I completely failed with her – an utter *fiasco*. I had recourse to a compensation to which she lent herself. Not knowing very well what to do, I wanted to return to this hand-play which she refused. She seemed surprised; I said a few words which were smart enough, considering the situation, and came away.

Hardly had Barot succeeded me when we heard bursts of laughter which reached us through three rooms. Suddenly Mme Petit dismissed the other girls, and Barot brought in Alexandrine in the simple array

'Of beauty that has just been snatched from sleep.'

'My admiration for Beyle,' said he, exploding with laughter, 'is going to make me imitate him; I've come to strengthen myself with champagne.' The roar of laughter lasted ten minutes: Poitevin was rolling on the carpet. The extreme astonishment of Alexandrine was unspeakably funny; it was the first time that the poor girl had met with a failure.

The gentlemen wanted to persuade me that I was dying with shame and that it was the most unhappy moment of my life. I was surprised, and that was all.

STENDHAL, *Memoirs of an Egotist*

Prostitution

Professed curtezans, if they be any good, it is because they are openly bad.

SIR THOMAS OVERBURY

Prostitution is essentially a matter of lack of choice.

CHARLES BAUDELAIRE

I love prostitution in and for itself ... In the very notion of prostitution there is such a complex convergence of lust and bitterness, such a frenzy of muscle and sound of gold, such a void in human relations, that the very sight of it makes one dizzy! And how much is learned there! And one is so sad! And one dreams so well of love!

GUSTAVE FLAUBERT

Advice to a Venetian Whore

Let her go along with the humour of these people, and speak as they wish, even though she hold them in scorn. Let her expressions be in general common ones, as my dear, my own heart, my soul, I am dying, let us die together, and such like, which will show a feigned sentiment, if not a true one. Let her add panting, and sighing, and the interrupting of her own words, and other such gallantries, which will give her out to be melting, to be swooning, to be totally consumed, whereas in fact she is not even moved, but more as if she were made of wood or of marble than of flesh. It is certain that the whore cannot take pleasure in all comers … She must nevertheless give pleasure through her words, if not her deeds, and let her put into operation what she can, authenticating her words by closing her eyes, by abandoning herself as if lifeless, and by then rising up again in full strength with a vehement sigh as if she were panting in the oppression of extreme joy, though in fact she be reduced and languid. These lies can be singularly useful, although they are discredited by too common feigning, and often obtain little credence.

FERRANTE PALLAVICINO, *La Retorica delle Puttane* (1642)

Assignations

While the war was still on, the seeds of our hateful peace were being sown.

A hysterical bitch, you could see what she'd be like just by watching her cavorting in the dance hall of the Olympia. In that long cellar room, you could see her squinting out of a hundred mirrors, stamping her feet in the dust and despair to the music of a Negro-Judeo-Saxon band. Britishers and Blacks, Levantines and Russians were everywhere, smoking and bellowing, military melancholics lined up on the red plush sofas. Those uniforms that people are beginning to find it hard to remember were the seeds of the present day, of something that is still growing and that won't become total shit for a while yet, but will in the long run.

Every week, after spending a few hours at the Olympia, warming up our desires, a few of us would go calling on our friend Madame Herote, who kept a lingerie, glove and bookshop in the Impasse des Bérésinas behind the Folies Bergère, a covered passage that isn't there any more, where little girls brought little dogs on leashes to do their business.

We went there to grope for our happiness, which all the world was threatening with the utmost ferocity. We were ashamed of wanting what we wanted, but something had to be done about it all the same. Love is harder to give up than life. In this world we spend our time killing or adoring, or both together. 'I hate you! I adore you!' We keep going, we fuel and refuel, we pass on our life to a biped of the next century, with frenzy, at any cost, as if it were the greatest of pleasures to perpetuate ourselves, as if, when all's said and done, it would make us immortal. One way or another, kissing is as indispensable as scratching.

My mental state had improved, but my military situation was still uncertain. I had leave to go out now and then. Anyway, the name of our lingerie lady was Madame Herote. Her forehead was low and so narrow that at first you felt uneasy in her presence, but her lips were so smiling and voluptuous that after a while you didn't see how you could get away from her. Under a surface of staggering volubility and unforgettable ardour, she concealed a set of simple, rapacious and piously mercantile aims.

In a few months she piled up a fortune, thanks to the Allies and thanks above all to her uterus. Her ovaries had been removed; to put it plainly, she had been operated for salpingitis the year before. That liber-ating castration had made her fortune. Gonorrhoea in a woman can be providential. A woman who spends her time worrying about pregnancy is a virtual cripple, she'll never go very far.

Old men and young men thought, and so did I, that love was easily and cheaply available in the backrooms of certain lingerie-bookshops. That was still true some twenty years ago, but today a lot of things aren't done any more, especially some of the most agreeable. Every month Anglo-Saxon puritanism is drying us up a little more, it has already reduced those impromptu backroom carousals to practically nothing. Now marriage and respectability are the thing.

In those days, for the last time, there was still freedom to fuck stand-ing up and cheap, and Madame Herote put it to good use. One Sunday an auction room appraiser with time on his hands sighted her shop and went in; he's still there. Their happiness aroused no interest in the neighbourhood. In the shadow of the newspapers with their delirious appeals for ultimate patriotic sacrifices, life went on, strictly rationed, larded with precautions, and more trickily resourceful than ever before. Those are the heads and tails, the light and shade, of the same coin.

Madame Herote's appraiser invested money in Holland for his better informed friends, and for Madame Herote as well once they became intimate. Her stock of neckties and brassières and scanty chemises attracted customers of both sexes and brought them back time and time again.

Any number of national and international encounters took place in the pink shadow of those curtains, amidst the incessant loquacity of Madame Herote, whose substantial, talkative, and overwhelmingly perfumed person would have put the most bilious of males in a lecherous mood. Far from losing her head in these miscellaneous gatherings, Madame Herote turned them to her advantage, first in terms of money, since she levied a tithe on all sentimental transactions, but also through her enjoyment of all the love-making that went on around her. She took pleasure in bringing couples together and as much or more in breaking them up by means of tale-telling, insinuations, and out and out treachery.

She never wearied of fomenting happiness and tragedy. She stoked the life of the passions, and her business prospered.

LOUIS-FERDINAND CÉLINE, *Journey to the End of the Night*

Child Prostitution

1 August 1920: The town of Bordeaux gave its name to the 'bordello'. I have visited them in many countries, out of curiosity and also because everyone else did. Each time I left one I experienced a feeling of disgust with human nature and hatred against men.

When I was at Bou Saada I passionately wanted to rescue that wonderful little Fally of the stormy eyes, slender and agile as a young gazelle; and her grandfather, like a good head of the family, refused to be seduced by even the most tempting offers. Finally, to convince me and get rid of me, I suppose, he told me: 'It is of the utmost importance that Fally should remain four or five years in the house of prostitution where her sisters, her aunts and her mother spent their youth.' I recoiled in horror. I tried to reason with him, to no avail. Nothing would shake him, sure as he was that he had made the right decision about the future of his wonderfully beautiful little grand-daughter who was alarmingly thin and shaken by a stubborn dry cough; his grand-daughter who at the age of eight was already dancing naked every evening in front of strangers. I sought out the commandant of the place, explained the situation and told him how I wanted to save pretty Fally's body and soul. He looked at me askance and sent me packing, politely but firmly. I heard afterwards that sometimes, after a good dinner, he made use of Fally.

So then, in despair, I went to see an elder sister of Fally's who was shut up in one of those houses, a café with dancing at night. The wretched girl's room had a dirty stone floor, its only furniture was a mahogany bed – like those of our country people – standing in a corner. On the bed, two torn and filthy mattresses. They made me feel sick. Filthy postcards and a few fair-ground ornaments on a shelf, a miserable white-wood table with bottle-marks all over it, and this sinister fat girl, her monstrous belly heaving with laughter at what I was saying. I left with gall in my heart. I can't even think about it without getting a lump in my throat, and to comfort myself a little I think: Fally must be dead. Surely, God, You must soon – very soon – have taken her away from this earth …

LIANE DE POUGY, *My Blue Notebooks*

The Country Whore

The front wall of the yard
often reflects the early sun
as the cowshed did. And the untidy room,
deserted in the morning when she wakes,
smells of the first, ingenuous perfume.
Even the body beneath the sheet is the same
as it was before, when her heart leapt in discovery.

Memories come when she wakes alone early
in the morning, and in the dark twilight returns
the ease of that other awakening: the cowshed
of childhood days, exhaustion from the hot
sun when she walked out slowly. A light
scent added to the customary sweat
of her hair, and the animals snuffling. Furtively
her body enjoyed the sun's caress,
insinuating, calm, as though it had touched her.

Getting out of bed deadens her limbs,
still young and stocky like a child's.
The innocent girl would search out the smell
of tobacco and hay and tremble at the fleeting
touch of a man: she liked playing.
Sometimes she would play lying down with the man
in the hay, but the man didn't smell her hair,
he searched in the hay for her tense limbs,
wearing them out, squeezing them as though he were her father.

The perfume was that of flowers crushed under stones.
Often as she wakes up slowly she smells again
that liquid smell of long-lost flowers,
cowshed and sun. No man would know
the subtle caress of that bitter memory.
No man sees beyond the body lying there
that tense and awkward childhood.

CESARE PAVESE

The Finest Men I Can Procure

I have purchased very extensive premises, which are situated between
two great thoroughfares, and are entered from each by means of
shops devoted entirely to such trades as are exclusively resorted to by
ladies. In the area between the two rows of houses I have erected a most

elegant temple, in the centre of which are large saloons entirely surrounded with boudoirs most elegantly and commodiously fitted up. In these saloons, according to their classes, are to be seen the finest men of their species I can procure, occupied in whatever amusements are adapted to their taste, and all kept in a high state of excitement by good living and idleness. The ladies will never enter the saloons even in their masks, but view their inmates from a darkened window in each boudoir. In one they will see fine, elegantly dressed young men playing at cards, music, &c. – in others athletic men wrestling or bathing, in a state of perfect nudity. In short, they will see such a variety of the animal that they cannot fail of suiting their inclinations. Having fixed upon one she should like to enjoy, the lady has only to ring for the chambermaid, call her to the window, point out the object, and he is immediately brought to the boudoir. She can enjoy him in the dark, or have a light and keep on her mask. She can stay for an hour or a night, and have one or a dozen men as she pleases, without being known to any of them. A lady of seventy or eighty years of age can at pleasure enjoy a fine, robust youth of twenty, and to elevate the mind to the sublimest raptures of love, every boudoir is surrounded with the most superb paintings of Aretino's Postures after Julio Romano and Ludovico Carracci, interspersed with large mirrors; also a sideboard covered with the most delicious viands and richest wines. The whole expense of the Institution is defrayed by a subscription from each lady of one hundred guineas per annum, with the exception of the refreshments which are to be paid for at the time.

The greatest possible pains have been taken to preserve order and regularity, and it is impossible that any discovery can take place by the intrusion of police or enraged cuckolds, as will be demonstrated to every lady before she pays her subscription, and as is more fully detailed in the private prospectus to be had of Madame de Gomez, the subdirectress, at the Institution, who will also furnish them with a catalogue of the most extensive collection of bawdy books in French, Italian and English, which has ever been collected, and which I have purchased at the expense of £2,000 for the use of my patronesses. The different saloons have been decorated by one of the first painters of the age, with designs from Mr Knight's work on the ancient worship of Priapus, which renders them one of the most singular exhibitions of Europe. No male creature is to be admitted into any part of the temple but the saloons, and those only the trusty, tried and approved functionaries who are well paid for their services, and not let in to gratify curiosity. Having thus made it my study to serve my own sex in a most essential point, I trust to their liberality for encouragement in my arduous undertaking, and am, Ladies, your most obedient servant, Mary Wilson.

MARY WILSON, *The Voluptuarian Cabinet*

The Game

Last night
A rather trite
Thought occurred to me. Exactly what pleasure
Is there in being a 'Lady of Leisure'?
One has to submit (and grit one's teeth) to a great many men who,
    when the 'fun' is at an end,
Pretend
They've 'never done this before'.
And it's really such a bore
To listen enthralled
As they tell you about having called
At the furriers to buy coats for their spouses
(Made from mouses)
And, while wrapped in gorilla-like embraces,
You lie making faces
At your big toe over a beefy shoulder,
And he becomes colder
Because you do not respond as he breathes garlic,
Or worse, alcoholic
Fumes over your pretty neck
And you fervently wish that he'd break his ...
There are of course so many different types:
Like the one who wipes

His hands all over your bedspread, and though you are very sweet to him
And entreat him
Not to do it again, he does – when you turn your back.
And you're just dying to whack
The man who is so 'thoughtful' and feels he really ought to give you
   'pleasure' too because you're really far too 'good'
For this life. (As if he could!)
And have you ever met the one who is just longing for sex,
But only ever pays with perfectly good cheques?
So when you're fool enough to agree –
(If you wish, he'll meet you at the bank next day, long before three)
You find he's hopped it –
And stopped it!
And how about the pound-of-flesher who insists
On being kissed
All over the place, and wants you to remove every bit of your clothes,
   including those nylons you spent your last pound on this afternoon,
Which will so soon
Be in shreds.
I'm forgetting the 'slave':
On bended knee he'll crave
To be allowed to clean your lavatory,
And when you've stripped him
And whipped him
Mercilessly,
Asks: 'Do you get many like me?'

A London prostitute of the 1960s

The Harlot's House

We caught the tread of dancing feet,
We loitered down the moonlit street,
And stopped beneath the harlot's house.

Inside, above the din and fray,
We heard the loud musicians play
The 'Treues Liebes Herz' of Strauss.

Like strange mechanical grotesques,
Making fantastic arabesques,
The shadows raced across the blind.

We watched the ghostly dancers spin
To sound of horn and violin,
Like black leaves wheeling in the wind.

Like wire-pulled automatons,
Slim silhouetted skeletons
Went sidling through the slow quadrille.

They took each other by the hand,
And danced a stately saraband;
Their laughter echoed thin and shrill.

Sometimes a clockwork puppet pressed
A phantom lover to her breast,
Sometimes they seemed to try to sing.

Sometimes a horrible marionette
Came out, and smoked its cigarette
Upon the steps like a live thing.

Then, turning to my love, I said,
'The dead are dancing with the dead,
The dust is whirling with the dust.'

But she – she heard the violin,
And left my side, and entered in:
Love passed into the house of lust.

Then suddenly the tune went false,
The dancers wearied of the waltz,
The shadows ceased to wheel and whirl.

And down the long and silent street,
The dawn, with silver-sandalled feet,
Crept like a frightened girl.

OSCAR WILDE

Harrison Street Court

I heard a woman's lips
Speaking to a companion
Say these words:

'A woman what hustles
Never keeps nothin'
For all her hustlin'.
Somebody always gets
What she goes on the street for.
If it ain't a pimp
It's a bull what gets it.
I been hustlin' now
Till I ain't much good any more.
I got nothin' to show for it.
Some man got it all,
Every night's hustlin' I ever did.'

CARL SANDBURG

A Masseuse and Prostitute

Nobody knows what love is anymore.
Nobody knows what happened to God.
After midnight, the lesbians and fairies
Sweep through the streets of the old tenderloin,
Like spirochetes in a softening brain.

347

The hustlers have all been run out of town.
I look back on the times spent
Talking with you about the idiocies
Of a collapsing world and the brutalities
Of my race and yours,
While the sick, the perverted, the malformed,
Came and went, and you cooked them,
And rolled them, and beat them,
And sent them away with a little taste
Of electric life from the ends of your fingers.
Who could ever forget your amiable body,
Or your unruffled good sense,
Or your smiling sex?
I suppose your touch kept many men
As sane as they could be kept.
Every hour there is less of that touch in the world.

KENNETH REXROTH

A Professed Courtezan

I am a profest Courtezan,
That live by peoples sinne:
With halfe a dozen Puncks I keepe,
I have great comming in.
Such store of Traders haunt my house,
To finde a lusty Wench,
That twentie Gallants in a weeke,
Doe entertaine the *French*:
Your Courtier, and your Citizen,
Your very rustique Clowne,
Will spend an Angell on the Poxe,
Even ready mony downe.
I strive to live most Lady-like,
And scorne those foolish Queanes,

That doe not rattle in their Silkes
And yet have able meanes.
I have my Coach, as if I were
A Countesse, I protest,
I have my daintie Musicke playes
When I would take my rest.
I have my Serving men that waite
Upon mee in blew Coates;
I have my Oares that do attend
My pleasure, with their boates:
I have my Champions that will fight,
My Lovers that do fawne:
I have my Hat, my Hood, my Maske,
My Fanne, My Cobweb Lawne;
To Give my Glove unto a Gull,
Is mighty favour found,
When for the wearing of the same,
It costs him twentie pound.
My Garter, as a gracious thing,
Another takes away:
And for the same, a silken Goune
The Prodigall doth pay ...
Another lowly-minded youth,
Forsooth my Shooe-string craves,
And that he putteth through his eare,
Calling the rest, base slaves.
Thus fit I Fooles in humour still,
That come to me for game,
I punish them for Venerie,
Leaving their Purses lame.

SAMUEL ROWLANDS, *Doctor Merrie-Man* (1609)

The Ruined Maid

'O 'Melia, my dear, this does everything crown!
Who could have supposed I should meet you in Town?
And whence such fair garments, such prosperi-ty?' –
'O didn't you know I'd been ruined?' said she.

– 'You left us in tatters, without shoes or socks,
Tired of digging potatoes, and spudding up docks;
And now you've gay bracelets and bright feathers three!' –
'Yes: that's how we dress when we're ruined,' said she.

– 'At home in the barton you said "thee" and "thou",
And "thik oon", and "theäs oon", and "t'other"; but now
Your talking quite fits 'ee for high compa-ny!' –
'Some polish is gained with one's ruin,' said she.

– 'Your hands were like paws then, your face blue and bleak
But now I'm bewitched by your delicate cheek,
And your little gloves fit as on any la-dy!' –
'We never do work when we're ruined,' said she.

– 'You used to call home-life a hag-ridden dream,
And you'd sigh, and you'd sock; but at present you seem
To know not of megrims or melancho-ly!' –
'True. One's pretty lively when ruined,' said she.

– 'I wish I had feathers, a fine sweeping gown,
And a delicate face, and could strut about Town!' –
'My dear – a raw country girl, such as you be,
Cannot quite expect that. You ain't ruined,' said she.

THOMAS HARDY

Safer Sex

O All ye Nymphs, in lawless Love's Disport
Assiduous! whose ever open Arms
Both Day and Night stand ready to receive
The fierce Assaults of Britain's am'rous Sons!
Whether with Golden Watch, or stiff Brocade,
You shine in Play-house or the Drawing-room,
Whores thrice magnificent; Delight of Kings,
And Lords of goodliest note; or in mean Stuffs
Ply ev'ry Evening near St Clement's Pile,
Or Church of fam'd St Dunstan, or in Lane,
Or Alley's dark Recess, or open Street,
Known by white Apron, bart'ring Love with Cit,
Or strolling Lawyer's Clerk at cheapest Rate;
Whether of Needham's or of Jordan's Train,
Hear, and attend: in Cundum's mighty Praise
I sing, for sure 'tis worthy of a Song.
Venus assist my Lays, Thou who presid'st
In City-Ball or Courtly-Masquerade,
Goddess supreme! sole Authoress of our Loves
Pure and impure! whose Province 'tis to rule
Not only o'er the chaster Marriage Bed,
But filthiest Stews, and Houses of kept Dames!
To thee I call, and with a friendly Voice,
Cundum I sing, by Cundum now secure
Boldly the willing Maid, by Fear awhile
Kept virtuous, owns thy Pow'r, and tastes thy Joys
Tumultuous; Joys untasted but for them.
Unknown big Belly, and the squawling Brat,
Best Guard of Modesty! She riots now
Thy vot'ry, in the Fullness of thy Bliss.
'Happy the Man, who in his Pocket keeps,
Whether with Green or Scarlet Ribband bound,
A well-made Cundum – He, nor dreads the Ills

Of Shankers, or Cordee, or Buboes dire!'
Thrice happy He – (for when in lewd Embrace
Of Transport-feigning Whore, Creature obscene!
The cold insipid Purchase of a Crown!
Bless'd chance! Sight seldom seen! and mostly given
By Templer, or Oxonian – best Support
Of Drury, or her starv'd Inhabitants);
With Cundum arm'd he wages am'rous Fight
Fearless, secure; nor Thought of future Pains
Resembling Prick of Pins and Needle's Point,
E'er checks his Raptures, or disturbs his Joys;
So Ajax, Grecian Chief, with Seven-fold Shield,
Enormous, brav'd the Trojan's fiercest Rage;
While the hot daring Youth, whose giddy Lust
Or taste too exquisite, in Danger's Spite
Resolves upon Fruition, unimpair'd
By intervening Armour, Cundum Height!
Scarce three Days past, bewails the dear-bought bliss.
For now, tormented sore with scalding Heat
Of Urine, dread Fore-runner of a Clap!
With Eye repentant, he surveys his Shirt,
Diversify'd with Spots of yellow Hue,
Sad Symptom of ten thousand Woes to come!
Now no Relief, but from the Surgeon's Hand,
Or Pill-prescribing Leach, tremendous Sight
To Youth diseas'd! In Garret high he moans
His wretched fate, where vex'd with nauseous draught
And more afflicting Bolus, he in Pangs
Unfelt before, curses the dire Result
Of lawless Revelling. ...

ANONYMOUS (early 18th century), *A Panegyric upon Cundums*

San Francisco Streets

I've had my eye on you
    For some time now.
You're getting by it seems,
    Not quite sure how.
But as you go along
    You're finding out
What different city streets
    Are all about.

Peach country was your home.
    When you went picking
You ended every day
    With peach fuzz sticking
All over face and arms,
    Intimate, gross,
Itching like family,
    And far too close.

But when you came to town
    And when you first
Hung out on Market Street
    That was the worst:
Tough little group of boys
    Outside Flagg's Shoes.
You learned to keep your cash.
    You got tattoos.

Then by degrees you rose
    Like country cream –
Hustler to towel boy,
    Bath house and steam;

Tried being kept a while –
   But felt confined,
One brass bed driving you
   Out of your mind.

Later on Castro Street
   You got new work
Selling chic jewelry.
   And as sales clerk
You have at last attained
   To middle class.
(No one on Castro Street
   Peddles his ass.)

You gaze out from the store.
   Watching you watch
All the men strolling by
   I think I catch
Half-veiled uncertainty
   In your expression.
Good looks and great physiques
   Pass in procession.

You've risen up this high –
   How, you're not sure.
Better remember what
   Makes you secure.
Fuzz is still on the peach,
   Peach on the stem.
Your looks looked after you.
   Look after them.

THOM GUNN

A Streetwalker Called Sabine

The other day, or rather the other night – it was four o'clock in the morning – we were in Room No 7 at the Maison d'Or, a room with the wall-panels edged with strips of gilded wood, and decorated with big flowers in bright red and white and broad leaves in relief imitating Coromandel lacquer. On the red velvet sofa a red-haired woman was sprawled on her belly, a street-walker called Sabine with something of the she-wolf, the lioness, and the cow about her, wearing neither a corset nor a dress, her breasts bare and her chemise hitched up above her knees. There was a basket of fruit standing untouched on the mantelpiece.

Now and then she uttered the cries of a drunken woman, her eyes red, her lips feverish. Then she would swear, grind her teeth, and try to bite; I raised her head whenever she let it fall. She vomited, swearing all the while.

In the meantime Charles was weeping on Edmond's shoulder, saying: 'Louise! I love her! I love her!' He was talking about La Rouvroy. There was some sort of coolness between them at this time. She was giving him the cold shoulder to get some more money out of him. The tart kept sitting up to watch him crying and in between hiccoughs she said to him: 'Cry, that's right, cry, Monsieur le Comte, I like to see a good cry! She doesn't love you! She'll never love you! Go on, Charles, you can cry better than that. And then, with a thousand-franc note ... Or take her two thousand-franc notes!' As for myself, I kept pouring the names of all her lovers over his head, like so much cold water.

'Come now,' said Edmond, 'dammit all, forget about that bitch and let's go to the brothel. La Rouvroy doesn't love you, it's time somebody told you that to your face. She's making a fool of you. Why, the other day I felt positively indignant: you send her your carriage to cart her family to the theatre, you go to see her in the box you have taken for her, and she fobs you off with a few words ... You are a laughing-stock at her theatre. They know she can do what she likes with you.'

'I've bought her twelve hundred francs' worth of jewels,' said Charles, and great tears trickled down one by one on to his big black beard.

'Oh, get along with you! You're young, you've got a review, a carriage and a theatre, and one day you'll have an income of eighty thousand francs a year. Why, with all that, I'd walk on a woman as if she were a pavement!'

The tart started vomiting again. Edmond, sitting opposite with his chin in his hands, seemed to be looking into Villedeuil's future. Villedeuil, his long hair falling into his red eyes, was sobbing and kissing a miniature of La Rouvroy. I threw some iced water over the tart's head.

And the crossing-sweepers on the boulevard below, raising their eyes, envied all the pleasure which seemed to shine in the fading light of the candles in Room No 7.

GONCOURT BROTHERS, *Journal*

Reading

Whenever I ask a certain acquaintance of mine to tell me what he knows about any subject, he consults a book: he would not dare tell me he had scabs on his arse without scanning his lexicon for the meanings of scab and arse.

MICHEL DE MONTAIGNE

The way to be esteemd Learned, is but only to have a Library, and to be able to Turn to the Indices.

SAMUEL BUTLER I

Critics are like brushers of noblemen's clothes.

GEORGE HERBERT

As in general, Reading improves the Judgment of a Man of Sense it only renders the Caprices of a Coxcomb more visible.

MATTHEW PRIOR

Extensive reading has brought us to a learned barbarism.

GEORG LICHTENBERG

Reading is like thinking with someone else's head instead of with one's own.

ARTHUR SCHOPENHAUER

Atrocities

It is impossible to scan any newspaper, no matter what the day, month or year, without finding on every line evidence of the most appalling human perversity, together with the most astonishing boasts of probity, goodness and charity and the most brazen claims about the progress of civilisation.

Every newspaper, from first line to last, is a tissue of horrors. Wars, crimes, thefts, lewdness, tortures, crimes by princes, crimes by nations, crimes by individuals, a debauch of universal atrocity.

And this is the disgusting appetiser that civilised people take at breakfast every morning. Everything in this world oozes crimes: the newspaper, the walls, human faces.

I cannot understand how any clean hand can touch a newspaper without a shudder of disgust.

CHARLES BAUDELAIRE

Australian Newspapers

[Sir George Fuller's government introduced a Bill to prohibit publication of details of divorce cases]

All the zoophaga and zygaena, the larger and fiercer carnivora and the hammer-headed sharks; all the social wolves, jackals, lynxes and hyenas;

all the social scavengers and refuse-eaters, and all the social sarcophaga and flesh-flies have been stirred into sympathetic and violent agitation by the yowl of the Sydney Dirt Merchants for 'the sacred right of the Free and Enlightened Press' ... All the friends of the Dirt-Merchants, the low-minded, depraved, corrupt and vitiated, and all the pimps, panderers, perverts and parasites, all the gutter-snipes and riff-raff, all the harridans and women of the pavement, and all the creatures, debauchees, derelicts, semi-idiots and criminals of the underworld, and all those who are past redemption and who crave for the company of the damned will, if the Legislative Assembly passed this Amendment, no longer have their gorge and glut of Dirt every evening, and a double supply on Sunday ... The Manager of the most notorious of the Yellow Journals remarked not long ago: 'A considerable section of the public wants literary garbage, and we give them what they want.' That is, he catered for the slugs, the sluts, the soss-bellies, the slubberdegullions, the slatterns, the slovens, the slabberers, the slush-swiggers, the swine snouts, and the sots.

'THE YOWL OF THE DIRT MERCHANTS',
The Australian Bystander, 9 October 1924

An Ethical Journalist

January 1852: 'Gentlemen,' said Nodier one day, getting almost inflamed at the end of dinner, 'to give you some idea of governmental corruption, Monsieur Laine, reputedly the most virtuous of all the Ministers, sent us on New Year's Day a 500 franc note to get a favourable article into our paper.'

'Did you send it back?' asked Leprevost.

'No,' replied Nodier, 'but I wrote an article against him.'

GONCOURT BROTHERS, *Journal*

A Gripping Read

He had begun to read the novel a few days before. He had put it down because of some urgent business conferences, opened it again on his way back to the estate by train; he permitted himself a slowly growing interest in the plot, in the characterisations. That afternoon, after writing a letter giving his power of attorney and discussing a matter of joint ownership with the manager of his estate, he returned to the book in the tranquillity of his study which looked out upon the park with its oaks. Sprawled in his favorite armchair, its back toward the door – even the possibility of an intrusion would have irritated him, had he thought of it – he let his left hand caress repeatedly the green velvet upholstery and set to reading the final chapters. He remembered effortlessly the names and his mental image of the characters; the novel spread its glamour over him almost at once. He tasted the almost perverse pleasure of disengaging himself line by line from the things around him, and at the same time feeling his head rest comfortably on the green velvet of the chair with its high back, sensing that the cigarettes rested within reach of his hand, that beyond the great windows the air of afternoon danced under the oak trees in the park. Word by word, licked up by the sordid dilemma of the hero and heroine, letting himself be absorbed to the point where the images settled down and took on color and movement, he was witness to the final encounter in the mountain cabin. The woman arrived first, apprehensive; now the lover came in, his face cut by the backlash of a branch. Admirably, she stanched the blood with her kisses, but he rebuffed her caresses, he had not come to perform again the ceremonies of a secret passion, protected by a world of dry leaves and furtive paths through the forest. The dagger warmed itself against his chest, and underneath liberty pounded, hidden close. A lustful, panting dialogue raced down the pages like a rivulet of snakes, and one felt it had all been decided from eternity. Even to those caresses which writhed about the lover's body, as though wishing to keep him there, to dissuade him from it; they sketched abominably the frame of that other body it was necessary to destroy. Nothing had been forgotten: alibis, unforeseen hazards, possible mistakes. From this hour on, each instant had its use minutely assigned. The cold-blooded, twice-gone-over re-examination of the details was barely broken off so that a hand could caress a check. It was beginning to get dark.

Not looking at one another now, rigidly fixed upon the task which awaited them, they separated at the cabin door. She was to follow the trail that led north. On the path leading in the opposite direction, he turned for a moment to watch her running, her hair loosened and flying. He ran in turn, crouching among the trees and hedges until, in the yellowish fog of dusk, he could distinguish the avenue of trees which led up to the house. The dogs were not supposed to bark, they did not bark. The estate manager would not be there at this hour, and he was not there. He went up the three porch steps and entered. The woman's words reached him over the thudding of blood in his ears: first a blue chamber, then a hall, then a carpeted stairway. At the top, two doors. No one in the first room, no one in the second. The door of the salon, and then, the knife in hand, the light from the great windows, the high back of an armchair covered in green velvet, the head of the man in the chair reading a novel.

JULIO CORTÁZAR, *End of the Game*

London Newspapers

Confining, room-keeping, thickest Winter, is yet more bearable here than the gaudy months. Among one's books at one's fire by candle, one is soothed into an oblivion that one is not in the country; but with the light the green fields return, till I gaze, and in a calenture can plunge myself into St Giles's. O let no native Londoner imagine that health, and rest, and innocent occupation, interchange of converse sweet, and recreative study, can make the country any thing better than altogether odious and detestable! A garden was the primitive prison, till man, with Promethean felicity and boldness, luckily sinned himself out of it. Thence followed Babylon, Nineveh, Venice, London, haberdashers, goldsmiths, taverns, playhouses, satires, epigrams, puns – these all came in on the town part, and the thither side of innocence. Man found out inventions. From my den I return you condolence for your decaying sight; not for any thing there is to see in the country, but for the miss of the pleasure of reading a London newspaper. The poets are as well to listen to; any thing high may, nay, must, be read out; you read it yourself with an imaginary auditor; but the light paragraphs must be glid over by the proper eye; mouthing mumbles their gossamery substance. 'Tis these trifles I should mourn in fading sight. A newspaper is the single gleam of comfort I receive here; it comes from rich Cathay with tidings of mankind.

CHARLES LAMB, *Letters*

Maggots for Triflers' Brains

Endless it were to sing the powers of all,
Their names, their numbers; how they rise and fall:
Like baneful herbs the gazer's eye they seize,
Rush to the head, and poison where they please:
Like idle flies, a busy, buzzing train,
They drop their maggots in the trifler's brain:
That genial soil receives the fruitful store,
And there they grow, and breed a thousand more.
Now be their arts display'd, how first they choose
A cause and party, as the bard his Muse;
Inspired by these, with clamorous zeal they cry,
And through the town their dreams and omens fly;
So the Sibylline leaves were blown about,
Disjointed scraps of fate involved in doubt;
So idle dreams, the journals of the night,
Are right and wrong by turns, and mingle wrong with right …
Some neutral powers, with secret forces fraught,
Wishing for war, but willing to be bought:

While some to every side and party go,
Shift every friend, and join with every foe;
Like sturdy rogues in privateers, they strike
This side and that, the foes of both alike;
A traitor crew, who thrive in troubled times,
Fear'd for their force, and courted for their crimes.

GEORGE CRABBE

Weak men are the worse for the good sense they read in Books, because it furnisheth them only with more matter to mistake.

MARQUIS OF HALIFAX

Let blockheads read what blockheads wrote.

EARL OF CHESTERFIELD

[Of the *Daily Mail*] Written for office boys by office boys.

MARQUESS OF SALISBURY

The most important service rendered by the Press and the magazines is that of educating people to approach printed matter with distrust.

SAMUEL BUTLER II

Man is by nature a liar. The London *Times*, in thirty-eight years I have known it, has never once told the truth, unless it was on indifferent matters.

HENRY ADAMS

The worst readers are those who behave like plundering troops: they carry off a few things they can use, soil and confound the rest, and revile all.

FRIEDRICH NIETZSCHE

Novels are longer than life.

NATALIE BARNEY

Nothing Beats a Death

Printers finde by experience that one Murther is worth two Monsters, and at least three walking Spirits. For the Consequence of Murther is hanging, with which the Rabble is wonderfully delighted. But where Murthers and walking Spirits meet, there is no other Narrative can come neare it.

SAMUEL BUTLER I, *Miscellaneous Observations*

Paris Newspapers

'Ideas and opinions can only be counteracted by opinions and ideas,' Vignon continued. 'By sheer terror and despotism, and by no other means, can you extinguish the genius of the French nation; for the language lends itself admirably to allusion and ambiguity. Epigram breaks out the more for repressive legislation; it is like steam in an engine without a safety-valve. The King, for example, does right; if a newspaper is against him, the Minister gets all the credit of the measure, and *vice versa*. A newspaper invents a scandalous libel – it has been misinformed. If the victim complains, the paper gets off with an apology for taking so great a freedom. If the case is taken into court, the editor complains that nobody asked him to rectify the mistake; but ask for redress, and he will laugh in your face and treat his offence as a mere trifle. The paper scoffs if the victim gains the day; and if heavy damages are awarded, the plaintiff is held up as an unpatriotic obscurantist and a menace to the liberties of the country. In the course of an article purporting to explain that Monsieur So-and-so is as honest a man as you will find in the kingdom, you are informed that he is no better than a common thief. The signs of the press? Pooh! mere trifles; the curtailers of its liberties are monsters; and give him time enough, the constant reader is persuaded to believe anything you please. Everything which does not suit the newspaper will be unpatriotic, and the press will be infallible. One religion will be played off against another, and the Charter against the King. The press will hold up the magistracy to scorn for meting out rigorous justice to the press, and applaud its action when it serves the cause of party hatred. The most sensational fictions will be invented to increase the circulation; Journalism will descend to mountebanks' tricks worthy of Bobêche; Journalism would serve up its father with the Attic salt of its own wit sooner than fail to interest or amuse the public; Journalism will outdo the actor who put his son's ashes into the urn to draw real tears from his eyes, or the mistress who sacrifices everything to her lover.'

'Journalism is, in fact, the People in folio form,' interrupted Blondet.

'The people with hypocrisy added and generosity lacking,' said Vignon. 'All real ability will be driven out from the ranks of Journalism, as Aristides was driven into exile by the Athenians. We shall see newspapers started in the first instance by men of honour, falling sooner or later into the hands of men of abilities even lower than the average, but endowed with the resistance and flexibility of indiarubber, qualities denied to noble genius; nay, perhaps the future newspaper proprietor will be the tradesman with capital sufficient to buy venal pens. We see such things already indeed, but in ten years' time every little youngster that has left school will take himself for a great man, slash his predecessors from the lofty height of a newspaper column, drag them down by the feet, and take their place.

'Napoleon did wisely when he muzzled the press. I would wager that the Opposition papers would batter down a government of their own setting up, just as they are battering the present government, if any demand was refused. The more they have, the more they will want in the way of concessions. The parvenu journalist will be succeeded by the starveling hack. There is no salve for this sore. It is a kind of corruption which grows more and more obtrusive and malignant; the wider it spreads, the more patiently it will be endured, until the day comes when newspapers shall so increase and multiply in the earth that confusion will be the result – a second Babel. We, all of us, such as we are, have reason to know that crowned kings are less ungrateful than kings of our profession; that the most sordid man of business is not so mercenary nor so keen in speculation; that our brains are consumed to furnish their daily supply of poisonous trash. And yet we, all of us, shall continue to write, like men who work in quick-silver mines, knowing that they are doomed to die of their trade.'

HONORÉ DE BALZAC, *Un Grand Homme de province à Paris*

A Perverted Taste

Luxury gives the mind a childish cast,
And while she polishes, perverts the taste;
Habits of close attention, thinking heads,
Become more rare as dissipation spreads,
Till authors hear at length, one general cry,
Tickle and entertain us, or we die.
The loud demand from year to year the same,
Beggars invention and makes fancy tame;
Till farce itself, most mournfully *jejune*,
Calls for the kind assistance of a tune,
And novels, (witness every month's Review)
Belie their name, and offer nothing new.

WILLIAM COWPER

Readers of Newspapers

It crawls, the underground snake,
crawls, with its load of people.
And each one   has his
newspaper, his skin
disease; a twitch of chewing;
newspaper *caries*.
Masticators of gum,
readers of newspapers.

And who are the readers? old men? athletes?
soldiers? No face, no features,
no age. Skeletons – there's no
face, only the newspaper page.

All Paris   is dressed
this way from forehead to navel.
Give it up, girl, or
you'll give birth to
a reader of newspapers.

Sway/he lived with his sister,
Swaying/he killed his father,
They blow themselves up with pettiness
as if they were swaying with drink.

For such gentlemen   what
is the sunset or the sunrise?
They swallow emptiness,
these readers of newspapers.

For news   read: calumnies,
For news   read: embezzling,
in every column   slander
every paragraph some   disgusting thing.

With what, at the Last Judgement
will you come before the light?
Grabbers of small moments,
readers of newspapers.

Gone! lost! vanished! so,
the old maternal terror.
But mother, the Gutenberg Press
is more terrible than Schwarz' powder.

It's better to go to a graveyard
than into the   prurient
sickbay of scab-scratchers,
these readers of newspapers.

And who is it rots our sons
now in the prime of their life?
Those corrupters of blood
the *writers* of newspapers.

Look, friends   much
stronger than in these lines, do
I think this, when with
a manuscript in my hand

I stand before the face
there is no   emptier place
than before the absent
face of an editor of news
                         papers' evil filth.

MARINA TSVETAYEVA

Schadenfreude

There is no spectacle more agreeable than watching an old friend fall from a roof.

CONFUCIUS

How pleasant to gaze out to sea, when the waves are lashed by the tempest and watch, from the safety of land, the desperate struggle of others.

LUCRETIUS

I detest that dark, dismal mentality which skims over life's pleasures but fastens on misfortunes, and feeds off them; like flies which cannot grip on smooth, polished surfaces, and so cling to rough, jagged spots, or leeches that suck off only bad blood.

MICHEL DE MONTAIGNE

Good Nature finds a great deal of Pleasure in having Compassion of the Miseries of others.

SAMUEL BUTLER I

A friend's ruin is relished by friends and foes alike.

DUC DE LA ROCHEFOUCAULD

Wine at a feast gives less joy than the mourning of an enemy.

MARQUISE DE SÉVIGNÉ

Friendship is a Cheat

Wise Rochefoucault a maxim writ,
Made up of malice, truth, and wit:
If what he says be not a joke,
We mortals are strange kind of folk.
But hold: before we farther go,
'Tis fit the maxim we should know.

    He says, 'Whenever Fortune sends
Disasters to our dearest friends,
Although we outwardly may grieve,
We oft are laughing in our sleeve.'
And, when I think upon't, this minute,
I fancy there is something in it.

    We see a comrade get a fall,
Yet laugh our hearts out, one and all.

    Tom for a wealthy wife looks round,
A nymph that brings ten thousand pound:
He nowhere could have better picked;
A rival comes, and Tom – is nicked.
See, how behave his friends professed,
They turn the matter to a jest;
Loll out their tongues, and thus they talk,
Poor Tom has got a plaguey baulk!

I could give instances enough,
That human friendship is but stuff.
Whene'er a flattering puppy cries
You are his dearest friend, he lies:
To lose a guinea at picquet,
Would make him rage and storm and fret,
Bring from his heart sincerer groans
Than if he heard you broke your bones.

Come, tell me truly, would you take well,
Suppose your friend and you were Equal,
To see him always foremost stand,
Affect to take the upper hand,
And strive to pass, in public view,
For much a better man than you?
Envy, I doubt, would powerful prove,
And get the better of your love;
'Twould please your palate, like a feast,
To see him mortified at least.

'Tis true, we talk of friendship much,
But who are they that can keep touch?
True friendship in two breasts requires
The same aversions and desires;
My friend should have, when I complain,
A fellow-feeling of my pain.

Yet, by experience, oft we find
Our friends are of a different mind;
And, were I tortured with the gout,
They'd laugh to see me make a rout,
Glad that themselves could walk about.

JONATHAN SWIFT

Most people enjoy the inferiority of their best friends.

EARL OF CHESTERFIELD

The worst human trait is *Schadenfreude*, which is akin to cruelty, indeed only differs from it as theory differs from practice. It usually occurs when its antithesis pity ought to be manifest, for pity is the source of all justice and love of humanity.

ARTHUR SCHOPENHAUER

A person seldom falls sick, but the bystanders are animated with a faint hope that he will die.

RALPH WALDO EMERSON

To think ill of mankind, and not wish ill to them, is perhaps the highest wisdom.

WILLIAM HAZLITT

Megatonnage

I decided to enroll at the University of Miami. It wasn't a bad place. Repetition gave way to the beginnings of simplicity. (A preparation thus for Texas.) I wanted badly to stay. I liked playing football and I knew that by this time I'd have trouble finding another school that would take me. But I had to leave. It started with a book, an immense volume about the possibilities of nuclear war – assigned reading for a course I was taking in modes of disaster technology. The problem was simple and terrible: I enjoyed the book. I liked reading about the deaths of tens of millions of people. I liked dwelling on the destruction of great cities. Five to twenty million dead. Fifty to a hundred million dead. Ninety percent population loss. Seattle wiped out by mistake. Moscow demolished. Airbursts over every SAC base in Europe. I liked to think of huge buildings toppling, of firestorms, of bridges collapsing, survivors roaming the charred country-side. Carbon 14 and strontium 90. Escalation ladder and subcrisis situa-tion. Titan, Spartan, Poseidon. People burned and unable to breathe. People being evacuated from doomed cities. People diseased and starv-ing. Two hundred thousand bodies decomposing on the roads outside Chicago. I read several chapters twice. Pleasure in the contemplation of millions dying and dead. I became fascinated by words and phrases like thermal hurricane, overkill, circular error probability, post-attack en-vironment, stark deterrence, dose-rate contours, kill-ratio, spasm war. Pleasure in these words. They were extremely effective, I thought, whis-pering shyly of cycles of destruction so great that the language of past world wars became laughable, the wars themselves somewhat naive. A thrill almost sensual accompanied the reading of this book. What was wrong with me? Had I gone mad? Did others feel as I did? I became seriously depressed. Yet I went to the library and got more books on the subject. Some of these had been published well after the original volume and things were much more up-to-date. Old weapons vanished. Megatonnage soared. New concepts appeared – the rationality of irra-tionality, hostage cities, orbital attacks. I became more fascinated, more depressed, and finally I left Coral Gables and went back home to my room and to the official team photo of the Detroit Lions. It seemed the only thing to do. My mother brought lunch upstairs. I took the dog for walks.

DON DELILLO, *End Zone*

373

Scuzzy People

The Patronising of Rascals is a form of the appetite for vice.

THEOPHRASTUS

Bad company is a disease;
Who lies with dogs, shall rise with fleas.

ROWLAND WATKYNS

Most men are cowards, all men should be knaves.

EARL OF ROCHESTER

Whoever contracts a friendship with a knave or a fool, has something bad to do or to conceal.

EARL OF CHESTERFIELD

You think I pursue weirdness because I do not know beauty; no, it is because you do not know beauty that I seek weirdness.

GEORG LICHTENBERG

Baseness attracts everybody.

JOHANN WOLFGANG GOETHE

Some persons make promises for the pleasure of breaking them.

WILLIAM HAZLITT

A Commissioner of Police

There was a Police Commissioner, a lively, political journalist, a moke of all trades who worked ambitiously in any shafts offered him, thinking he would one day have a chance to sit on the driver's seat and show a long head despite his ass's ears. He had been a Minister in a Government, but he drove one day into some too, too slippery mass of garbage, and he had been obliged to take a long rest in the country in the clover, biding his time. In the country, he had improved his manners, taken an eye-glass, studied fine eating, invented a few dishes, written two romances and a book of aphorisms and learned to seem wise by ignoring questions. He had a wife with whom he lived at times in hotels, and then the pair would quarrel so loudly that everyone would rap on the walls and the manager, red in face, would endeavour to silence the domestic ululations, pacifying madam, expostulating with the gentleman, bidding him remember the next elections. And when his wife was ill and went to a sanatorium in Switzerland, the Commissioner published in modern liter-ary journals, post-dada-ist laments on his tubercular love. When he had put his finger successfully into several lucrative scandals in Persia, Thibet and China, he retired for a season again, but now to Biarritz, where he met the best people, including princes of the blood, cinema stars, champion Aberdeen terriers and bathing-suits by Patou, and distinguished himself at water-polo. His supporters then thought him groomed for another public appearance and he emerged as Police Commissioner and was given the Order of Merit by the king of his country. There, he revolutionised the police, introduced military discipline, gave military pay, studied machine-guns and tear-gas bombs and went on long voyages. During these, he visited America and studied their automatic prisons and the adroit way they broadcast robberies so that their police can give the burglar a fair avenue of escape; went to London, admired Dartmoor and crossed the crossing at the Bank; went to Paris to see how they provide one policeman for each citizen, and visited the Quai d'Orsay where they entertained him at dinner: went to Germany and learned how to turn recidivists into citizens by kindness, and how to discover non-existent documents. Then he returned home, made a secret report, was fêted in the streets, received bouquets, an Order, and proposals of marriage from ladies, invented a new dish, appeared in the films, improved the munition factories and once more went into retirement to be groomed for a *coup d'état*. This man of his time had come to Salzburg to polish himself off by rubbing shoulders with the cultivated, and to meet the Gold Trust. In the meantime, he spread sedulously his reputation for caustic repartee and looked through the proofs of a slight volume of neo-symbolist poems dedicated to his Lady of the Snows.

CHRISTINA STEAD, *The Salzburg Tales*

The Destructive Character

The destructive character knows only one watchword: make room; only one activity: clearing away. His need for fresh air and open space is stronger than any hatred.

The destructive character is young and cheerful. For destroying rejuvenates in clearing away the traces of our own age; it cheers because everything cleared away means to the destroyer a complete reduction, indeed eradication, of his own condition. But what contributes most of all to this Apollonian image of the destroyer is the realisation of how immensely the world is simplified when tested for its worthiness of destruction. This is the great bond embracing and unifying all that exists. It is a sight that affords the destructive character a spectacle of deepest harmony.

The destructive character is always blithely at work. It is nature that dictates his tempo, indirectly at least, for he must forestall her. Otherwise she will take over the destruction herself.

No vision inspires the destructive character. He has few needs, and the least of them is to know what will replace what has been destroyed. First of all, for a moment at least, empty space, the place where the thing stood or the victim lived. Someone is sure to be found who needs this space without its being filled.

The destructive character does his work, the only work he avoids is being creative. Just as the creator seeks solitude, the destroyer must be constantly surrounded by people, witnesses to his efficacy.

The destructive character is a signal. Just as a trigonometric sign is exposed on all sides to the wind, so is he to rumour. To protect him from it is pointless.

The destructive character has no interest in being understood. Attempts in this direction he regards as superficial. Being misunderstood cannot harm him. On the contrary he provokes it, just as oracles, those destructive institutions of the state, provoked it. The most petty bour geois of all phenomena, gossip, comes about only because people do not wish to be misunderstood. The destructive character tolerates misunderstanding; he does not promote gossip.

WALTER BENJAMIN, *One Way Street*

The Duellist

In all bad counsels, sat a third,
By birth a lord; O sacred word!
O word most sacred, whence men get
A privilege to run in debt;

Whence they at large exemption claim
From Satire, and her servant Shame;
Whence they, depriv'd of all her force,
Forbid bold Truth to hold her course.
    Consult his person, dress, and air,
He seems, which strangers well might swear,
The master, or, by courtesy,
The captain of a colliery.
Look at his visage, and agree
Half-hang'd he seems, just from the tree
Escap'd; a rope may sometimes break,
Or men be cut down by mistake.
    He hath not virtue (in the school
Of Vice bred up) to live by rule,
Nor hath he sense (which none can doubt
Who know the man) to live without.
His life is a continued scene
Of all that's infamous and mean;
He knows not change, unless grown nice
And delicate, from vice to vice;
Nature design'd him, in a rage,
To be the Wharton of his age,
But having giv'n all the sin,
Forgot to put the virtues in.
To run a horse, to make a match,
To revel deep, to roar a catch;
To knock a tott'ring watchman down,
To sweat a woman of the Town;
By fits to keep the peace, or break it,
In turn to give a pox, or take it;
He is, in faith, most excellent,
And, in the word's most full intent,
A true Choice Spirit we admit;
With wits a fool, with fools a wit.
Hear him but talk, and you would swear
Obscenity herself was there;

And that Profaneness had made choice,
By way of trump, to use his voice;
That, in all mean and low things great,
He had been bred at Billingsgate;
And that, ascending to the earth
Before the season of his birth,
Blasphemy, making way and room,
Had mark'd him in his mother's womb:
Too honest (for the worst of men
In forms are honest now and then)
Not to have, in the usual way,
His bills sent in; too great to pay:
Too proud to speak to, if he meets
The honest tradesman whom he cheats:
Too infamous to have a friend;
Too bad for bad men to commend,
Or good to name; beneath whose weight
Earth groans; who hath been spar'd by Fate
Only to shew, on mercy's plan,
How far and long God bears with man.

CHARLES CHURCHILL

Famous

Fame requires every kind of excess. I mean true fame, a devouring neon, not the somber renown of waning statesmen or chinless kings. I mean long journeys across gray space. I mean danger, the edge of every void, the circumstance of one man imparting an erotic terror to the dreams of the republic. Understand the man who must inhabit these extreme regions, monstrous and vulval, damp with memories of violation. Even if half-mad he is absorbed into the public's total madness; even if fully rational, a bureaucrat in hell, a secret genius of survival, he is sure to be destroyed by the public's contempt for survivors. Fame, this special kind, feeds itself on outrage, on what the counselors of lesser men would consider bad publicity – hysteria in limousines, knife fights in the audience, bizarre litigation, treachery, pandemonium and drugs. Perhaps the only natural law attaching to true fame is that the famous man is compelled, eventually, to commit suicide.

(Is it clear I was a hero of rock 'n' roll?)

DON DELILLO, *Great Jones Street*

The Fly

7 March 1858: A strange person with whom Gavarni took pleasure in dining recently. He is an Italian, origin unknown, who once lived in London where he made acquaintances from whom, almost every day, he would cadge a few shillings with which he would gamble in the low gaming houses of the town. He frequented a stew where one was not allowed to sleep and where there was not so much as a chair to sit upon. There his nickname was The Fly, because of his habit of dropping off to sleep leaning against a wall. One evening play became very lively and a sovereign rolled off the table and over to his feet. He put forth a foot naked beneath a shoe with almost no sole, and, seizing the coin with his big toe, he stood still until dawn, not daring to pick the coin up for fear of being accused of theft. That morning, rich for the first time in his life, the first thought of this man who never went to bed was to go to bed. He knocked on the door of a lodginghouse and was admitted. At ten o'clock he was woken by the servant who asked if he would like to take breakfast with her mistresses, two ex-governesses. They liked him; in a few days he became the lover of one of them; married her; inculcated in them both a taste for gambling; and ruined them. Having ruined them, he persuaded first his wife and then his sister-in-law to become Roman Catholics; and with money received from English Catholics he went off to Hamburg to try his luck at the table, won 200,000 francs, lost them again, and now ... Imagine what he does: he goes from pub to pub, in the Étoile Quarter, organising a gambling syndicate among journeyman masons, he to go off to gamble in Germany for them under the surveillance of a committee of ten masons in evening clothes who, themselves, will have nothing to do but eat, drink, and stroll about while he works for them.

GONCOURT BROTHERS, *Journals*

Gigolo

Pocket watch, I tick well.
The streets are lizardy crevices
Sheer-sided, with holes where to hide.
It is best to meet in a cul-de-sac,

A palace of velvet
With windows of mirrors.
There one is safe,
There are no family photographs,

No rings through the nose, no cries.
Bright fish hooks, the smiles of women
Gulp at my bulk
And I, in my snazzy blacks,

Mill a litter of breasts like jellyfish.
To nourish
The cellos of moans I eat eggs –
Eggs and fish, the essentials,

The aphrodisiac squid.
My mouth sags,
The mouth of Christ
When my engine reaches the end of it.

The tattle of my
Gold joints, my way of turning
Bitches to ripples of silver
Rolls out a carpet, a hush.

And there is no end, no end of it.
I shall never grow old. New oysters
Shriek in the sea and I
Glitter like Fontainebleau

Gratified,
All the fall of water an eye
Over whose pool I tenderly
Lean and see me.

SYLVIA PLATH

A Knowledgeable Host

Lord Hertford had not invited one person to us; but his excellent dinner, good wine, and very intelligent conversation, kept us alive, till a very late hour. I mean no compliment to Lord Hertford; for he has acted very rudely to me, of late; but he is a man possessing more general knowledge than anyone I know. His Lordship appears to be *au fait* on every subject one can possibly imagine. Talk to him of drawing, or horse riding; painting or cock-fighting; rhyming, cooking, or fencing; profligacy or morals; religion of whatever creed; languages living or dead; claret, or burgundy; champagne or black strap; furnishing houses, or riding hobbies; the flavour of venison, or breeding poll-parrots; and you might swear he had served his apprenticeship to every one of them.

HARRIETTE WILSON, Memoirs (1825)

Lord Hertford Again

19 March 1842: This day Lord Hertford is buried at Ragley, a man whose death excited much greater interest than anything he ever did in his life, because the world was curious to learn the amount of his wealth, and how he had disposed of it. A pompous funeral left Dorchester House three days ago, followed by innumerable carriages of private individuals, pretending to show a respect which not one of them felt for the deceased; on the contrary, no man ever lived more despised or died less regretted. His life and his death were equally disgusting and revolting to every good and moral feeling. As Lord Yarmouth he was known as a sharp, cunning, luxurious, avaricious man of the world, with some talent, the favourite of George 4th (the worst of Kings) when Lady Hertford, his mother, was that Prince's mistress. He was celebrated for his success at play, by which he supplied himself with the large sums of money required for his pleasures, and which his Father had no inclination to give him, and the Son had none to ask of him. He won largely, not by any cheating or unfairness, but by coolness, calculation, always backing the best players, and getting the odds on his side. He was a Bon Vivant, and when young and gay his parties were agreeable, and he contributed his share to their hilarity. But after he became Lord Hertford and the Possessor of an enormous property he was puffed up with vulgar pride, very unlike the real scion of a noble race; he loved nothing but dull pomp and ceremony, and could only endure people who paid him court and homage. After a great deal of coarse and vulgar gallantry, generally purchased at a high rate, he formed a connexion with Lady Strachan, which thenceforward determined all the habits of his life. She was a very infamous and shameless woman, and his love after some years was changed to hatred; and She, after getting very large sums out of him, married a Sicilian. But her children, three daughters, he in a manner adopted; though eventually all his partiality centred upon one, Charlotte by name, an ugly little thing, who married Count Zichy, a Hungarian. She continued to live with Hertford on and off, here and abroad, until his habits became in his last years so ostentatiously crapulous that her residence in his house (in England at least) ceased to be compatible with common decency. She was, however, here till within a week or ten days of his death, and her departure appears curiously enough to have led to the circumstances which immediately occasioned it. There has been, as far as I know, no example of undisguised debauchery exhibited to the world like that of Lord Hertford, and his age and infirmities rendered it at once the more remarkable and the more shocking. Between sixty and seventy years old, broken with various infirmities, and almost unintelligible from a paralysis of the tongue, he has been in the habit of travelling about with a company of prostitutes, who formed his principal society, and by whom he was surrounded up to the moment of his death, generally picking them up from the dregs of that class, and changing them according to his fancy and caprice. Here he was to be seen driving about the town, and lifted by two Footmen from his carriage into the Brothel, and he never seems to have thought it necessary to throw the slightest veil over the habits he pursued. For some months or weeks past he lived at Dorchester House, and the Zichys with him; but every day at a certain hour his women, who were quartered elsewhere, arrived, passed the greater part of the day, and one or other of them all the night in his room. He found the presence of the Countess Zichy troublesome and embarrassing to his pleasures, and he made her comprehend that her absence would not be disagreeable to him, and accordingly she went away. He had then been ill in bed for many days, but as soon as she was gone, as if to celebrate his liberation by a Jubilee, he got up and posted with his seraglio down to Richmond. No room was ready, no fire lit, nevertheless he chose to dine there amidst damp and cold, drank a quantity of champagne, came back chilled and exhausted, took to his bed, grew gradually worse, and in ten days he died. And what a life, terminating in what a death! without a serious thought or a kindly feeling, lavishing sums incalculable on the worthless objects of his pleasures or caprices, never doing a generous or a charitable action, caring and cared for by no human being, the very objects of his bounty only regarding him for what they could get out of him; faculties, far beyond mediocrity, wasted and degraded, immersed in pride without dignity, in avarice and sensuality; all his relations estranged from him, and surrounded to the last by a venal harem, who pandered to the disgusting exigencies *lassatae sed nondum satiatae libidinis*. He left vast sums to the Strachan family, a considerable legacy to Croker, to whom he had been formerly under obligations, largely provided for his Servants, and, with the exception of a few bequests to his Executors and one or two other people, and a very large property to an old mistress (formerly Lady Strachan's maid), he left everything to Yarmouth, with whom he had always been on very moderate terms.

CHARLES GREVILLE, *Memoirs*

A Swagger Beau

He brought in with him, a lawyer from Buda-Pesth, a swagger beau who spent his nights in night-clubs and paid attention to every woman he met, dark or fair, pretty or plain, sweet or forbidding, out of incontinence. He read all the gossip sheets and liked to pretend that he could find out the truth of every affair in the city, by fraud, bribery, threats and natural cunning. He believed whatever his client believed, affected to be cynical and saturnine, speaking in innuendoes; or jovial, sly and hail-fellow-well-met, according to the case. He soothed and flattered his client as if the client were a prince and he the prince's vizier. He examined a contract so closely for a flaw or deceitful intent, that he often missed the nature of the business and he was astonished to observe that a business could be unsound when a contract was watertight. He loved to crack a walnut with a sledge-hammer. He gulped down all the information thrown at him, went ahead in business and conversation by leaps and bounds, was called for that a bounder, loved to interrupt a business conversation with a quotation from his schoolbook poets, read the memoirs of diplomats with fervour and credulity, rejoiced at the crashing fall of magnates and kings, and was an ardent patriot and a conservative voter. He was like a man who has got into a pair of bewitched shoes by accident and must always be hopping and pirouetting, curtseying and leaping in the air, malapropos. He was a handsome young man of thirty-two with thick curly hair, brown eyes and a red mouth: he wore a morning coat in the morning and an eyeglass and evening dress every evening. He had learned, in two or three hours, all about the people in the hotel, and he now flattered and fawned on them shamelessly; he went about the place with dancing steps and his head in the air, delighted to be able to show his glittering talents to so cultivated a crowd. He was not a bad man, but very foolish: he was rich, because he had married a rich wife: he flattered her to her heart's content, and was a gay man about town.

CHRISTINA STEAD, *The Salzburg Tales*

The Tyrant

I know a castle set upon a fearful precipice, exposed to the winds above perilous waters. There I saw a tyrant seated at his high table in a great palace, in his sumptuous hall, surrounded by his haughty retinue, all full of deceit, envy, and discontent, devoid of loyalty and love and happy peace, slavish and fawning because of their rapacious greed.

Viands and wines he had beyond all measure, and flesh and fish also served in many a fashion, soups and sauces of different colours, and dishes skilfully made up to suit his fancy. The swinish wretch is ever watchful and alert to find an appetite, seeking means by which his mouth, afire with gluttony, can fill his belly like a beggar's pouch.

But this bag of excrement, this stinking cemetery, sepulchre of wine, with body puffed and swollen belly, for all his wealth has yet no gladness in him; for an overfull stomach finds no delight in savour, nor can he be pleased by laughter, sport, song, or dance, for he desires and covets and craves so many things that he finds true satisfaction in nothing that he has. He wants to seize a whole kingdom or an empire.

He suffers grievous martyrdom through avarice, he dreads treason, he trusts no man. His heart is cruel, swollen with pride and anger, gloomy, full of care and melancholy. Alas! far better is the life of honest Gontier, in sober happiness and cleanly poverty, than haunting tyrants' courts and wealthy misery to satisfy foul greed.

PIERRE D'AILLY

An Unwelcome Guest

12 September, 1920: The sun is brilliant, bright and warm. The sea is calm and blue. One threat in my sky: Max Jacob, in Quimper visiting his mother, is going to come and 'say hello', or so he writes. Now – I know that he will stay here as long as he is able. Now – he is not livable-with. He will eat all the plump part of a fish, empty the cream jug without thinking of those who have not yet had any, take half a cheese, the best part of a cake, almost all the jam, scrape the bottom of the sauce-boat, cynically refuse potatoes, ask for coffee every day and sweeten it with three lumps of sugar. Such a guest is a real disaster, disorganising his hosts' larder with an unfailing touch even while he tells them in a childish voice 'How you do spoil me! In Paris I often go without dinner after lunching on a pickled herring and a hunk of bread.' One smiles; one tells the maid: 'Don't put the butter on the table, serve it in a little shell for each person; make the desserts in separate ramckins, like in a restaurant; put the fish or roast in front of me, and I will do the serving.' One becomes thoroughly ratty, one mumbles and grumbles. At last the guest takes his leave and one says 'Ouf!'

Max goes to six o'clock mass every morning, waking everyone up. He upsets the serving of breakfast. He leans with all his weight on frail white-lacquered chairs as he puts on his dirty espadrilles. He broke a bidet worth ten louis without using it, and I have seen him lying in his filthy clothes and muddy shoes on a precious bedspread of white silk damask. Every one of his boy's loutish gestures irritates me like a fly buzzing perpetually round my head.

LIANE DE POUGY, *My Blue Notebooks*

The Wanton

Alberta having looked not very long into life, had not looked very far. She put out her hands to touch things that pleased her and her lips to kiss them. Her eyes were deep brown wells that were drinking, drinking impressions and treasuring them in her soul. They were mysterious eyes and love looked out of them.

Alberta was very fond of her mama who was really not her mama; and the beatings which alternated with the most amiable and generous indulgence, were soon forgotten by the little one, always hoping that there would never be another, as she dried her eyes.

She liked the ladies who petted her and praised her beauty, and the artists who painted it naked, and the student who held her upon his knee and fondled and kissed her while he taught her to read and spell.

387

There was a cruel beating about that one day, when her mama happened to be in the mood to think her too old for fondling. And the student had called her mama some very vile names in his wrath, and had asked the woman what else she expected.

There was nothing very fixed or stable about her expectations – whatever they were – as she had forgotten them the following day, and Alberta, consoled with a fantastic bracelet for her plump little arm and a shower of bonbons, installed herself again upon the student's knee. She liked nothing better, and in time was willing to take the beating if she might hold his attentions and her place in his affections and upon his knee.

Alberta cried very bitterly when he went away. The people about her seemed to be always coming and going. She had hardly the time to fix her affections upon the men and the women who came into her life before they were gone again.

Her mama died one day – very suddenly; a self-inflicted death, she heard the people say. Alberta grieved sorely, for she forgot the beatings and remembered only the outbursts of a torrid affection. But she really did not belong anywhere then, nor to anybody. And when a lady and gentleman took her to live with them, she went willingly as she would have gone anywhere, with any one. With them she met with more kindness and indulgence than she had ever known before in her life.

There were no more beatings; Alberta's body was too beautiful to be beaten – it was made for love. She knew that herself; she had heard it since she had heard anything. But now she heard many things and learned many more. She did not lack for instruction in the wiles – the ways of stirring a man's desire and holding it. Yet she did not need instruction – the secret was in her blood and looked out of her passionate, wanton eyes and showed in every motion of her seductive body.

At seventeen she was woman enough, so she had a lover. But as for that, there did not seem to be much difference. Except that she had gold now – plenty of it with which to make herself appear more beautiful, and enough to fling with both hands into the laps of those who came whining and begging to her.

Alberta is a most beautiful woman, and she takes great care of her body, for she knows that it brings her love to squander and gold to squander.

Some one has whispered in her ear:

'Be cautious, Alberta. Save, save your gold. The years are passing. The days are coming when youth slips away, when you will stretch out your hands for money and for love in vain. And what will be left for you but – ' Alberta shrank in horror before the pictured depths of hideous degradation that would be left for her. But she consoles herself with the thought that such need never be – with death and oblivion always within her reach.

Alberta is capricious. She gives her love only when and where she chooses. One or two men have died because of her withholding it. There is a smooth-faced boy now who teases her with his resistance; for Alberta does not know shame or reserve.

One day he seems to half-relent and another time he plays indifference, and she frets and she fumes and rages.

But he had best have a care; for since Alberta has added much wine to her wantonness she is apt to be vixenish; and she carries a knife.

KATE CHOPIN, *Two Portraits*

The Worst Man Ever Born: a Scrivener

Ciappelletto's manner of life was this. He was a Scrivener, and his pride was to make false documents; he would make them whenever he was asked, and more readily without fee than another at a great price; few indeed that he made were not false, and great was his shame when they were discovered. False witness, he bore, solicited or unsolicited, with boundless delight; he had no scruples about perjury, and as oaths in those times were held in utmost respect in France, he corruptly carried the day in every law-suit in which he was called upon to tell the truth upon his faith. He took inordinate pleasure, and showed mighty zeal, in stirring up strife, enmities and scandal between friends, kinsfolk and everyone else; the more calamitous the mischief, the better he was pleased. Set on murder, or any other foul crime, he never hesitated, but went at it with zest; more than once of his choice he wounded men, or did them to death with his own hand. He was a terrible blasphemer of God and His saints, and even over trifles was the most irritable man alive. He never went to church, flouted the sacraments, and derided them with vile ribaldry. On the other hand he haunted taverns and lewd places. He was as fond of women as a dog was of the stick; in acts against nature he delighted more than any other filthy fellow alive. He robbed and pillaged as a matter of conscience, as a holy man would make oblation to God; he was very gluttonous, and inordinately fond of wine, so much so that it sometimes brought him shame and suffering. He was a notorious gamester and thrower of false dice. But why enlarge upon him any more? Enough that he was, perhaps, the worst man ever born.

GIOVANNI BOCCACCIO, *Decameron*

Seduction

I will not say in what particular year of his life the Duke of Argyle succeeded with me. Ladies scorn dates! Dates make ladies nervous and stories dry.

HARRIETTE WILSON

In Russia before the war six Christs came to save St Petersburg every year, and were every year seduced by six great ladies of that capital.

LOGAN PEARSALL SMITH

[Of Lord Rosebery] My readers will agree that when a young man is privileged to have sexual intercourse with a Prime Minister, any proposal regarding the *modus operandi* must emanate from the latter.

SIR EDMUND BACKHOUSE

Most virtue is a demand for greater seduction.

NATALIE BARNEY

The Coastguard and the Tramp

Every two or three miles along the coast of Spain the coastguards have put up little sheds overlooking the sea. One night someone entered the shed where I had lain down to sleep ...

All doubled up, wrapped in my coat so as to keep out the ocean dampness, I forgot my body and its fatigue by imagining details which would make the cane and reed hut a perfect dwelling, built expressly for the man I became in a few seconds, so that my soul might be in perfect harmony with the site – sea, sky, rocks and heaths – and the fragility of the structure. A man stumbled against me. He swore. I was no longer afraid at night. Quite the contrary. It was a coast-guard of about thirty. Armed with his rifle, he was on the lookout for the fishermen and sailors who engaged in smuggling between Morocco and Spain. He wanted to put me out; then, turning his flashlight on my face and seeing that I was young, he told me to stay. I shared his supper (bread, olives and a few herrings) and I drank some wine. We talked for a while and then he began to caress me. He told me that he was Andalusian. I don't remember whether he was good-looking. The water could be seen through the opening. We heard oars striking the water and voices speaking, but were unable to see any boat. He knew he ought to leave, but my caresses grew more artful. He couldn't tear himself away; the smugglers must have landed peacefully.

In submitting to the whims of the coast-guard I was obeying a dominating order which it was impossible not to serve, namely, the Police. For a moment I was no longer a hungry, ragged vagabond whom dogs and children chased away, nor was I the bold thief flouting the cops, but rather the favourite mistress who, beneath a starry sky, soothes the conqueror. When I realised that it was up to me whether or not the smugglers landed safely, I felt responsible not only for them but for all outlaws. I was being watched elsewhere and I could not back out. Pride bore me up. After all, since I held back the guard by feigning love, I shall hold him back more surely, I thought to myself, if my love is more potent, and, unable to do better, I loved him with all my might. I granted him the loveliest of my nights. Not so that he might be happy but that I might take upon myself – and deliver him from – his own ignominy.

JEAN GENET, *The Thief's Journal*

The Man Who Did Not Deliver

He did not belong to reality, and yet he had much to do with it. He was constantly running beyond it, but just at the time he most completely abandoned himself to it, he had already finished with it. But it was not the good which beckoned him away, nor was it the bad; even at this moment I dare not say that about him. He suffered from mental excitement, for which reality did not afford a sufficient stimulus, at most only a temporary one. He did not break down under reality; he was not too weak to endure it, not at all, he was too strong; but this strength was really a sickness. As soon as reality had lost its significance as a stimulus, he was disarmed, and this constituted the evil in him. He was conscious of this in the moment of stimulation, and the evil lay in this consciousness ...

He had known how to tempt a young girl and attract her to himself, without really caring to possess her. I can imagine that he knew how to excite a girl to the highest pitch, so that he was certain that she was ready to sacrifice everything. When the affair reached this point, he broke it off without himself having made the slightest advances, and without having spoken a single word of love, let alone a declaration, a promise. And still it had happened, and the consciousness of it was doubly bitter for the unhappy girl because there was not the slightest thing to which she could appeal, because she was constantly tossed about by her varying moods in a terrible witches' dance, in which she alternately reproached herself and forgave him, then presently reproached him, and then, since the relation-ship had had reality only in a figurative sense, she must constantly struggle with the doubt as to whether the whole affair was not a figment of the imagination. She could not confide in anyone, for she had nothing defin-ite to confide. When one has had a dream it can be told to another per-son, but this which she had to tell was no dream, it was real, and yet when she wished to speak of it and relieve her troubled mind, there was nothing to tell. She felt it keenly. No one knew about it except herself, and yet it rested upon her with alarming weight ...

How, I wonder, does he regard himself? As he has led others astray, so he ends by going astray himself. The others he perverted not outwardly, but in their inward natures. There is something revolting when a man directs a traveller, perplexed about his way, to the wrong road, and then leaves him alone in his error; but what is that compared with causing a man to go astray inwardly? The lost wayfarer always has the consolation that the scene is constantly changing before him, and with every change there is born the hope of finding a way out. He who goes astray inwardly has not so great a range; he soon discovers that he is going about in a circle from which he cannot escape. I think it will be this way with him later, to a still more terrible extent. I can imagine nothing more excruciating than an intriguing mind, which has lost the thread of its continuity and turns against itself, when conscience awakens and compels the schemer to extricate himself from this confusion. It is in vain that he has many exits from his foxhole; at the moment his anxious soul believes that it already sees daylight breaking through, it turns out to be a new entrance, and like a startled deer, pursued by despair, he constantly seeks a way out, and finds only a way in, through which he goes back into himself. Such a man is not always what we might call a criminal, he is even frequently disappointed by his intrigues, and yet a more terrible punishment overtakes him than befalls a criminal; for what is even the pain of remorse in comparison with this conscious madness?

SØREN KIERKEGAARD, *Diary of the Seducer*

My Conquests

11 July 1922: Today I want to talk about my conquests. Rediscovered Nathalie comes to coax and caress me, and murmur 'My first love, and my last.' I see her bending over to enfold me, and it seems that I have never left her arms. Inconstant Nathalie, so faithful, in spite of her infidelities. She celebrates my body down to the waist. That is all that I allow myself to grant. The rest belongs to Georges and no one else in the world can touch it. The rest would make the sin too big; and anyway that rest is so accustomed to Georges that it throbs for no one but him.

In second place comes Thérèse Diehl of the beaky nose, the wicked eye, the sensual mouth, very chic, candid as a child, unaffected, impudent, artful, simultaneously boring and attractive. She amused me; her skin is resilient. She is a good healthy Basque. She goes to mass every Sunday and doesn't at all allow her disorderly life to disturb her relationship with God. She shares a mad apartment with her brother Carl, a charming and well set-up invert who gets on very well with her and runs the family factory. Thérèse pursues happiness in pleasure, she drinks hard, talks too much, is a bad hostess, pays out generously, but lacks flair. Her head is charming when she tips it back. We went no further than kisses on the mouth. Then I went to dinner with her. There her furniture and her guests enlightened me: I was bored to death. I wrote her very charmingly, truly my letter was a song: 'Forgive me for having loved you because I can no longer tell you that I do.' That is a splendid sentence and always works. I have used it a good deal in my time.

It was then that poor Dora turned up. I had to pretend that I'd gone away. The telephone rang day and night. Pépé would answer: 'The princess is in Saint-Germain for a few days.' She loathed Nathalie and would never consent to meet us there. She did, however, bring her orchestra to the Countess de La Béraudière's. Funny little woman; she told me she was forty, because in an attempt to put her off I had advanced my fiftieth birthday. God! when a woman gets something into her head, how hard it is to get it out again!

My other conquest was Madame Bonin, heavy and hot. We met at Nathalie's and sat hand in hand during the whole two hours of that tea party. Another time I invited her to Pépé's house. I was alone. She arrived trembling and panting, fell on my bed and wanted to offer me everything. I drew her attention to the barrier raised by my principles across the bodies of women, just a little below their hearts and their breasts. She tore off her clothes to bare the latter, neither beautiful nor ugly, too big and a bit squeezed together. The top part of her arms was ravishing. She is a woman for men, designed to serve them, amuse them and then, very soon, to bore them. I took it into my head to offer her something to eat and dragged her into the dining-room where she devoured a bowl of cherries, reproaching me the while for getting her 'into such a state'.

LIANE DE POUGY, My Blue Notebooks

Protests Too Much

No, no; for my virginity,
When I lose that, says Rose, I'll die;
Behind the elms, last night, cried Dick,
Rose, were you not extremely sick?

MATTHEW PRIOR

The Real Thing

He had a concession at the bowling alley. He called it the pro shop, sold equipment, and drilled and plugged bowling balls with some rented machinery. It was dark that afternoon, but you could see him in the darkness, talking into a wall telephone. He had been talking for three-quarters of an hour. He lowered his voice when I came in, but I heard him say, 'She's wild, that one, I was into her three times, and she *buzzbuzzbuzz.*' He said he'd call back, hung up, and turned on a light. He was a tall, bulky man with a vast belly – proof of the fact that there is little connection between erotic sport and physical beauty. His thin hair was most neatly oiled and combed with the recognisable grooming of the lewd. On his little finger he wore a flashy diamond, flanked by two rubies. His voice was reedy, and when he turned his face into the light you saw the real thing, a prince of barroom and lunch-counter pickups, reigning over a demesne of motels, hotels, and back bedrooms – proud, stupid, and serene. His jaw was smooth, well shaven,

and anointed, a piney fragrance came from his armpits, his breath smelled
of chewing gum, and he had the eyes of an adder. He was the real thing.

JOHN CHEEVER, *Journals*

The Siege

'Tis now since I sat down before
    That foolish fort, a heart;
(Time strangely spent) a year, and more,
    And still I did my part:

Made my approaches, from her hand
    Unto her lip did rise,
And did already understand
    The language of her eyes.

Proceeding on with no less art,
    My tongue was engineer;
I thought to undermine the heart
    By whispering in the ear.

When this did nothing, I brought down
    Great cannon-oaths, and shot
A thousand thousand to the town,
    And still it yielded not.

I then resolved to starve the place
    By cutting off all kisses,
Praising and gazing on her face,
    And all such little blisses.

To draw her out, and from her strength,
    I drew all batteries in:
And brought myself to lie at length,
    As if no siege had been.

When I had done what man could do
  And thought the place mine own,
The enemy lay quiet too,
  And smiled at all was done.

I sent to know from whence, and where,
  These hopes, and this relief?
A spy informed, Honour was there,
  And did command in chief.

March, march (quoth I) the word straight give,
  Let's lose no time, but leave her:
That giant upon air will live,
  And hold it out for ever.

To such a place our camp remove
  As will no siege abide;
I hate a fool that starves her love
  Only to feed her pride.

SIR JOHN SUCKLING

Tête à Tête

I sigh, I faint, I tremble at your touch,
And in your Absence, all the World I shun,
I hate Mankind, and curse the cheering Sun;
Still as I fly, ten thousand Swains persue;
Ten thousand Swains I sacrifice to you:
I shew you all my Heart, without Disguise:
But these are tender proofes that you despise –
I see too well what Wishes you persue;
You would not only Conquer, but undo.
You, Cruel Victor, weary of your Flame,
Would seek a Cure in my Eternal Shame;

And not content my Honor to subdue,
Now strive to triumph o're my Virtue too. ...
    Could I forget the Honor of my Race,
And meet your wishes, fearless of Disgrace;
Could Passion o'er my tender Youth prevail,
And all my Mother's pious Maxims fail:
Yet to preserve your Heart (which still must be,
False as it is, for ever dear to me)
This fatal proofe of Love, I would not give,
Which you contemn the moment you receive.
The wretched she who yields to guilty Joys,
A Man may pity, but he must despise.

    Your Ardour ceas'd, I then should see you shun
The wretched victim by your Arts undone,
Yet if I could that cold Indifference bear,
What more would strike me with the last Despair,
With this Refflection would my Soul be torn,
To know I merited your cruel Scorn.

    Has Love no pleasures free from Guilt or Fear?
Pleasures less fierce, more lasting, more sincere?
Thus let us gently kiss, and fondly Gaze,
Love is a Child, and like a Child he plays.

    Oh Strephon! if you would continu Just,
If Love be something more than Brutal Lust;
Forbear to ask, what I must still deny,
This bitter Pleasure, this Destructive Joy;
So closely follow'd by the Dismal Train
Of cutting Shame, and Guilt's heart piercing Pain.

    She paus'd; and fix'd her Eyes upon her Fan,
He took a pinch of snuff, and thus began,
Madam, if Love could touch that Gentle Breast
With halfe that ardour with which mine's oppress'd,
You would not blast my more than vestal Fire
And call it Brutal, or impure Desire.
The Lusty Bull professes not, nor vows,
But Bellows equal for a Herd of Cows,

The Stately Horse persues no chosen Fair,
But neighs, and prances for each common Mare.
This is impure desire, this Brutal Lust,
Man sighs for One, and to that One is just.
Why, Lovely Delia, do these sighs arise?
Why heaves your Breast? why sparkle thus your Eyes?
Examine your own Heart, and you will find
Some Wish still left unsatisfy'd behind.
Oh take me, press me to your panting Breast!
Let me be now, and I'm for ever blest.
He spoke, and on her Bosom laid his Cheek,
Fair Delia sigh'd, but had no power to speak,
Fair Delia blush'd, while he put out the Light,
And all that follow'd was Eternal Night.

LADY MARY WORTLEY MONTAGU

The Train from Bordeaux

I was sixteen years old. I still looked like a child. It was when we'd come back from Saigon, after the Chinese lover. It was on a night train, the train from Bordeaux, in about 1930. I was with my family – my two brothers and my mother. We were in a third-class compartment with eight seats in it, and I think there were two or three other people besides us. There was also a young man sitting opposite me and looking at me. He must have been about thirty. It must have been in the summer. I was still wearing the sort of light-coloured dress I used to wear in the colonies, with sandals and no stockings. The man asked me about my family, and I told him about what it was like living in the colonies: the rains, the heat, the veranda, how different it was from France, the walks in the forest, and the *baccalauréat* exam I was going to take that year. That sort of thing – the usual kind of conversation you have in a train when you pour out your own and your family's life history. And then all of a sudden we noticed everyone else was asleep. My mother and brothers had dropped off soon after we left Bordeaux. I spoke quietly so as not to wake them. If they'd heard me telling someone else all our business their yells and threats would soon have put a stop to it. And our whispered conversation had sent the other three or four passengers to sleep too. So the man and I were the only two still awake. And that was how it started, suddenly, at exactly the same moment, and with a single look. In those days people didn't speak about such things, especially in circumstances like that. All at once we couldn't go on talking. We couldn't go on looking at one another either; we felt weak, shattered. I was the one who said we ought to get some sleep so as not to be too tired when we got to Paris in the morning. He was sitting near the door so he switched out the light. There was an empty seat between us. I curled up on it and closed my eyes. I heard him open the door. He went out and came back with a blanket and spread it over me. I opened my eyes to smile and say thank you. He said: 'They turn off the heating at night and it gets cold towards morning.' I went to sleep. I was wakened by his warm soft hand on my legs; very slowly it straightened them out and tried to move up towards my body. I opened my eyes just a fraction. I could see he was looking at the other people in the carriage, watching them; he was afraid. I very slowly moved my body towards him and put my feet against him. I gave them to him. He took them. With my eyes shut, I followed all his movements. They were slow even at first, then more and more slow and controlled until the final paroxysm of pleasure, as upsetting as if he'd cried out.

For a long while there was nothing except the noise of the train. It was going faster and the noise was deafening. Then it became bearable again. He put his hand on me. Distraught, still warm, afraid. I held it in mine for a moment, then let it go, let it do as it liked.

The noise of the train came back again. The hand went away, stayed away for some time. I don't remember how long – I must have drowsed off.

Then it came back.

It stroked me all over first, then my breasts, stomach and hips, in a kind of overall gentleness disturbed every so often by new stirrings of desire. Sometimes it would stop. It halted over my sex, trembling, about to take the bait, burning hot again. Then it moved on. Finally it resigned itself, quietened down, became kind in order to bid the child goodbye. All around the hand was the noise of the train. All around the train, the darkness. The silence of the corridors within the noise of the train. The stops, waking people up. He got off into the darkness. When I opened my eyes in Paris his seat was empty.

MARGUERITE DURAS, *Practicalities*

Shopping

An American Millionairess

With Nicole's help Rosemary bought two dresses and two hats and four pairs of shoes with her money. Nicole bought from a great list that ran two pages, and bought the things in the windows besides. Everything she liked that she couldn't possibly use herself, she bought as a present for a friend. She bought coloured beads, folding beach cushions, artificial flowers, honey, a guest bed, bags, scarfs, love birds, miniatures for a doll's house, and three yards of some new cloth the colour of prawns. She bought a dozen bathing suits, a rubber alligator, a travelling chess set of gold and ivory, big linen handkerchiefs for Abe, two chamois leather jackets of kingfisher blue and burning bush from Hermes – bought all these things not a bit like a high class courtesan buying underwear and jewels, which were after all professional equipment and insurance, but with an entirely different point of view. Nicole was the product of much ingenuity and toil. For her sake trains began their run at Chicago and traversed the round belly of the continent to California; chicle factories fumed and link belts grew link by link in factories; men mixed toothpaste in vats and drew mouthwash out of copper hogsheads; girls canned tomatoes quickly in August or worked rudely at the Five-and-Tens on Christmas Eve; half-breed Indians toiled on Brazilian coffee plantations and dreamers were muscled out of patent rights in new tractors – these were some of the people who gave a tithe to Nicole and, as the whole system swayed and thundered onward, it lent a feverish bloom to such processes of hers as wholesale buying, like the flush of a fireman's face holding his post before a spreading blaze. She illustrated very simple principles, containing in herself her own doom, but illustrated them so accurately that there was grace in the procedure, and presently Rosemary would try to imitate it.

It was almost four. Nicole stood in a shop with a love bird on her shoulder, and had one of her infrequent outbursts of speech.

'Well, what if you hadn't gone in that pool that day – I sometimes wonder about such things. Just before the war we were in Berlin – I was twelve, it was just before Mother died. My sister was going to a court ball and she had three of the royal princes on her dance card, all arranged by a chamberlain and everything. Half an hour before she was going to start she had a side ache and a high fever. The doctor said it was appendicitis and she ought to be operated on. But Mother had her plans made, so Baby went to the ball and danced till two with an ice pack strapped on under her evening dress. She was operated on at seven o'clock next morning.'

It was good to be hard, then; all nice people were hard on themselves.

F. SCOTT FITZGERALD, *Tender is the Night*

A Cobbler's Sales Patter

Sit ye down, Metro. Pistos, open the casket up there, not this one but that one up there, and bring down those fair works from the third shelf. Oh, Metro, how fortunate you are! What noble works you will view! Bring me the shoe-case gently, you glutton. Now this shoe first, Metro, is a perfect whole of perfect parts consisting – look ye, too, ladies; see how firm the sole is fixed, and how precisely it is rounded off with straps; the handiwork is not part fair, part ugly, but all equal. And the colour – as I hope that Pallas may grant you enjoyment of all you yearn for – never will you find such colour at the tanner's, nor could painter's pallet vie with its hues. Three minae my buyer gave Kandas only the day before yesterday for it and one other – I swear by all that is holy ever up till to-day have I spoken the truth without concealment, since a lie weighs not the scales down a fraction, or may Kerdon have no profit in estate or goodly bargains – and he asked me actually to thank him; for the tanners are putting up their prices.

You Metro will get the works of my art, while I, the poor cobbler, will get nothing but wretched lamentation. Day after day and night after night I keep my seat warm. What does any of us get to bite till evening? Then there are all the morning cries – not Micion's animals, I fancy, are so well off for voice.

Then more – I keep thirteen slaves – they are a pack of idleness; even in rainy times they have but one song 'Give, give'; for the rest they sit as silent as chicks, idly warming their buttocks. But, say they, words are no good on 'change – it is cash we want; so if you don't like this pair, Metro, my man will bring you another and again another, till you are quite decided that Kerdon is telling the truth. Pistos, bring me all the shoe-cases – it were hard, ladies, if you went home without even trying on. You will see; here are all kinds, Sicyonian, Ambraciot, Nossis-shoes, Chian, parrots, hempen, saffron shoes, common shoes, Ionian button-boots, 'nighthoppers', 'ankle-tops', red shoes, Argive sandals, scarlet, 'youths', 'steps'; just say each of you what your heart desires; that you may know why women like dogs find leather goods so attractive.

HERODAS, Mimes and Fragments

The Fish Market

When Florent made his appearance on the first morning, at seven o'clock, he felt quite distracted; his eyes were dazed, his head ached with all the noise and riot. Retail dealers were already prowling about the auction pavilion; clerks were arriving with their ledgers, and consigners' agents, with leather bags slung over their shoulders, sat on overturned chairs by the salesmen's desks, waiting to receive their cash. Fish was being unloaded and unpacked not only in the enclosure, but even on the footways. All along the latter were piles of small baskets, an endless arrival of cases and hampers, and sacks of mussels, from which streamlets of water trickled. The auctioneers' assistants, all looking very busy, sprang over the heaps, tore away the straw at the tops of the baskets, emptied the latter, and tossed them aside. They then speedily transferred their contents in lots to huge wickerwork trays, arranging them with a turn of the hand so that they might show to the best advantage. And when the large tray-like baskets were all set out, Florent could almost fancy that a whole shoal of fish had got stranded there, still quivering with life, and gleaming with rosy nacre, scarlet coral, and milky pearl, all the soft, pale, sheeny hues of the ocean.

The deep-lying forests of seaweed, in which the mysterious life of the ocean slumbers, seemed at one haul of the nets to have yielded up all they contained. There were cod, keeling, whiting, flounders, plaice, dabs, and other sorts of common fish of a dingy grey with whitish splotches; there were conger-eels, huge serpent-like creatures, with small black eyes and muddy, bluish skins, so slimy that they still seemed to be gliding along, yet alive. There were broad flat skate with pale under-sides edged with a soft red, and superb backs bumpy with vertebrae, and marbled down to the tautly-stretched ribs of their fins with splotches of cinnabar, intersected by streaks of the tint of Florentine bronze – a dark medley of colour suggestive of the hues of a toad or some poisonous flower. Then, too, there were hideous dog-fish, with round heads, widely-gaping mouths like those of Chinese idols, and short fins like bats' wings; fit monsters to keep yelping guard over the treasures of the ocean grottoes. And next came the finer fish, displayed singly on the osier trays; salmon that gleamed like chased silver, every scale seemingly outlined by a graving-tool on a polished metal surface; mullet with larger scales and coarser markings; huge turbot and huge brill with firm flesh white like curdled milk; tunny-fish, smooth and glossy, like bags of blackish leather; and rounded bass, with widely-gaping mouths which a soul too large for the body seemed to have rent asunder as it forced its way out amidst the stupefaction of death. And on all sides there were soles, brown and grey, in pairs; sand-eels, slim and stiff, like shavings of pewter; herrings, slightly twisted, with bleeding gills showing on their silver-worked skins; fat dories tinged with just a suspicion of carmine; burnished mackerel with green-streaked backs, and sides gleaming with ever-changing iridescence; and rosy gurnets with white bellies, their heads towards the centre of the baskets and their tails radiating all around, so that they simulated some strange florescence splotched with pearly white and brilliant vermilion. There were rock mullet, too, with delicious flesh, flushed with the pinky tinge peculiar to the Cyprinus family; boxes of whiting with opaline reflections; and baskets of smelts – neat little baskets, pretty as those used for strawberries, and exhaling a strong scent of violets. And meantime the tiny black eyes of the shrimps dotted as with beads of jet their soft-toned mass of pink and grey; and spiny crawfish and lobsters striped with black, all still alive, raised a grating sound as they tried to crawl along with their broken claws.

Florent gave but indifferent attention to Monsieur Verlaque's explanations. A flood of sunshine suddenly streamed through the lofty glass roof of the covered way, lighting up all these precious colours, toned and softened by the waves – the iridescent flesh-tints of the shell-fish, the opal of the whiting, the pearly nacre of the mackerel, the ruddy gold of the mullets, the plated skins of the herrings, and massive silver of the salmon. It was as though the jewel-cases of some sea-nymph had been emptied there – a mass of fantastical, undreamt-of ornaments, a streaming and heaping of necklaces, monstrous bracelets, gigantic brooches, barbaric gems and jewels, the use of which could not be divined. On the backs of the skate and the dog-fish you saw, as it were, big dull green and purple stones set in the dark metal, while the slender forms of the sand eels and the tails and fins of the smelts displayed all the delicacy of finely wrought silver-work.

And meantime Florent's face was fanned by a fresh breeze, a sharp, salt breeze redolent of the sea. It reminded him of the coasts of Guiana and his voyages. He half fancied that he was gazing at some bay left dry by the receding tide, with the seaweed steaming in the sun, the bare rocks drying, and the beach smelling strongly of the brine. All around him the fish in their perfect freshness exhaled a pleasant perfume, that slightly sharp, irritating perfume which depraves the appetite.

ÉMILE ZOLA, *Le Ventre de Paris*

Floorwalker, or What?

It was the season of sales. The august establishment of Walpurgis and Nettlepink had lowered its prices for an entire week as a concession to trade observances, much as an Archduchess might protestingly contract an attack of influenza for the unsatisfactory reason that influenza was locally prevalent. Adela Chemping, who considered herself in some measure superior to the allurements of an ordinary bargain sale, made a point of attending the reduction week at Walpurgis and Nettlepink's.

'I'm not a bargain hunter,' she said, 'but I like to go where bargains are.'

Which showed that beneath her surface strength of character there flowed a gracious undercurrent of human weakness.

With a view to providing herself with a male escort Mrs Chemping had invited her youngest nephew to accompany her on the first day of the shopping expedition, throwing in the additional allurement of a cinematograph theatre and the prospect of light refreshment. As Cyprian was not yet eighteeen, she hoped he might not have reached that stage in masculine development when parcel-carrying is looked on as a thing abhorrent.

'Meet me just outside the floral department,' she wrote to him, 'and don't be a moment later than eleven.'

Cyprian was a boy who carried with him through early life the wondering look of a dreamer, the eyes of one who sees things that are not visible to ordinary mortals, and invests the commonplace things of this world with qualities unsuspected by plainer folk – the eyes of a poet or a house agent. He was quietly dressed – that sartorial quietude which frequently accompanies early adolescence, and is usually attributed by novel-writers to the influence of a widowed mother. His hair was brushed back in a smoothness as of ribbon seaweed and seamed with a narrow furrow that scarcely aimed at being a parting. His aunt particularly noted this item of his toilet when they met at the appointed rendezvous, because he was standing waiting for her bareheaded.

'Where is your hat?' she asked.

'I didn't bring one with me,' he replied.

Adela Chemping was slightly scandalised.

'You are not going to be what they call a Nut, are you?' she inquired with some anxiety, partly with the idea that a Nut would be an extravagance which her sister's small household would scarcely be justified in incurring, partly, perhaps, with the instinctive apprehension that a Nut, even in its embryo stage, would refuse to carry parcels.

Cyprian looked at her with his wondering, dreamy eyes.

'I didn't bring a hat,' he said, 'because it is such a nuisance when one is shopping; I mean it is so awkward if one meets any one one knows and has to take one's hat off when one's hands are full of parcels. If one hasn't got a hat on one can't take it off.'

Mrs Chemping sighed with great relief; her worst fear had been laid at rest.

'It is more orthodox to wear a hat,' she observed, and then turned her attention briskly to the business in hand.

'We will go first to the table-linen counter,' she said, leading the way in that direction; 'I should like to look at some napkins.'

The wondering look deepened in Cyprian's eyes as he followed his aunt; he belonged to a generation that is supposed to be over-fond of the rôle of mere spectator, but looking at napkins that one did not mean to buy was a pleasure beyond his comprehension. Mrs Chemping held one or two napkins up to the light and stared fixedly at them, as though she half expected to find some revolutionary cypher written on them in scarcely visible ink; then she suddenly broke away in the direction of the glassware department.

'Millicent asked me to get her a couple of decanters if there were any going really cheap,' she explained on the way, 'and I really do want a salad bowl. I can come back to the napkins later on.'

She handled and scrutinised a large number of decanters and a long series of salad bowls, and finally bought seven chrysanthemum vases.

'No one uses that kind of vase nowadays,' she informed Cyprian, 'but they will do for presents next Christmas.'

Two sunshades that were marked down to a price that Mrs Chemping considered absurdly cheap were added to her purchases.

'One of them will do for Ruth Colson; she is going out to the

Malay States, and a sunshade will always be useful there. And I must get her some thin writing paper. It takes up no room in one's baggage.'

Mrs Chemping bought stacks of writing paper; it was so cheap, and it went so flat in a trunk or portmanteau. She also bought a few envelopes – envelopes somehow seemed rather an extravagance compared with notepaper.

'Do you think Ruth will like blue or grey paper?' she asked Cyprian.

'Grey,' said Cyprian, who had never met the lady in question.

'Have you any mauve notepaper of this quality?' Adela asked the assistant.

'We haven't any mauve,' said the assistant, 'but we've two shades of green and a darker shade of grey.'

Mrs Chemping inspected the greens and the darker grey, and chose the blue.

'Now we can have some lunch,' she said.

Cyprian behaved in an exemplary fashion in the refreshment department, and cheerfully accepted a fish cake and a mince pie and a small cup of coffee as adequate restoratives after two hours of concentrated shopping. He was adamant, however, in resisting his aunt's suggestion that a hat should be bought for him at the counter where men's head-wear was being disposed of at temptingly reduced prices.

'I've got as many hats as I want at home,' he said, 'and besides, it rumples one's hair so, trying them on.'

Perhaps he was going to develop into a Nut after all. It was a disquieting symptom that he left all the parcels in charge of the cloak-room attendant.

'We shall be getting more parcels presently,' he said, 'so we need not collect these till we have finished our shopping.'

His aunt was doubtfully appeased; some of the pleasure and excitement of a shopping expedition seemed to evaporate when one was deprived of immediate personal contact with one's purchases.

'I'm going to look at those napkins again,' she said, as they descended the stairs to the ground floor. 'You need not come,' she added, as the dreaming look in the boy's eyes changed for a moment into one of mute protest, 'you can meet me afterwards in the cutlery department; I've just remembered that I haven't a corkscrew in the house that can be depended on.'

Cyprian was not to be found in the cutlery department when his aunt in due course arrived there, but in the crush and bustle of anxious shoppers and busy attendants it was an easy matter to miss any one. It was in the leather goods department some quarter of an hour later that Adela Chemping caught sight of her nephew, separated from her by a rampart of suitcases and portmanteaux and hemmed in by the jostling crush of human beings that now invaded every corner of the great shopping emporium. She was just in time to witness a pardonable but rather embarrassing mistake on the part of a lady who had wriggled her way with unstayable determination towards the bareheaded Cyprian, and was now breathlessly demanding the sale price of a handbag which had taken her fancy.

'There now,' exclaimed Adela to herself, 'she takes him for one of the shop assistants because he hasn't got a hat on. I wonder it hasn't happened before.'

Perhaps it had. Cyprian, at any rate, seemed neither startled nor embarrassed by the error into which the good lady had fallen. Examining the ticket on the bag, he announced in a clear, dispassionate voice:

'Black seal, thirty-four shillings marked down to twenty-eight. As a matter of fact, we are clearing them out at a special reduction price of twenty-six shillings. They are going off rather fast.'

'I'll take it,' said the lady, eagerly digging some coins out of her purse.

'Will you take it as it is?' asked Cyprian; 'it will be a matter of a few minutes to get it wrapped up, there is such a crush.'

'Never mind, I'll take it as it is,' said the purchaser, clutching her treasure and counting the money into Cyprian's palm.

Several kind strangers helped Adela into the open air.

'It's the crush and the heat,' said one sympathiser to another; 'it's enough to turn any one giddy.'

When she next came across Cyprian he was standing in the crowd that pushed and jostled around the counters of the book department. The dream look was deeper than ever in his eyes. He had just sold two books of devotion to an elderly Canon.

SAKI, *The Dreamer*

He asked About the Quality

He left the office where he had been hired
for a menial, low paid job,
(about eight pounds a month, including bonuses)
left at the end of the dreary work
that had bowed him down all afternoon,
came out at seven, and walked off slowly,
idling down the street. Handsome;
and interesting: he looked like a man
at the peak of his sensual capacity.
He had turned twenty-nine a month before.

He loitered on the streets, and in the poor
alleys that led to his lodgings.

Passing in front of a little shop
where they sold cheap and nasty
merchandise for workmen,
he saw a face inside, a figure
that attracted him, and he went in, pretending
to look at some coloured handkerchieves.

He asked about the quality,
and what they cost, his voice choking,
almost dumb with desire.
And the answers came in the same tone,
distracted, muted,
giving secret assent.

They kept talking about the purchase –
but their only aim: the touching of their hands
over the handkerchieves; the coming close
of faces and lips, as if by chance;
a momentary contact of limbs.

Furtive and fast, so that the owner
sitting at the back should notice nothing.

CONSTANTINE CAVAFY

The Ladies' Paradise

It was the cathedral of modern commerce, light but solid, made for a nation of customers. Below, in the central gallery, after the door bargains, came the cravat, the glove, and the silk departments; the Monsigny Gallery was occupied by the linen and the Rouen goods; the Michodière Gallery by the mercery, the hosiery, the drapery, and the woollen departments. Then, on the first floor were installed the ready-made, the under-linen, the shawl, the lace, and other new departments, whilst the bedding, the carpets, the furnishing materials, all the cumbersome articles difficult to handle, had been relegated to the second floor. The number of departments was now thirty-nine, with eighteen hundred employees, of whom two hundred were women. Quite a little world operated there, in the sonorous life of the high metallic naves.

Mouret's unique passion was to conquer woman. He wished her to be queen in his house, and he had built this temple to get her completely at his mercy. His sole aim was to intoxicate her with gallant attentions, and traffic on her desires, work on her fever. Night and day he racked his brain to invent fresh attractions. He had already introduced two lifts lined with velvet for the upper storeys, in order to spare delicate ladies the trouble of mounting the stairs. Then he had just opened a bar where the customers could find, gratis, some light refreshment, syrups and biscuits, and a reading-room, a monumental gallery, decorated with excessive luxury, in which he had even ventured on an exhibition of pictures. But his most profound idea was to conquer the mother through the child, when unable to do so through her coquetry; he neglected no means, speculated on every sentiment, created departments for little boys and girls, arresting the passing mothers by distributing pictures and air-balls to the children. A stroke of genius this idea of distributing to each buyer a red air-ball made of fine gutta-percha, bearing in large letters the name

413

of the shop, and which, held by a string, floated in the air, parading in the streets a living advertisement.

But the greatest power of all was the advertising. Mouret spent three hundred thousand francs a year in catalogues, advertisements, and bills. For his summer sale he had launched forth two hundred thousand catalogues, of which fifty thousand went abroad, translated into every language. He now had them illustrated with engravings, even accompanying them with samples, gummed between the leaves. It was an overflowing display; The Ladies' Paradise became a household word all over the world, invading the walls, the newspapers, and even the curtains at the theatres. He declared that woman was powerless against advertising, that she was bound to follow the crowd. Not only that, he laid still more seductive traps for her, analysing her like a great moralist. Thus he had discovered that she could not resist a bargain, that she bought without necessity when she thought she saw a cheap line, and on this observation he based his system of reductions in price, progressively lowering the price of unsold articles, preferring to sell them at a loss, faithful to his principle of the continual renewal of the goods. He had penetrated still further into the heart of woman, and had just thought of the 'returns', a masterpiece of Jesuitical seduction. 'Take whatever you like, madame; you can return the article if you don't like it.' And the woman who hesitated was provided with the last excuse, the possibility of repairing an extravagant folly, she took the article with an easy conscience.

ÉMILE ZOLA, *Au bonheur des dames*

The Saleswoman

At the hat shop. With the arrival of a client, the saleswoman rushes up: twenty-five years old, with the eyes of a young tyrant, a tower of blonde hair on the top of her head. Her hands, her figure, her mouth, her feet, all are thin to excess, witty, and aggressive.

'Ah, Madame! At last; you've come back to us! I had almost given up hope. I was saying to myself, "That's it! She must have gone to Harry's to have some Berlin-style hats made for herself!" But … what is that you have on your head?'

'...?'

'Yes, that thing with the blue wing on the side and the velour all around it?'

'...?'

'What, you made it yourself? All by yourself. Why, that's incredible, it's miraculous! If I may indulge in a little joke, you have a future in fashion. Would you do our *maison* the honour of entering it as trimmer?'

'...?'

'The trimmer? She's ... well, heavens, she's the one who puts the linings inside the hats, who ... well ... who does a lot of little things. Give me your lovely little "creation"; oh, I'll give it back to you! Here, I'll give it back ... let's see ... tomorrow. Yes, tomorrow. Exactly, the car is making a delivery tomorrow in your suburb.'

'...?'

'Yes, well, in your neighbourhood, I meant. It's so far! I'm just a poor little Parisian girl who never has time to leave her post, you understand. The boulevard shop in winter, Deauville in the summer, the Biarritz shop in September, Monte Carlo in January ... Oh, not everybody can live in Auteuil. Quick, come with me, I have a nice corner in the little fitting room facing the street. It's poorly lit? You don't like being with your back to the light? But it's the best place for trying on hats! Your silhouette is projected on the window, and with hats, it's primarily a question of silhouette, this season; one disregards the details. And, you see, you're between Mademoiselle X, the "little diva", who's trying on hats for her tour right now, and Princess Z, who's just back from the south.'

'...'

'Yes, that one, the fat old lady. In the shop, we call her the "Pink Pompon".

'...?'

'Because whenever she doesn't like a hat, she always says, "I think it's missing something, here, in the hollow ... a little nothing, a little flower ... a bouquet of pompon roses!" Mademoiselle X, that one there, to your left, she's not what you'd normally call pretty, but she has such a good heart!'

'...?'

'Oh, a heart of gold. Look, the lady who's with her, yes, that sort of little shark in black, is a poor friend she's taken in. She takes her with her everywhere, to her couturier's, to her jeweller's; she stays here for hours trying on twenty-five different hats under her poor friend's nose – to distract her.

'Let's see now, how about if we talk a little more seriously now? I've got it into my head that I could really do a job on you today. It's days like this when my mind is set on business. Okay, for starters, pull this little cloche down over your beautiful hair for me! ... You haven't changed colour?"

'...'

'Excuse me, it's a reflection from the outside light. I was saying to myself: it has more gold in it than usual. You might have got the urge to change, just for a change. And then there are some people who go grey very early. On the side, on the side, completely covering one ear! There! ... What do you think of it?'

'...!'

'I can see it's not a hit. Besides, you're right, it's not your style. On you, it looks a little ... a little too ladylike. It's funny, I just sold the same hat to Mrs W. She is ravishing in it, Mrs W, with her long neck, and especially her, you see, her chin, her cheeks, so fresh and the ear ... Let's say good-bye to this style here for a minute; one lost, ten found. Look at that, what was I telling you! This is what we're after. Way down, all right?'

'...'

'More than that, more than that! I can still see the hair on your temple, and on the back of your neck! I believe you're familiar with the "great hat principle of the season", as the owner herself says?'

'...'

'The great hat principle is that when you meet a woman on the street and her hat allows you to see whether she's a brunette, a blonde, or a red-head, the woman in question is not wearing a chic hat. There! ... Notice I'm not saying anything, I'll let you make up your own mind. Well?'

'...'

'You prefer the navy-blue one? That one there, on the mushroom? Yes? ... Well, really!'

'...'

'No, no, it's not sold.'

'…?'

'Why no, Madame, I don't want to keep you from buying it! I wasn't suggesting it to you because I didn't think I was talented enough to sell hats like that one. But it's true, it does seem to go with your face. Ah, you really know what it is you want! Like I always say: there are only two categories of clients whose minds can't be changed: artists and lower-middle-class women.'

'…'

'You're not an artist, but you still have a very independent sense of judgment. Try on this one here, just for me. It's not at all excessive, but I think it's both rich and discreet, because of this polished cotton fantasia which gives it all its cachet … No? Ah, I'm not having any luck at all, you're just trying to mortify me. If your two sons have your personality, they'll be terrible men! Are those two big boys doing all right?'

'…'

'Already? How time flies, my Lord! And still good-looking, I'm sure. Well, there's nothing surprising about that.'

'…'

'No, Madame, there's no flattery intended at all; anyway, everybody in the shop agrees with me, it's just what everybody says about the presence, the charm, the intelligence of your husband … and everyone knows that your two gorgeous children also inherited your beautiful health! What a shame they're not daughters! I'd already be fitting them for hats, and spoiling them as much as you. So, nothing more today, except the little blue hat? Shall I have it sent down to you in your car?'

'…'

'Yes, yes, don't worry, I give the description of the car to the messenger boy myself. You think I don't know the brown sedan you've had for six years? Goodbye, Madame, and thank you for your lovely visit, don't go so long without coming to see your faithful saleswoman; I enjoy seeing you so much … it gives me a rest from our American clientele: all I feel like telling those women are disagreeable things.'

COLETTE, *Collected Stories*

This Terrible Mart

The Wooden Galleries of the Palais Royal used to be one of the most famous sights of Paris. Some description of the squalid bazaar will not be out of place; for there are few men of forty who will not take an interest in recollections of a state of things which will seem incredible to a younger generation.

The great dreary, spacious Galerie d'Orléans, that flowerless hothouse, as yet was not; the space upon which it now stands was covered with booths; or, to be more precise, with small, wooden dens, pervious to the weather, and dimly illuminated on the side of the court and the garden by borrowed lights styled windows by courtesy, but more like the filthiest arrangements for obscuring daylight to be found in little wineshops in the suburbs.

The Galleries, parallel passages about twelve feet in height, were formed by a triple row of shops. The centre row, giving back and front upon the Galleries, was filled with the fetid atmosphere of the place, and derived a dubious daylight through the invariably dirty windows of the roof; but so thronged were these hives, that rents were excessively high, and as much as a thousand crowns was paid for a space scarce six feet by eight. The outer rows gave respectively upon the garden and the court, and were covered on that side by a slight trellis-work painted green, to protect the crazy plastered walls from continual friction with the passers-by. In a few square feet of earth at the back of the shops, strange freaks of vegetable life unknown to science grew amid the products of various no less flourishing industries. You beheld a rosebush capped with printed paper in such a sort that the flowers of rhetoric were perfumed by the cankered blossoms of that ill-kept, ill-smelling garden. Handbills and ribbon streamers of every hue flaunted gaily among the leaves; natural flowers competed unsuccessfully for an existence with odds and ends of millinery. You discovered a knot of ribbon adorning a green tuft; the dahlia admired afar proved on a nearer view to be a satin rosette.

The Palais seen from the court or from the garden was a fantastic sight, a grotesque combination of walls of plaster patchwork which had once been whitewashed, of blistered paint, heterogeneous placards, and all the most unaccountable freaks of Parisian squalor; the green trellises were prodigiously the dingier for constant contact with the Parisian public. So, upon either side, the fetid, disreputable approaches might have been there for the express purpose of warning away fastidious people; but fastidious folk no more recoiled before these horrors than the prince in the fairy stories turns tail at sight of the dragon or of the other obstacles put between him and the princess by the wicked fairy.

There was a passage through the centre of the Galleries then as now; and, as at the present day, you entered them through the two peristyles begun before the Revolution, and left unfinished for lack of funds; but in place of the handsome modern arcade leading to the Théâtre-Français, you passed along a narrow, disproportionately lofty passage, so ill-roofed that the rain came through on wet days. All the roofs of the hovels indeed were in very bad repair, and covered here and again with a double thickness of tarpaulin. A famous silk mercer once brought an action against the Orleans family for damages done in the course of a night to his stock of shawls and stuffs, and gained the day and a considerable sum. It was in this last-named passage, called 'The Glass Gallery' to distinguish it from the Wooden Galleries, that Chevet laid the foundations of his fortunes.

Here, in the Palais, you trod the natural soil of Paris, augmented by importations brought in upon the boots of foot passengers; here, at all seasons, you stumbled among hills and hollows of dried mud swept daily by the shopman's besom, and only after some practice could you walk at your ease. The treacherous mud-heaps, the window-panes encrusted with deposits of dust and rain, the mean-looking hovels covered with ragged placards, the grimy unfinished walls, the general air of a compromise between a gipsy camp, the booths of a country fair, and the temporary structures which we in Paris build round about public monuments that remain unbuilt; the grotesque aspect of the mart as a whole was in keeping with the seething traffic of various kinds carried on within it; for here in this shameless, unblushing haunt, amid wild mirth and a babel of talk, an immense amount of business was transacted between the Revolution of 1789 and the Revolution of 1830.

For twenty years the Bourse stood just opposite, on the ground floor of the Palais. Public opinion was manufactured, and reputations made and ruined here, just as political and financial jobs were arranged. People made appointments to meet in the Galleries before or after 'Change; on showery days the Palais Royal was often crowded with weather-bound capitalists and men of business. The structure which had grown up, no one knew how, about this point was strangely resonant, laughter was multiplied; if two men quarrelled, the whole place rang from one end to the other with the dispute. In the daytime milliners and booksellers enjoyed a monopoly of the place; towards nightfall it was filled with women of the town. Here dwelt poetry, politics, and prose, new books and classics, the glories of ancient and modern literature side by side with political intrigue and the tricks of the bookseller's trade. Here all the very latest and newest literature were sold to a public which resolutely declined to buy elsewhere. Sometimes several thousand copies of such and such a pamphlet by Paul-Louis Courier would be sold in a single evening; and people crowded thither to buy *Les aventures de la fille d'un Roi* – that first shot fired by the Orleanists at the Charter promulgated by Louis XVIII.

When Lucien made his first appearance in the Wooden Galleries, some few of the shops boasted proper fronts and handsome windows, but these in every case looked upon the court or the garden. As for the centre row, until the day when the whole strange colony perished under the hammer of Fontaine the architect, every shop was open back and front like a booth in a country fair, so that from within you could look out upon either side through gaps among the goods displayed or through the glass doors. As it was obviously impossible to kindle a fire, the tradesmen were fain to use charcoal chafing-dishes, and formed a sort of brigade for the prevention of fires among themselves; and, indeed, a little carelessness might have set the whole quarter blazing in fifteen minutes, for the plank-built republic, dried by the heat of the sun, and haunted by too inflammable human material, was bedizened with muslin and paper and gauze, and ventilated at times by a thorough draught.

The milliners' windows were full of impossible hats and bonnets, displayed apparently for advertisement rather than for sale, each on a separate iron spit with a knob at the top. The galleries were decked out in all the colours of the rainbow. On what heads would those dusty bonnets end their careers? – for a score of years the problem had puzzled frequenters of the Palais. Saleswomen, usually plain-featured, but vivacious, waylaid the feminine foot passenger with cunning importunities, after the fashion of market-women, and using much the same language; a shop-girl, who made free use of her eyes and tongue, sat outside on a stool and harangued the public with 'Buy a pretty bonnet, madame?' – 'Do let me sell you something!' – varying a rich and picturesque vocabulary with inflexions of the voice, with glances, and remarks upon the passers-by. Booksellers and milliners lived on terms of mutual good understanding.

But it was in the passage known by the pompous title of the 'Glass Gallery' that the oddest trades were carried on. Here were ventriloquists and charlatans of every sort, and sights of every description, from the kind where there is nothing to see to panoramas of the globe. One man who has since made seven or eight-hundred thousand francs by travel-ling from fair to fair began here by hanging out a signboard, a revolving sun in a blackboard, and the inscription in red letters – 'Here Man may see what God can never see. Admittance, two sous.' The showman at the door never admitted one person alone, nor more than two at a time. Once inside, you confronted a great looking-glass; and a voice, which might have terrified Hoffmann of Berlin, suddenly spoke as if some spring had been touched, 'You see here, gentlemen, something that God can never see through all eternity, that is to say, your like. God has not His like.' And out you went, too shamefaced to confess to your stupidity.

Voices issued from every narrow doorway, crying up the merits of Cosmoramas, views of Constantinople, marionettes, automatic chess-players, and performing dogs who would pick you out the prettiest woman in the company. The ventriloquist Fitz-James flourished here in the Café Borel before he went to fight and fall at Montmartre with the young lads from the École polytechnique. Here, too, there were fruit and flower shops, and a famous tailor whose gold-laced uniforms shone like the sun when the shops were lighted at night.

Of a morning the galleries were empty, dark, and deserted; the shop-keepers chatted among themselves. Towards two o'clock in the after-noon the Palais began to fill; at three, men came in from the Bourse, and Paris, generally speaking, crowded the place. Impecunious youth, hunger-ing after literature, took the opportunity of turning over the pages of the books exposed for sale on the stalls outside the booksellers' shops; the men in charge charitably allowed a poor student to pursue his course of free studies; and in this way a duodecimo volume of some two hundred pages, such as *Smarra* or *Pierre Schlemihl*, or *Jean Sbogar* or *Jocko*, might be devoured in a couple of afternoons. There was something very French in this alms given to the young, hungry, starved intellect. Circulating libraries were not as yet; if you wished to read a book, you were obliged to buy it, for which reason novels of the early part of the century were sold in numbers which now seem well nigh fabulous to us.

But the poetry of this terrible mart appeared in all its splendour at the close of the day. Women of the town, flocking in and out from the neighbouring streets, were allowed to make a promenade of the Wooden Galleries. Thither came prostitutes from every quarter of Paris to 'do the Palais'. The Stone Galleries belonged to privileged houses, which paid for the right of exposing women dressed like princesses under such and such an arch, or in the corresponding space of garden; but the Wooden Galleries were the common ground of women of the streets. This was *the* Palais, a word which used to signify the temple of prostitution. A woman might come and go, taking away her prey whithersoever seemed good to her. So great was the crowd attracted thither at night by the women, that it was impossible to move except at a slow pace, as in a procession or at a masked ball. Nobody objected to the slowness; it facilitated examination. The women dressed in a way that is never seen nowadays. The bodices cut extremely low both back and front; the fantastical head-dresses, designed to attract notice; here a cap from the Pays de Caux, and there a Spanish mantilla; the hair crimped and curled like a poodle's, or smoothed down in bandeaux over the forehead; the close-fitting white stockings and limbs, revealed it would not be easy to say how, but always at the right moment – all this poetry of vice has fled. The licence of question and reply, the public cynicism in keeping with the haunt, is now unknown even at masquerades or the famous public balls. It was an appalling, gay scene. The dazzling white flesh of the women's necks and shoulders stood out in magnificent contrast against the men's almost invariably sombre costumes. The murmur of voices, the hum of the crowd, could be heard even in the middle of the garden as a sort of droning bass, interspersed with *fioriture* of shrill laughter or clamour of some rare dispute. You saw gentlemen and celebrities cheek by jowl with gallows-birds. There was something indescribably piquant about the anomalous assemblage; the most insensible of men felt its charm, so much so, that until the very last moment, Paris came hither to walk up and down on the wooden planks laid over the cellars where men were at work on the new buildings; and when the squalid wooden erections were finally taken down, great and unanimous regret was felt.

HONORÉ DE BALZAC, *Un Grand Homme de Province à Paris*

Two Pounds of Goose-Fat

The goose-fat is shown in glass jars, each containing, as the handwritten label says, 'two limbs of plump goose (a leg and a wing), goose-fat, salt and pepper. Net weight: two pounds.' In the thick, soft whiteness that fills the jars the clangour of the world is muffled: a dark shadow rises from the bottom and, as in the fog of memories, allows a glimpse of the goose's severed limbs, lost in its fat.

Mr Palomar is standing in line in a Paris charcuterie. It is the holiday season, but here the throng of customers is usual even at less ceremonial times, because this is one of the good gastronomical shops of the city, miraculously surviving in a neighbourhood where the levelling of mass trade, taxes, the low income of the consumers, and now the depression have dismantled the old shops, one by one, replacing them with anonymous supermarkets.

Waiting in line, Mr Palomar contemplates the jars. He tries to find a place in his memories for *cassoulet*, a rich stew of meats and beans, in which goose-fat is an essential ingredient; but neither his palate's memory nor his cultural memory is of any help to him. And yet the name, the sight, the idea attract him, awaken an immediate fantasy not so much of appetite as of eros: from a mountain of goose-fat a female figure surfaces, smears white over her rosy skin, and he already imagines himself making his way towards her through those thick avalanches, embracing her, sinking with her.

He dispels this incongruous thought from his mind, raises his eyes to the ceiling bedecked with salamis, hanging from the Christmas wreaths like fruit from boughs in the land of Cockaigne. All round, on the marble

423

counters, abundance triumphs in the forms developed by civilisation and art. In the slices of game pâté, the pursuits and flights of the moor are fixed forever, sublimated in a tapestry of flavours. The galantines of pheasant are arrayed in grey-pink cylinders surmounted, to certify their origin, by two birdly feet like talons that jut from a coat-of-arms or from a Renaissance chest.

Through the gelatine sheaths the thick beauty-spots of black truffle stand out, aligned like buttons on a Pierrot's tunic, like the notes of a score, dotting the roseate, variegated beds of pâtés de foie gras, of head-cheese, terrines, galantines, fans of salmon, artichoke hearts garnished like trophies. The leading motive of the little truffle discs unifies the variety of substances like the black of dinner-jackets at a masked ball, distinguishing the festive dress of the foods.

Grey and opaque and sullen, on the contrary, are the people who make their way among the counters, shunted by salesladies in white, more or less elderly, brusquely efficient. The splendour of the salmon canapés radiant with mayonnaise disappears, swallowed by the dark shopping-bags of the customers. Certainly every one of these men and women knows exactly what he wants, heads straight for his objective with a decisiveness admitting no hesitancy; and rapidly he dismantles mountains of vol-au-vents, white puddings, cervelats.

Mr Palomar would like to catch in their eyes some reflection of those treasures' spell, but the faces and actions are only impatient and hasty, of people concentrated on themselves, nerves taut, each concerned with what he has and what he does not have. Nobody seems to him worthy of the pantagruelian glory that unfolds in those cases, on the counters. A greed without joy or youth drives them; and yet a deep, atavistic bond exists between them and those foods, their consubstance, flesh of their flesh.

He realises he is finding something closely akin to jealousy: he would like the duck and hare pâtés, from their platters, to show they prefer him to the others, recognising him as the only one deserving of their gifts, those gifts that nature and culture have handed down for millennia and that must not now fall into profane hands! Is not the sacred enthusiasm that he feels pervading him perhaps a sign that he alone is the elect, the one touched by grace, the only one worthy of the deluge of good things brimming from the cornucopia of the world?

He looks around, waiting to hear the vibration of an orchestra of flavours. No, nothing vibrates. All those delicacies stir in him imprecise, blurred memories; his imagination does not instinctively associate flavours with images and names. He asks himself if his gluttony is not chiefly mental, aesthetic, symbolic. Perhaps, for all the sincerity of his love of galantines, galantines do not love him. They sense that his gaze transforms every food into a document of the history of civilisation, a museum exhibit.

Mr Palomar wishes the line would advance more rapidly. He knows that if he spends a few more hours in this shop, he will end up convincing himself that he is the profane one, the alien, the outsider.

ITALO CALVINO, Mr Palomar

Short Views on Mean Vices

Every other sin hath some pleasure annexed to it, or will admit of some excuse; but envy wants both.

ROBERT BURTON

Envy is more implacable than hatred.

DUC DE LA ROCHEFOUCAULD

Those who are the most distrustful of themselves, are the most envious of others; as the most weak and cowardly are the most revengeful.

WILLIAM HAZLITT

Envy is the most stupid of vices, for it yields nothing.

HONORÉ DE BALZAC

The gilded sheath of pity conceals the dagger of envy.

FRIEDRICH NIETZSCHE

The arch flatterer, with whom all the petty flatterers have intelligence, is a man's self.

FRANCIS BACON

The more we love our friends, the less we flatter them.

JEAN BAPTISTE MOLIÈRE

He who cannot love must learn to flatter.

JOHANN WOLFGANG VON GOETHE

Weak characters cannot be sincere.

DUC DE LA ROCHEFOUCAULD

Being kind to a liar is abetting a treason against mankind.

MARQUESS OF HALIFAX

As universal a Practice as Lying is, and as easy a one as it seems; I do not remember to have heard three good Lyes in all my Conversation.

JONATHAN SWIFT

The man who lies to himself can be more easily offended than anyone else.

FEDOR DOSTOEVSKY

Paternity, vanity's last and most uncertain refuge.

NATALIE BARNEY

Intelligent vanity does not exist.

LOUIS-FERDINAND CÉLINE

Modesty is a timid confession of pride.

REMY DE GOURMONT

His scorn of the great is repeated too often to be real; no man thinks much of that which he despises.

SAMUEL JOHNSON

Great riches have sold more men than they have bought.

FRANCIS BACON

Ambition hath no mean, it is either upon all fours or upon tiptoes.

MARQUESS OF HALIFAX

All great men are monsters.

HONORÉ DE BALZAC

What is glory? It is to have a lot of nonsense talked about you.

GUSTAVE FLAUBERT

A Nice Man is a Man of nasty ideas.

JONATHAN SWIFT

Distrust all those in whom the urge to punish is strong.

JOHANN WOLFGANG VON GOETHE

Prudery is a kind of avarice, the worst of all.

STENDHAL

A man prone to suspect evil is mostly looking in his neighbour for what he sees in himself.

JULIUS HARE

Society takes its revenges on any happiness it does not share.

HONORÉ DE BALZAC

We suffer less in renouncing our desires when we have trained our imagination to recall the past as ugly.

FRIEDRICH NIETZSCHE

Moral indignation is jealousy with a halo.

H. G. WELLS

The obscene is the sexual fact treated seriously.

REMY DE GOURMONT

The passion for setting people right is in itself an afflictive disease. Distaste which takes no credit to itself is best.

MARIANNE MOORE

The first and only principle of sexual ethics: the accuser is always in the wrong.

THEODOR ADORNO

Snobbery

The man who has not anything to boast of but his illustrious ancestors is like a potato – the only good belonging to him is underground.

SIR THOMAS OVERBURY

He that eats cherries with noblemen shall have his eyes spirted out with the stones.

THOMAS FULLER

I should be happy to *enlighten* the lower classes, but not to dine with them.

BENJAMIN ROBERT HAYDON

One who meanly admires mean things.

WILLIAM MAKEPEACE THACKERAY

The working man who tries to desert his class and rise above it, enters into a lie.

CHARLES KINGSLEY

The crush of minor litterrateurs whom one sees at funerals, distributing handshakes and trying to catch the attention of the obituarist.

CHARLES BAUDELAIRE

After the Emperor had taken a bath at the Prefecture during his tour of the south of France, Chapuys-Montlaville, the senator, had the bath-water drawn off and bottled. He decanted it as if it were from the waters of Jordan. This was in the middle of the nineteenth century, when we laugh at a nation which worships the Grand Lama's shit. In life there are two infinites: God above, and human vice below.

GONCOURT BROTHERS

A Darwinian

Pavel Ilitch Rashevitch marched up and down the room, stepping softly on the Little Russian parquet, and casting a long shadow on the walls and ceiling; and his visitor, Monsieur Meyer, Examining Magistrate, sat on a Turkish divan, with one leg bent under him, smoked, and listened. It was eleven o'clock, and from the next room came the sound of preparations for supper.

'I don't dispute it for a moment!' said Rashevitch. 'From the point of view of fraternity, equality, and all that sort of thing the swineherd Mitka is as good a man as Goethe or Frederick the Great. But look at it from the point of view of science; have the courage to look actuality straight in the face, and you cannot possibly deny that the white bone [blue blood] is not a prejudice, not a silly woman's invention. The white bone, my friend, has a natural-historical justification, and to deny it, in my mind, is

432

as absurd as to deny the antlers of a stag. Look at it as a question of fact! You are a jurist, and never studied anything except the humanities, so you may well deceive yourself with illusions as to equality, fraternity, and that sort of thing. But, on my side, I am an incorrigible Darwinian, and for me such words as race, aristocracy, noble blood are no empty sounds.'

Rashevitch was aroused, and spoke with feeling. His eyes glittered, his pince-nez jumped off his nose, he twitched his shoulders nervously, and at the word 'Darwinian' glanced defiantly at the mirror, and with his two hands divided his grey beard ...

As a rule he loved the sound of his own voice; and it always seemed to him that he was saying something new and original. In the presence of Meyer he felt an unusual elevation of spirits and flow of thought. He liked the magistrate, who enlivened him by his youthful ways, his health, his fine manners, his solidity, and, even more, by the kindly relations which he had established with the family. Speaking generally, Rashevitch was not a favourite with his acquaintances. They avoided him, and he knew it. They declared that he had driven his wife into the grave with his perpetual talk, and called him, almost to his face, a beast and a toad. Meyer alone, being an unprejudiced new-comer, visited him often and willingly, and had even been heard to say that Rashevitch and his daughters were the only persons in the district with whom he felt at home. And Rashevitch reciprocated his esteem – all the more sincerely because Meyer was a young man, and an excellent match for his elder daughter, Zhenya.

And now, enjoying his thoughts and the sound of his own voice, and looking with satisfaction at the stout, well-groomed, respectable figure of his visitor, Rashevitch reflected how he would settle Zhenya for life as the wife of a good man, and, in addition, transfer all the work of managing the estate to his son-in-law's shoulders. It was not particularly agreeable work. The interest had not been paid into the bank for more than two terms, and the various arrears and penalties amounted to over twenty thousand roubles.

'There can hardly be a shadow of doubt,' continued Rashevitch, becoming more and more possessed by his subject, 'that if some Richard the Lion-hearted or Frederick Barbarossa, for instance, a man courageous and magnanimous, has a son, his good qualities will be inherited by the son, together with his bumps; and if this courage and magnanimity are fostered in the son by education and exercise, and he marries a princess also courageous and magnanimous, then these qualities will be transmitted to the grandson, and so on, until they become peculiarities of the species and descend organically, so to speak, in flesh and blood. Thanks to severe sexual selection, thanks to the fact that noble families instinctively preserve themselves from base alliances, and that young people of position do not marry the devil knows whom, their high spiritual qualities have reproduced themselves from generation to generation, they have been perpetuated, and in the course of ages have become even more perfect and loftier. For all that is good in humanity we are indebted to Nature, to the regular, natural-historical, expedient course of things, strenuously in the course of centuries separating the white bone from the black. Yes, my friend! It is not the potboy's child, the cookmaid's brat who has given us literature, science, art, justice, the ideas of honour and of duty ... For all these, humanity is indebted exclusively to the white bone; and in this sense, from the point of view of natural history, worthless Sobakevitch [a stupid, coarse country gentleman in Gogol's novel *Dead Souls*], merely because he is a white bone, is a million times higher and more useful than the best tradesman, let him endow fifty museums! You may say what you like, but if I refuse to give my hand to the potboy's or the cookmaid's son, by that refusal I preserve from stain the best that is on the earth, and subserve one of the highest destinies of mother Nature, leading us to perfection ...'

Rashevitch stood still, and smoothed down his beard with both hands. His scissors-like shadow stood still also.

'Take our dear Mother Russia!' he continued, thrusting his hands into his pockets, and balancing himself alternately on toes and heels. 'Who are our best people? Take our first-class artists, authors, composers ... Who are they? All these, my dear sir, are representatives of the white bone. Pushkin, Gogol, Lermontoff, Turgenieff, Tolstoy ... Were these cookmaids' children?'

'Gontcharoff was a tradesman,' said Meyer.

'What does that prove? The exception, my friend, proves the rule. And as to the genius of Gontcharoff there can be two opinions. But let us leave names and return to facts. Tell me how you can reply, sir, to the eloquent fact that when the potboy climbs to a higher place than he was born in – when he reaches eminence in literature, in science, in local government, in law – what have you to say to the fact that Nature herself intervenes on behalf of the most sacred human rights, and declares war against him? As a matter of fact, hardly has the potboy succeeded in stepping into other people's shoes when he begins to languish, wither, go out of his mind, and degenerate; and nowhere will you meet so many dwarfs, psychical cripples, consumptives, and starvelings as among these gentry. They die away like flies in autumn. And it is a good thing. If it were not for this salutary degeneration, not one stone of our civilisation would remain upon another – the potboy would destroy it all … Be so good as to tell me, please, what this invasion has given us up to the present time? What has the potboy brought with him?' …

Up to this Meyer had said nothing, and sat motionless. Now he rose from the sofa, and looked at the clock.

'Excuse me, Pavel Ilitch,' he said, 'but it's time for me to go.'

But Rashevitch, who had not finished, took him by the arm, set him down forcibly upon the sofa, and swore he should not leave the house without supper. Meyer again sat motionless and listened; but soon began to look at Rashevitch with an expression of doubt and alarm, as if he were only just beginning to understand his character …

'Just as western chivalry repelled the onslaught of the Mongols, so must we, before it is too late, combine and strike together at the enemy.' Rashevitch spoke apostolically, and lifted his right hand on high. 'Let me appear before the potboy no longer as plain Pavel Ilitch, but as a strong and menacing Richard the Lion-Heart! Fling your scruples behind you – enough! Let us swear a sacred compact that when the potboy approaches we will fling him words of contempt straight in the face! Hands off! Back to your pots! Straight in the face!' In ecstasy, Rashevitch thrust out a bent forefinger, and repeated: 'Straight in the face! In the face! In the face!'

Meyer averted his eyes. 'I cannot tolerate this any longer!' he said.

'And may I ask why?' asked Rashevitch, scenting the beginnings of a prolonged and interesting argument.

'Because I myself am the son of an artisan.'

And having so spoken, Meyer reddened, his neck seemed to swell, and tears sparkled in his eyes.

'My father was a plain working man,' he said in an abrupt, broken voice. 'But I can see nothing bad in that.'

Rashevitch was thunderstruck. In his confusion he looked as if he had been detected in a serious crime; he looked at Meyer with a dumbfounded face, and said not a word. Zhenya and Iraida blushed, and bent over their music. They were thoroughly ashamed of their tactless father. A minute passed in silence, and the situation was becoming unbearable when suddenly a sickly, strained voice – it seemed utterly *mal à propos* – stammered forth the words:

'Yes, I am a tradesman's son, and I am proud of it.'

And Meyer, awkwardly stumbling over the furniture, said good-bye, and walked quickly into the hall, although the trap had not been ordered.

ANTON CHEKHOV, *At the Manor*

Epitaph on a Tuft-Hunter

Lament, lament, Sir Isaac Heard,
    Put mourning round thy page, Debrett,
For here lies one, who ne'er preferr'd
    A Viscount to a Marquis yet.

Beside him place the God of Wit,
    Before him Beauty's rosiest girls,
Apollo for a *star* he'd quit,
    And Love's own sister for an Earl's.

Did niggard fate no peers afford,
    He took, of course, to peers' relations;
And, rather than not sport a Lord,
    Put up with even the last creations.

Even Irish names, could he but tag 'em
    With 'Lord' and 'Duke', were sweet to call;
And, at a pinch, Lord Ballyraggum
    Was better than no Lord at all.

Heaven grant him now some noble nook,
    For, rest his soul! he'd rather be
Genteelly damn'd beside a Duke,
    Than sav'd in vulgar company.

THOMAS MOORE

We justify our vices, compromises and snobberies by protesting: 'It's for the children's sake.'

ANTON CHEKHOV

The romantic impulse of our nature to people the world with Gods seems to us pretty in lovers: in snobs we dislike it.

LOGAN PEARSALL SMITH

All children are snobs, and the aristocracy of childhood is age.

DUFF COOPER

Treachery is of the very essence of snobbery.

GEOFFREY MADAN

For the snob like the politician there is no retirement age.

JEAN-FRANÇOIS REVEL

Successive ducs de Levis in France reckoned themselves to be the only people to address the Virgin Mary with the familiar *tutoiement*.

Parents

Parents who barely can afford it
Should not send their children to public schools
    ill will reward it
That skimping and saving and giving up
That seems so unselfish will buy you a pup
Oh what an ugly biting bow-wow
Well Colonel, how does it go now?
Your son aged twenty-two wears a glittering blazer
His conversation about ponds and ducks, oh happy fool,
Is interrupted to speak of his school
As if at fault he'd allowed
Momentarily that pond to draw him from being proud.
Ah, so hardly won through to it, Colonel,
Is to attach too much importance to it.
But he's saved; ponds, duck, fish in dark water
Have a tight hold of him. It is your daughter
Colonel, who is wholly corrupted.
Women when they are snobbish do not loaf
Look at fish, are not oafish
But are persistently mercenary, cold, scheming and calculating,
This in a young girl is revolting.
Oh beautiful brave mother, the wife of the colonel,
How could you allow your young daughter to become aware
    of the scheming?
If you had not, it might have stayed a mere dreaming
Of palaces and princes, girlish at worst.
Oh to become sensible about social advance at seventeen is to
    be lost.

STEVIE SMITH

People Who Want To Be Less Mere

By the desk was seated a tall man of 35 with very nice eyes of a twinkly nature and curly hair he wore a quite plain suit of palest grey but well made and on the table reposed a grey top hat which had evidently been on his head recently. He had a rose in his button hole also a signet ring.

Hullo said this plesant fellow as Mr Salteena was spell bound on mat.

Hullo your Lord Ship responded our hero bowing low and dropping his top hat do I adress of Earl of Clincham.

You do said the Earl with a homely smile and who do I adress eh.

Our hero bowed again Alfred Salteena he said in deep tones.

Oh I see said the kindly earl well come in my man and tell me who you are.

Mr Salteena seated himself gingerly on the edge of a crested chair.

To tell you the truth my Lord I am not anyone of import and I am not a gentleman as they say he ended getting very red and hot.

Have some whiskey said lord Clincham and he poured the liquid into a glass at his elbow. Mr Salteena lapped it up thankfully.

Well my man said the good natured earl what I say is what dose it matter we cant all be of the Blood royal can we.

No said Mr Salteena but I suppose you are.

Lord Clincham waved a careless hand. A small portion flows in my veins he said but it dose not worry me at all and after all he added piously at the Day of Judgement what will be the odds.

Mr Salteena heaved a sigh. I was thinking of this world he said.

Oh I see said the Earl but my own idear is that these things are as piffle before the wind.

Not being an earl I can't say answered our hero but may I beg you to read this letter my Lord. He produced Bernards note from his coat tails. The Earl of Clincham took it in his long fingers. This is what he read.

My dear Clincham

The bearer of this letter is an old friend of mine not quite the right side of the blanket as they say in fact he is the son of a first rate butcher but his mother was a decent family called Hyssopps of the Glen so you see he is not so bad and is desireus of being the correct article. Could you rub him up a bit in Socierty ways. I dont know much details about him but no doubt he will supply all you need. I am keeping well and hope you are. I must run up to the Compartments one day and look you up.

Yours as ever your faithfull friend

BERNARD CLARK

The Earl gave a slight cough and gazed at Mr Salteena thourghtfully.

Have you much money he asked and are you prepared to spend a good deal.

Oh yes quite gasped Mr Salteena I have plenty in the bank and £10 in ready gold in my purse.

You see these compartments are the haunts of the Aristockracy said the earl and they are kept going by peaple who have got something funny in their family and who want to be less mere if you can comprehend.

Indeed I can said Mr Salteena.

Personally I am a bit parshial to mere people said his Lordship but the point is that we charge a goodly sum for our training here but however if you cant pay you need not join.

I can and will proclaimed Mr Salteena and he placed a £10 note on the desk. His Lordship slipped it in his trouser pocket. It will be £42 before I have done with you he said but you can pay me here and there as convenient.

Oh thankyou cried Mr Salteena.

Not at all said the Earl and now to bissness. While here you will live in compartments in the basement known as Lower Range. You will get many hints from the Groom of the Chambers as to clothes and ettiquett to menials. You will mix with me for grammer and I might take you out hunting or shooting sometimes to give you a few tips. Also I have lots of ladies partys which you will attend occasionally.

Mr Salteenas eyes flashed with excitement. I shall enjoy that he cried.

His Lordship coughed loudly. You may not marry while under instruction he said firmly.

Oh I shall not need to thankyou said Mr Salteena.

You must also decide on a profeshion said his Lordship as your instruction will vary according.

Could I be anything at Buckingham Pallace said Mr Salteena with flashing eyes.

Oh well I dont quite know said the noble earl but you might perhaps gallopp beside the royal baroushe if you care to try.

Oh indeed I should cried Mr Salteena I am very fond of fresh air and royalties.

Well said the earl with a knowing smile I might arrange it with the prince of Wales who I am rarther intimate with.

Not really gasped Mr Salteena.

Dear me yes remarked the earl carelessly and if we decide for you to gallopp by the royal viacle you must be mesured for some plush knickerbockers at once.

Mr Salteena glanced at his rarther fat legs and sighed.

Well I must go out now and call on a few Dowigers said his Lordship picking up his elegent top hat. Well au revoir he added with a good french accent.

Adieu my Lord cried Mr Salteena not to be out done we meet anon I take it.

Not till tomorrow answered the earl you will now proceed to the lower regions where you will nr doubt find tea. He nodded kindly and glided out in silence.

Here I will end my chapter.

DAISY ASHFORD, *The Young Visiters*

Precepts for a Social Climber

Choose judiciously thy friends; for to discard them is undesirable,
Yet it is better to drop thy friends, O my daughter, than to drop thy 'H's'.
Dost thou know a wise woman? yea, wiser than the children of light?
Hath she a position? and a title? and are her parties in the Morning Post?
If thou dost, cleave unto her, and give up unto her thy body and mind;

Think with her ideas, and distribute thy smiles at her bidding:

So shalt thou become like unto her; and thy manners shall be 'formed',

And thy name shall be a Sesame, at which the doors of the great shall fly
    open:

Thou shalt know every Peer, his arms, and the date of his creation,

His pedigree and their intermarriages, and cousins to the sixth remove;

Thou shalt kiss the hand of Royalty, and lo! in next morning's papers,

Side by side with rumours of wars, and stories of shipwrecks and sieges,

Shall appear thy name, and the minutiae of thy head-dress and petticoat,

For an enraptured public to muse upon over their matutinal muffin.

Read not Milton, for he is dry; nor Shakespeare, for he wrote of
    common life:

Nor Scott, for his romances, though fascinating, are yet intelligible:

Nor Thackeray, for he is a Hogarth, a photographer who flattereth not:

Nor Kingsley, for he shall teach thee that thou shouldest not dream, but
    do.

Read incessantly thy Burke; that Burke who, nobler than he of old,

Treateth of the Peer and Peeress, the truly Sublime and Beautiful:

Likewise study the 'creations' of 'the Prince of modern Romance';

Sigh over Leonard the Martyr, and smile on Pelham the puppy:

Learn how 'love is the dram-drinking of existence';

And how we 'invoke, in the Gadara of our still closets,

The beautiful ghost of the Ideal, with the simple wand of the pen'.

Listen how Maltravers and the orphan 'forgot all but love',

And how Devereux's family chaplain 'made and unmade kings';

How Eugene Aram, though a thief, a liar, and a murderer,

Yet, being intellectual, was amongst the noblest of mankind.

So shalt thou live in a world peopled with heroes and master-spirits;

And if thou canst not realise the Ideal, thou shalt at least idealise the
    Real.

C. S. CALVERLEY

A South Kensington Landlady

Undemanding though Mrs Roxburgh was, she simply loved gossip. I was not averse to listening to it, although I had precious little to contribute. It was amazing to me how someone so apparently cut off from the great world as my landlady, knew so much about it. There was no titled woman with whom she was not on the most familiar terms, and to whom she did not refer by her christian name, and if she had one, her nickname. Thus Lady Ilchester, who if Burke's Peerage may be relied upon was baptised Helen, became on Mrs Roxburgh's lips Birdie, and Lady Shaftesbury's prosaic Constance turned to Cuckoo. I would learn how Birdie was complaining only the other day to Ethel (Mrs Roxburgh, who was above a nickname) how Cuckoo's pin money was five times more than hers, just because Shaftesbury's earldom was of older creation, which seemed a shame. 'And what, Mrs Roxburgh, did you say to Lady Ilchester?' I asked. 'I advised her,' came the considered answer, 'to dispute the date of Cuckoo's husband's creation.' Then, 'I never did think much of that Fruity,' Mrs Roxburgh resumed, jumping rapidly like the bright little hen she was from perch to perch. 'And I was only saying yesterday to Louey Liverpool that he'll bring the monarchy down, sure as eggs are eggs – not that you can be sure they are anything of the sort these days – if David will be seen driving to night clubs with Fruity, and if you please, in one of May's Daimlers! Baba's all right of course. Still, perhaps Fruity's less dangerous than Ramsay. And have you seen Lossiemouth, my dear? I couldn't even find the place. I doubt if it actually is a *place*. Circe Londonderry must be mad.'

JAMES LEES-MILNE, *Another Self*

Suburbanite

I've miscalculated in every way and I've always known it; but is there anything in life except miscalculations? Born into a poor but snobbish family, instead of getting rid of snobbery and accepting poverty, I rejected poverty and devoted myself to snobbery. I had some excuse, anyhow, owing to the atmosphere in my family. All I need say of my father is that he acted as administrator to a Roman prince and was as faithful and lachrymose as an ancient watchdog; my mother, poor dear, longed to make friends with the aristocratic ladies, even, it must be admitted, by means of such improbable devices as asking by telephone for information about a servant-girl; as for my brother Piero, he was the perfect product of such a situation, always, and in vain, chasing heiresses with historic names. I was no less of a snob than they, but I had the advantage over them of being conscious of it. Of what use was this knowledge to me? That is quickly said: absolutely none at all.

In my family we were always waiting for invitations that did not materialise, for meetings that did not take place, for friendships that did not consolidate. My mother had been queuing up for years in front of the doors of drawing-rooms hermetically sealed to her; my father had been blackballed when seeking admission to the same club as his employer, the prince; my brother addressed his noble contemporaries by the familiar *tu* and found himself answered with the formal *lei*. We were, in short, a family which specialised in stoically-borne loss of face, in bitter pills swallowed without batting an eyelid.

Piero and I had a singular relationship. Eaten up with snobbery as we were, we nevertheless never spoke about it. To make up for this, we gave one another mutual support, by tacit agreement, in a loyal alliance. He would urge me on, whenever he could; and I would do the same for him. However, in spite of our efforts, we remained for ever in the antechamber of real, genuine high society, in an expectation that threatened to be prolonged for the whole of our lives. Finally I had an inspiration: I must not besiege only the feet, but must aim at the head, of the fetish. At that time the recognised, undisputed leader of youthful high society was Edoardo, the mocking, indolent, fickle heir of a great family. I had never been introduced to him in a formal way, even though I met him everywhere; it seemed to me that he avoided me and this dubious situation was wearing me out. One night I awoke with a start and then, with the spontaneity of an action long premeditated, I seized the telephone and dialled my idol's number. Strange to say, I felt I was telephoning out of indignation towards him, as though he were someone who had tried one's patience to the utmost limit. I remember thinking, as I listened to the tone of the receiver, 'It's time it was brought to an end, yes, I've had enough.' I waited a long time and then, finally, a voice well known to me but irritated and fatigued, said, 'Please may I know who it is?'

'Someone who knows you very well but whom you avoid because you are frightened of her.'

'One of the usual suburban girls, I suppose. Where are you?'

'I'm in my nightdress.'

'What are you doing in your nightdress? You'll catch cold.'

'What do you say to my slipping my fur coat over my nightdress and coming to see you?'

'I should tell you to stay where you are. Who are you, anyhow?'

'I'll describe myself. Then you'll get an idea of what I'm like. I'm tall, with a small head, a long neck, broad shoulders, a very well-developed bosom, and a very slim waist. My legs are long and slender and come straight down from my stomach. I have round, black eyes, a broad nose, thick lips. My skin is dark.'

'You're a negress, then.'

'Well, well, at last you've understood.'

Goodness knows why I described myself in this way. Possibly because his definition of me as a 'suburbanite' had made me fear that that was what I really was. Whereas it seemed to me that the African exoticism, so much in fashion, would somehow or other escape any snobbish ostracism. But he, being a true superior snob who can see deep into the minds of inferior snobs, immediately unmasked me: 'Let's say, then, that you must be a black suburbanite.'

'Well, am I to come or not?'

He was silent for a moment, then he replied, 'Not tonight. Come tomorrow, but not here in Rome. Come to B.,' and he named a village in the Castelli Romani, 'tomorrow afternoon. You can't go wrong; our palazzo is in the village square. Go in, go upstairs, I'll be there expecting you.'

He flung down the telephone; and I, elated, went straight to my brother's bedroom. I went over to his bed, in the dark, and called him. He woke up and turned on the light. I told him all in one breath, 'I've just been telephoning to Edoardo and he's given me an appointment, in his palazzo at B.'

Although awakened from a deep sleep, although, as I have said, we had never confided in one another on the subject of snobbism, my brother at once understood what it was all about. He exclaimed joyfully, 'You telephoned Edoardo!'

'Yes, but I didn't tell him who I was. I passed myself off as a negress. Goodness knows if he believed it. Anyhow he gave me this appointment.'

We looked at each other in triumph. I went on, 'However, you'll have to lend me your car.'

'I'll drive you there myself.'

I went back to my room, lay down and went to sleep. But my sleep was restless and filled with nightmares. In the morning I felt ill; I took my temperature and saw that I was feverish. What a misfortune! I could have punched my head with rage. I called my brother and told him that for this time I would have to give up the trip to Edoardo's village. He at once protested violently, 'You absolutely must go. Even with a high temperature.'

'Yes, I *have* got a high temperature.'

'You must wrap up well and we'll take great care.'

So I resigned myself, reflecting that, after all, the fever would make my love-making more passionate – if love-making there was to be, as seemed probable. We drove those thirty kilometres in darkened air, in pouring, icy rain. I was trembling and my teeth were chattering from the fever; everything seemed to be happening in a sort of delirium. As we reached the village it stopped raining. There we found the palazzo, gloomy and smoke-blackened, with crooked walls and gratings over the big windows, in a deserted square of black, shiny cobbles, surrounded by a circle of miserable hovels. My brother and I entered a big courtyard with a long portico and made our way up the flight of stairs at the far end of the courtyard. The place had a strange look of abandonment and rusticity: there was straw and hens' excrement on the step; the window-shutters were loose and unbarred; sacks were piled up on the landings. We found the door of Edoardo's apartment half-open and went through into a vast and entirely empty antechamber. It was extremely cold, and the strangely livid light and a pool of water that had formed on the floor caused me to look upwards; and then, up there between the black beams of the ceiling, I saw the sky, grey and already reddening from the early winter sunset. A door opened and a woman appeared, asking us what we wanted. My brother mentioned Edoardo's name. The woman shook her head: 'He never comes here.'

'But it was here that he gave us an appointment.'

'He lives in Rome. The palazzo has never been repaired since it was bombed during the war. We live in one room, my husband and I and our children. The other rooms are like this anteroom: the rain comes in.'

We said good-bye to the woman who, mistrustful, did not even answer us; we went back into the square. My brother, without uttering a word, took the wheel and we left. Then, all of a sudden, I started laughing, with irresponsible, sobbing, hysterical laughter. I laughed for a long time and then I did not laugh any more; my brother did not open his mouth. At home, I went straight to the telephone and dialled Edoardo's number. I heard his drawling, contemptuous voice. I said to him, 'It was I who spoke to you yesterday.'

'Ah yes. The black suburban girl. How did your trip go off?'

'You're an idiot, a scoundrel and a degenerate.'

I saw my brother make a sign to me, in a nervous way, as if to advise me to be cautious; but I shrugged my shoulders. I went on, 'If you wished to make me see what sort of a person you are, you couldn't have done better. That ruined palazzo, empty and with the rain coming in – that's you all over.'

'How intolerant you are! One sees you must be an African.'

'I'm not an African, I'm a Roman.'

'Well, really! And what are you doing now?'

'I'm in bed, I've got a temperature.'

'Indeed! I'm very sorry. However, that needn't prevent you from slipping on your famous fur coat over your famous nightdress and coming here, to see me. Here in Rome, in my own flat.'

'Do you want me to come?'

'But of course. Why, d'you think I'm joking?'

'All right, then, I'll come at once.'

And so I did. Well, well, it's not enough to know that one makes miscalculations. What is needed, as I have already said, is to have something in one's life that goes beyond miscalculations.

ALBERTO MORAVIA, *Lady Godiva*

Some Unpretentious English Names

Lyulph Ydwallo Odin Nestor Egbert Lyonel Toedmag Hugh Erchenwyne
  Saxon Esa Cromwell Orma Nevill Dysart Plantagenet Tollemache-
  Tollemache-de Orellana-Plantagenet-Tollemache-Tollemache
  (1876–1961) and his brother Lyonulph Cospatrick Bruce Berkeley
  Jermyn Tullibardine Petersham de Orellana Dysart Plantagenet
  Tollemache-Tollemache-de Orellana-Plantagenet-Tollemache-
  Tollemache (1892–1960) (cousins of the Earl of Dysart)
Temple-Nugent-Brydges-Chandos-Grenville (surname of the Dukes of
  Buckingham and Chandos)
Borlase-Warren-Venables-Vernon (surname of Lord Vernon's kinsmen)
William Lehmann Ashmead Burdett-Coutts-Bartlett-Coutts (husband of
  the Victorian philanthropist)
Hepburn-Stuart-Forbes-Trefusis (surname of Lords Clinton)
Lane Fox-Pitt-Rivers (surname of good plain gentry)
Montagu-Stuart-Wortley-Mackenzie (surname of Earls of Wharncliffe)
Plunkett-Erle-Ernle-Drax (cousins of Lord Dunsany)
Pole-Tylney-Long-Wellesley (surname of Earls of Mornington)
Shaw-Lefevre-St John-Mildmay (baronet: grandson of Viscount
  Eversley)
Hamilton-Temple-Blackwood (Marquesses of Dufferin and Ava)
Milborne-Swinnerton-Pilkington (baronets)
Pelham-Clinton-Hope (Dukes of Newcastle)
Twistleton-Wykeham-Fiennes (surname of Lords Saye and Sele)
Wooster-Mannering-Phipps (original surname of Bertie Wooster)

Solitary Vice

The intimate, exalted, utterly refined vice of the solitary.

CAMILO JOSÉ CELA

Masturbation is reckoned disgraceful – it cannot be sentimentalised.

W. H. AUDEN (paraphrasing Laura Riding)

In a Stalinist Prison

The tapping started again, this time very loudly and ringingly – No. 402 had obviously taken off a shoe in order to give more weight to his words:
LONG LIVE H.M. THE EMPEROR!

So that's it, thought Rubashov. There still exist genuine and authentic counter-revolutionaries – and we thought that nowadays they only occurred in the speeches of No. 1, as scapegoats for his failures. But there sits a real one, an alibi for No. 1 in flesh and blood, roaring, just as he should: long live the Monarch ...

AMEN, tapped out Rubashov, grinning. The answer came immediately, still louder if possible:

SWINE!

Rubashov was amusing himself. He took off his pince-nez and tapped with the metal edge, in order to change the tone, with a drawling and distinguished intonation:

DIDN'T QUITE UNDERSTAND.

No. 402 seemed to go into a frenzy. He hammered out HOUN' –, but the D did not come. Instead, his fury suddenly flown, he tapped:

WHY HAVE YOU BEEN LOCKED UP?

What touching simplicity ... The face of No. 402 underwent a new transformation. It became that of a young Guards officer, handsome and stupid. Perhaps he even wore a monocle. Rubashov tapped with his pince-nez:

POLITICAL DIVERGENCIES.

A short pause. No. 402 was obviously searching his brain for a sarcastic answer. It came at last:

BRAVO! THE WOLVES DEVOUR EACH OTHER.

Rubashov gave no answer. He had had enough of this sort of entertainment and started on his wanderings again. But the officer in 402 had become conversational. He tapped:

RUBASHOV ...

Well, this was just about verging on familiarity.

YES? answered Rubashov.

No. 402 seemed to hesitate; then came quite a long sentence:

WHEN DID YOU LAST SLEEP WITH A WOMAN?

Certainly No. 402 wore an eye-glass; probably he was tapping with it and the bared eye was twitching nervously. Rubashov did not feel repelled. The man at least showed himself as he was; which was pleasanter than if he had tapped out monarchist manifestos. Rubashov thought it over for a bit, and then tapped:

THREE WEEKS AGO.

The answer came at once:

TELL ME ALL ABOUT IT.

Well, really, that was going a bit far. Rubashov's first impulse was to break off the conversation; but he remembered the man might later become very useful as a connecting link to No. 400 and the cells beyond. The cell to the left was obviously uninhabited; there the chain broke off.

Rubashov racked his brain. An old pre-war song came to his memory, which he had heard as a student, in some cabaret where black-stockinged ladies danced the French can-can. He sighed resignedly and tapped with his pince-nez:

SNOWY BREASTS FITTING INTO CHAMPAGNE GLASSES ...

He hoped that was the right tone. It was apparently, for No. 402 urged:

GO ON. DETAILS.

By this time he was doubtless plucking nervously at his moustache. He certainly had a little moustache with twirled-up ends. The devil take the man; he was the only connecting link; one had to keep up with him. What did officers talk about in the mess? Women and horses. Rubashov rubbed his pince-nez on his sleeve and tapped conscientiously:

THIGHS LIKE A WILD MARE.

He stopped, exhausted. With the best will in the world he could not do more. But No. 402 was highly satisfied.

GOOD CHAP! he tapped enthusiastically. He was doubtless laughing boisterously, but one heard nothing; he slapped his thighs and twirled his moustache, but one saw nothing. The abstract obscenity of the dumb wall was embarrassing to Rubashov.

GO ON, urged No. 402.

He couldn't. THAT'S ALL – tapped Rubashov and regretted it immediately. No. 402 must not be offended. But fortunately No. 402 did not let himself be offended. He tapped on obstinately with his monocle:

GO ON – PLEASE, PLEASE ...

Rubashov was now again practised to the extent of no longer having to count the signs; he transformed them automatically into acoustic perception. It seemed to him that he actually heard the tone of voice in which No. 402 begged for more erotic material. The begging was repeated:

PLEASE – PLEASE ...

No. 402 was obviously still young – probably grown up in exile, sprung from an old Army family, sent back into his country with a false passport – and he was obviously tormenting himself badly. He was doubtless plucking at his little moustache, had stuck his monocle to his eye again and was staring hopelessly at the whitewashed wall.

451

MORE – PLEASE, PLEASE.

... Hopelessly staring at the dumb, whitewashed wall, staring at the stains caused by the damp, which gradually began to assume the outlines of the woman with the champagne-cup breasts and the thighs of a wild mare.

TELL ME MORE – PLEASE.

ARTHUR KOESTLER, *Darkness at Noon*

Itching Fires

I now shunned all company in which there was no hopes of coming at the object of my longings, and used to shut myself up, to indulge in solitude some tender meditation on the pleasures I strongly perceived the overture of, in feeling and examining what nature assured me must be the chosen avenue, the gates for the unknown bliss to enter at, that I panted after.

But these meditations only increased my disorder, and blew the fire that consumed me. I was yet worse when, yielding at length to the insupportable irritations of the little fairy charm that tormented me, I seized it with my fingers, teasing it to no end. Sometimes, in the furious excitations of desire, I threw myself on the bed, spread my thighs abroad, and lay as it were expecting the longed-for relief, till finding my illusion, I shut and squeezed them together again, burning and fretting. In short, this devilish thing, with its impetuous girds and itching fires, led me such a life, that I could neither, night or day, be at peace with it or myself. In time, however, I thought I had gained a prodigious prize, when figuring to myself that my fingers were something of the shape of what I pined for, I worked my way in with one of them with great agitation and delight; yet not without pain too did I deflour myself as far as it could reach; proceeding with such a fury of passion, in this solitary and last shift of pleasure, as extended me at length breathless on the bed in an amorous melting trance.

JOHN CLELAND, *Memoirs of Fanny Hill*

Madame's Jewels

At Feignies we passed through customs. It was at night, and the master was so sleepy that he stayed behind in the train compartment. Madame and I went to the shed where the baggage was being examined.

'Anything to declare?' asked a huge great customs officer who, seeing that the mistress was so elegant, was delighted at the thought of fingering all her pretty things. There really are officials for whom the chance of rummaging through a pretty woman's knickers is a real turn on.

'No,' Madame answered, 'nothing to declare.'

'Would you mind opening this suitcase?'

Of our six cases, he had picked the biggest and heaviest, made of pigskin, with a grey cloth cover.

'But I tell you, I have nothing to declare,' Madame insisted crossly.

'Never mind, open it,' the lout demanded, excited by the mistress's resistance.

The mistress – I know why, now – took her key-ring from her handbag and unlocked the suitcase. With a despicable show of pleasure, the customs officer inhaled the delicious scent that wafted from it, and then started fumbling the exquisite underwear and dresses with his dirty, clumsy paws. Madame was livid, and protested when, with obvious spite, the brute turned everything upside down, crumpling the clothes which we had so meticulously folded and packed.

Then, just when it seemed his inspection was over, he dug a long red velvet case from the bottom of the trunk and demanded: 'And this? What does this contain?'

'My jewellery,' Madame replied smoothly.

'Do you mind opening it?'

'But what's the point? I've told you, it only contains my personal jewellery.'

'Open it.'

'No, I refuse. You're abusing your authority, and I refuse. Besides, I haven't the key.'

By now Madame was betraying agitation. She tried to snatch the case from the officer, but he drew back, and said ominously, 'If you refuse, I will be obliged to summon the chief inspector.'

'But this is preposterous! Shameful!'

'If you can't produce the key, we will just have to force the lock.'

In mounting exasperation Madame shouted: 'You have no right to do anything of the kind! I shall complain to our ambassador, to the ministers! I shall report the matter to the King who is a personal friend of ours! I shall have you dismissed, do you understand? You shall go to prison for this.'

Her fury had no effect on the customs officer who merely repeated blandly, 'Will you please open the case?'

Madame had paled and was nervously twisting her hands. 'No,' she said, 'I will not open it. I don't want to, and in any case I can't.'

For the umpteenth time the stubborn official repeated 'Open the case.'

This disturbance had interrupted everyone, and a little bevy of travellers had collected around us. As for me, I was fascinated by it all, especially by the mysterious case, which I did not recognise, and indeed had never seen before, let alone packed. Next Madame changed tactics, taking a gentler even endearing tone with the intractable official. Drawing closer to him, as though to enchant him with the scent of her perfume, she quietly begged, 'Just send these people away, and I will open the case.'

The official, suspecting Madame of a trick, shook his stubborn old head and replied, 'I've had just about enough of your nonsense, and won't have any more of it. Open the case.'

At last, blushing but resigned, Madame took a tiny key from her purse, a pretty little golden key, and keeping a firm grip on the red velvet case, trying to shield it from onlookers, she opened it. As soon as he saw what it contained, the officer recoiled as though in fear of being bitten by a venomous snake.

'For Christ's sake,' he swore. Then, mastering himself, he said more chirpily, 'Why on earth didn't you tell me in the first place? If only I'd known that you were a widow!' He shut the case, but not before the sniggers and whispers of the crowd, their offensive and even indignant remarks, had made it only too clear to Madame that her jewels had been seen by everyone.

She was mortified. Still, I must admit, she showed considerable pluck under very trying circumstances although she always had plenty of cheek. She helped me to repack the suitcase which was in a terrible mess, and we left the custom shed to a chorus of whistles and insulting laughter.

I accompanied her to the sleeper, carrying her bag into which she thrust the famous case. When we reached the platform, she stopped a moment, and with cool insolence said to me, 'Heaven, what a fool I was! I should have told him that it belonged to you.'

With equal impertinence I retorted: 'I appreciate the honour, ma'am. You are really too kind. But personally I prefer that particular type of "jewel" in its natural form.'

OCTAVE MIRBEAU, The Diary of a Chambermaid

Manikins

6 May 1858: Maria told us that there exist – this is a fact, she was shown one by another midwife – there exist imitation women, complete in every detail, with all the charms and uses of real women: manikins with flesh which you can push in and which comes out again, a tongue which darts in and out for five minutes, eyes which roll, hair which you would swear was the real thing, and moistness and warmth where you would expect to find them, on sale at the manufacturer's for 15,000 francs, for the use of religious communities or rich sailors. This one was for a ship whose name Maria has forgotten; but there are others to suit all pockets, down to male and female parts in gilded boxes which cost only 300 francs. Maria told us that the one she saw was a wonderful sight. It was nearly finished; there were only the toe-nails which still had to be stuck on.

The artist who makes these things – this public benefactor, this moralist endeavouring to avoid so many evils, to spare man, for instance, apart from anything else, that tempestuous age of woman, that unbearable period, the change of life – this rare artist was prosecuted six months ago and sent to prison, no doubt on a charge of immorality.

GONCOURT BROTHERS, Journal

Secret Shadows

The moment of desire! the moment of desire! the virgin
That pines for man shall awaken her womb to enormous joys
In the secret shadows of her chamber: the youth shut up from
The lustful joy shall forget to generate and create an amorous image
In the shadows of his curtains and in the folds of his silent pillow.
Are not these the places of religion, the rewards of continence,
The self-enjoyings of self-denial? Why dost thou seek religion?
Is it because acts are not lovely that thou seekest solitude,
Where the horrible darkness is impressed with reflections of desire?

WILLIAM BLAKE

Signior Dildo

You ladies all of merry England
Who have been to kiss the Duchess's hand,
Pray, did you lately observe in the show
A noble Italian called Signior Dildo?

This signior was one of Her Highness's train,
And helped to conduct her over the main;
But now she cries out, 'To the Duke I will go!
I have no more need for Signior Dildo.'

At the Sign of the Cross in St James's Street,
When next you go thither to make yourselves sweet
By buying of powder, gloves, essence, or so,
You may chance t' get a sight of Signior Dildo.

You'll take him at first for no person of note
Because he appears in a plain leather coat,
But when you his virtuous abilities know,
You'll fall down and worship Signior Dildo.

My Lady Southesk, heavens prosper her for 't!
First clothed him in satin, then brought him to Court;
But his head in the circle he scarcely durst show,
So modest a youth was Signior Dildo.

The good Lady Suffolk, thinking no harm,
Had got this poor stranger hid under her arm.
Lady Betty by chance came the secret to know,
And from her own mother stole Signior Dildo.

The Countess of Falmouth, of whom people tell
Her footmen wear shirts of a guinea an ell,
Might save the expense if she did but know
How lusty a swinger is Signior Dildo.

By the help of this gallant the countess of Ralph
Against the fierce Harrys preserved herself safe.
She stifled him almost beneath her pillow,
So closely sh' embraced Signior Dildo.

Our dainty fine duchesses have got a trick
To dote on a fool for the sake of his prick:
The fops were undone, did Their Graces but know
The discretion and vigour of Signior Dildo.

That pattern of virtue, Her Grace of Cleveland,
Has swallowed more pricks than the ocean has sand;
But by rubbing and scrubbing so large it does grow,
It is fit for just nothing but Signior Dildo.

The Duchess of Modena, though she looks high,
With such a gallant is contented to lie,
And for fear the English her secrets should know,
For a Gentleman Usher took Signior Dildo.

The countess o' th' Cockpit (Who knows not her name?
She's famous in story for a killing dame),
When all her old lovers forsake her, I trow
She'll then be contented with Signior Dildo.

Red Howard, red Sheldon, and Temple so tall
Complain of his absence so long from Whitehall;
Signior Bernard has promised a journey to go
And bring back his countryman Signior Dildo.

Doll Howard no longer with 's Highness must range,
And therefore is proffered this civil exchange:
Her teeth being rotten, she smells best below,
And needs must be fitted for Signior Dildo.

St Albans, with wrinkles and smiles in his face,
Whose kindness to strangers becomes his high place,
In his coach and six horses is gone to Borgo
To take the fresh air with Signior Dildo.

Were this signior but known to the citizen fops,
He'd keep their fine wives from the foremen of shops;
But the rascals deserve their horns should still grow
For burning the Pope and his nephew Dildo.

Tom Killigrew's wife, north Holland's fine flower,
At the sight of this signior did fart and belch sour,
And her Dutch breeding farther to show,
Says, 'Welcome to England, Mynheer Van Dildo!'

He civilly came to the Cockpit one night,
And proffered his service to fair Madam Knight.
Quoth she, 'I intrigue with Captain Cazzo;
Your nose in mine arse, good Signior Dildo!'

This signior is sound, safe, ready, and dumb
As ever was candle, carrot, or thumb;
Then away with these nasty devices, and show
How you rate the just merits of Signior Dildo.

Count Cazzo, who carries his nose very high,
In passion he swore his rival should die;
Then shut up himself to let the world know
Flesh and blood could not bear it from Signior Dildo.

A rabble of pricks who were welcome before,
Now finding the Porter denied 'em the door,
Maliciously waited his coming below
And inhumanly fell on Signior Dildo.

Nigh wearied out, the poor stranger did fly,
And along the Pall Mall they followed full cry;
The women, concerned, from every window
Cried, 'Oh! for heavens' sake, save Signior Dildo!'

The good Lady Sandys burst into a laughter
To see how the ballocks came wobbling after,
And had not their weight retarded the foe,
Indeed 't had gone hard with Signior Dildo.

EARL OF ROCHESTER

Theatricals

To write a comedie kindly grave old men should instruct, younge men should showe the imperfections of youth, strumpets should be lascivious, Boyes unhappy, and Clownes should speak disorderlye; entermingling all these actions in such sort as the grave matter may instruct, and the pleasant delight.

GEORGE WHETSTONE

All the chief forms of amusement endanger Christian life; but of all those devised by the world, none is so fearful as the theatre.

BLAISE PASCAL

Hypocritical and Zealous Teachers that Cry down Plays most, are the greatest Actors themselves in the world. For they do not all indeavour to convince their Hearers, with strength of Reason, and Soundness of Doctrine, but with Laborious vehemence and Noyse, Forcd Tones, and Fantastique extravagant expressions, to impose upon their Naturall Infirmitys.

SAMUEL BUTLER I

Always On

Though the television droned all day, and though by day's end, to save my head from decapitation, I could not have related to my tormentors a smidgen of anything I had seen, now I remember the shows clearly. I saw the quiz shows in which contestants stood as tremulous as condemned men in outhouse-like glass prisons, the flanks of their skulls encased in great Buck Rogers-like earphones. Watching them strain, look abstracted, purse, wet their lips, and roll their eyes while searching so zealously for an answer, I laughed heartily and knew that the show was either rigged – the contestants were such abominable actors – or – watching them, all phony sighs of relief, give their farcically esoteric answers – that the con- testants were mental freaks unworthy of the homage a boy-minded country was paying them. I watched the jolly comedies that induced no laughter save on that Orwellian laugh track. Implying, as in its sinister intimidation it did imply, that there was a green and salutary land just off the wings where pink-cheeked, wittily precious people were grasping things beyond my brutal sense of humor, that laughter soured me utterly. The louder the belly laughs grew, the more puritanically severe became my distaste until I began to feel like an obtuse Presbyterian perusing Rabelais.

I watched – but there is no need to enumerate. Not once during those months did there emanate from the screen a genuine idea or emotion, and I came to understand the medium as subversive. In its deceit, its out- right lies, its spinelessness, its weak-mindedness, its pointless violence, in the disgusting personalities it holds up to our youth to emulate, in its endless and groveling deference to our fantasies, television undermines strength of character, saps vigor, and irreparably perverts notions of real- ity. But it is a tender, loving medium; and when it has done its savage job completely and reduced one to a prattling, salivating infant, like a buxom mother it stands always poised to take one back to the shelter of its brown-nippled bosom. Save for football I no longer watch the tube, and yet my set is always on. In the way one puts a ticking clock in a six-week- old puppy's pillowed box to assure him that Mom is always there, I come in from having one too many beers, flick on the switch, and settle comfortably on the davenport. The drone reassures me that life is there, life is simple, life is unending. Starting up abruptly at 3 a.m., I am at first chagrined and terrified by the darkness; then suddenly I am conscious of the hot hum of the voiceless tube and turn to receive the benediction from the square of brilliant light shining directly upon me from out of the darkness. How I envy those people who live in areas where all-night movies are shown.

To say that I took no pleasure from television is untrue. The endearing world of the soap operas captivated me completely. I don't remember the names of any of them; nor do I remember anything of the plots save that the action moved along with underwater creepiness. I do remember the picture of America they apostrophised was truer than either the tongue-in-cheek writer or the lumbering actors imagined (the latter all walked left-handedly through their parts, letting us know they were between roles in The Legitimate Theater).

The world of the soap opera is the world of the Emancipated American Woman, a creature whose idleness is employed to no other purpose but creating mischief. All these women had harsh crow's feet about the eyes, a certain fullness of mouth that easily and frequently distended into a childish poutiness, and a bosomless and glacial sexuality which, taken all together, brought to their faces a witchy, self-indulgent suffering that seemed compounded in equal parts of unremitting menstrual periods, chronic constipation, and acute sexual frustration. Though I do not remember the plots, I remember there was a recurring scene in which these females, like the witches about the cauldron in *Macbeth*, gathered together in shiny kitchens with checkered muslin curtains and ovens built into beige bricks; that there, seated over snowy porcelain tables adorned with exquisite china coffee cups and artificial flowers, they planned for, plotted against, and passed judgment upon all the shadowy and insubstantial characters who made their flickering entrances and exits through the kitchen. They produced plans and plots and judgments which the writer, for all his cynicism, his two thousand dollars a week, and the corny lines he gave them to speak, never questioned as being any less than their right to make. If Kit's stepson Larry was so ungratefully and willfully contumacious as to want to buy a hot-dog stand instead of accepting his engineering scholarship to Yale, a means was devised to dissuade him. If Pamela's husband Peter was drinking (and how the women lingered on and gave pregnancy to words like *drinking*, rolling them lovingly around on the palate like hot pecan pie), it was determined, not that Peter might be buckling under too much responsibility but that he did not have enough and that 'Pammy ought to have children.' Woe unto that philanderer Judson, now having a fling with his new secretary from out of town (as with the Southern mind, all the evil influences in the soap operas came from 'out of town'); within days he was certain to meet his horrifying death in the holocaust of his overturned Jaguar.

Wondering constantly how accurate a portrait of America it was, I saw this world as one in which these witches were without motive save that of keeping everyone about them locked and imprisoned within the illiterate and banal orbit of their days, a world to which the passionate and the singular aspiration were forbidden.

FREDERICK EXLEY, *A Fan's Notes*

Between the Acts

At eight o'clock the curtain went up on *Tristan and Isolde*, before a house hushed into the proper frame of mind already by the Overture.

A house – the expression is inaccurate. Upper circles and gallery were full; the stalls and boxes but sparsely occupied. Into the stalls, people trickled in parties of two and four, tip-toeing in the semi-darkness; into the boxes, parties came with less circumspection, having no resentful feet to stumble over, no whispered apologies to make; they came in, with a gleam of light as the door opened, and took their places amid scarcely suppressed chatter and laughter. Sh-sh-sh, came from the circles and gallery, but the disturbers glanced round, although unseen, into the dim amphitheatre as though chidden by an intruder in their own home. As the first act wore on, these gleamings and rustlings diminished and subsided; the stalls filled up; and the house began to await the final chords of the orchestra and the turning-up of the lights, when the full splendour of Covent Garden in mid-season should be revealed.

How dark they were, those minutes filled by the rumble of impending tragedy! A doom-laden ship — strange, accepted convention upon the stage — when everybody knew that the tiers around the house were filled by the galaxy of London fashion, light-hearted and care-free people who took this in the natural course of the things they had to do. Little clerks, putting aside half a crown out of a weekly wage of five-and-twenty shillings, felt no grievance; they merely awaited the turning up of the lights to admire a spectacle which was as much part of their evening's treat as the music itself. Dr John Spedding, who had at last brought his wife Teresa to Covent Garden because she gave him no peace until he consented to do so, and who, being himself a sincere lover of music, had taken his seat full of prejudice against this elegant performance, now found himself infected by the general atmosphere of luxury and sophistication, and leant back in his seat definitely enjoying the sensation that around him were hundreds of spoilt, leisured people, soon to be on show like regal animals or plumaged birds, well-accustomed and seemingly indifferent to excited gaze.

Teresa, at his side, could scarcely sit still, such was her impatience. She wriggled herself against him like a kitten, and whispered to know how soon the act would be over. She was terribly bored by King Mark. Hush, said the people behind them, and she subsided, giving herself up again to the warmth and the mysterious presence of all those men and women, nonchalant in their boxes between the dim pink lights of the sconces, which just permitted them to be seen, quiet, silent, and attentive. Teresa Spedding was frankly and childishly fascinated by high life. She had quite a collection of photographs which she had cut out of the newspapers and stuck into an album, so that she was confident she would be able to recognise many of these celebrities although she had never yet seen them in the flesh. She spent a great deal of her time wondering about them; had they any feelings, she wondered? did husbands and wives ever quarrel? did they know how many servants they had, or was all that left to a secretary? did they call the King sir or sire? And were they all dreadfully wicked? It excited her beyond measure to know that she was actually within reach of them: would brush against some of them as they left the building when the opera was over. If only one of them would slip and twist an ankle, so that John might push his way forward professionally —

'Allow me, Lady Warwick, I am a doctor –' and then a few weeks later would come an invitation on paper with a gilt embossed coronet, 'Dear Mrs Spedding, it would give me so much pleasure if you and your husband would spend the following week-end with us at Warwick Castle.' Thus Teresa's mind galloped along, until she became aware that the orchestra was playing the finale, and that in a few moments everyone would begin to clap and the lights would go up.

The music ceased, applause broke out, and the curtain came magnificently down, but it must be raised again, and the singers must bow, twice, three times. 'Don't clap, John, don't clap,' implored Teresa, in agonies lest her husband's enthusiasm should swell the delaying noise; but like all evils it came to an end, the applause died away, the curtain remained finally lowered, and Covent Garden blazed suddenly into light. It was like the first day of Creation, let there be light, and there was light, thought Teresa, but hastily checked her irreverence. The whole house was full of movement; people were getting up in the stalls; conversation roared; the orchestra was creeping away through a trap-door. The great red velvet curtain alone hung motionless. But Teresa's eyes were devouring the boxes; she clutched John's arm, she pinched it; 'Oh John, look, there's Princess Patricia in the Royal box, and Lord Chesterfield talking to her – they say he's the best dressed man in London –', but Teresa had no time to linger over Lord Chesterfield; her eyes were roaming too greedily; like a child before a Christmas tree, she felt dazzled by the glitter and variety presented to her sight. Tier upon tier of boxes, those dark squares cut in a wall of light. Within them, visible to the waist, sat the queens of fashion and beauty – or so thought Teresa, undiscriminating between the rightful holder and the parvenue – dazzling in tiaras and *rivières*, resplendent in their satins and *décolletés*, they allowed their arms in long white gloves to repose on the velvet ledge, while a fan slowly waved, and their eyes slowly travelled over the house, to find and acknowledge a friend, many friends; and the well-bred minimum of attention was accorded to the men who with suitable gallantry leaned over the backs of their chairs. This, in truth, was the great world as Teresa had conceived it. She regretted only that the men were in ordinary evening dress; somehow she had imagined that they would all be in uniform. Still, the black and white was a good foil; and the ladies gave her no cause for complaint, so generously had they emptied the contents of their safes on to their persons: from head to waist they trickled in diamonds. But it was not so much the diamonds that dazzled Teresa, for those she had fully expected; what she had not foreseen was this coming and going, this interchange of groupings, this indication of familiarity; so that a young man but recently observed in one box appeared in another on the opposite side of the house, and lounged there in the same accepted way; and what delighted her almost beyond control was to see famous people stopping to chat together, Lord Curzon with Mr Balfour down in the gangway, laughing together as they enjoyed a joke. Now her album of photographs served her well, for many were the personalities she could point out to John; 'Do you see, John?' she said, still squeezing his arm, 'there in the third box on the left, in the grand tier – there's Mrs Asquith with the Duchess of Rutland – and in the next box there's Lady Savile and Sir Ernest Cassel – look, they're talking to Mrs Asquith now, across the partition – what do you think they're saying? – and there's the Marquis de Soveral with his little imperial – and oh John, look! in the box opposite them, that's Lady Roehampton surely? yes, it must be; I've seen her before, once in the Park –' and Teresa's excitement reached its height, as she contemplated the beauty through her opera-glasses and thought that nothing could ever be more exquisite than this apparition of the renowned Lady Roehampton in the framing of a grand tier box. What self-possession, she thought, was expressed in the set of the magnificent shoulders, emerging from clouds of tulle! how divinely her head was poised, under its crown of diamonds! how royally she sat, surveying the house while a faint smile played about her lips! how much Teresa envied her, so calm and languorous and queenly, without a care in the world! Even the impassive John agreed that she was a handsome woman. And now a young man entered the box, a dark, slim young man, and sat beside her for a moment, speaking to her, but she seemed scarcely to take any notice of him, but turned to another man instead, a foreigner evidently, who came in and bowed very low over her hand; and the dark, slim young man got up and went away.

V. SACKVILLE-WEST, *The Edwardians*

Country House Melodramatics

'Salsie, won't you play something?' said Hermione, breaking off completely. 'Won't somebody dance? Gudrun, you will dance, won't you? I wish you would. *Anche tu, Palestra, ballerai? – si, per piacere.* You too, Ursula.'

Hermione rose and slowly pulled the gold-embroidered band that hung by the mantel, clinging to it for a moment, then releasing it suddenly. Like a priestess she looked, unconscious, sunk in a heavy half-trance.

A servant came, and soon reappeared with armfuls of silk robes and shawls and scarves, mostly oriental, things that Hermione, with her love for beautiful extravagant dress, had collected gradually.

'The three women will dance together,' she said.

'What shall it be?' asked Alexander, rising briskly.

'Vergini Delle Rocchette,' said the Contessa at once.

'They are so languid,' said Ursula.

'The three witches from *Macbeth*,' suggested Fräulein usefully. It was finally decided to do Naomi and Ruth and Orpah. Ursula was Naomi, Gudrun was Ruth, the Contessa was Orpah. The idea was to make a little ballet, in the style of the Russian Ballet of Pavlova and Nijinsky.

The Contessa was ready first, Alexander went to the piano, a space was cleared. Orpah, in beautiful oriental clothes, began slowly to dance the death of her husband. Then Ruth came, and they wept together, and lamented, then Naomi came to comfort them. It was all done in dumb show, the women danced their emotion in gesture and motion. The little drama went on for a quarter of an hour.

Ursula was beautiful as Naomi. All her men were dead, it remained to her only to stand alone in indomitable assertion, demanding nothing. Ruth, woman-loving, loved her. Orpah, a vivid, sensational, subtle widow, would go back to the former life, a repetition. The inter-play between the women was real and rather frightening. It was strange to see how Gudrun clung with heavy, desperate passion to Ursula, yet smiled with subtle malevolence against her, how Ursula accepted silently, unable to provide any more either for herself or for the other, but dangerous and indomitable, refuting her grief.

Hermione loved to watch. She could see the Contessa's rapid, stoat-like sensationalism, Gudrun's ultimate but treacherous cleaving to the woman in her sister, Ursula's dangerous helplessness, as if she were helplessly weighted, and unreleased.

'That was very beautiful,' everybody cried with one accord. But Hermione writhed in her soul, knowing what she could not know. She cried out for more dancing, and it was her will that set the Contessa and Birkin moving mockingly in Malbrouk.

Gerald was excited by the desperate cleaving of Gudrun to Naomi. The essence of that female, subterranean recklessness and mockery penetrated his blood. He could not forget Gudrun's lifted, offered, cleaving, reckless, yet withal mocking weight. And Birkin, watching like a hermit crab from its hole, had seen the brilliant frustration and helplessness of Ursula. She was rich, full of dangerous power. She was like a strange unconscious bud of powerful womanhood. He was unconsciously drawn to her. She was his future.

Alexander played some Hungarian music, and they all danced, seized by the spirit. Gerald was marvellously exhilarated at finding himself in motion, moving towards Gudrun, dancing with feet that could not yet escape from the waltz and the two-step, but feeling his force stir along his limbs and his body, out of captivity. He did not know yet how to dance their convulsive, rag-time sort of dancing, but he knew how to begin. Birkin, when he could get free from the weight of the people present, whom he disliked, danced rapidly and with a real gaiety. And how Hermione hated him for this irresponsible gaiety.

'Now I see,' cried the Contessa excitedly, watching his purely gay motion, which he had all to himself. 'Mr Birkin, he is a changer.'

Hermione looked at her slowly, and shuddered, knowing that only a foreigner could have seen and have said this.

'*Cosa vuol' dire, Palestra?*' she asked, sing-song.

'Look,' said the Contessa, in Italian. 'He is not a man, he is a chameleon, a creature of change.'

'He is not a man, he is treacherous, not one of us,' said itself over in Hermione's consciousness. And her soul writhed in the black subjugation to him, because of his power to escape, to exist, other than she did, because he was not consistent, not a man, less than a man. She hated him in a despair that shattered her and broke her down, so that she suffered sheer dissolution like a corpse, and was unconscious of everything save the horrible sickness of dissolution that was taking place within her, body and soul.

D. H. LAWRENCE, *Women in Love*

Everything and Nothing

There was no one in him; behind his face (which even in the poor paintings of the period is unlike any other) and his words, which were copious, imaginative, and emotional, there was nothing but a little chill, a dream not dreamed by anyone. At first he thought everyone was like him, but the puzzled look on a friend's face when he remarked on that emptiness told him he was mistaken and convinced him forever that an individual must not differ from his species. Occasionally he thought he would find in books the cure for his ill, and so he learned the small Latin and less Greek of which a contemporary was to speak. Later he thought that in the exercise of an elemental human rite he might well find what he sought, and he let himself be initiated by Anne Hathaway one long June afternoon. At twenty-odd he went to London. Instinctively, he had already trained himself in the habit of pretending that he was someone, so it would not be discovered that he was no one. In London he hit upon the profession to which he was predestined, that of the actor, who plays on stage at being someone else. His playacting taught him a singular happiness, perhaps the first he had known; but when the last line was applauded and the last corpse removed from the stage, the hated sense of unreality came over him again. He ceased to be Ferrex or Tamburlaine and again became a nobody. Trapped, he fell to imagining other heroes and other tragic tales. Thus, while in London's bawdyhouses and taverns his body fulfilled its destiny as body, the soul that dwelled in it was Caesar, failing to heed the augurer's admonition, and Juliet, detesting the lark, and Macbeth, conversing on the heath with the witches, who are also the fates. Nobody was ever as many men as that man, who like the Egyptian Proteus managed to exhaust all the possible shapes of being. At times he slipped into some corner of his work a confession, certain that it would not be deciphered; Richard affirms that in his single person he plays many parts, and Iago says with strange words, 'I am not what I am'. His passages on the fundamental identity of existing, dreaming, and acting are famous.

Twenty years he persisted in that controlled hallucination, but one morning he was overcome by the surfeit and the horror of being so many kings who die by the sword and so many unhappy lovers who converge, diverge, and melodiously agonise. That same day he disposed of his theatre. Before a week was out he had returned to the village of his birth, where he recovered the trees and the river of his childhood; and he did not bind them to those others his muse had celebrated, those made illustrious by mythological allusions and Latin phrases. He had to be someone; he became a retired impresario who has made his fortune and who interests himself in loans, law-suits, and petty usury. In this character he dictated the arid final will and testament that we know, deliberately excluding from it every trace of emotion and of literature. Friends from London used to visit his retreat, and for them he would take on again the role of poet.

The story goes that, before or after he died, he found himself before God and he said: 'I, who have been so many men in vain, want to be one man: myself.' The voice of God replied from a whirlwind: 'Neither am I one self; I dreamed the world as you dreamed your work, my Shakespeare, and among the shapes of my dream are you, who, like me, are many persons – and none.'

JORGE LUIS BORGES, Dreamtigers

Garrick Not Appreciated

As soon as the play, which was *Hamlet, Prince of Denmark*, began, Partridge was all attention, nor did he break silence till the entrance of the ghost; upon which he asked Jones, 'What man that was in the strange dress; something,' said he, 'like what I have seen in a picture. Sure it is not armour, is it?' Jones answered, 'That is the ghost.' To which Partridge replied with a smile, 'Persuade me to that, sir, if you can. Though I can't say I ever actually saw a ghost in my life, yet I am certain I should know one, if I saw him, better than that comes to. No, no, sir, ghosts don't appear in such dresses as that, neither.' In this mistake, which caused much laughter in the neighbourhood of Partridge, he was suffered to continue, till the scene between the ghost and Hamlet, when Partridge gave that credit to Mr Garrick, which he had denied to Jones, and fell into so violent a trembling, that his knees knocked against each other. Jones asked him what was the matter, and whether he was afraid of the warrior upon the stage? 'O la! sir,' said he, 'I perceive now it is what you told me. I am not afraid of anything; for I know it is but a play. And if it was really a ghost, it could do one no harm at such a distance, and in so much company; and yet if I am frightened, I am not the only person.' 'Why, who,' cries Jones, 'dost thou take to be such a coward here besides thyself?' 'Nay, you may call me a coward if you will; but if that little man there upon the stage is not frightened, I never saw any man frightened in my life. Ay, ay: go along with you! Ay, to be sure! Who's fool then? Will you? Lud have mercy upon such fool-hardiness? – Whatever happens, it is good enough for you. – Follow you? I'd follow the devil as soon. Nay, perhaps, it is the devil for they say he can put on what likeness he pleases. – Oh! here he is again. – No farther! No, you have gone far enough already; farther than I'd have gone for all the King's dominions.' Jones offered to speak, but Partridge cried 'Hush, hush! dear sir, don't you hear him?' And during the whole speech of the ghost, he sat with his eyes fixed partly on the ghost and partly on Hamlet, and with his mouth open; the same passions which succeeded each other in Hamlet, succeeding likewise in him ...

When the ghost made his next appearance Partridge cried out, 'There, sir, now; what say you now? is he frightened now or no? As much frightened as you think me, and, to be sure, nobody can help some fears. I would not be in so bad a condition as what's his name, squire Hamlet, is there, for all the world. Bless me! what's become of the spirit? As I am a living soul, I thought I saw him sink into the earth.' 'Indeed, you saw right,' answered Jones. 'Well, well,' cries Partridge, 'I know it is only a play: and besides, if there was anything in all this, Madam Miller would not laugh so; for as to you, sir, you would not be afraid, I believe, if the devil was here in person. – There, there – Ay, no wonder you are in such a passion, shake the vile wicked wretch to pieces. If she was my own mother, I would serve her so. To be sure all duty to a mother is forfeited by such wicked doings. – Ay, go about your business, I hate the sight of you.'

Our critic was now pretty silent till the play, which Hamlet introduces before the King. This he did not at first understand, till Jones explained it to him; but he no sooner entered into the spirit of it, than he began to bless himself that he had never committed murder. Then turning to Mrs Miller, he asked her, 'If she did not imagine the King looked as if he was touched; though he is,' said he, 'a good actor, and doth all he can to hide it. Well, I would not have so much to answer for, as that wicked man there hath, to sit upon a much higher chair than he sits upon. No wonder he run away; for your sake I'll never trust an innocent face again.'

The grave-digging scene next engaged the attention of Partridge, who expressed much surprise at the number of skulls thrown upon the stage. To which Jones answered, 'That it was one of the most famous burial-places about town.' 'No wonder then,' cried Partridge, 'that the place is haunted. But I never saw in my life a worse grave-digger. I had a sexton, when I was clerk, that should have dug three graves while he is digging one. The fellow handles a spade as if it was the first time he had ever had one in his hand. Ay, ay, you may sing. You had rather sing than work, I believe.' – Upon Hamlet's taking up the skull, he cried out, 'Well! it is strange to see how fearless some men are: I never could bring myself to touch anything belonging to a dead man, on any account. – He seemed frightened enough too at the ghost, I thought. *Nemo omnibus horis sapit.*'

Little more worth remembering occurred during the play, at the end of which Jones asked him, 'Which of the players he had liked best?' To this he answered, with some appearance of indignation at the question, 'The King, without doubt.' 'Indeed, Mr Partridge,' says Mrs Miller, 'you are not of the same opinion with the town; for they are all agreed, that Hamlet is acted by the best player who ever was on the stage.' 'He the best player!' cried Partridge, with a contemptuous sneer, 'why, I could act as well as he myself. I am sure, if I had seen a ghost, I should have looked in the very same manner, and done just as he did. And then, to be sure, in that scene, as you called it, between him and his mother, where you told me he acted so fine, why, Lord help me, any man, that is, any good man, that had such a mother, would have done exactly the same. I know you are only joking with me; but, indeed, madam, though I was never at a play in London, yet I have seen acting before in the country; and the King for my money; he speaks all his words distinctly, half as loud again as the other. – Anybody may see he is an actor.'

HENRY FIELDING, *Tom Jones*

The rabble of little people are more pleas'd with *Jack Puddings* being soundly kick'd, or having a Custard handsomely thrown in his face, than with all the wit in Plays; and the higher sort of Rabble (as there may be a rabble of very fine people in this illiterate age) are more pleascd with the extravagant and unnatural actions, the trifles and fripperies of a Play, or the trappings and ornaments of Nonsense, than with all the wit in the world.

THOMAS SHADWELL

I cannot understand people who spend hours at the theatre watching scenes between those whom in real life they would not listen to for five minutes.

NATALIE BARNEY

An actor is a guy who, if you ain't talking about him, ain't listening.

MARLON BRANDO

Hints for Young Players

1. There is no necessity to subject yourself to the slavery of studying your part: *what's* the use of the prompter? Besides, it's ten to one, that in a modern play, you substitute something from your own mother wit much

better than the author wrote. If you are entirely at a loss and out, you will get noticed both by the audience and the critic, which would otherwise, perhaps, have never been the case. As to the feelings of the poet, did he shew any for you, when he put you in the part? And, as he is paid for his play by your master, why mayn't you do what you like with it?

2. Another excellent mode of acquiring *notice*, is never to be ready to go on the stage, and to have apologies made for you as often as possible.

3. Never attend to another actor in the same scene with you. You may be much better employed in arranging your dress, or in winking and nodding at your friends in the boxes. You must always keep your eye on your *benefit*.

4. As you take no notice of him, it is very likely he'll take none of you; therefore you may as well, out of respect to the understanding of your audience, and much better to shew yourself, address all your speeches to the pit, looking them full in the face, and making them quite uneasy in their seats, lest you should expect an answer. This will render you an *interesting* performer; and you will find *judicious* persons saying, 'Lord, I do like Mr —, you hear every word he says.'

5. If you have any witticism, or good saying to deliver *aside*, bawl it out as loud as you can. How are they to laugh and applaud at the back of the one shilling gallery, if they don't hear what you say? If you have no lungs, give up the profession.

6. Never part with your hat: *what are you to do with your fingers?*

7. After you've very indifferently sung a very indifferent song, do not quit the side scenes; but, if, amidst a hundred hisses, you hear a little boy in the gallery cry *encore*, come on and sing it again. That's the *sense* of the house. Nothing like respect.

8. If in a tragedy, your friend, the hero, is dying at the farther end of the stage, let him die and be damned. You come forward, and look about you. *Every man attend to his own business.*

9. To dine out when you are going to play, is thought wrong, but foolishly so, unless there is some other objection besides that of getting drunk. Recollect that you are in England. The audience is English, and the greater part will have a fellow feeling for you. Some two or three sober blockheads may hiss, but you'll benefit by this, for it will bring down all your friends. When you *can't speak*, and they hiss, don't leave the

stage, but *make a speech*. Press your hand to your heart, turn up your eyes, and give them to understand that it is grief, and not liquor, and you have them at once. If you feel hurt, (*as you ought*, and indignant too) at their disapprobation, when you quit the scene, drink more; you are with Pope:

> 'Shallow draughts intoxicate the brain,
> And *drinking largely sobers us again.*'

10. If you don't like a part, be sick – it will give you consequence!

11. In singing, never mind the music – observe what time you please. It would be a pretty degradation indeed, if you were obliged to run after a fiddler – '*horse hairs and cat's guts*' – no, let him keep your time, and play your tune. *Dodge him.*

12. If you can force another actor to laugh, by making ugly faces at him – you'll get the character of being – *so droll!* The play may suffer by this – but *you* must look to your *reputation*.

13. Never speak a good word of the manager. I can't well explain why, but mind, I caution you not to do it! This is certain, that *he* will always be trying to thwart *your genius*, by putting you in parts, in which he thinks you will appear to most advantage. This is not to be borne without a murmur by an actor of any spirit.

14. When you are not in a good humour, walk through the character. If you always play well, there will be so much *sameness*, that they'll take no notice of you.

15. Ever avoid speaking favourably of any actor in your own line. Nothing is unhandsome that *seems* prudent!

16. Be sure not to read or inform yourself about any part except your own. It will only confuse you! To try to make your countenance expressive of your sentiments will have the same effect. You can't *do two things at once.*

17. In an interesting scene blow your nose, and generally have a cough – it will excite pity; and, if it's the right kind of *pity*, you know 'pity is akin to love'.

18. Go to rehearsal very rarely. You are not a schoolboy, nor are you to think yourself a parrot, that nothing but repetition will beat the words into your head. Assert the dignity of your character, and constantly rely on your own wit and ingenuity for a happy issue.

19. In a modern piece, when you are in haste, leave out what you like. If they discover it, they will have no reason to complain; but, most probably, commend your judgment.

20. Hug the side where the prompter sits. It will shew your anxiety to be correct.

21. After you have *said your say*, drop your character directly. *You are only paid to play your own part, and not to assist another to play his.* Never aid to set him off – it may make the scene better, but it will surely lead to comparisons to your disadvantage. *Complain, if he serves you so.*

22. Attitude is a great thing. When you speak, always clap your left hand to your hip, making an angle with your elbow, and stretch out your right. Other positions are, I know, by some preferred, but take common sense with you, and is it not clear that what is most easily recognised, will be most approved? Then what figure is known better than that of a *tea-pot?*

23. Coming on out of your turn is sure to attract notice.

24. When you have spoken your last speech, walk off instantly, and leave the other to do the same, when he has done. Knowing that there was no more for *you* to say, will prove that you have read your part. It's a mere waste of time to stay.

25. In making love always whine. These are the tones that go to the heart.

26. Avoid forming any style of acting of your own. In this imitate the dramatists, who copy one another. That, which has been tried, *must* be safest.

27. Never stir your left hand, unless according to rule – it is unnecessary trouble, and you ought to be better taught than to let your right hand know what your left hand doth.

28. Remember the Horatian maxim, *qualis ab incaepto*. Be always *Mr Whatever's your name*, in every thing, and throughout every part. Variety is destructive of consistency.

29. The less you enter into your part, the more command you'll have over yourself, and the beauty of your dress. Always wear the smartest clothes you have; never mind the character. Why should you make yourself look ugly?

30. In the middle of a speech, if there's the least applause, stop, turn

round, come forward, and bow. It's respectful. In general, the plaudits will arise from the sentiment, and not at all from your acting – bow nevertheless.

I have now nothing further to add but this. Give way to envy and jealousy, and make yourself as miserable as you can at home. It will save your gaiety and spirits, and you'll have the more to waste in the green-room, and at public dinners, as well as to expend on the stage, in the performance of these essential rules.

WILLIAM OXBERRY, *Dramatic Biography*

How Gallants Should Behave

By sitting on the stage, you may (with small cost) purchase the deere acquaintance of the boys: have a good stoole for sixpence: at any time know what particular part any of the infants present: get your match lighted, examine the playsuits lace, and perhaps win wagers upon laying 'tis copper, etc. And to conclude, whether you be a foole or a Justice of peace, or a Capten, a Lord-Mayor's sonne, or a dawcocke, a knave, or an under-Sherife; of what stamp soever you be, currant, or counterfet, the Stage, like time, will bring you to most perfect light and lay you open; neither are you to be hunted from thence, though the Scarecrows in the yard hoot at you, hisse at you, spit at you, yea, throw durt even in your teeth: 'tis most Gentlemanlike patience to endure all this, and to laugh at the silly Animals: but if the Rabble, with a full throat, crie, away with the foole, you were worse then a madman to tarry by it: for the Gentleman, and the foole should never sit on the Stage together.

THOMAS DEKKER, *How a Gallant should Behave Himself in a Playhouse*

My First Play

A little while after that something happened which marked an epoch in my life: I went to my first play. My parents were no great theatre-goers, and for them to take me to the theatre an extraordinary conjunction of circumstances was required. It was necessary that my father, by his skill and attention, should cure a certain playwright's wife of a dangerous illness, and that, shortly afterwards, that playwright should be having one of his pieces, an historical drama, enacted at the Porte-Saint-Martin; then it was further necessary that the grateful husband should offer my father a box, available for the one and only night in the week on which I could be allowed to stay up late, which meant Saturday – not a day when theatrical managers are lavish of their favours as a rule; and, finally, it was necessary that the play should be of such a nature as would bring no offence to innocent ears. For twenty-four hours I lived torn betwixt hope and fear, devoured by fever, awaiting this undreamt-of felicity which any sudden blow of fate might utterly destroy. I was on thorns up to the last minute lest the doctor should suddenly be called away to a case. When the day came I thought the sun would never set. The dinner, of which I did not eat a mouthful, seemed interminable, and I was in mortal terror lest we should arrive late. My mother seemed as if she would never finish dressing. She was afraid of missing the beginning, and so offending the author, and yet she wasted the all too precious time in arranging the flowers in her bodice and in her hair. My mother stood before the glass of her wardrobe studying her white muslin dress, over which she was wearing a transparent tunic with green spots, and she seemed to attach a serious importance to the way her hair was done, to the arrangement of her tippet, to the hang of the lace on her short sleeves, and to various other details of her toilet which, to me, seemed utterly trivial. I have since modified that opinion. Justine had been to fetch a fiacre, and it was waiting at the door. Mother sprinkled some lavender water on her handkerchief, and came downstairs. When she got to the bottom she found she had left her smelling-salts on the dressing table, and sent me up to fetch them. At last we reached the theatre. The attendant showed us into a box that was red all over. It looked out on to an immense hall buzzing like a hive of bees, whence there arose the discordant sounds of the instruments which the musicians were tuning up. There was something tremendously solemn about the three raps on the stage and the dead silence that followed. When the curtain went up it was really like going from one world to another. And how splendid was the one into which I was passing! Peopled by knights and pages, dames and damozels of high degree, life was on a broader and grander scale than in the world into which I had been born; passions were more terrible there, and beauty more beautiful. In those spacious Gothic halls the dresses, the gestures, the voices of those who moved therein charmed the senses, dazzled the brain, and captivated the heart. From that moment nothing existed for me save that enchanted world thus suddenly opened to my curious and adoring gaze. An irresistible illusion had taken hold of me, and things that might well have destroyed it by reminding me that it was all only theatrical make-believe, such as the boards, the friezes, the strips of painted canvas that represented the sky, the curtain that framed the stage, all combined to hold me more closely than ever in the magic circle. The play took me back to the later years of the reign of Charles VII, and not one of the characters that came upon the scene, not even the night watchman or the sergeant of the guard, but left a vivid impression on my mind. But when Margaret of Scotland appeared I became extraordinarily excited. I felt burning hot and icy cold at the same time, and I almost fainted away. I loved her. She was beautiful. Never would I have believed that mortal woman could be so lovely. She looked pale and melancholy in the subdued light. The moon, which was immediately recognisable as a medieval moon by reason of the procession of gloomy clouds that accompanied it, and by its obvious predilection for church towers, poured down its silver beams upon the youthful princess. In the riot of memories that come thronging in upon me, I know not what sequence to keep or how to finish off my story. I marvelled that Margaret was so white, and, perceiving that she had blue eyelashes, I deemed it a sign of noble birth. Wedded to Louis the Dauphin, she loves Raoul, the young and handsome archer. He knows neither father nor mother – a circumstance which makes him exceeding sad. None dare blame the princess for loving Raoul the archer, when they know that that same archer is a son of Charles VII. The King, having been warned by the astrologers that he would meet his death at the hands of his son, causes him to be left naked as soon as he was born, and substitutes for him a foundling who marries Margaret of Scotland, and becomes the Dauphin Louis. Thus it was for Raoul that Margaret was really destined. She knows it not, nor does Raoul, but a mysterious power draws them one to the other.

The intervals between the acts brought me rudely back to the work-a-day world. They struck me as being detestably coarse, and the shouts of 'chocolates, lemonade, bottled ale', though new to my ears and consequently devoid of commonness, wounded me by reason of their profane character ...

During the last interval, the author, a tall man with a pimply face and hair turning grey, came into our box, and I saw him bow politely to my mother. He laid his hand on my head as Rachel once did, he talked to me kindly about my work at school, he congratulated me on being so fond of literature at my age, and he exhorted me to make a thorough study of Latin. He knew Latin himself, he said, and that was why his style was so different from his fellow dramatists', who wrote like hacks. But all these condescensions were in vain. I answered hardly a word, and never looked at him at all. Had he known the cause of my indifference, he would have felt flattered, but he probably thought me stupid, never dreaming that my stupidity was due to the prodigious impression his work had made on me. The curtain went up again. Once more I began to live. Margaret of Scotland was restored to me. Alack, I had found her only to lose her again forthwith. She perished at the hand of the Dauphin Louis just as the archer Raoul was casting himself at her feet. The archer Raoul fell stabbed by the same dagger and learnt, as he breathed his last, that he was loved. How I envied his lot!

ANATOLE FRANCE, *The Bloom of Life*

If You Will Learn to Play the Vice

Do they not maintaine bawdrie, insinuat solery, & renue the remembrance of hethen ydolatrie? Do they not induce whordom & unclennes? nay, are they not rather plaine devourers of maydenly virginitie and chastitie? For proofe whereof, but marke the flocking and running to Theaters & curtens, daylie and hourely, night and daye, tyme and tyde, to see Playes and Enterludes; where such wanton gestures, such bawdie speaches, such laughing and sneering, such kissing and bussing, such clipping and culling, such winkinge and glancinge of wanton eyes, and the like, is used, as is wonderfull to behold. Then, these goodly pageants being done, every mate sorts to his mate, every one bringes another homeward of their waye verye freendly, and in their secret conclaves (covertly) they play *the Sodomists*, or worse. And these be the fruits of Playes and Enterluds for the most part. And whereas you say there are good Examples to be learned in them, Trulie so there are: if you will learne falshood; if you will learn cosenage; if you will learn to deceive; if you will learn to play the Hipocrit, to cogge, lye, and falsifie; if you will learn to jest, laugh, and sneer, to grin, to nodd, and mow; if you will learn to playe the vice, to swear, teare, and blaspheme both Heaven and Earth: If you will learn to become a bawde, uncleane, and to deverginat Mayds, to deflour honest Wyves: if you will learne to murther, slaie, kill, picke, steal, robbe, and rove: If you will learn to rebel against Princes, to commit treasons, to consume treasurs, to practise ydleness, to sing and talke of bawdie love and venery: if you will lerne to deride, scoffe, mock, & flowt, to flatter & smooth: If you will learn to play the whore-maister, the glutton, Drunkard, or incestuous person: if you will learn to become proude, hawtie, & arrogant; and, finally, if you will learne to contemne GOD and al his lawes, to care neither for heaven nor hel.

PHILIP STUBBES, *The Anatomie of Abuses* (1583)

Incidents on an American Tour

8 November, 1848: Acted King Lear, with a Goneril – perhaps sober, but acting the distressful! – with a Cordelia talking nonsense, haggard and old as Tisiphone, and affecting the timid; a Fool singing *horribly out of tune*, but by far the best of bunch; that great lout, Mr Ryder, as bad as the worst of them. I acted *against* it all, striving to keep my self-possession, and I acted *well*. The curtain fell, and the audience, who would have cheered on a thick-headed, thick-legged *brute* like Mr Forrest, took no notice of this, my best performance. This is the civilisation – the growing *taste* of the United States!!!

10 November: Rehearsed with care, but I have *brutes* to deal with – not *intelligences* – '*ignorance made drunk*' will well describe American actors from Mr Forrest downwards! Acted Cardinal Wolsey and Oakley – with a Catherine and a Mrs Oakley to make a dog *vomit*! Did my best.

20 November: Acted Macbeth. Before the play Mr Ryder came to inform me there would be a disturbance. I would take no stimulant; had fortunately eaten a light dinner, conscious of having done nothing even questionable. I was prepared. I heard great shouting at Mr Ryder, who was evidently mistaken by the deputed rioters for myself. Went on, and applause, with the hissing, coarse noises, etc., of the ruffians there, attended my entry. I received it unmoved, and went on braving it. It continued growing more and more faint through the scenes, the rioters, sometimes well informed, trying to interrupt the more effective parts of the performance, but becoming gradually subdued until applause aroused them again. They were sufficiently quiet before the end of the first act. They heard the dagger soliloquy, manifestly enrapt, and the applause was a genuine burst, but of course again a signal for the ruffian blackguards assembled. The murder went triumphantly, and the second act ended as having stilled them. I went through cheerily and defyingly, pointing at the scoundrels such passages as 'I dare do all', etc. The third act also had evidently a strong hold upon them; in the early part a copper cent was thrown at me, missing me, which particularly excited the indignation of the audience, and when I went on a bouquet was thrown to me. I mention all I can recollect. The fourth act passed smoothly after my entrance. In the fifth act, as if the scoundrels were aware that it was a strong point for me, they began with more than their primary violence of noise and outrage. A rotten egg was thrown on the stage. I went in active and cheerful defiance through it, though injured in the more touching and delicate effects, and in the last scene threw all my heart into the contest, and wound up with great effect. The majority – the large majority – of the audience were enthusiastic in their demonstrations of sympathy with me, and of indignation against these ruffians. I was called, and I went on – of course the tumult of applause, and of the attempts of those wretches was very great.

WILLIAM MACREADY, *Reminiscences*

The TV Set

So, more of the same. Every day, everywhere, it's on the rise. The television malady. The set is dirty. It's a household object now, an old pot, a kitchen sink, but old and dirty. We've been hearing them, seeing them, for a very long time. They come into your house, they show off for us. You turn on the set and there they are, you turn it off. You turn on this poor set once more and there's another one. You see their life-size heads, they stretch their necks, they look toward you, then you stand in front of them to block them, you turn it off. They give us the same presumptuous, profoundly conniving smile. They talk to us in the singular language that likewise presumes to be self-evident, with the same staggering force of conviction, the same postures, the same zoom, then they go off in another vein to speak to you about France, about the quality of life, about the Olympic games, and *we* see they have a tooth missing, they have laryngitis or a cold, a Cardin outfit, clean fingernails, a château in Périgord. The lie, they're all in it, we see that they lie the way they breathe, every one of them, we see it, see it so much we don't see it anymore. They come there to lie. It's when they have to lie still more than usual that they order television to come look for them so they can show off. *We* know, we see the lie on television the way we see them, every one of them. There are the ones who are on the spot, and there are their commentators, their scavengers. Their phrasing in French is the same; sometimes we confuse them. What a gang. In general we tend to prefer the ones on late-night television, the ones who are on at four in the morning, because they're so tired. But what a strange effect they have on what they're talking about. Where they come from there aren't any more books, any more films, there's no one, no more news briefs. There's nothing but the show. It's mysterious. It's no longer a question of them alone but of the set, maybe, hard to believe that everything they approach they trivialise. And yet, as soon as they appear, a screen comes up between their image and we who are watching. As if the colour were changing, as if the set were turning to grey, to the malady of grey.

Sometimes, you have to admit, what a joy, the great whales of Hawaii go by and chase them. Sometimes it's the baby seals, they are strange, they are painted different colours; the inspired youth of Canada discovered this, painting them in indelible colour to make their fur unusable so as to save them from horrible slaughter.

MARGUERITE DURAS, *Green Eyes*

Tobacco

Tobacco I love and tobacco I'll take,
And hope good tobacco I ne'er shall forsake.
'Tis drinking and wenching destroys still the creature;
But this noble fume does dry up ill nature.

ANONYMOUS, 16th century

Tobacco is a filthy weed,
That from the devil doth proceed;
That drains your purse, that burns your clothes,
That makes a chimney of your nose.

ANONYMOUS, early 17th century

Tobacco reek, Tobacco reek,
When I am well, it makes me sick:
Tobacco reek, Tobacco reek,
It makes me well when I am sick.

ANONYMOUS, early 19th century

Chewing

Their launch rounded the bend; at the head of the lake, under a mountain slope, they saw the little central dining-shack of their hotel and the crescent of squat log cottages which served as bedrooms. They landed, and endured the critical examination of the habitués who had been at the hotel for a whole week. In their cottage, with its high stone fireplace, they hastened, as Babbitt expressed it, to 'get into some regular he-togs'. They came out; Paul in an old grey suit and soft white shirt; Babbitt in khaki shirt and vest and flapping khaki trousers. It was excessively new khaki; his rimless spectacles belonged to a city office; and his face was not tanned, but a city pink. He made a discordant noise in the place. But with infinite satisfaction he slapped his legs and crowed, 'Say, this is getting back home, eh?'

They stood on the wharf before the hotel. He winked at Paul and drew from his back pocket a plug of chewing-tobacco, a vulgarism forbidden in the Babbitt home. He took a chew, beaming and wagging his head as he tugged at it. 'Um! Um! Maybe I haven't been hungry for a wad of eating-tobacco! Have some?'

They looked at each other in a grin of understanding. Paul took the plug, gnawed at it. They stood quiet, their jaws working. They solemnly spat, one after the other, into the placid water. They stretched voluptuously, with lifted arms and arched backs. From beyond the mountains came the shuffling sound of a far-off train. A trout leaped, and fell back in a silver circle. They sighed together.

SINCLAIR LEWIS, *Babbitt*

Children Smoking

'They sent over from Grigorievitch's for some book, but I said that you were not at home. The postman has brought the newspapers and two letters. And, Yevgénii Petróvitch, I really must ask you to do something in regard to Serózha. I caught him smoking the day before yesterday, and again to-day. When I began to scold him, in his usual way he put his hands over his ears, and shouted so as to drown my voice.'

Yevgénïï Petróvitch Buikovsky, Procurator of the District Court, who had only just returned from the Session House and was taking off his gloves in his study, looked for a moment at the complaining governess and laughed:

'Serózha smoking!' He shrugged his shoulders. 'I can imagine that whipper-snapper with a cigarette! How old is he?'

'Seven. Of course you may not take it seriously, but at his age smoking is a bad and injurious habit, and bad habits should be rooted out in their beginning.'

'Very true. But where does he get the tobacco?'

'On your table.'

'On my table! Ask him to come here.'

When the governess left the room, Buikovsky sat in his armchair in front of his desk, shut his eyes, and began to think. He pictured in imagination his Serózha with a gigantic cigarette a yard long, surrounded by clouds of tobacco smoke. The caricature made him laugh in spite of himself; but at the same time the serious, worried face of his governess reminded him of a time, now long passed by, a half-forgotten time, when smoking in the schoolroom or nursery inspired in teachers and parents a strange and not quite comprehensible horror. No other word but horror would describe it. The culprits were mercilessly flogged, expelled from school, their lives marred, and this, although not one of the school-masters or parents could say what precisely constitutes the danger and guilt of smoking. Even very intelligent men did not hesitate to fight a vice which they did not understand. Yevgénïï Petróvitch remembered the director of his own school, a benevolent and highly educated old man, who was struck with such terror when he caught a boy with a cigarette that he became pale, immediately convoked an extraordinary council of masters, and condemned the offender to expulsion. Such indeed appears to be the law of life; the more intangible the evil the more fiercely and mercilessly is it combated ...

'In my time these questions were decided very simply,' he thought. 'Every boy caught smoking was flogged. The cowards and babies, therefore, gave up smoking, but the brave and cunning bore their floggings, carried the tobacco in their boots and smoked in the stable. When they were caught in the stable and again flogged, they smoked on the river-bank ... and so on until they were grown up. My own mother in order to keep me from smoking used to give me money and sweets. Nowadays all these methods are regarded as petty or immoral. Taking logic as his standpoint, the modern teacher tries to inspire in the child good principles not out of fear, not out of wish for distinction or reward, but consciously.'

ANTON CHEKHOV, *At Home*

Cigars

The Havannah cigar is unquestionably at the head. You know it by the peculiar beauty of the firm, brown, smooth, delicately textured, and *soft* leaf: and, if you have anything of a nose, you can never be deceived as to its odour, for it is a perfect *bouquet*. The *Chinese* cheroots are the next in order; but the devil of it is that one can seldom get them, and then they are always dry beyond redemption. The best Chinese cheroots have a delicate greyish tinge; and, if they are not complete sticks, put them into an airtight vessel with a few slices of a good juicy melon, and in the course of a few hours they will extract some humidity from their neigh-bours. Some people use a sliced apple, others a carrot, either of which may do when a melon is not to be had: but that is the real article when attainable. As to all the plans of moistening cigars by means of tea-leaves, rum-grog, etc., they are utterly absurd, and no true smoker ever thinks of them. Manilla cigars occupy the third station in my esteem, but their enormous size renders them inconvenient. One hates to be seen sucking away at a thing like a walking cane. I generally find that Gliddon of London has the best cigars in the market. George Cotton of Edinburgh is also very *recherché* in these articles. But, as I believe I once remarked before, a man must smuggle, in the present state of the code.

WILLIAM MAGINN, *Maxims of Sir Morgan O'Doherty, Bart.*

Excels All Medicine

It is *Tobacco*, whose sweet substantiall fume
The hellish torment of the teeth doth ease,
By drawing downe, and drying up the rewme,
The Mother and the Nurse of each disease.
It is *Tobacco* which doth colde expell,
And cleares the obstructions of the Arteries,
And surfets threatning Death digesteth well,
Decocting all the stomackes crudities.
It is *Tobacco* which hath power to clarifie
The clowdie mists before dim eyes appearing,
It is *Tobacco* which hath power to rarifie
The thick grose humour which doth stop the hearing.
The wasting Hectique, and the Quartain Fever,
Which doth of Physique make a mockerie,
The gowt it cures, and helps ill breaths for ever,
Whether the cause in Teeth or stomacke be.
And though ill breaths were by it but confounded,
Yet that Medicine it doth Farre excell,
Which by sir *Thomas Moore* hath bin propounded,
For this is thought a Gentleman-like smell.

SIR JOHN DAVIES, *Of Tobacco*

Giving Up

Mr Bradish wanted a change. He did not mean at all by this that he wanted to change himself – only his scenery, his pace, and his environment, and that for only a space of eighteen or twenty days. He could leave his office for that long. Bradish was a heavy smoker, and the Surgeon General's report had made him self-conscious about his addiction. It seemed to him that strangers on the street regarded the cigarette in his fingers with disapproval and sometimes with commiseration. This was manifestly absurd, and he needed to get away. He would take a trip. He was divorced at the time, and would go alone.

One day after lunch he stopped in a travel agency on Park Avenue to see what rates were in force. A receptionist directed him to a desk at the back of the office, where a young woman offered him a chair and lit his cigarette from a matchbook flying the ensign of the Corinthian Yacht Club. She had, he noticed, a dazzling smile and a habit of biting it off when it had served its purpose, as a tailor bites off a thread. He had England in mind. He would spend ten days in London and ten in the country with friends. When he mentioned England, the clerk said that she had recently come back from England herself. From Coventry. She flashed her smile, bit it off. He did not want to go to Coventry, but she was a young woman with the determination and single-mindedness of her time of life, and he saw that he would have to hear her out on the beauties of Coventry, where she seemed to have had an aesthetic and spiritual rebirth. She took from her desk drawer an illustrated magazine to show him pictures of the cathedral. What impressed him, as it happened, was a blunt advertisement in the magazine, stating that cigarettes caused lung cancer. He dismissed England from his mind – the clerk was still on Coventry – and thought that he would go to France. He would go to Paris. The French government had not censured smoking, and he could inhale his Gauloise without feeling subversive. However, the memory of a Gauloise stopped him. Gauloises, Bleues and Jaunes. He recalled how their smoke seemed to drop from an altitude into his lungs and double him up with paroxysms of coughing. In his imagination clouds of rank French tobacco smoke seemed to settle like a bitter fog over the City of Light, making it appear to him an unsavory and despondent place. So he would go to the Tyrol, he thought. He was about to ask for information on the Tyrol when he remembered that tobacco was a state monopoly in Austria and that all you could get to smoke there were flavorless ovals that came in fancy boxes and smelled of perfume. Italy, then. He would cross the Brenner and go down to Venice. But he remembered Italian cigarettes – Esportaziones and Giubeks – remembered how the crude tobacco stuck to his tongue and how the smoke, like a winter wind, made him shiver and think of death. He would go on to Greece, then; he would take a cruise through the islands, he thought –

until he recalled the taste of that Egyptian tobacco that is all you can get to smoke in Greece. Russia. Turkey. India. Japan. Glancing above the clerk's head to a map of the world, he saw it all as a chain of tobacco stores. There was no escape. 'I think I won't go anywhere,' he said. The clerk flashed her smile, bit it off like a thread, and watched him go out the door.

The quality of discipline shines through a man's life and all his works, giving them a probity and a fineness that preclude disorder, or so Bradish thought. The time had come for him to discipline himself. He put out his last cigarette and walked up Park Avenue with the straitened, pleasant, and slightly dancy step of an old athlete who has his shoes and his suits made in England. As a result of his decision, toward the end of the afternoon he began to suffer from something that resembled a mild case of the bends. His circulatory system was disturbed. His capillaries seemed abraded, his lips were swollen, and now and then his right foot would sting. There was a marked unfreshness in his mouth that seemed too various and powerful to be contained by that small organ; seemed by its power and variety to enlarge his mouth, giving it, in fact, the dimensions and malodorousness of some ancient burlesque theatre like the Howard Athenaeum. Fumes seemed to rise from his mouth to his brain, leaving him with an extraordinary sense of light-headedness. Since he felt himself committed to this discipline, he decided to think of these symptoms in the terms of travel. He would observe them as they made themselves felt, as one would observe from the windows of a train the changes in geology and vegetation in a strange country.

As the day changed to night, the country through which he traveled seemed mountainous and barren. He seemed to be on a narrow-gauge railroad traveling through a rocky pass. Nothing but thistles and wire grass grew among the rocks. He reasoned that once they were over the pass they would come onto a fertile plain with trees and water, but when the train rounded a turn on the summit of the mountain, he saw that what lay ahead was an alkali desert scored with dry stream beds. He knew that if he smoked, tobacco would irrigate this uninhabitable place, the fields would bloom with flowers, and water would run in the streams, but since he had chosen to take this particular journey, since it was quite literally an escape from an intolerable condition, he settled down to study the unrelieved aridity. When he made himself a cocktail in his apartment that night, he smiled – he actually smiled – to observe that there was nothing to be seen in the ashtrays but a little dust and a leaf he had picked off his shoe.

He was changing, he was changing, and like most men he had wanted to change, it seemed. In the space of a few hours, he had become more sagacious, more comprehensive, more mature. He seemed to feel the woolly mantle of his time of life come to rest on his shoulders. He felt himself to be gaining some understanding of the poetry of the force of change in life, felt himself involved in one of those intimate, grueling, and unseen contests that make up the story of a man's soul. If he stopped smoking, he might stop drinking. He might even curtail his erotic tastes. Immoderation had been the cause of his divorce. Immoderation had alienated his beloved children. If they could only see him now, see the clean ashtrays in his room, mightn't they invite him to come home? He could charter a schooner and sail up the coast of Maine with them. When he went, later that night, to see his mistress, the smell of tobacco on her breath made her seem to him so depraved and unclean that he didn't bother to take off his clothes and went home early to his bed and his clean ashtrays.

Bradish had never had any occasion to experience self-righteousness other than the self-righteousness of the sinner. His censure had been aimed at people who drank clam juice and cultivated restrained tastes. Walking to work the next morning, he found himself jockeyed rudely onto the side of the angels; found himself perforce an advocate of abstemiousness, and discovered that some part of this condition was an involuntary urge to judge the conduct of others – a sensation so strange to him, so newly found, so unlike his customary point of view that he thought it exciting. He watched with emphatic disapproval a stranger light a cigarette on a street corner. The stranger plainly had no will power. He was injuring his health, trimming his life span, and betraying his dependents, who might suffer hunger and cold as a result of this self-indulgence. What's more, the man's clothing was shabby, his shoes were unshined, and if he could not afford to dress himself decently he could surely not afford the vice of tobacco. Should Bradish take the cigarette out of his hand? Lecture him? Awaken him? It seemed a little early in the game, but the impulse was there and he had never experienced it before. Now he walked up Fifth Avenue with his newly possessed virtuousness, looking neither at the sky nor at the pretty women but instead raking the population like a lieutenant of the vice squad employed to seek out malefactors. Oh, there were so many! A disheveled old lady, colorless but for a greasy smear of crimson lipstick, stood on the corner of Forty-fourth Street, lighting one cigarette from another. Men in doorways, girls on the steps of the library, boys in the park all seemed determined to destroy themselves.

His light-headedness continued through the morning, so that he found it difficult to make business decisions, and there was some definite injury to his eyesight. He felt as if he had taken his eyes through a dust storm. He went to a business lunch where drinks were served, and when someone passed him a cigarette he said, 'Not right now, thank you.' He blushed with self-righteousness, but he was not going to demean his struggle by confiding in anyone. Having abstained triumphantly for nearly twenty-four hours, he thought he deserved a reward, and he let the waiter keep filling his cocktail glass. In the end he drank too much, and when he got back to his office he was staggering. This, on top of his disturbed circulatory system, his swollen lips, his bleary eyes, the stinging sensation in his right foot, and the feeling that his brain was filled with the fumes and the malodorousness of an old burlesque theatre made it impossible for him to work, and he floundered through the rest of the day. He seldom went to cocktail parties, but he went to one that afternoon, hoping that it would distract him. He definitely felt unlike himself. The damage by this time had reached his equilibrium, and he found crossing streets difficult and hazardous, as if he were maneuvering over a high and narrow bridge.

The party was large, and he kept going to the bar. He thought that gin would quench his craving. It was hardly a craving, he noticed – nothing like hunger or thirst or the need for love. It felt like some sullen and stubborn ebbing in his bloodstream. The lightness in his head had worsened. He laughed, talked, and behaved himself up to a point, but this was merely mechanical. Late in the party, a young woman wearing a light sack or tube-shaped dress, her long hair the color of Virginia tobacco, came in at the door. In his ardor to reach her he knocked over a table and several glasses. It was, or had been up to that point, a decorous party, but the noise of broken glass, followed by the screaming of the stranger when he wrapped his legs around her and buried his nose in her tobacco-colored hair, were barbarous. Two guests pried him loose. He stood there, crouched with ardor, snorting through his distended nostrils. Then he flung away the arms of the men who held him and strode out of the room.

He went down in the elevator with a stranger whose brown suit looked and smelled like a Havana Upman, but Bradish kept his eyes on the floor of the carriage and contented himself with breathing in the stranger's fragrance. The elevator man smelled of a light, cheap blend that had been popular in the fifties. The doorman, he noticed, looked and smelled like a briar pipe with a Burley mixture. And on Fifty-seventh Street he saw a woman whose hair was the color of his favorite blend and who seemed to trail after her its striking corrupt perfume. Only by grinding his teeth and bracing his muscles did he keep from seizing her, but he realized that his behavior at the party, repeated on the street, would take him to jail, and there were, as far as he knew, no cigarettes in jail. He had changed – he had changed, and so had his world, and watching the population of the city pass him in the dusk, he saw them as Winstons, Chesterfields, Marlboros, Salems, hookahs, meerschaums, cigarillos, Corona-Coronas, Camels, and Players. It was a young woman – really a child – whom he mistook for a Lucky Strike that was his undoing. She screamed when he attacked her, and two strangers knocked him down, striking and kicking him with just moral indignation. A crowd gathered. There was pandemonium, and presently the sirens of the police car that took him away.

JOHN CHEEVER, *Metamorphoses*

A good cigar is as great a comfort to a man as a good cry is to a woman.

EDWARD BULWER LYTTON

It has been the companionship of smoking that I have loved, rather than the habit.

ANTHONY TROLLOPE

18 July 1868: There is a basic antagonism between tobacco and women. One reduces the other. This is so true that sooner or later men in love with women stop smoking because they feel or imagine that tobacco deadens sexual desire and sexual acts. Love in fact is gross compared with the spirituality of a pipe.

GONCOURT BROTHERS

[Of his brother, Sir James FitzJames Stephen] He once smoked a cigar, and found it so delicious that he never smoked again.

SIR LESLIE STEPHEN

[His recipe for political success] Smoke all day, and take no exercise.

JOSEPH CHAMBERLAIN

It is to the cigarette that the temperate habits of the twentieth century are due. Nicotine knocked port and claret out in the second round.

LORD FREDERICK HAMILTON

Hack! Hack! Hack!

Here Severance had a coughing attack. One of these accompanied his first cigarette almost every morning and they recurred with grisly frequence all day and all evening until he dropped his final butt down the toilet, flushed it away, and reeled or crept into bed. They did not for some reason occur in lecture or seminar, but everywhere else they convulsed without mercy, horrible to all within hearing. Hundreds had clapped him on the back, men as well as women had run for water, and to the near-prostration of the seizures themselves – he often half-expected to *die* at the third or fourth next hack – was superadded the exasperating need to reassure his stricken company: 'Just cigarettes (hack!) – three packs (hack!) a day for (hack!) thirty-five years. My internist says I have a (hack hack hack) chronic mild bronchitis. Die of cancer of the trachea, caught too late to (hack! hack!) operate.' So they'd all laugh together (hack!). Theatres were worst, sometimes he gave up and slunk out. Not a problem, really, except social; and the agony of the throat. He had tried everything, cutting down (many devices), pipes, cigars, even cold turkey. He had quit once in Rome, for seven hours after breakfast, during the last two of which his (first) wife was begging him to take it up again.

JOHN BERRYMAN, *Recovery*

An International Vice

If we run over those countries where Tobacco is made use of, we may observe the various manners of using it; some Americans will mix it with a powder of shells, to chew it, salivating all the time, which, they fancy, does refresh them in their journeys and labours: others in New Spain will daub the ends of reeds with the gum, or juice of tobacco; and, setting them on fire, will suck the smoke to the other end. The Virginians were observed to have pipes of clay before ever the English came there; and, from those Barbarians, we Europeans have borrowed our mode and fashion of smoaking. The Moors and Turks have no great kindness for tobacco; yet, when they do smoak, their pipes are very long, made of reeds or wood, with an earthen head. The Irishmen do most commonly powder their tobacco, and snuff it up their nostrils, which some of our Englishmen do, who often chew and swallow it. I know some persons

that do eat every day some ounces of tobacco, without any sensible altera-
tion; from whence we may learn, that use and custom will tame and
naturalize the most fierce and rugged poison, so that it will become civil
and friendly to the body.

ANON., *The Natural History of Coffee, Thee, Chocolate and Tobacco* ... (1682)

The Joy of Mortals

Others affirme the gods were ignorant
Of the confection of so sweet a plant;
For had they knowne this smoke's delicious smack
The vault of heav'n ere this time had been black,
And by the operation of this fume
Been purg'd for ever of her clowdie rheume.
Daintie ambrosia with a loth'd disdaine
Had been made meate for each milk-pottage braine
Iove's Ganymede had never smelt of drinke
The heav'nly Mazers' flowing ore the brinke,
Nor fixen Iuno ever broke his head
For spilling nectar on the gorgeous bed:
Gods would have revel'd at their feasts of mirth
With the pure distillation of the Earth:
The marrow of the world, starre of the West,
The pearle, whereby this lower orbe is blest,
The ioy of mortals, umpire of all strife,
Delight of nature, Mithridate of life,
The daintiest dish of a delicious feast,
By taking which man differs from a beast.

SIR JOHN BEAUMONT, *The Metamorphosis of Tobacco*

A Loathsome Custom

Is it not both great vanitie and uncleannessee that at the table, a place of respect, of cleanlinesse, of modestie, men should not be ashamed to sit tossing of *Tobacco pipes*, and puffing of the smoke of *Tobacco* one to another, making the filthy smoke and stinke thereof to exhale athwart the dishes and infect the aire, when, very often, men that abhor it are at their repast? ... And is it not a great vanitie, that a man cannot heartily welcome his friend now, straight they must bee in hand with *Tobacco*? ... He but that will refuse to take a pipe of *Tobacco* among his fellowes, (though by his own election he would rather feele the savour of a Sinke) is accounted peevish and no good company, even as they doe with tippling in the cold Eastern Countries ...

A custome lothsome to the eye, hatefull to the Nose, harmfull to the braine, dangerous to the Lungs, and in the blacke stinking fume thereof, neerest resembling the horrible Stigian smoke of the pit that is bottomlesse.

KING JAMES VI, *A Counterblast to Tobacco*

A Pipe of Tobacco

Little tube of mighty power,
Charmer of an idle hour,
Object of my warm desire,
Lip of wax, and eye of fire,
And thy snowy taper waist
With my finger gently braced,
And thy pretty smiling crest
With my little stopper press'd,
And the sweetest bliss of blisses
Breathing from thy balmy kisses,
Happy thrice and thrice again
Happiest he of happy men,

Who, when again the night returns,
When again the cricket's gay,
(Little cricket full of play)
Can afford his tube to feed
With the fragrant Indian weed.
Pleasure for a nose divine
Incense of the God of wine,
Happy thrice and thrice again,
Happiest he of happy men.

ISAAC HAWKINS BROWNE

Poison from the Devil

In this island, as also in other provinces of these new countries, there are some bushes, not very large, like reeds, that produce a leaf in shape like that of the walnut, though rather larger, which (where it is used) is held in great esteem by the natives, and very much prized by the slaves whom the Spaniards have brought from Ethiopia.

When these leaves are in season, they pick them, tie them up in bundles, and suspend them near their fire-place till they are very dry; and when they wish to use them, they take a leaf of their maize and putting one of the others into it, they roll them round tight together; then they set fire to one end, and putting the other end into the mouth, they draw their breath up through it, wherefore the smoke goes into the mouth, the throat, the head, and they retain it as long as they can, for they find a pleasure in it, and so much do they fill themselves with this cruel smoke, that they lose their reason. And there are some who take so much of it, that they fall down as if they were dead, and remain the greater part of the day or night stupefied ... See what a pestiferous and wicked poison from the devil this must be. It has happened to me several times that, going through the provinces of *Guatemala* and *Nicaragua*, I have entered the house of an Indian who had taken this herb, which in the Mexican language is called *tabacco*.

GIROLAMO BENZONI, *La Historia del mondo nuovo* (1565)

499

The Smoking Room at the Club

Very delightful must be the sensations of the man who has just lit a 'weed', and sunk deep into the recesses of an arm-chair, very soothing, very dreamy, very lazy, very languid, very everything that is free and easy ... The Smoking-Room of a Club is the place of all others where the characteristics of the man under the influence of his cigar may be best seen and studied. Sometimes he is by way of reading a novel, the last new novel, as he reclines at full length on an ottoman, or lies buried in a huge arm-chair. But only a small portion of his thoughts are given to the book; it is quite impossible that he can follow the story attentively, or can form a correct estimate of its literary merits – more than half his mind is in his cigar. Sometimes he sits puffing, the picture of contentment, but not bright-looking, perhaps even slightly obfuscated in appearance, the intellect as well as the countenance obscured as it were in clouds of smoke, the eyes almost closed in sleep, the utterances infrequent, and when they come not too clear. The happiness derived from the smoke must be so great that neither thought, nor talk of any kind, can add to it, or equal it.

When those curls of cloud go wafting slowly upwards, perhaps they sometimes obscure for the moment a misfortune, or shut out for the time some of the worries of life: or it may be that the smoker, his head thrown back and his eye turned up towards the sky and to the ceiling, beholds a whole panorama of splendid castles in the air. But they begin in smoke and end in smoke.

Cornhill Magazine, Volume 6 (1862)

Tobacco

When tobacco came, when Raleigh did first bring
The unfabled herb; the plant of peace, the known king
Of comfort bringers, then indeed new hope
Came to the host of poets – with new scope,

New range of power, since henceforth one still might sit
Midnight – on and still further, while the war of wit
More kindly became and coloured till dawn came in;
Piercing blind shutter chinks with pale daylight thin,
Talk went on other things than the rich night did relate.

Raleigh he knew, but could not the impossible
War of swift steel and hurtled bronze foretell –
Nor the imaginary hurt on the body's vessel;
Nor how tobacco ever would steady disastered
Nerves, courage by gay terror almost mastered.
Gloucester men, half a day or more; they would hide
Five cigarettes and damp matches well inside
Their breasts, the only thing unsodded, while despair, despair
Dripped incessantly without interest from the air;
Or go supperless
The better next day's tobacco taste to bless.
Wonder at frogs, stars, posts till headaches came
Those chief of trouble-comforts still in number the same.
Watch Verey lights, sand-bags, grasses, rifle sights, mud –
Crampt in uncouth postures men crouched or stood –
A Woodbine breakfast inspiriting the blood.

Or in those caves of dugouts, men talking lazily
Smoke in luxuriously, of Woodbines, Goldflakes easily –
For one gift condoning Fate and its unnatural mazily
Self-tangled knots. Easing the strained back –
Somehow or other slipping unseen from the rack
Into tobacco scent, or tobacco savour or look;
The divine virtue of some content long-golden book
Multiplying; or in the sunniest quiet resting
Loll into restlessness or sleepy jesting.

Tobacco truly taken, as poetry, as a real thing.
Tobacco tasted exactly; in waves or odd ring
Noted; tobacco blown to the wind, or still watched
Melt into ether's farthest smother unmatched.

Keen sentries hid whiffing surreptitiously –
Sly fatigue parties hidden from scrutiny –
Last breath favours begged desperately.
Over all the breath of the airy vapour is known,
Life's curtain rises on it and Death's trembles down.
Heroism has taken smoke for sufficient crown.
Wires hang bodies for such courage as makes tobacco so known –
Machine guns sweep in heaps those who such honour keep.

When I think of the Ark slapping hopeless eternal waters –
Of Aeneas' sailors cursed with unclean hunger –
Or Irus and his scorn, or the legions Germanicus
Met, and was nearly scotted by whose just anger;
I know, I realise, and am driven to pity –
As by sunscorched eternal days of Babylon City –
And any unsoothed restless war people's clamour;
As hunger for Empire, any use of War's evil hammer;
Tea and tobacco after decent day body-clean labour,
Would bring again England of madrigal, pipe and tabor –
Merry England again of Daniel, after four centuries,
Of dawn rising and late talking, and go-as-you please.
But by Laventie or Ypres, or Arras the thing
Kept heart and soul together, and the mud out of thinking.
There was no end to the goodness, and Raleigh who journeyed
Far over waters to Virginia – and risked life and there did
Things like the heroes' things – but felt want never as we
Carefully guarding the fragments, and finishing the half spents –
Knew joy never so, nor pain; two hours and miles over sea.
How tell the poetic end and comfort of pain past any sustain?

IVOR GURNEY

The Tobacconist

There were two maids talking of husbands; for that is for the most part the theme of maids' discourse, and the subject of their thoughts.

Said one to the other: 'I would not marry a man that takes tobacco for anything.'

Said the second: 'Then it is likely you will have a fool for a husband; for though it doth not always work to wise effects, by reason some fools are beyond improvement, it never fails where improvement is to be made.'

'Why,' said the first, 'how doth it work such wise effects?'

'It composes the mind – it busies the thoughts – it attracts all outward objects to the mind's view – it settles and soothes the senses – it clears the understanding – strengthens the judgment – spies out errors – evaporates follies – it heats ambition – it comforts sorrow – it abates passions – it digests conceptions – it elevates imaginations – it creates fancies – it quickens wit.'

Said the first: 'It makes the breath stink.'

DUCHESS OF NEWCASTLE, *Allegories*

Triumph of Tobacco over Sack and Ale

> Tobacco engages
> Both sexes, all ages,
>   The poor as well as the wealthy;
> From the court to the cottage,
> From childhood to dotage,
>   Both those that are sick and the healthy.

It plainly appears
That in a few years
   Tobacco more custom hath gain'd
Than sack or than ale,
Though they double the tale
   Of the times wherein they have reign'd.

And worthily too,
For what they undo,
   Tobacco doth help to regain,
On fairer conditions
Than many physicians,
   Puts an end to much grief and pain.

It helpeth digestion,
Of that there's no question;
   The gout and the toothache it eases;
Be it early or late,
'Tis ne'er out of date,
   He may safely take it that pleases.

Tobacco prevents
Infections by scents,
   That hurt the brain and are heavy,
An antidote is
Before you're amiss,
   As well as an after remedy.

The cold it doth heat,
Cools them that do sweat,
   And them that are fat maketh lean,
The hungry doth feed,
And if there be need,
   Spent spirits restoreth again.

The Poets of old
Many Fables have told,
   Of the gods and their symposia,

But Tobacco alone,
Had they known it, had gone
For their *Nectar* and *Ambrosia*.

Ballad, *circa* 1640

Turkish Tobacco

The most ordinary pastime here, as in all the other countries of Turkey, is smoking and drinking coffee. From morning to night, the inhabitants have their pipe in their mouth; at home, in each other's houses, in the streets, on horseback, they keep their pipe lighted, and the tobacco-bag is hung at their waist. These are two articles of luxury; the bags, which serve to contain the stock, are of silken stuffs richly embroidered, and the shank of the pipes, which are excessively long, are of the most rare and odoriferous wood. I brought home one of jasmine that was upwards of six feet: an idea may be formed of the beauty of the jasmines of those countries, from their producing branches of such a size, straight and thick enough to be bored. The pipes of commoner wood are wrapped round with silk fastened with gold wire. The poor, to whom the smoking of tobacco is a call of the first necessity, make use of common shanks of reed. The top of the pipe is covered with a kind of factitious alabaster, as white as milk, and enriched with precious stones. Among persons less opulent, they are adorned with false ones. What is put in the mouth is a bit of *succinum*, or yellow amber, the sweet and agreeable odour of which, when it is heated or slightly pressed, contributes to correct the pungent taste of the tobacco. To the extremity of these shanks are fitted very pretty cups of baked clay, commonly called *noix de pipes* (pipe-bowls). Some are marbled with various colours, and inlaid with *or moulu*. They are to be had of different sizes; those which are most generally made use of in Egypt are large, and shaped like a vase. They almost all come from Turkey, and the reddish clay of which they are formed is procured from the environs of Constantinople ...

It is difficult for Frenchmen, especially for those who are not in the habits of burning their mouths with our short pipes and our strong tobacco, to conceive how it is possible to be incessantly smoking. In the first place, the tobacco of Turkey is the best and the mildest in the world; it has not that acrid taste which in our countries provokes a continual spitting; then the length of the shanks, in which the smoke rises, the odoriferous nature of the wood of which they are made, the amber tube that is held in the mouth, the aloes wood with which the tobacco is scented, contribute to make it still milder, and to render the smoke of it not unpleasant in a room. Even the beautiful women are fond of passing their time in pressing the yellow amber with their rosy lips, and gently inhaling the smoke of Syrian tobacco, perfumed with that of aloes. Neither is it necessary to draw up the smoke strongly: it almost rises of itself. People turn aside their pipe, chat, look, now and then rest it in the middle of the lips, and gently inhale the smoke, which immediately escapes from the half-open mouth. Sometimes they amuse themselves with making it pass through the nose; at others they fill their mouth with it, and blow it with art upon the extended hand, where it forms a spiral column, which remains there some moments.

C. S. SONNINI, *Travels in Upper and Lower Egypt*

A cigarette is the perfect type of a perfect pleasure. It is exquisite and it leaves one unsatisfied.

OSCAR WILDE

In principle, I'm entirely against smoking – it is unchristian and unnecessary – it makes me sick to see a gang of little punks puffing at coffin nails – I know for a fact that all labor agitators smoke cigarettes. But my doctor, a Christian man, advises me to take an occasional cigar for the sake of my throat.

SINCLAIR LEWIS

If alcohol is queen, then tobacco is her consort. It's a fond companion for all occasions, a loyal friend through fair weather and foul. People smoke to celebrate a happy moment, or to hide a bitter regret. Whether you're alone or with friends, it's a joy for all the senses. What lovelier sight is there than that double row of white cigarettes, lined up like soldiers on parade and wrapped in silver paper? If I were blindfolded and a lighted cigarette placed between my lips, I'd refuse to smoke it. I love to touch the packet in my pocket, open it, savour the feel of the cigarette between my fingers, the paper on my lips, the taste of tobacco on my tongue. I love to watch the flame spurt up, love to watch it come closer and closer, filling me with its warmth.

LUIS BUÑUEL

The Dame

The most fearsome of the three Aspects of Aphrodite Philomastrix is the *Dame* – Discipline's Hecate, the cold and heartless Hag, concerned, not with the improvement of the character of those under her rule, or the elegant performance of an ancient Eleusinian Mystery, but simply and exclusively with being obeyed. I call her the Dame, not only because of the children's Pantomime character (drawn from a universal model we can all recognise) but because the great exemplar of the whipping crone is the cross old woman so often found in the Dame Schools of the last century and earlier.

> For brandishing the rod, she doth begin
> To Loose the brogues, the stripling's late delight;
> And down they drop; appears his dainty skin,
> Fair as the furry coat of whitest ermilin …
> But ah! what pen his piteous plight may trace?
> Or what device his loud laments explain –
> The form uncouth of his disguised face –
> The pallid hue that dyes his looks amain –
> The plenteous shower that doth his cheek distain?

When he, in abject wise, implores the dame,
Ne hopeth aught of sweet reprieve to gain;
Or when from high she levels well her aim,
And through the thatch, his cries each falling stroke proclaim.

WILLIAM SHENSTONE, *The Schoolmistress*

There is little mercy, or even patience, in such a *régime*; and the rule of the Dame should be reserved for the 'bad cases' that deserve it. A sound flogging is her first as well as her last reaction to wrongdoing. Justice does not greatly concern her – she is beyond such refinements. All that matters to her is not to have her will crossed in even the minutest respect. She is both arbitrary and cruel, and takes considerable satisfaction in laying low those who fall under her rod. The only way for a pupil to 'scape whipping is to obey – instantly. Even then he may not escape, because the occasional arbitrariness of her youth (when she appeared as the Nurse) and the capacity for tactical fury (which she occasionally employed in her character as Mistress) have now been magnified into a senescent unreasonableness; though there is nothing venerable or withered about her physical strength.

The Dame needs no excuses or justification for administering a flogging, beyond her own opinion that it is probably necessary and certainly desirable. The relentless application of the birch causes her no misgivings: on the contrary, she is wholly expert at this craft, seeks opportunities to display it, and does not trouble to conceal her enjoyment. She prefers the grosser effects: the shrill, hopeless pleas of a penitent are like love-poems in her ears; the swishy percussions of the rod, interpolated with heartbreaking *roulades* and *glissandi*, the sweetest of musics. To use a maligned and misunderstood word in its correct sense – for once – she is a sadist. Yet she is necessary.

Her favourite instrument is the venerable birch-rod, almost to the exclusion of all other weapons. She administers whippings, not in the grave, ceremonious – even courtly – manner of the Mistress, but in a blur of verbal and physical violence: denouncing; threatening; seizing;

untrussing; forcing into position, and finally, laying on the astonishing fusillade of strokes which bite deep and reduce even the most hardened of juvenile criminals to instant, abject submission. If she deigns to order him to prepare, she does so in a harsh and furious manner which turns his blood to water, even while he fumbles frantically with his buttons in an effort to obey as rapidly as possible ...

Special *régimes* of this type call for many specific alterations (of surroundings, furniture, equipment, routine and overall style), but the vital ingredient is the personality of the governess. Where before she blended the sharp and the sweet in due measure, now she is wholly transformed into a terrifying flagellatrix, an ogress devoid of mercy and capable, if crossed even for a moment, of the most stupendous rages and the most painful and prolonged punishments.

ALICE KERR-SUTHERLAND, *A Guide to the Correction of Young Gentlemen, or the Successful Administration of Physical Discipline to Young Males* (1924)

The Great Unrestrained Sadist

Before his immense window high as a cathedral window, the great unrestrained sadist vibrates like an electric gut filled with rubber of nothingness. The great unrestrained sadist is stark naked and rubbed all over with phosphorus, which makes him decorative and macabre. His eyes and his long, womanly tresses are as white as currycombed air. His face is proud and ruthless like the faces of all the truly great sadists who are stylised, certified, and eligible for government pensions. The great unrestrained sadist does not deign to eat his perfumed time in extinct grass, to wear the rosy-white gloves of those who carry their ransom in a litter of depraved light. He vibrates like an electric gut stuffed with rubber of nothingness, I said, I repeat it, and I'll repeat it as often as necessary. He is impatient to continue his august task or his alphonse task – however you want to christen it. The domestics are already arriving with crocodiles, grandmothers, dandies, airplanes, flies, etc., and putting them down before the great window.

In a diabolical and remunerated *élan*, with the joyous cry of a Tirolean defenestrator dancing around a lake of dirty grease, he pounces upon the piled-up objects and hurls them out of the majestic window of sublime works. He spends his life hurling everything in existence out the window. He even takes whole, live elephants and hurls them out the window. Quack, quack, quack, beg the gallant but terrified elephants. The great unrestrained sadist refuses to stop in his venerable *élan*. Anything his dead or alive, sweetened or salted, heavy or light servants bring him he hurls out the window: cigars, navies, apartments, railroads, regular coffees, sex appeals, houses, mushrooms, etc. The window is high enough to let the fallen objects change into orange marmalade, and billions of little children come swarming like flies to lick it up with their little mouths. The little children joyfully clap their hands and cry: *Marmalade, marmalade, marmalade* up to the window of the great unrestrained sadist. And without respite, over and over again, he hurls pianos, zeppelins, monuments, diplomats, etc., out the window. He foams, perspires, grinds his teeth, and realises that he must outdo himself and crown his already inconceivable labour. Not having anything else at hand, he pulls out his white hair, his hands, his feet, hurls them out the window, and finally hurls anything remaining of himself out the window, uttering a dreadful shriek, and after his fall changes like all the other objects, and to the great pleasure of the billions of little children – into orange marmalade.

JEAN ARP, Collected French Writings

Swishing Wet and Dry

Two days after his arrival, Denham saw good to open fire upon his pupil, and it was time indeed to apply whip and spur, bit and bridle, to the flanks and mouth of such a colt; the household authorities supported and approved the method of the breaker, under whose rigorous hand and eye he began to learn his paces bit by bit; a breaker who was hardly over-strict, and out of school hours amiable enough; and idle as the boy often was, he soon began to move on except in the mournful matter of sums. As Friday was consecrated to the worship of that numerical Moloch at whose altar more boys have bled than ever at that of Artemis,

Herbert was horsed afresh every Friday for some time. He was soon taught not to appeal to his sister; once assured that he was in good train- ing and not overworked, she gave him all condolence but no interces- sion. Nothing excessive was in effect expected of the boy; Denham had always a fair pretext for punishment and was not unjust or unkind; and in time Herbert learnt to be quiet and perverse; it had grown into a point of honour with him to take what fate sent him at his tutor's hands with a rebellious reticence, and bear anything in reason rather than expose him- self to an intercession which he could not but imagine contemptuous; and thus every flogging became a duel without seconds between the man and the boy. These encounters did both of them some good; Herbert, fearless enough of risk, had a natural fear of pain, which lessened as he grew familiar with it, and a natural weight of indolence which it helped to quicken and lighten; Denham eased himself of much superfluous dis- comfort and fretful energy by the simple exercise of power upon the mind and body of his pupil: and if the boy suffered from this, he gained by it often; the talk and teaching of his tutor, the constant contact of a clear trained intellect, served to excite and expand his own, he grew read- ier and sharper, capable of new enjoyment and advance. And Denham, a practised athlete whose strength of arm Herbert knew to his cost, encouraged him to swim and ride and won his esteem by feats which his slighter limbs were never to emulate. In summer they went daily into the sea together, and the rougher it was the readier they were for it; Herbert wanted no teaching to make him face a heavy sea; he panted and shouted with pleasure among breakers where he could not stand two minutes; the blow of a roller that beat him off his feet made him laugh and cry out in ecstasy: he rioted in the roaring water like a young sea-beast, sprang at the throat of waves that threw him flat, pressed up against their soft fierce bosoms and fought for their sharp embraces; grappled with them as lover with lover, flung himself upon them with limbs that laboured and yielded deliciously, till the scourging of the surf made him red from the shoulders to the knees, and sent him on shore whipped by the sea into a single blush of the whole skin, breathless and untired. Denham had to drive him out of the water once or twice; he was insatiable and would have revelled by the hour among waves that lashed and caressed him with all their might and all their foam. Standing where it was so shallow in the interval from wave to wave that the seething water in its recoil only touched the boy's knees, they waited for a breaker that rose to the whole height of the man. Herbert would creep out to it quivering with delight, get under the curve of it and spring right into the blind high wall of water, then turn and dive straight with it as it broke and get his feet again upon dry ground, sand or shingle as it pleased the water to throw him; and return, a little cut or beaten as it might be, with fresh laughter and appetite, into the sweet white trouble of the waters. Denham, though not such a seagull, had a taste for all work of this kind, and perhaps gave the boy something more than his fair credit; for the magnetism of the sea drew all fear out of him, and even had there been any discomfort or peril to face, it was rather desire than courage that attracted and attached him to the rough water. Once in among green and white seas, Herbert forgot that affliction was possible on land, and in his rapture of perfect satisfaction was glad to make friends with the man he feared and hated in school hours. The bright and vigorous delight that broke out at such times nothing could repress or resist; he appealed to his companion as to a schoolfellow, and was answered accordingly. 'He was a brick in the water,' Herbert told young Lunsford; 'like another fellow you know, and chaffs one about getting swished, and I tell him it's a beastly chouse and he only grins.' This intimacy was broken by one tragic incident; bathing had been forbidden on all hands one stormy day before the sea had gone down, and Herbert, drawn by the delicious intolerable sound of the waves, had stolen down to them and slipped in; having had about enough in three or four minutes, he came out well buffeted and salted, with sea-water in his throat and nostrils and eyes; and saw his tutor waiting just above the watermark between him and his clothes. Finding him gone, Denham had quietly taken a tough and sufficient rod and followed without a superfluous word of alarm. He took well hold of Bertie, still dripping and blinded; grasped him round the waist and shoulders, wet and naked, with the left arm and laid on with the right as long and as hard as he could. Herbert said afterwards that a wet swishing hurt most awfully; a dry swishing was a comparative luxury. The sting of every cut was doubled or trebled, and he was not released till blood had been drawn from his wet skin, soaked as it was in salt at every pore: and came home at once red and white, drenched and dry. Nothing in his life had ever hurt him as much as these. He did not care to face again the sharp superfluous torture of these stripes on the still moist flesh; and from that day he was shy of facetious talk in the water or out: thus the second stage of his apprenticeship began.

ALGERNON SWINBURNE, *Lesbia Brandon*

Venus in Furs

While I was unfolding the documents and reading them, Wanda got pen and ink. She then sat down beside me with her arm around my neck and looked over my shoulder at the papers.

The first one read:

AGREEMENT BETWEEN MME VON DUNAJEW

AND SEVERIN VON KUSIEMSKI

Severin von Kusiemski ceases with the present day being the affianced of Mme Wanda von Dunajew and renounces all the rights appertaining thereunto; he on the contrary binds himself on his word of honour as a man and nobleman that hereafter he will be her *slave* until such time that she herself sets him at liberty again.

As the slave of Mme von Dunajew he is to bear the name Gregor, and he is unconditionally to comply with every one of her wishes and to obey every one of her commands; he is always to be submissive to his mistress and is to consider her every sign of favour as an extraordinary mercy.

Mme von Dunajew is entitled not only to punish her slave as she deems best, even for the slightest inadvertence or fault, but also is herewith given the right to torture him as the mood may seize her or merely for the sake of whiling away the time. Should she so desire, she may kill him whenever she wishes; in short, he is her unrestricted property.

Should Mme von Dunajew ever set her slave at liberty, Severin von Kusiemski agrees to forget everything that he has experienced or suffered as her slave and promises *never under any circumstances and in no wise to think of vengeance or retaliation.*

Mme von Dunajew on her behalf agrees as his mistress to appear as often as possible in her furs, especially when she purposes some cruelty toward her slave.

Appended at the bottom of the agreement was the date of the present day.

The second document contained only a few words.

Having since many years become weary of existence and its illusions, I have of my own free will put an end to my worthless life.

I was seized with a deep horror when I had finished. There was still time, I could still withdraw, but the madness of passion and the sight of the beautiful woman that lay all relaxed against my shoulder carried me away ...

'You are trembling,' said Wanda calmly. 'Shall I help you?'

She gently took hold of my hand, and my name appeared at the bottom of the second paper. Wanda looked once more at the two documents, and then locked them in the desk that stood at the head of the ottoman.

'Now then, give me your passport and money.'

I took out my wallet and handed it to her. She inspected it, nodded, and put it with the other things while in a sweet drunkenness I kneeled before her, leaning my head against her breast.

Suddenly she thrusts me away with her foot, leaps up, and pulls the bellrope. In answer to its sound three young, slender negresses enter; they are as if carved of ebony and are dressed from head to foot in red satin; each one has a rope in her hand.

Suddenly I realise my position and am about to rise. Wanda stands proudly erect, her cold, beautiful face with its sombre brows and contemptuous eyes is turned toward me. She stands before me as mistress, commanding, gives a sign with her hand, and before I really know what has happened to me, the negresses have dragged me to the ground and have tied me hand and foot. As in the case of one about to be executed, my arms are bound behind my back so that I can scarcely move.

'Give me the whip, Haydée,' commands Wanda, with unearthly calm.

The negress hands it to her mistress, kneeling.

'And now take off my heavy furs,' she continues. 'They impede me.'

The negress obeyed.

'The jacket there!' Wanda commanded.

Haydée quickly brought her the *kazabaika* set with ermine, which lay on the bed, and Wanda slipped into it with two inimitably graceful movements.

'Now tie him to the pillar here!'

The negresses lifted me up and, twisting a heavy rope around my body, tied me standing against one of the massive pillars which supported the top of the wide Italian bed.

Then they suddenly disappeared, as if the earth had swallowed them.

Wanda swiftly approached me. Her white satin dress flowed behind her in a long train, like silver, like moonlight; her hair flared like flames against the white fur of her jacket. Now she stood in front of me with her left hand firmly planted on her hips, her right hand holding the whip. She uttered an abrupt laugh.

'Now play has come to an end between us,' she said with heartless coldness. 'Now we will begin in dead earnest. You fool, I laugh at you and despise you; you who in your insane infatuation have given yourself as a plaything to me, a frivolous and capricious woman. You are no longer the man I love, but my *slave*, at my mercy even unto life and death.

'You shall know me!

'First of all you shall have a taste of the whip in all seriousness, without having done anything to deserve it, so that you may understand what to expect if you are awkward, disobedient, or refractory.'

With a wild grace she rolled back her fur-lined sleeve and struck me across the back.

I winced, for the whip cut like a knife into my flesh.

'Well, how do you like that?' she exclaimed.

I was silent.

'Just wait, you will yet whine like a dog beneath my whip,' she threatened, and simultaneously began to strike me again.

The blows fell quickly, in rapid succession, with terrific force upon my back, arms, and neck; I had to grit my teeth not to scream aloud. Now she struck me in the face, warm blood ran down, but she laughed and continued her blows.

'It is only now I understand you,' she said. 'It really is a joy to have someone so completely in one's power, and a man at that, who loves you – you do love me? – No – Oh! I'll tear you to shreds yet, and with each blow my pleasure will grow. Now, twist like a worm, scream, whine! You will find no mercy in me!'

Finally she seemed tired. She tossed the whip aside, stretched out on the ottoman, and rang.

The negresses entered.

'Untie him!'

As they loosened the rope, I fell to the floor like a lump of wood. The black women grinned, showing their white teeth.

'Untie the rope around his feet.'

They did it, but I was unable to rise.

'Come over here, Gregor.'

I approached the beautiful woman. Never did she seem more seductive to me than today in spite of all her cruelty and contempt.

'One step further,' Wanda commanded. 'Now kneel down, and kiss my foot.'

She extended her foot beyond the hem of white satin, and I, the suprasensual fool, pressed my lips upon it.

'Now, you won't lay eyes on me for an entire month, Gregor,' she said seriously. 'I want to become a stranger to you so you will more easily adjust yourself to our new relationship. In the meantime you will work in the garden and await my orders. Now, off with you, slave!'

LEOPOLD VON SACHER-MASOCH, *Venus in Furs*

Vice and Virtue

There is almost no man, but hee sees clearlier, and sharper, the vices in a speaker, than the vertues.

BEN JONSON

The vices we scoff at in others, laugh at us within.

SIR THOMAS BROWNE

Vices are part of the composition of virtues, just as poisons are in medicines: prudence blends and tempers them, using them against the ills of life.

DUC DE LA ROCHEFOUCAULD

No vice exists which does not pretend to resemble some virtue and which does not exploit this supposed resemblance.

JEAN DE LA BRUYÈRE

A Saint's Opinions

Pride is the beginning of all sin. But seven principal vices, as its first progeny, spring doubtless from this poisonous root, namely vain glory, envy, anger, melancholy, avarice, gluttony, lust ... these several sins have each their army against us. For from vain glory there arise disobedience, boasting, hypocrisy, contentions, obstinacies, discords, and the presumptions of novelties. From envy there spring hatred, whispering, detraction, exultation at the misfortunes of a neighbour, and affliction at his prosperity. From anger are produced strifes, swelling of mind, insults, clamour, indignation, blasphemies. From melancholy there arise malice, rancour, cowardice, despair, slothfulness in fulfilling the commands, and a wandering of the mind on unlawful subjects. From avarice there spring treachery, fraud, deceit, perjury, restlessness, violence, and hardnesses of heart against compassion. From gluttony are propagated foolish mirth, scurrility, uncleanness, babbling, dullness of sense in understanding. From lust are generated blindness of mind, inconsiderateness, inconstancy, precipitation, self-love, hatred of God, affection for this present world, but dread or despair of that which is to come. Because, therefore, seven principal vices produce from themselves so great a multitude of vices, when they reach the heart, they bring, as it were, the bands of an army after them.

ST GREGORY THE GREAT

For vices of the sences, custome is all.

KING JAMES VI OF SCOTLAND

Every great vice is a pike in a pond, that devours vertues and lesse vices.

SIR THOMAS OVERBURY

Vice and intemperance is but an inward persecution. 'Tis here the violence begins.

EARL OF SHAFTESBURY

If vice cannot wholly be eradicated, it ought to be confined to particular objects.

JONATHAN SWIFT

It is a very easy thing to devise good laws; the difficulty is to make them effective. The great mistake is of looking upon men as virtuous, or thinking that they can be made so by laws; and consequently the greatest art of a politician is to render vices serviceable to the cause of virtue.

VISCOUNT BOLINGBROKE AND ST JOHN

Ye Joys of Virtue have ye Misfortune of being Unprohibited goods.

EDWARD YOUNG

What maintains one vice would bring up two children.

BENJAMIN FRANKLIN

How like herrings and onions our vices are in the morning after we have committed them.

SAMUEL TAYLOR COLERIDGE

There is an air of interest about Vice, when joined to a person of beauty and grace.

BENJAMIN ROBERT HAYDON

Three American Vices

The three great American vices seem to be efficiency, punctuality and the desire for achievement and success. They are the things that make the Americans so unhappy and so nervous. They steal from them their inalienable right of loafing and cheat them of many a good, idle and beautiful afternoon. One must start out with a belief that there are no catastrophes in this world, and that, besides the noble art of getting things done, there is a nobler art of leaving things undone. On the whole, if one answers letters promptly, the result is about as good or as bad as if he had never answered them at all. After all, nothing happens, and while one may have missed a few good appointments, one may have also avoided a few unpleasant ones. Most of the letters are not worth answering, if you keep them in your drawer for three months; reading them three months afterwards, one might realise how utterly futile and what a waste of time it would have been to answer them all. Writing letters really can become a vice. It turns our writers into fine promotion salesmen and our college professors into good efficient business executives. In this sense, I can understand Thoreau's contempt for the American who always goes to the post office.

LIN YUTANG, *The Importance of Living*

Discretion is a virtue that ought to be practised with true friends.

SEIGNEUR DE SAINT EVREMONDE

Vanity is the foundation of the most ridiculous and contemptible vices – the vices of affectation and common lying.

ADAM SMITH

Impudence, though really a vice, has the same effects on a man's fortune, as if it were a virtue.

DAVID HUME

Often habit is a vice. It makes us mistake injustice for justice, and falsity for truth.

GEORG LICHTENBERG

I loathe that low vice – curiosity.

LORD BYRON

The most irreparable vice is to do evil without knowing it.

CHARLES BAUDELAIRE

Early in the morning, at dawn, in one's first burst of vigour, to read a *book* – I call that vice.

FRIEDRICH NIETZSCHE

Patriotism is the virtue of the vicious.

OSCAR WILDE

Of all virtues, magnanimity is the rarest.

WILLIAM HAZLITT

Pity, the tenderest, the most natural and useful of virtues.

ANATOLE FRANCE

The greatest vice of all, lack of will.

MARCEL PROUST

Vice Is More Violent Than Fire

Vice makes all men completely miserable, since as a creator of unhappiness it is clothed with absolute power, for it has no need of either instruments or ministers. But whereas despots, when they desire to make miserable those whom they punish, maintain executioners and torturers, or devise branding-irons and wedges; vice, without any apparatus, when it has joined itself to the soul, crushes and overthrows it, and fills the man with grief and lamentation, dejection and remorse. And this is the proof: many are silent under mutilation and endure scourging and being tortured by the wedge at the hands of despots and tyrants without uttering a cry, whenever by the application of reason the soul abates the pain and by main force, as it were, checks and represses it; but you cannot order anger to be quiet nor grief to be silent, nor can you persuade a man possessed by fear to stand his ground, nor one suffering from remorse not to cry out or tear his hair or smite his thigh. So much more violent is vice than either fire or sword.

PLUTARCH, Moralia

Vices of Adoption

If people had no vices but their own, few would have so many as they have. For my own part, I would sooner wear other people's clothes than their vices; and they would sit upon me just as well. I hope you will have none; but if ever you have, I beg, at least, they may be all your own. Vices of adoption are, of all others, the most disgraceful and unpardonable. There are degrees in vices as well as in virtues; and I must do my countrymen the justice to say, they generally take their vices in the lowest degree. Their gallantry is the infamous mean debauchery of stews, justly attended and rewarded by the loss of their health, as well as their character. Their pleasures of the table end in beastly drunkenness, low riot, broken windows, and very often (as they well deserve) broken bones. They game for the sake of the vice, not of the amusement; and therefore carry it to excess; undo, or are undone by, their companions. By such conduct, and in such company abroad, they come home, the unimproved, illiberal, and ungentlemanlike creatures that one daily sees them; that is, in the park and in the streets, for one never meets them in good company; where they have neither manners to present themselves, nor merit to be received. But, with the manners of footmen and grooms, they assume their dress too; for you must have observed them in the streets here, in dirty-blue frocks, with oaken sticks in their hands, and their hair greasy and unpowdered, tucked up under hats of an enormous size. Thus finished and adorned by their travels, they become the disturbers of playhouses; they break the windows, and commonly the landlords, of the taverns where they drink; and are at once the support, the terror, and the victims of the bawdy-houses they frequent. These poor mistaken people think they shine, and so they do indeed; but it is as putrefaction shines in the dark.

EARL OF CHESTERFIELD, letter of 15 May 1749

I prefer an accommodating vice to an obstinate virtue.

JEAN BAPTISTE MOLIÈRE

Our virtues and our vices depend too much on our circumstances.

JOHN CLELAND

Virtue knows to a farthing what it has lost by not having been vice.

HORACE WALPOLE

Few vices prevent one from having many friends, as having too many virtues may do.

SEBASTIEN CHAMFORT

Premeditated virtue is almost worthless.

GEORG LICHTENBERG

The drawing a certain positive line in morals, beyond which a single false step is irretrievable, makes virtue formal, and vice desperate.

WILLIAM HAZLITT

Every day confirms my opinion on the superiority of a vicious life – and if Virtue is not its own reward I don't know any other stipend annexed to it.

LORD BYRON

No evil is pure, nor hell itself without its extreme satisfactions.

RALPH WALDO EMERSON

How sad that one's vices, however horrible, contain the proof of our craving for the Infinite.

CHARLES BAUDELAIRE

Debauchery is an act of despair in the face of infinity.

GONCOURT BROTHERS

Virtue and Vice

She was so good, and he was so bad:
A very pretty time they had!
A pretty time, and it lasted long:
Which of the two was more in the wrong?
He befouled in the slough of sin;
Or she whose piety pushed him in?
He found her yet more cold and staid
As wedded wife than courted maid:
She filled their home with freezing gloom;
He felt it dismal as a tomb:
Her steadfast mind disdained his toys
Of worldly pleasures, carnal joys;
Her heart firm-set on things above
Was frigid to his earthly love.

So he came staggering home at night;
Where she sat chilling, chaste, and white:
She smiled a scornful virtuous smile,
He flung good books with curses vile.
Fresh with the early morn she rose,
While he yet lay in a feverish doze:
She prayed for blessings from the Throne,
He called for 'a hair of the dog' with a groan:
She blessed God for her strength to bear
The heavy load – he 'gan to swear:
She sighed, Would Heaven, ere yet too late,
Bring him to see his awful state!
The charity thus sweetly pressed
Made him rage like one possessed.

So she grew holier day by day,
While he grew all the other way.
She left him: she had done her part
To wean from sin his sinful heart,

But all in vain; her presence might
Make him a murderer some mad night.
Her family took her back, pure saint,
Serene in soul, above complaint:
The narrow path she strictly trod,
And went in triumph home to God:
While he into the Union fell,
Our halfway house on the road to Hell.
With which would you rather pass your life
The wicked husband or saintly wife?

JAMES THOMSON

You can't expect a boy to be vicious till he's been to a good school.

SAKI

Sensuality is the vice of young men and old nations.

W. E. H. LECKY

Members of the same profession recognise each other, and so it is with a common vice.

MARCEL PROUST

We think we have escaped the vices of the common run of men when we indulge in those of great men; without realising that, in that respect, they are part of the common run too.

BLAISE PASCAL

A virtuous king is a king who has shirked his proper function – to embody for his subjects an ideal of illustrious misbehaviour beyond their reach.

LOGAN PEARSALL SMITH

In England towers so seldom mellowed rightly. They were too rain-washed, weather-beaten, wind-kissed, rugged; they turned tragic and outlived themselves; they became such hags of things; they grew dowdy and wore snapdragons; objects for picnics; rendezvous of lovers, haunts of vice.

RONALD FIRBANK

Whether Vice is a Virtue

The Commission met every morning at the Royal Library, under the presidency of Monsieur de Quatrefeuilles, assisted by Messieurs Trou and Boncassis, on special duty. At every sitting it examined an average of fifteen hundred reports. After a session of four months it had not yet secured a happy man.

As the President, Quatrefeuilles, was bewailing the situation, Monsieur Boncassis exclaimed:

'Alas, it is vice that causes us to suffer, and all men have vices!'

'I have none,' said Monsieur Chaudesaigues, 'and the result is that I am in despair. Life without vice is nothing but weariness, despondency, and sadness. Vice is the only distraction that one can taste in this world: vice is the colour of life, the salt of the soul, and the light of the mind. What do I say? Vice is original, man's only creative power; it is the attempt of a natural organisation against nature itself, of the enthronement of human sovereignty over animal sovereignty, of human creation over animal creation, of a conscious world in the midst of the universal unconsciousness: vice is man's sole personal property, his real patrimony, his true virtue in the correct sense of the word, since virtue is the fact of being man (*virtus, vir*).

'I have tried to acquire some; I have been unable to do so; it requires genius, a natural gift – an assumed vice is not a vice.'

'Well,' asked Quatrefeuilles, 'what do you call vice?'

'I call vice an habitual predisposition to what the majority regard as evil and abnormal: that is to say, individual morality, individual strength, individual virtue, beauty, power, and genius.'

'That's all right,' said the Counsellor Trou, 'it's only a matter of understanding one another.'

But Saint-Sylvain strongly combated the librarian's opinion.

'Don't talk of vices,' he said, 'since you have none. You don't know what they are. I have some; I have several, and I can assure you that I derive thence less pleasure than inconvenience. There is nothing more fatiguing than a vice. One worries, heats oneself, and exhausts oneself in satisfying it, and when it is satisfied one only experiences an immense disgust.'

'You would not speak thus, sir,' answered Chaudesaigues, 'if you had fine vices, noble, proud, imperious, lofty, really virtuous vices. But you have nothing but mean, fearful, ridiculous little vices. You are not, sir, a great affronter of the gods.'

At first Saint-Sylvain felt hurt by this remark, but the librarian explained that there was nothing offensive in it. Saint-Sylvain agreed with a good grace, and with calmness and resolution made the following reflection:

'Alas, virtue, like vice, and vice, like virtue, consists in effort, constraint, conflict, trouble, toil, and exhaustion! That is why we are all unhappy.'

But the President, Quatrefeuilles, complained that his head would burst.

'Gentlemen,' he said, 'please do not let us argue. We are not here for that.'

And he closed the meeting.

ANATOLE FRANCE, *The Shirt*

If we had no vices ourselves we should take less pleasure in identifying those of others.

DUC DE LA ROCHEFOUCAULD

They that endeavour to abolish vice, destroy also vertue; for contraries, though they destroy one another, yet are the life of one another.

SIR THOMAS BROWNE

When one seeks to pursue virtues to extremes, vices emerge.

BLAISE PASCAL

Beginning with the best intentions in the world, such societies [for the suppression of vice] must in all probability degenerate into a receptacle for every species of tittle-tattle, impertinence and malice. Men whose trade is rat-catching love to catch rats; the bug-destroyer seizes on his bug with delight; and the suppressor is gratified by finding his vice. The last soon becomes a mere tradesman like the others.

REV. SYDNEY SMITH

When the imagination is continually led to the brink of vice by a system of terror and denunciations, people fling themselves over the precipice from the mere dread of falling.

WILLIAM HAZLITT

Nothing is more unpleasant than a virtuous person with a mean mind.

WALTER BAGEHOT

More people are flattered into virtue than bullied out of vice.

ROBERT SURTEES

I never came across anyone in whom the moral sense was dominant who was not heartless, cruel, vindictive, log-stupid, and entirely lacking in the smallest sense of humanity. Moral people, as they are termed, are simple beasts. I would sooner have fifty unnatural vices than one unnatural virtue.

OSCAR WILDE

Every virtue has its own indecent literature.

LOUIS-FERDINAND CÉLINE

Voyeurism

I saw a plump canon, lying beside a stove in a well-carpeted room, with
Dame Sidonie beside him, white, soft, smooth and elegant, drinking
hippocras, both day and night, laughing, playing, toying, kissing, naked
side by side, for their bodies' pleasure – I saw them through a keyhole.
Then I knew that nothing beats living at your ease.

FRANÇOIS VILLON

It is a dangerous thing, when mens minds come to sojourne with their
affections, and their diseases eate into their strength: that when too much
desire, and greediness of vice, hath made the body unfit, or unprofitable;
it is yet gladded with the sight, and spectacle of it in others: and for want
of ability to be an Actor; is content to be a Witnesse.

BEN JONSON

9 May 1865: Flaubert told us, 'Such was my vanity when I was young that
when I visited a brothel with my friends I always took the ugliest girl and
insisted on screwing her in front of them all without taking my cigar out
of my mouth. It was no fun for me: I just did it for the spectators.'

GONCOURT BROTHERS

A Night with Henry Miller

Henry's whores. I feel curious and friendly towards Henry's whores.

The taxi drops us in a narrow little street. A red light painted with number 32 shines over the doorway. We push a swinging door. It is like a café full of men and women, but the women are naked. There is heavy smoke, much noise, and women are trying to get our attention even before the *patronne* leads us to a table. Henry smiles. A very vivid, very fat Spanish-looking woman sits with us and she calls a woman we had not noticed, small, feminine, almost timid.

'We must choose,' says Henry. 'I like these well enough.'

Drinks are served. The small woman is sweet and pliant. We discuss nail polish. They both study the pearly nail polish I use and ask the name of it. The women dance together. Some are handsome, but others look withered and tired and listless. So many bodies all at once, big hips, buttocks, and breasts. 'The two girls will amuse you,' says the *patronne*.

I had expected a man for the demonstration of sixty-six ways of making love. Henry barters over the price. The women smile. The big one has bold features, raven black hair in curls which almost hide her face. The smaller one has a pale face with blonde hair. They are like mother and daughter. They wear high-heeled shoes, black stockings with garters at the thighs, and a loose open kimono. They lead us upstairs. They walk ahead, swinging their hips.

Henry jokes with them. They open the door on a room which looks like a velvet-lined jewel casket. The walls are covered with red velvet. The bed is low, and has a canopy which conceals a mirror on the ceiling of the bed. The lights are rosy and dim. The women are at ease and cheerful. They are washing themselves in the bidet which is in the room. It is all done so casually and with so much indifference that I wonder how one can become interested. The women are joking, between themselves. The big woman ties a rubber penis around her waist. It is of an impossible pink. They lie on the bed after slipping their shoes off, but not the black stockings.

And they begin to take poses.

'*L'amour dans un taxi.*'

'*L'amour à l'Espagnole.*'

'*L'amour* when you do not have the price of a hotel room.' (For this, they stand up against the wall.)

'*L'amour* when one of them is sleepy.'

The small woman pretended to be asleep. The big woman took the smaller woman from behind, gently and softly.

As they demonstrate they make humorous remarks.

It is all bantering and mockery of love until … The small woman has been lying on her back with her legs open. The big woman removed the penis and kissed the small woman's clitoris. She flicked her tongue over it, caressed it, kissed. The small woman's eyes closed and we could see she was enjoying it. She began to moan and tremble with pleasure. She offered to our eyes her quivering body and raised herself a little to meet the voracious mouth of the bigger woman. And then came the climax for her and she let out a cry of joy. Then she lay absolutely still. Breathing fast. A moment later they both stood up, joking, and the mood passed.

ANAIS NIN, *Journals 1931–1934*

Once More, & None Can Mend It

Walking in a meadow green,
    fair flowers for to gather,
where primrose ranks did stand on banks
    to welcome comers thither,
I heard a voice which made a noise,
    which caused me to attend it,
I heard a lass say to a lad,
    'Once more, & none can mend it.'

They lay so close together,
    they made me much to wonder;
I know not which was wether,
    until I saw her under.

Then off her came, & blushed for shame
   so soon that he had ended;
yet still she lies, & to him cries,
   'Once more, & none can mend it.'

His looks were dull & very sad,
   his courage she had tamed;
she bade him play the lusty lad
   or else he quite was shamed;
'then stiffly thrust, he hit me just,
   fear not, but freely spend it,
& play about at in & out;
   once more, & none can mend it.'

And then he thought to venter her,
   thinking the fit was on him;
but when he came to enter her,
   the point turned back upon him.
Yet she said, 'stay! go not away
   although the point he bended!
but toot again, & hit the vane!
   once more, & none can mend it.'

Then in her armes she did him fold,
   & oftentimes she kissed him,
yet still his courage was but cold
   for all the good she wished him;
yet with her hand she made it stand
   so stiff she could not bend it,
& then anon she cries 'come on
   once more, & none can mend it!'

'Adieu, adieu, sweet heart,' quoth he,
   'for in faith I must be gone.'
'Nay, then you do me wrong,' quoth she,
   'to leave me thus alone.'

Away he went when all was spent,
whereat she was offended;
Like a Trojan true she made a vow
she would have one should mend it.

ANONYMOUS, 17th century

A Shocking Proposal

This Candaules then was enamoured of his own wife, and being so, thought that she was by far the most beautiful of all women. Now being of this opinion, Gyges, son of Dascylus, one of his body-guard, happened to be his especial favourite, and to him Candaules confided his most important affairs, and moreover extolled the beauty of his wife in exaggerated terms. In lapse of time (for Candaules was fated to be miserable) he addressed Gyges as follows: 'Gyges, as I think you do not believe me when I speak of my wife's beauty (for the ears of men are naturally more incredulous than their eyes) you must contrive to see her naked.' But he, exclaiming loudly, answered, 'Sire, what a shocking proposal do you make, bidding me behold my queen naked! With her clothes a woman puts off her modesty. Wise maxims have been of old laid down by men, from these it is our duty to learn: amongst them is the following – "Let every man look to the things that concern himself." I am persuaded that she is the most beautiful of her sex, but I entreat of you not to require what is wicked.' Saying thus, Gyges fought off the proposal, dreading lest some harm should befall himself: but the king answered, 'Gyges, take courage, and be not afraid of me, as if I desired to make trial of you, by speaking thus, nor of my wife, lest any harm should befall you from her. For from the outset I will so contrive that she shall not know she has been seen by you. I will place you behind the open door of the apartment in which we sleep; as soon as I enter my wife will come to bed; there stands by the entrance a chair, on this she will lay her garments one by one as she takes them off, and then she will give you an opportunity to look at her at your leisure; but when she steps from the chair to the bed, and you are at her back, be careful that she does not see you as you are going out by the door.'

Gyges therefore, finding he could not escape, prepared *to obey*. And Candaules, when it seemed to be time to go to bed, led him to the chamber, and the lady soon afterwards appeared, and Gyges saw her enter and lay her clothes *on the chair*: when he was at her back, as the lady was going to the bed, he crept secretly out, but she saw him as he was going away. Perceiving what her husband had done, she neither cried out through modesty, nor appeared to notice it, purposing to take vengeance on Candaules; for among the Lydians and almost all the barbarians, it is deemed a great disgrace even for a man to be seen naked. At the time therefore, having shown no consciousness of what had occurred, she held her peace, and as soon as it was day, having prepared such of her domestics as she knew were most to be trusted, she sent for Gyges. He, supposing that she knew nothing of what had happened, came when he was sent for, for he had been before used to attend whenever the queen sent for him. When Gyges came, the lady thus addressed him: 'Gyges, I submit two proposals to your choice, either kill Candaules and take possession of me and of the Lydian kingdom, or expect immediate death, so that you may not, from your obedience to Candaules in all things, again see what you ought not. It is necessary however that he who planned this, or that you who have seen me naked, and have done what is not decorous, should die.' Gyges for a time was amazed at what he heard; but, afterwards, he implored her not to compel him to make such a choice. He however could not persuade, but saw a necessity imposed on him, either to kill his master Candaules or die himself by the hands of others; he chose therefore to survive, and made the following inquiry: 'Since you compel me to kill my master against my will, tell me how we shall lay hands on him.' She answered, 'The assault shall be made from the very spot whence he showed me naked; the attack shall be made on him while asleep.'

When they had concerted their plan, on the approach of night he followed the lady to the chamber: then (for Gyges was not suffered to depart, nor was there any possibility of escape, but either he or Candaules must needs perish) she, having given him a dagger, concealed him behind the same door: and after this, when Candaules was asleep,

Gyges having crept stealthily up and slain him, possessed himself both of the woman and the kingdom.

HERODOTUS, *Clio I*

Two Sparks Romping

I had, on a visit intended to Harriet, who had taken lodgings at Hampton-court, hired a chariot to go out thither, Mrs Cole having promised to accompany me; but some indispensable business intervening to detain her, I was obliged to set out alone; and scarce had I got a third of my way, before the axle-tree broke down, and I was well off to get out, safe and unhurt, into a public-house, of a tolerable handsome appearance, on the road. Here the people told me that the stage would come by in a couple of hours at farthest; upon which, determining to wait for it, sooner than lose the jaunt I had got so far forward on, I was carried into a very clean decent room, up one pair of stairs, which I took possession of for the time I had to stay, in right of calling for sufficient to do the house justice.

Here, whilst I was amusing myself with looking out of the window, a single horse-chaise stopt at the door, out of which lightly leaped two young gentlemen, for so they seemed, who came in only as it were to bait and refresh a little, for they gave their horse to be held in readiness against they came out. And presently I heard the door of the next room, where they were let in, and called about them briskly; and as soon as they were served, I could just hear that they shut and fastened the door on the inside.

A spirit of curiosity, far from sudden, since I do not know when I was without it, prompted me, without any particular suspicion, or other drift or view, to see what they were, and examine their persons and behaviour. The partition of our rooms was one of those moveable ones that, when taken down, served occasionally to lay them into one, for the conveniency of a larger company; and now, my nicest search could not shew me the shadow of a peep hole, a circumstance which probably had not escaped the review of the parties on the other side, whom much it stood upon not to be deceived in it; but at length I observed a paper patch of the same colour as the wainscot, which I took to conceal some flaw: but then it was so high, that I was obliged to stand upon a chair to reach it, which I did as soft as possible; and, with a point of a bodkin, soon pierced it, and opened myself espial-room sufficient. And now applying my eye close, I commanded the room perfectly, and could see my two young sparks romping and pulling one another about, entirely, to my imagination, in frolic and innocent play.

The eldest might be, on my nearest guess, towards nineteen, a tall comely young man, in a white fustian frock, with a green velvet cape, and cut bob-wig.

The youngest could not be above seventeen, fair, ruddy, completely well made, and to say the truth, a sweet pretty stripling: he was too, I fancy, a country lad by his dress, which was a green plush frock, and breeches of the same, white waistcoat and stockings, a jockey cap, with his yellowish hair, long and loose, in natural curls.

But after a look of circumspection, which I saw the eldest cast every way round the room, probably in too much hurry and heat not to over-look the very small opening I was posted at, especially at the height it was, whilst my eye close to it kept the light from shining through and betraying it, he said something to his companion that presently changed the face of things.

For now the elder began to embrace, to press and kiss the younger, to put his hands into his bosom, and give him such manifest signs of an amorous intention, as made me conclude the other to be a girl in disguise: a mistake that nature kept me in countenance for, for she had certainly made one, when she gave him the male stamp.

In the rashness then of their age, and bent as they were to accomplish their project of preposterous pleasure, at the risk of the very worst of consequences, where a discovery was nothing less than improbable, they now proceeded to such lengths as soon satisfied me what they were.

For presently the eldest unbuttoned the other's breeches, and remov-ing the linen barrier, brought out to view a white shaft, middle sized, and scarce fledged, when after handling and playing with it a little, with other dalliance, all received by the boy without other opposition than certain wayward coynesses, ten times more alluring than repulsive, he got him to turn round, with his face from him, to a chair that stood hard by, when knowing, I suppose, his office, the Ganymede now obsequiously leaned his head against the back of it, and projecting his body, made a fair mark, still covered with his shirt, as he thus stood in a side view to me, but fronting his companion, who, presently unmasking his battery, produced an engine that certainly deserved to be put to a better use, and very fit to confirm me in my disbelief of the possibility of things being pushed to odious extremities, which I had built on the disproportion of parts: but this disbelief I was now to be cured of, as by my consent all young men should likewise be, that their innocence may not be betrayed into such snares, for want of knowing the extent of their danger, for nothing is more certain than that ignorance of a vice is by no means a guard against it.

Slipping, then, aside the young lad's shirt, and tucking it up under his cloaths behind, he shewed to the open air those globular fleshy eminences that compose the Mount Pleasants of Rome, and which now, with all the narrow vale that intersects them, stood displayed and exposed to his attack; nor could I without a shudder behold the dispositions he made for it. First, then, moistening well with spittle his instrument, obviously to make it glib, he pointed, he introduced it, as I could plainly discern, not only from its direction, and my losing sight of it, but by the writhing, twisting, and soft murmured complaints of the young sufferer; but at length, the first straights of entrance being pretty well got through, every thing seemed to move and go pretty currently on, as on a carpet road, without much rub or resistance; and now, passing one hand round his minion's hips, he got hold of his redtopped ivory toy, that stood perfectly stiff, and shewed, that if he was like his mother behind, he was like his father before; this he diverted himself with, whilst with the other he wantoned with his hair, and leaning forward over his back, drew his face, from which the boy shook the loose curls that fell over it, in the posture he stood him in, and brought him towards his, so as to receive a long breathed kiss; after which, renewing his driving, and thus continuing to harass his rear, the height of the fit came on with its usual symptoms, and dismissed the action.

The criminal scene they acted, I had the patience to see to an end, purely that I might gather more facts and certainty against them in my design to do their deserts instant justice; and accordingly, when they had re-adjusted themselves, and were preparing to go out, burning as I was with rage and indignation, I jumped down from the chair, in order to raise the house upon them, but with such an unlucky impetuosity, that some nail or ruggedness in the floor caught my foot, and flung me on my face with such violence, that I fell senseless on the ground, and lay there some time before any one came to my relief; so that they, alarmed, I suppose, by the noise of my fall, had more than the necessary time to make a safe retreat. This they effected, as I learnt, with a precipitation nobody could account for, until, when come to myself, and composed enough to speak, I acquainted those of the house with the whole transaction I had been evidence to.

JOHN CLELAND, *Fanny Hill: Memoirs of a Woman of Pleasure*

Under Father's Eyes

It was during a spell of very hot weather; my parents, who had been obliged to go away for the whole day, had told me that I might stay out as late as I pleased; and having gone as far as the Montjouvain pond, where I enjoyed seeing again the reflection of the tiled roof of the hut, I had lain down in the shade and gone to sleep among the bushes on the steep slope that rose up behind the house, just where I had waited for my parents, years before, one day when they had gone to call on M. Vinteuil. It was almost dark when I awoke, and I wished to rise and go away, but I saw Mlle Vinteuil (or thought, at least, that I recognised her, for I had not seen her often at Combray, and then only when she was still a child, whereas she was now growing into a young woman), who probably had just come in, standing in front of me, and only a few feet away from me, in that room in which her father had entertained mine, and which she had now made into a little sitting-room for herself. The window was partly open; the lamp was lighted; I could watch her every movement without her being able to see me; but, had I gone away, I must have made a rustling sound among the bushes, she would have heard me, and might have thought that I had been hiding there in order to spy upon her.

She was in deep mourning, for her father had but lately died. We had not gone to see her; my mother had not cared to go, on account of that virtue which alone in her fixed any bounds to her benevolence – namely, modesty; but she pitied the girl from the depths of her heart. My mother had not forgotten the sad end of M. Vinteuil's life, his complete absorption, first in having to play both mother and nursery-maid to his daughter, and, later, in the suffering which she had caused him; she could see the tortured expression which was never absent from the old man's face in those terrible last years ...

At the far end of Mlle Vinteuil's sitting-room, on the mantelpiece, stood a small photograph of her father which she went briskly to fetch, just as the sound of carriage wheels was heard from the road outside, then flung herself down on a sofa and drew close beside her a little table on which she placed the photograph, just as, long ago, M. Vinteuil had 'placed' beside him the piece of music which he would have liked to play over to my parents. And then her friend came in. Mlle Vinteuil greeted her without rising, clasping her hands behind her head, and drew her body to one side of the sofa, as though to 'make room'. But no sooner had she done this than she appeared to feel that she was perhaps suggesting a particular position to her friend, with an emphasis which might well be regarded as importunate. She thought that her friend would prefer, no doubt, to sit down at some distance from her, upon a chair; she felt that she had been indiscreet; her sensitive heart took fright; stretching herself out again over the whole of the sofa, she closed her eyes and began to yawn, so as to indicate that it was a desire to sleep, and that alone, which had made her lie down there. Despite the rude and hectoring familiarity with which she treated her companion I could recognise in her the obsequious and reticent advances, the abrupt scruples and restraints which had characterised her father. Presently she rose and came to the window, where she pretended to be trying to close the shutters and not succeeding.

'Leave them open,' said her friend. 'I am hot.'

'But it's too dreadful! People will see us,' Mlle Vinteuil answered. And then she guessed, probably, that her friend would think that she had uttered these words simply in order to provoke a reply in certain other words, which she seemed, indeed, to wish to hear spoken, but, from prudence, would let her friend be the first to speak. And so, although I could not see her face clearly enough, I am sure that the expression must have appeared on it which my grandmother had once found so delightful, when she hastily went on: 'When I say "see us" I mean, of course, see us reading. It's so dreadful to think that in every trivial little thing you do some one may be overlooking you.'

With the instinctive generosity of her nature, a courtesy beyond her control, she refrained from uttering the studied words which, she had felt, were indispensable from the full realisation of her desire. And perpetually, in the depths of her being, a shy and suppliant maiden would kneel before that other element, the old campaigner, battered but triumphant, would intercede with him and oblige him to retire.

'Oh, yes, it is so extremely likely that people are looking at us at this time of night in this densely populated district!' said her friend, with bitter irony. 'And what if they are?' she went on, feeling bound to annotate with a malicious yet affectionate wink these words which she was repeating, out of good nature, like a lesson prepared beforehand which, she knew, it would please Mlle Vinteuil to hear. 'And what if they are? All the better that they should see us.'

Mlle Vinteuil shuddered and rose to her feet. In her sensitive and scrupulous heart she was ignorant what words ought to flow, spontaneously, from her lips, so as to produce the scene for which her eager senses clamoured. She reached out as far as she could across the limitations of her true character to find the language appropriate to a vicious young woman such as she longed to be thought, but the words which, she imagined, such a young woman might have uttered with sincerity sounded unreal in her own mouth. And what little she allowed herself to say was said in a strained tone, in which her ingrained timidity paralysed her tendency to freedom and audacity of speech; while she kept on interrupting herself with: 'You're sure you aren't cold? You aren't too hot? You don't want to sit and read by yourself? ...

'Your ladyship's thoughts seem to be rather "warm" this evening,' she concluded, doubtless repeating a phrase which she had heard used, on some earlier occasion, by her friend.

In the V-shaped opening of her crape bodice Mlle Vinteuil felt the sting of her friend's sudden kiss; she gave a little scream and ran away;

and then they began to chase one another about the room, scrambling over the furniture, their wide sleeves fluttering like wings, clucking and crowing like a pair of amorous fowls. At last Mlle Vinteuil fell down exhausted upon the sofa, where she was screened from me by the stooping body of her friend. But the latter now had her back turned to the little table on which the old music-master's portrait had been arranged. Mlle Vinteuil realised that her friend would not see it unless her attention were drawn to it, and so exclaimed, as if she herself had just noticed it for the first time: 'Oh! there's my father's picture looking at us; I can't think who can have put it there; I'm sure I've told them twenty times, that is not the proper place for it.'

I remembered the words that M. Vinteuil had used to my parents in apologising for an obtrusive sheet of music. This photograph was, of course, in common use in their ritual observances, was subjected to daily profanation, for the friend replied in words which were evidently a liturgical response: 'Let him stay there. He can't trouble us any longer. D'you think he'd starting whining, d'you think he'd pack you out of the house if he could see you now, with the window open, the ugly old monkey?'

To which Mlle Vinteuil replied, 'Oh, please!' – a gentle reproach which testified to the genuine goodness of her nature, not that it was prompted by any resentment at hearing her father spoken of in this fashion (for that was evidently a feeling which she had trained herself, by a long course of sophistries, to keep in close subjection at such moments), but rather because it was the bridle which, so as to avoid all appearance of egotism, she herself used to curb the gratification which her friend was attempting to procure for her. It may well have been, too, that the smiling moderation with which she faced and answered these blasphemies, that this tender and hypocritical rebuke appeared to her frank and generous nature as a particularly shameful and seductive form of that criminal attitude towards life which she was endeavouring to adopt. But she could not resist the attraction of being treated with affection by a woman who had just shewn herself so implacable towards the defenceless dead; she sprang on to the knees of her friend and held out a chaste brow to be kissed; precisely as a daughter would have done to her mother, feeling with exquisite joy that they would thus, between them, inflict the last turn of the screw of cruelty, in robbing M. Vinteuil, as though they were actually rifling his tomb, of the sacred rights of fatherhood. Her friend took the girl's head in her hands and placed a kiss on her brow with a docility prompted by the real affection she had for Mlle Vinteuil, as well as by the desire to bring what distraction she could into the dull and melancholy life of an orphan.

'Do you know what I should like to do to that old horror?' she said, taking up the photograph. She murmured in Mlle Vinteuil's ear something that I could not distinguish.

'Oh! You would never dare.'

'Not dare to spit on it? On that?' shouted the friend with deliberate brutality.

I heard no more, for Mlle Vinteuil, who now seemed weary, awkward, preoccupied, sincere, and rather sad, came back to the window and drew the shutters close; but I knew now what was the reward that M. Vinteuil, in return for all the suffering that he had endured in his lifetime, on account of his daughter, had received from her after his death.

MARCEL PROUST, *Swann's Way*

Voyeur

Find the hidden face. A prize is offered.
The scene is green and summer. On the grass
The dresses spread, exhausted butterflies,
And smooth brown legs make soft confessions to
Rough trousers. Excited air
Is hushed with kissing.
Now search for the solitary, the uncoupled one:
Not in the leafy tentacles of trees,
He is no climber,
But close to earth, well-hidden, squat.
You see him now? Yes, there! His snarling grin
Bearded with leaves, his body bushed,
Invisible. See how his eyes are fat with glee
And horror. They fizz with unfulfilment's booze.

His tongue makes sure his lips are still in place
With quick red pats.
You've found him now, and you can take your prize,
Though, as you see, we do not offer cash:
Just recognition and its loaded cosh.

VERNON SCANNELL

Copyright
Acknowledgements

Co for Don DeLillo, *End Zone* (Penguin) and *Great Jones Street* (Picador); David Higham Associates for James Lees-Milne, *Another Self*, for 'The Waltz' from Dame Edith Sitwell's *Collected Poems*, for Dylan Thomas's *Poems* and his *Selected Letters*; James MacGibbon for *The Collected Poems of Stevie Smith* (Penguin 20th Century Classics); John Murray Publishers Ltd for Sir John Betjeman, *Collected Poems*, and for Sir Rupert Hart-Davis's *Lyttleton-Hart David Letters*; Peter Owen publishers, London, for Paul Bowles, *Pages from Cold Point* (1968), Anais Nin, *Journals 1931–34* (1966) and Cesare Pavese's poem 'The Country Whore', from *A Mania for Solitude: Selected Poems*, translated by Margaret Crosland (1969); Laurence Pollinger Limited & the Estate of Christina Stead for Christina Stead, *The Salzburg Tales* (Virago); estate of Daisy Ashford for *The Young Visiters* (Chatto & Windus); Sir Kingsley Amis, *Nothing to Fear* (Jonathan Cape); the estate of John Cheever for his *Journals* (Jonathan Cape); the estate of Malcolm Lowry for his *Under the Volcano* (Jonathan Cape); the estate of William Plomer for his *Collected Poems* (Jonathan Cape); Random Century Group UK and Tom Wolfe for his *Bonfire of the Vanities* (Jonathan Cape); Martin Secker & Warburg for Wole Soyinka's *Poems of Black Africa*, for Italo Calvino's *Adam, One Afternoon*, for Italo Calvino's Mr Palomar, Colette's *Short Stories*, Kafka's *Collected Short Stories*, Alberto Moravia's Lady Godiva and *More Roman Tales*; Wm. Heinemann for Fedor Dostoevsky's *The Gambler*, translated by C. Garnett, and for Vernon Scannell's *Walking Wounded*; Robson Books Ltd for Vernon Scannell's *New and Collected Poems*, Routledge & Kegan Paul for John Hayward, *Letters of Saint Evremonde*; Souvenir Press Educational & Academic Ltd for Jorge Luis Borges, *Dreamtigers*; Virago Press for Anne Lister, *I Know My Own Heart*, edited by Helena Whitbread; Watson, Little Ltd for D. J. Enright, *Collected Poems* (Oxford University Press, 1987); A. P. Watt Ltd on behalf of Timothy d'Arch Smith for Pamela Frankau, *The Bridge* (Heinemann); Weidenfeld & Nicolson for Vladimir Nabokov, *Tyrants Destroyed and Other Stories* and for Charles Baudelaire, *My Heart Laid Bare*, translated by N. Cameron and edited by P. Quennell.

Grateful thanks also to Carol Ann Duffy; Martyn Goff; John Hughes; Lord Kennet; Professor Edward Mendelson; Sir Ferdinand Mount; and Nigel Nicolson.

The selection from 'The Way the Dead Love' copyright © 1973 by

Jovanovich Inc. for Walter Benjamin, *One Way Street, and Other Writings*, translated by Edmund Jephcott and Kingsley Shorter. Harcourt Brace Jovanovich Inc. for Italo Calvino, *Adam One Afternoon* and *Mr Palomar*. Nikki Smith for extract from V. Nabokov, 'A Matter of Chance', in *Tyrant Destroyed, and Other Stories*. Janklow & Nesbit for Frederick Exley, *A Fan's Notes*. The Estate of John Cheever for extract from his story 'Metamorphoses' in *The Brigadier and the Golf Widow*, copyright the Estate of John Cheever, together with Random UK and Alfred A. Knopf Inc. Macmillan Publishing Company of New York for Marianne Moore, 'Snakes, Mongooses, Snake-Charmers and the Like' in *Collected Poems*. William Morris Agency Inc. for extract from 'The Delicate Prey' by Paul Bowles, in *Pages from Cold Point*. Pantheon Books for W. H. Auden, 'A Curse', *Collected Poems*, copyright © 1976 the Executors of the Estate of W. H. Auden. Julio Cortázar, *All Fires the Fire*, translated by Suzanne Levine, 1979. Liane de Pougy, *Mes cahiers bleu*, copyright © 1977 Libraire Plon, English translation © 1979 by Diana Athill. Editorial Sudamerica SA for Julio Cortázar, *End of the Game*, translated by Paul Blackburn. Urizen Books for Gavino Ledda, *Padre Padrone*, translated by George Salmanazar. 'Please Master' from *Collected Poems 1947–1980* by Allen Ginsberg. Copyright © 1968 by Allen Ginsberg. Reprinted by permission of HarperCollins Publishers Inc. From *Franz Kafka: The Complete Stories* by Franz Kafka, edited by Nahum N. Glatzer. Copyright 1946, 1947, 1948, 1949, 1954, 1958, 1971 by Schocken Books Inc. Reprinted by permission of Pantheon Books, a division of Random House, Inc. 'Sad Strains of a Gay Waltz' from *Collected Poems* by Wallace Stevens. Copyright 1936 by Wallace Stevens and renewed 1964 by Holly Stevens Stephenson. Reprinted by permission of Alfred A. Knopf, Inc. Reprinted by permission of Farrar, Straus & Giroux Inc. Excerpts from *Recovery* by John Berryman. Copyright © 1973 by the Estate of John Berryman. 'The Saleswoman' and 'The Master' from *The Collected Stories* by Colette, edited by Robert Phelps. Translation copyright © 1983 by Farrar, Straus & Giroux, Inc. Excerpt from *The Hive* by Camilo José Cela, translated by J. M. Cohen. Copyright © 1953 and copyright renewed © 1981 by Camilo José Cela. 'San Francisco Streets' from *The Passages of Joy* by Thom Gunn. Copyright © 1982 by Thom Gunn. 'In Time of Plague' from *The Man With Night Sweats* by Thom Gunn. Copyright © 1992 by Thom

Index Of Authors